OWNERSHIP, LEADERSHIP AND TRANSFORMATION

400 sd
6/12

D1456104

OWNERSHIP, LEADERSHIP AND TRANSFORMATION

CAN WE DO BETTER FOR CAPACITY DEVELOPMENT?

Carlos Lopes and Thomas Theisohn

Earthscan Publications Ltd
London and Sterling, Virginia

First published in the UK and USA in 2003
by Earthscan Publications Ltd

Copyright © 2003
United Nations Development Programme
One United Nations Plaza
New York, NY, 10017

All rights reserved

ISBN: 1-84407-058-1 paperback
          1-84407-057-3 hardback

DISCLAIMER
The responsibility for opinions in this book rests solely with its authors. Publication does not
constitute an endorsement by the United Nations Development Programme or the institutions
of the United Nations system.

Design and layout by Karin Hug
Printed in the UK by Cambrian Printers Ltd.

A catalogue record for this book is available from the British Library.

Library of Congress Cataloging-in-Publication Data

Lopes, Carlos.
        Ownership, leadership, and transformation : can we do better for capacity development? /
Carlos Lopes, Thomas Theisohn.
            p. cm.
        Includes bibliographical references and index.
        ISBN 1-84407-058-1 (pbk.) -- ISBN 1-84407-057-3 (hardback)
        1. Industrial capacity--Developing countries. 2. Economic development projects--Developing
countries. 3. Technical assistance--Developing countries. 4. Organizational learning--
Developing countries. 5. Organizational change--Developing countries. 6. Leadership--
Developing countries. 7. Intellectual property--Developing countries. I. Theisohn, Thomas,
1961- II. Title.

        HC59.72.C3L67 2003
        338.4'5--dc21

                                                                        2003012070

Earthscan Publications Ltd
120 Pentonville Road, London, N1 9JN, UK
Tel: +44 (0)20 7278 0433. Fax: +44 (0)20 7278 1142
Email: earthinfo@earthscan.co.uk. Web: www.earthscan.co.uk

22883 Quicksilver Drive, Sterling, VA 20166-2012, USA

Earthscan is an editorially independent subsidiary of Kogan Page Ltd and publishes in association
with WWF-UK and the International Institute for Environment and Development.

This book is printed on elemental chlorine-free paper.

CONTENTS

PART B: A CASEBOOK OF EXPERIENCES AND LESSONS 167

Country Cases

FIGURES, TABLES AND BOXES

Figures

Tables

Boxes

Foreword

As this book goes to press, we have about 12 years to reach or miss the targets set in the Millennium Declaration and the eight Millennium Development Goals (MDGs). These targets represent promises that every country in the world have already pledged to keep. The Monterrey Consensus shows how those promises *can* be kept: through a new partnership that imposes mutual obligations on developed and developing countries.

The overall success or failure of this new global partnership will hinge on the commitments of rich countries to help poorer counterparts who are undertaking good faith economic, political and social reforms. The success of the MDGs also depends on their being translated into nationally owned priorities and targets, and adapted to the particular local conditions. National ownership means that a country needs to decide for itself the difficult questions of how to allocate scarce resources – choosing, for instance, whether girls' education should be a bigger budget priority than clean water. If we want to succeed, this new global partnership needs to be an honest compact to empower people, to build and sustain institutions with a solid level of performance, and to create space for vibrant civic engagement and societies to shape and pursue their own destiny.

For that reason, this research project has focused on the question of capacity development. This volume, the third book in the series, explores the operational implications, from the standpoint of capacity development, for dealing with long-standing development dilemmas. It aims to provide additional impetus to the current drive for harmonization of donor practices as convergence around country priorities, processes and systems. It also addresses head on some of the most problematic issues related to incentives, such as compensation schemes, project implementation units, brain drain and corruption. I am hopeful that this book will prove useful to decision makers and development practitioners alike, in particular in developing countries, and inspire new ways to care for the fertile ground on which local ownership and capacity grow.

MARK MALLOCH BROWN
Administrator
United Nations Development Programme

Preface

No other agency can claim more practical knowledge of development problems than the United Nations Development Programme (UNDP). Since its inception, UNDP has been the main source of concrete thinking and expertise in practically all areas of development policies. It has been an engine of change in the way development is conceived and implemented, constantly pushing forward the frontiers of international cooperation. Beyond those of its achievements that are visible in the field, UNDP's main merit is its continuous and humble revisiting of conceptual frameworks and operational instruments of development policies. It reflects on what the dynamics of the economy mean for development goals: they are moving targets entailing moving values, since policy agendas at both the international and the national levels evolve in tandem with the pace of changes in technology, information, transnational flows and cross-cutting phenomena.

This book is part of the process of reviewing and reassessing what we know about development and how we provide technical assistance to developing countries. It is an important contribution to the ongoing task of understanding development processes. It improves and enlarges on the current basic concepts that sustain the technical cooperation policies of the UN agencies, and it points the way forward for all of them. We can be sure that this publication will be the starting point of discussions and research in development agencies and in developing and developed countries alike, thus enriching the participation of all sorts of stakeholders in the shaping of development actions.

The evolving vocabulary of North-South relations mirrors changes in attitude. During the 1960s, the only way to foresee and design development aid policies was summed up in the concept of "technical assistance". These words connoted the idea that rich countries have a monopoly on knowledge. Technical "cooperation" was coined more than a decade later, as a way to re-establish some balance in the North-South relationship. Then, in the 1980s and 1990s, following that logical sequence, "capacity-building" appeared as a key concept of development aid, and was widely recognized as its main goal. At the same time, UNDP introduced full-fledged changes in the way of measuring the impact of aid by launching the human development index and the annual *Human Development Report.* The instruments of development operations further evolved to give an important role to human resources development and institutional development. Therefore, more than the words, what has been constantly evolving is the "technology" of development cooperation.

This book introduces the additional and provocative notion of capacity development, defined by the authors as an endogenous course of action that builds on existing capacities and assets, and the ability of people, institutions and societies to perform functions, solve problems and set and achieve objectives.

The idea that capacities exist in developing countries and need to be developed synthesizes the acknowledgement that development strategies do not have to, and indeed should not, be imported from outside. This, in turn, leads to two conclusions: one, that only home-grown policies based on local capacities are sustainable and potentially successful; and two, that there is no "one-size-fits-all" economic development model, applicable to all situations and all national realities. These conclusions can help us understand the limited success – and sometimes the downright failure – of development policies that have been designed and applied in recent years: the predominance of uniform economic thinking has affected almost all developing countries and policy makers, and has determined the content and the objectives of development aid provided by donors. Fulfilling the paradigm of economic liberalization without paying attention to the local conditions required to benefit from it has been the main model applied to development policies all over the world. We now know that opening trade and investment regimes, modernizing and diversifying productive structures, and ensuring social equity and democratic systems entail a great deal more than implementing what manuals say. "Ownership" is another notion that has appeared in recent years as a *sine qua non* for the starting point of development operations rather than at the end. It is amazing how many aid programmes or financial loans are being implemented in such a way that the recipients are supposed to "own" timetables and reform processes that have in fact been designed far away from their reality. Common sense dictates that sustainability will not be achieved unless the truly committed involvement of local players is ensured in the transformations aimed at by the development programmes. Common sense, however, is not automatically guaranteed in this field. Too often, short-sighted economic or political interests prevail and distort the long-term goals of technical cooperation. The book rightly highlights what should have been common sense but was ignored in too many cases: "there are no simple blueprints." The willingness to question conventional wisdom, which has characterized UNDP's behavior, emerges here as a code of conduct for all those involved in development policies, in both industrialized and developing countries.

There is an even more fundamental conclusion stemming from the idea of capacity development: the main objective of technical cooperation should be to contribute to the utilization and expansion of local capacities. Drawing from the United Nations Conference on Trade and Development's (UNCTAD) experiences on trade and development issues, this means, for instance, supporting the capacity of national trade ministries to formulate and implement home-grown trade policies. This also means ensuring that national research capacity is developed in order to match the scope of the trade agenda that the country requires; that the government officials in charge of decisions affecting the trade and investment regime are fully aware of the features of the country's production and export goals; and that the various institutions needed to manage the complexities of economic liberalization are in place – from customs to environmental authorities, from negotiators to financial intermediaries, from private sector groupings to technology transfer mechanisms. In other words, this means giving a predominant role to local expertise and local institutions, while also providing them with the tools they need to be effective in their functions.

The authors make two types of contribution to the debate on how to be effective in development operations. On the one hand, there is a set of basic principles underlying the concept of capacity development and its practical implementation, presented in user-friendly fashion meant to stimulate discussion by several types of participants. These principles describe the best practices that ensure quality in development aid. On the other hand, the book contains a compendium of 56 case experiences illustrating concrete situations where a capacity development approach has been applied. These demonstrate the variety of development problems that have to be addressed, and the solutions that have to be devised, reiterating the limitations of standardized approaches. In many cases, endorsing the notion of capacity development will inevitably imply sweeping changes in donors' views, in agencies' routines and in recipients' approaches. The process leading to full implementation of the necessary changes will take some time and will be uneven. It will also be cumbersome; we should not expect quick results. Let us recognize that changing attitudes in the realm of development policies is not an easy endeavor. Routine and well-known procedures are the main characteristics of development operations within the UN system as well as outside it. Indeed, it is easier to send an "expert" to a developing country for a few days or weeks than to figure out how to help a national-based institution cope with new issues. It is easier to produce a report on rural development when one is comfortably installed in a high-tech office in an industrialized country than to actually spend time visiting rural communities in remote areas, understanding their needs and formulating a project proposal that will develop their own capacity. And we should not forget that sometimes, vested interests determine the nature of development initiatives more than neutral goals. Technical cooperation is – and will probably continue to be – a tool of domestic economic objectives. One of the main challenges raised by this book is to eliminate that danger.

Development is an international public good. The Millennium Development Goals provide a strong, unequivocal political framework to orient international development aid. Let us hope that the notion of capacity development will soon find its place at the heart of new thinking and action.

RUBENS RICUPERO
Secretary-General
United Nations Conference on Trade and Development

June 2003

Acknowledgements

This volume emerged from two years of research, dialogue and creative thinking to which many people have contributed directly and indirectly. While development thought and practice have evolved significantly since the seminal UNDP study *Rethinking Technical Cooperation: Reforms for Capacity Building in Africa* (Berg et al. 1993), long-standing dilemmas persist. UNDP, therefore, launched an initiative, called Reforming Technical Cooperation for Capacity Development, in early 2001, intending to revisit the same issues in light of new concepts, approaches and challenges. The project was funded by the Netherlands Government, which is gratefully acknowledged. *Ownership, Leadership and Transformation* is the final product of the work that took place; a wealth of related materials can be found on the Internet (www.undp.org/capacity).

Our deep recognition goes to those who have contributed the most to this effort, through the provision of background papers, reports and detailed peer reviewing. We acknowledge in particular Gus Edgren and Paul Matthews as well as Selim Jahan, Terry McKinley and Pauline Tamesis, who have offered their rich professional experience; Daniela Mitrovitch, who has helped us with research, in compiling references and in tying up loose ends; Bozena Blix, Georgina Fekete, Marina Miranda Guedes, Lina Hamadeh-Banerjee and Christopher Ronald for their inputs; and Niloy Banerjee and Tony Land, who have been instrumental in composing and skillfully editing the case book (Part B), in close collaboration with the individuals and institutions mentioned in each case.

This volume would not have been possible without the tireless work of Fe Conway, who managed all aspects of production. Our appreciation is particularly directed to Gretchen Sidhu for a thorough job of editing and proofing the full manuscript. Karin Hug did a very appealing cover design and the entire layout. Patricia Eisenberg and Zaida Omar have interpreted and digitalized our handwritten scribbles on worked and reworked manuscripts and kept us on track. Lavone Mason and Arleen Verendia alternated to ensure the administrative support required.

The draft manuscript underwent a thorough review process that included a full session of the initiative's Advisory and Facilitation Group in Johannesburg, South Africa, from 31 March to 2 April 2003. A candid and intense exchange and constructive spirit helped to significantly improve the book. Geraldine Fraser-Moleketi was our congenial and inspiring host. Hans Peter Boe, Harry Buikema, Liang Dan, Gus Edgren, Eckhard Hein, Mary Hilderbrand, Pim de Keizer, Oscar Monteiro, Joseph Mugore, Ndioro Ndiaye, John Ohiorhenuan, Michael Sarris and Helen Sutch offered their precious time and advice. We acknowledge the opportunity to exchange views in a meeting with Southern African Public Service Ministers as well as the public colloquium hosted by the Southern African Poverty

Reduction Network (SAPRN) during the same occasion. Gillian Chan-Sam and Nina Tumbare ably ensured logistical support for the three meetings, always with a smile.

The internal UNDP review process included a reader's group, several in-house consultations, brainstorming sessions, and feedback through knowledge networks. Particular thanks for their contributions are due to William Andrianasolo, Barbara Barungi, Bob Boase, Stephen Browne, Suely Carvalho, Nicholas Gouede, Girma Hailu, Ameerah Haq, Bruce Jenks, Terence D. Jones, Leonard Joy, Douglas Keh, Nigist Mekonnen, Mehrnaz Mostafavi, Thord Palmlund, Serra Reid, Monica Sharma, Dagmar Schumacher, Mark Suzman, John Taylor, Grace Wamala and Patrick Van Weerelt. UNDP country offices have reviewed and cleared the case experiences.

The leadership provided by Mark Malloch Brown, Administrator of UNDP, Zephirin Diabre, Associate Administrator of UNDP, and Shoji Nishimoto, Director of the Bureau for Development Policy, was essential for this book to come to fruition. We want to thank them deeply, particularly the Administrator for his patience and encouragement. As the authors, we remain responsible for all the views that appear on the following pages, which do not reflect any official stance on the part of UNDP.

In taking on the subject of capacity development, we surely have been humbled by reality, which is so multifaceted that no single mind or book can ever grasp it adequately. Each assertion opened new questions. As we tried to understand what helps capacities grow, we had the precious opportunity to learn ourselves. In advocating the departure from blueprints, we left some of our own conceptions behind. We now hope that *Ownership, Leadership and Transformation* will prove useful to decision makers and other stakeholders in developing countries in strengthening domestic development management for sustainable results. We trust that it will help stimulate a constructive policy dialogue with development partners, as well as stir concrete innovations in development cooperation, including for UNDP, that are firmly grounded in capacity development as a default setting.

CARLOS LOPES AND THOMAS THEISOHN

Brasilia and Vauvenargues, July 2003

Acronyms

CBOs: Community-based organizations
CCA: Common Country Assessments
CCF: Country Cooperation Framework
CIDA: Canadian International Development Agency
DANIDA: Danish Agency for Development Assistance
DFID: (British) Department for International Development
ECDPM: European Centre for Development Policy Management
EGDI: Expert Group on Development Issues
FDI: Foreign direct investment
GEF: Global Environment Facility
GTZ: German Technical Cooperation
HIPC: Heavily indebted poor countries
IBRD: International Bank for Reconstruction and Development
IDA: International Development Association
IFC: International Finance Corporation
ILO: International Labour Organization
IMF: International Monetary Fund
IOM: International Organization for Migration
IT/ICT: Information technology/ Information and communication technology
LDC: Least developed country
LICUS: Low-income countries under stress
MDG: Millennium Development Goal
NEPAD: The New Partnership for Africa's Development
OECD/DAC: Organisation for Economic Co-operation and Development/Development Assistance Committee
PER: Public expenditure review
PRSP: Poverty reduction strategy paper
Sida: Swedish International Development Agency
SWAP: Sector-wide approaches
SWOT: Strengths, weaknesses, opportunities and threats
TRIPS: Trade-related aspects of intellectual property rights
UNCDF: United Nations Capital Development Fund
UNCTAD: United Nations Conference on Trade and Development
UNDAF: United Nations Development Assistance Framework
UNDP: United Nations Development Programme
UNESCO: United Nations Educational, Scientific and Cultural Organization
UNHCR: United Nations High Commissioner for Refugees
UNIFEM: United Nations Development Fund for Women
UNV: United Nations Volunteers
USAID: US Agency for International Development
VSO: Voluntary Services Overseas
WTO: World Trade Organization

Overview:
Turning dilemmas into opportunities

"Give someone a fish and he eats for a day;
Teach someone to fish, and he can feed himself for a lifetime."

It is an intriguing and powerful message, one understood universally by individuals, communities and societies. Premised on inequality, it puts the destiny of those who lack the knowledge to fish in the hands of those "in the know". Yet in a world now driven by technology and drawn close by satellites beaming information even to the most remote corners, highly industrialized countries no longer have the monopoly on knowledge that they once enjoyed. Global partnerships and networking are creating opportunities to learn "how to fish on your own". Societies have more choices and more means to determine their destiny than ever before.

This book is about developing the capacity to transform these choices and means into real progress. Grounded in ownership, guided by leadership, and informed by confidence and self-esteem, capacity development is the ability of people, institutions and societies to perform functions, solve problems, and set and achieve objectives. It embodies the fundamental starting point for improving people's lives.

There is now a growing understanding that capacity development unfolds over the long-term, and can easily be undercut by insistence on short-term results. An endogenous strengthening of existing capacities and assets, it takes place across three overlapping layers: individual, institutional and societal. Each point involves learning and adopting acquired knowledge to meet local needs. This learning is always voluntary, includes trial and error, and is open to the wealth of opportunities from "scanning globally and reinventing locally" (Stiglitz, 1999).

Capacity development is not power neutral. Questions of capacity "for what?" and "for whom?" quickly touch on power differentials, and are subject to political influence and vested interests. Capacity development flourishes where incentives — monetary and non-monetary — are conducive, and dwindles where they are not. It thrives upon civic engagement and in places where people have control over the systems and resources that shape their lives.

Today, there is a rich body of literature on capacity development. A difficulty remains, however, in pinning down what it actually implies in practical terms. This may be due to the fact that the discussion often relies upon abstract notions that are hard to translate into actions and objectives. As well, countries vary so widely that generalizations tend to become broad and meaningless, skirting the real issues. Yet a set of core principles can still be identified and applied.

This starts with a reconsideration of the default setting for conceiving, negotiating and charting a locally appropriate path towards transformation. With development long viewed mainly from the cooperation side, it is first of all time to switch to a national perspective. As much a matter of changing mindsets as it is of bringing people together around national priorities and processes, the onus for this will rest primarily on national leaders and their constituencies. In addition, the understanding needs to grow among all development practitioners that the fundamentals of capacity development are universal. Principles of national ownership and stakeholder accountability need to be upheld even in difficult circumstances, and in no situation should the size of the task detract from the commitment to the effort.

Even with basic principles in place, there are no simple blueprints. In a constantly changing world, innovations are generated or reinvented locally, power shifts, interests arise, and "chemistry", whether between individuals or institutions, opens and shuts doors. Successful development responses account for this reality, and tend to be found where national agents, local communities, academia, the private sector and external partners come together and devise tailored responses, taking into account the uniqueness of each situation.

Part A of this book explores these issues, examining a range of long-standing development dilemmas that relate to capacity development, and demonstrating how it is driven by the learning and advancement that stem from particular circumstances and experiences. Key considerations are summarized in bullets under each section. Subsequently, Part B presents a compilation of case histories from around the globe that support the strong links between ownership, leadership and transformation. These real-world examples show that capacity development is not a utopian idea. Never intended as recipes for replication, the cases instead document promising practices and innovations, and underline critical factors that strengthen capacities. They should be regarded as *good* rather than *best* practices.

If there is one central message to single out, it is that we can do better for capacity development. Development literature in the 1960s and 1970s emphasized the need for implementation, only to replace this notion in the 1980s by commitment and political will. We are now in a phase of talking about ownership, even if understanding varies widely on the meaning of this word. By one definition, it is the exercise of control and command, from the idea to the process, from input to output, from ability to results (Edgren, 2003). Still, while a strong case can be made that ownership is a pre-condition for commitment and capacity development, true transformation requires an important additional element: qualified leadership.

The following overview summarizes issues and arguments discussed in this book, presenting ten default principles that inspire ownership and transfigure leadership, and in the process help ensure capacity development.

1. Don't rush

Building and developing sustainable capacities is a long endeavour, whether that involves educating individuals, establishing viable organizations or fomenting major societal changes. Nevertheless, countries tend to operate on a short-term horizon, encouraged in this direction by regular democratic elections or other political and financial imperatives. Similarly, external cooperation is seldom designed to cover more than five years – often less – and budgets are virtually all determined on an annual basis. With 2015 as a target date, the MDGs[1] now provide at least a medium-term development framework, structured around a set of outcome indicators, that is consistent with capacity development.

In recognizing a longer timeframe, benchmarking for capacity development likewise needs to be realistic, informed by a sense of history and social influences. As the MDGs acknowledge, the routes to development goals can differ significantly. While obviously not all means are justified, what matters are the ultimate results. Measuring progress must take place, but without introducing rigidities that fail to accommodate emerging realities. Furthermore, understanding historical dimensions and the often painful upheavals that have sculpted the modern world may help external agents to engage with a sense of humility, one that allows them to see and respond clearly to the situation in which they work.

2. Respect the value system and foster self-esteem

Society brings together all elements of a population, giving rise to an ethos that largely determines the value system within which people function. Elements such as trust and honesty, or corruption and greed, consequently have a major influence on the direction and performance of development efforts.

Values, identity, self-esteem and creativity all nurture a vision for the future. It is by no means a given that there will be mutual understanding when different worlds of knowledge, ways of thinking and arguing, culture and values meet. This is often evident with external cooperation, with its disproportionately dominant role in many host countries. Donors bring along finance, goodwill, values, agendas, priorities, interests and constraints, yet quantity often exceeds quality, and interests motivate action that may not be aligned with a common development objective. Mistrust and cynicism also stand in the way, with talk of "us and them". This division is not necessarily just between expatriates and nationals; there is

---

[1] The MDGs include: 1. eradicate extreme poverty and hunger; 2. achieve universal primary education; 3. promote gender equality and empower women; 4. reduce child mortality; 5. improve maternal health; 6. combat HIV/AIDS, malaria and other diseases; 7. ensure environmental sustainability; and 8. develop a global partnership for development.

often an alignment between the interests of external partners and the national elite that comes from a homogeneity of education and aspirations.

The result is a tendency to overlook the fact that there may be different ways of achieving the same target. While the best global knowledge should be shared and put to use, developing countries in the end need policy choices that are based on their own development model. They need to be able to make decisions that can be nationally negotiated and agreed on – in ways that seriously respect stakeholders' rights.

3. Scan locally and globally; reinvent locally

Even with a broad grasp of capacity development, the pinpointing of specific capacities can remain more elusive. Traditionally, the notion of capacity came from the engineering world, and was understood to involve using particular processes to transfer knowledge, especially technical and scientific skills (Morgan, 2001). Little attention was paid to less sector-specific realms, including policy formulation, social and economic research, systems analysis, and review and feedback mechanisms.

Today we know better: knowledge cannot be transferred. It has to be acquired, learned and reinvented. And it encompasses both the deep pool of local under-standing that is the very foundation of learning, and the wealth of global information that can be reconceived to meet local needs. When adaptation fails to happen, however, there is no ownership and likely no lasting capacity development.

There are now more opportunities than ever before for global knowledge to be applied at all levels. The remarkable reductions in the costs of transportation and communication have provided unprecedented access. However, while information and communications technology (ICT) enables collection, storage and access to explicit knowledge, much remains tacit, or embodied in individuals and institutions. So the real benefits of ICT lie not in the provision of technology per se, but rather in improving communication and information exchange through networks of people.

Targeted directly towards specific development goals, ICT can have a dramatic impact, becoming a powerful enabler of capacity development. As local communities become part of global networks, they transcend cultural barriers, and challenge policy, legal and regulatory structures within and between nations. At the same time, a knowledge-rich world is striking down many of the traditional rules that governed organizations, with some parallels for countries as well. For organizations to survive and prosper, they need to adapt and learn, sustaining transformational change through a combination of individual and institutional learning. This new knowledge guides the use of resources, the fostering of team-building, the management of complex matrix relationships – all relevant issues for countries (Khadar et al., 2003).

4. Challenge mindsets and power differentials

While widely regarded as intangible, mindsets, vested interests and power differentials may make the biggest contribution to development success or failure. Mindsets and personalities, informed by language and culture, dictate the course of communication and collaboration. They create influential virtual realities determining how people, institutions and societies behave. One example is the sense of entitlement found in many developing countries, or the myth of superiority that haunts the minds of donors and their experts in subtle and not-so-subtle ways. The language of development is full of metaphors of hierarchy and inequality: aid, assistance, developed, developing world, donor, recipients, etc. (Ribeiro, 2002).

In addition to mindsets, every intervention that involves resource transfers is subject to numerous influences, favourable or opposed. Vested interests may steer efforts away from the development purpose, inducing significant opportunity costs for capacity development as gatekeepers at all levels jealously guard their privileges. And despite well-accepted rhetoric, power differentials can fuel profound mistrust and a vicious cycle of exclusion and disempowerment.

These are highly sensitive issues that often are not talked about and thus are difficult to address. Change starts from acknowledging unproductive vested interests and conditions that do not guarantee a level playing field. Systematically, space must be reduced for illegitimate interests, while clear rules of engagement are established.

Opening room for dialogue in turn sparks an irresistible energy that may encounter resistance. Yet it is difficult today for any party to argue that public participation and transparency are not the way to go. Freedom of expression, an active media, diverse political activities and a functioning judicial system all foster vibrant civil society participation and turn mindsets towards the service of capacity development.

5. Think and act in terms of sustainable capacity outcomes

It may sound like common sense, and in fact, it is. But if decision makers and practitioners do not think and act in terms of sustainable capacity development outcomes, as some have been reluctant to do, they are not likely to achieve much. Capacity development needs to be a national priority, an issue that is discussed in domestic priority setting, strategizing and work planning. Equally, it needs to be firmly on the agendas of policy dialogues between a government and its donors, and continue to be a prime objective throughout programming, implementation and monitoring.

Strong leaders can ensure that capacity development receives proper emphasis in all forums, which is why the relationship between capacity development and leadership is fundamental for transformation. It is critical to foster leadership to protect capacity investments from the beginning, because poor leaders can destroy decades of patient building of human skills or institutions, or even use available knowledge to provoke social regression. They can confuse ownership claims and leave a vacuum that other less legitimate leaders, including experts, readily fill. The bottom line: high capacity with poor leadership can make an organization or country stumble, but even with low capacities, sound leadership can move a country forward.

From national to local authorities, leaders are most effective when they are inclusive and proactive, and ensure allocation of adequate domestic resources. They must have the courage to take risks and overcome obstacles, while empowering others. With clarity about their own personal goals and how these fit with collective aspirations, leaders cultivate self-awareness, manage themselves in stressful environments, empathize with other people, and address blocks to individual and team performance in order to get the job done.

6. Establish positive incentives

Development interventions, like all actions, are driven by incentive systems, some of which are conducive to capacity development, while others are clearly not. Although incentives can be intended to spark positive results, some actually end up discouraging local initiative, ignoring sustainability and indirectly encouraging brain drain.

Incentives that help preserve capacities and maximize their use are grounded in governance systems based on the rule of law and human rights. Using a rights-based approach to development is one step towards a larger ambition for the entire society, even though transformation requires much more. Many examples of good governance have dominated the literature on this subject, and even without entering into the debate on the issue, it is important to acknowledge the immense consensus attained by the international community on what constitutes good governance.

Many developing countries, however, still struggle with public services that are riddled with negative or perverse incentives, including low remuneration, skewed recruitment and promotion criteria, compression of salary differentials and downsizing. All of these factors have been blamed for capacity erosion. To shield their sponsored initiatives, while ensuring sustained delivery, donors often hand out incentives in the form of salary supplements, and travel and meeting allowances. Yet such practices drain the public service of its most able employees and reduce the motivation for a comprehensive reform. While there is no quick fix, there is a need for locally led, harmonized solutions, optimally integrated in national budgets. Independent mechanisms can support reform of public programmes and procedures, while partnerships between the government and civil society actors can foster consensus for larger public administration reforms.

The use of external expertise, still often regarded as a bonus or free good, is another example of perverse incentives. Foreign consultants are never free, and their costs have to be known, budgeted and compared with alternatives in the most transparent fashion. Governments can negotiate greater use of local and regional consultants, short-term advisors and volunteers. Coaching models and independent oversight mechanisms, as well as institutional twinning, time-bound gap-filling and costing of technical cooperation attributed to national budget systems are all initiatives that have been successfully tested.

Incentives also have to be examined in the arena of procurement, where policies for donors as well as recipients should explicitly address the requirements for capacity development. Procurement transparency is central to the establishment of a culture of accountability and cost-effectiveness, but complex procedures tend to overwhelm recipient country governments and local agents. The best course of action is to adhere to minimum operating standards.

One of the biggest threats to capacity development is corruption, which siphons away resources and weakens systems. Instead of indulging in witch-hunts, however, anti-corruption efforts should focus on prevention, through incentives that arise from fostering positive values, creating a culture of professionalism and meritocracy, improving transparency and disclosure, and building accountability. De-mystifying and de-personalizing government through civic education not only reduces opportunities for corruption, but also enlarges the capacity for participation. It is also important to strengthen and protect the integrity of the media, civic groups and other non-governmental organizations, which offer checks-and-balances. Without the threat of exposure, corrupt officials act with impunity.

Even when all is done to create the optimum set of incentives for capacity development, qualified labour is subject to global trends. To deal with brain drain, push factors have to be turned into pull factors, with the ability to monitor, evaluate and respond to the emigration of the highly skilled becoming particularly essential for countries with weak talent pools. In addition to stimulating return migration, it is important to encourage reverse flows of income, through remittances and investments, and channel them towards development efforts. Diaspora networks can be an important medium for knowledge sharing.

7. Integrate external inputs into national priorities, processes and systems

Development agencies, even with all good intentions, have invented a jungle of multiple rules, procedures and requirements. Developing countries have been expected to adapt to these. But this accommodation involves high transaction costs and strains domestic capacities. It is time to shift the onus of flexibility from developing countries to donors, even if it means that doing business may differ significantly from one country to another. Recipient countries, on the other hand, should be prepared to refuse offers of extrabudgetary support that divert national resources to lower priority activities, and obscure the true costs of development efforts.

Increasingly, developing countries are taking charge of the process of development aid, starting with the mechanisms for policy dialogue with donors. National development forums are replacing consultative groups and round table mechanisms. Recipient countries should in general insist on the primacy of one single development framework, such as the poverty reduction strategy paper (PRSP) process, a national development plan, or similar approaches that are nationally derived and owned.

PRSP preparation can be driven merely by the desire to obtain continued concessional assistance – as some recent cases have shown. But PRSP design has put stakeholder consultation and participation at the centre of defining national priorities and actions, which gives PRSP countries a tremendous opportunity to reclaim ownership of their development. The MDGs offer another option, and in some cases may be integrated with the PRSPs. Where governments are not committed to these goals, societal forces need to exert pressure to make them more responsive.

Project aid, programmatic or sector-wide approaches (SWAP), and budget support all present both risks and possibilities to increase ownership. From a capacity point of view, there is clear reason for integrating aid into national priorities and systems. Where a government is not representative or fails to meet minimum operating standards, budget support may not be feasible, but it may remain a good starting point for exploring options.

In general, external partners must respect national procedures for the selection and approval of priorities and related budgetary allotments, with the implementation of programmes ultimately the responsibility of national agents. However, management and oversight still require clear delineation of responsibility, relationships and accountability through established institutions and systems. In countries with weak capacities, integrating external expertise directly into the administration through gap-filling "without shame" is preferable to establishing parallel institutions, such as project implementation units.

Monitoring should be a mechanism for learning and adjusting to evolving conditions, but when approached primarily as a reporting and control instrument, this fundamental purpose tends to get lost. A broader approach is the public expenditure review (PER), which emphasizes national participation. Results-based management, when used as a part of national planning systems, can also become an important instrument for empowerment.

When piecemeal alignments among groups of donors become standard practice, they fragment development efforts and further diffuse national control. Multilateral development banks, Organisation for Economic Co-operation and Development/Development Assistance Committee (OECD/DAC) members, the European Union and United Nations agencies have pledged to become more coordinated and responsive to country conditions, which implies commensurate changes within their legislative and regulatory frameworks. For developing countries, this level of international momentum on harmonization opens the door for renegotiating aid systems on more beneficial terms.

8. Build on existing capacities rather than creating new ones

Each generation learns from earlier ones, with language, values, culture and customs strong determining influences on any individual. So it is appropriate for capacity development, as an endogenous course of action, to begin with existing capacities and assets. For any country, it is useful to identify current capacities and determine those that need bolstering. Even if an entire systemic analysis cannot be carried out, capacity self-assessments start the process of asking hard questions and set the right tone for internal discussion.

With current incentive structures for the development industry heavily stacked in favour of "getting the job done" over sustainability, a gap-filling approach prevails and tends to be donor driven. Everyone stands to benefit, however, when technical cooperation is directed towards fostering organic capacities (see figure 0.1). This begins with restricting the use of technical cooperation to where it is most needed, or by infusing consulting and strategy formulation with participatory techniques, such as a future search. The challenge is to work with agents of change within society and government, while cultivating and protecting existing social capital. Fragile countries pose particular difficulties, although scenario building and prospective studies have been successful in building consensus in post-conflict and crisis situations.

9. Stay engaged under difficult circumstances

Where crisis or post-crisis conditions constrain government functions and competencies are weak, external partners typically react by tightening conditionalities, taking control of vital functions, or in some cases disengaging altogether. Corrupt or exploitative governments tend to see their aid flows sharply decrease. Yet people in the weakest societies need capacity development support most, or even capacity replenishment, as in the case of the devastating consequences wrought by HIV/AIDS. Operational responses will naturally vary, even as fundamental capacity development principles must remain in place.

FIGURE 0.1: ORGANIC CAPACITY DEVELOPMENT

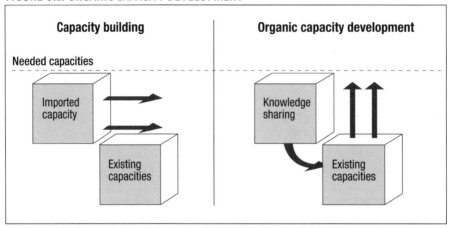

In post-crisis situations, each phase in crossing from relief to development offers the potential for capacity development. Area development programmes have been successful in some places because they take a comprehensive approach, building on local ownership, and focusing on reinforcing the capacities of local and district governments as well as traditional institutions. Reconstruction phases in particular may provide significant openings for leapfrogging administrative gaps.

The challenge of finding appropriate ways of intervening is highest in countries where government ownership has strayed far from the common good, human rights are violated, and the personal interests of the powerful overshadow any develop- ment effort. The most desperate situations may be those where semi-legal but irresponsible leaders betray their people and wreck their country by gutting national capacity and assets. Protecting what remains of existing social capital becomes an urgent priority, while finding and working with change agents requires sensitivity and ingenuity. Instead of fully bypassing government, it may be preferable to maintain pressure points in strategic areas that can foster change and increased accountability. Basic social service delivery, for instance, may become an entry point allowing continuous engagement as well as potential short- and long-term support for the population.

As a crisis wanes, donors also need to stay engaged, instead of simply over- whelming a country during its darkest hours and then moving on just when the long-term agenda must begin. Donors also often inadvertently target the same sectors, neglecting others that offer less political mileage and visibility. Their over- powering presence makes local authorities look impotent, while the flood of assessment missions creates astronomical expectations often followed by an excruciating hiatus of activity that leads directly to alienation.

Such uncoordinated and disruptive support does little to help a country find a sustainable development path. To avoid some of these problems, external agents must be willing to accept coordination by a national institution wherever possible, or pool their resources in a temporary arrangement. This encourages the emergence of ownership and leadership, yielding a lasting benefit.

10. Remain accountable to ultimate beneficiaries

Any responsible government is answerable to its people, and accountability among both national governments and donors is essential. But while accountability mechanisms that prevent wrongdoing are important, they do not necessarily steer a course towards the actions that make a difference in poor people's lives.

Far more important is a general culture of transparency, the foremost instrument of public accountability, not just in terms of financial resources, but also with regard to institutional management practices, planning and service delivery. Transparency gives a powerful opportunity for stakeholders to monitor and apply pressure, with information about positive experiences and success stories becoming as important as the monitoring of failure and misconduct.

Systematic feedback from intended beneficiaries of development and from those responsible for development activities always carries the promise of a response – after all, no large famine has ever occurred in societies characterized by democracy and freedom of expression (Sen, 1999). When public service managers, for example, come to depend on feedback for their portion of public resources, they soon appreciate mechanisms such as suggestion boxes, user satisfaction surveys and public hearings. National reporting on the MDGs is another avenue that will provide stakeholders with a potent tool to assess the actual achievements of both their leaders and the international community.

Ideally, monitoring should be seen as a mechanism for learning and adjusting to circumstances, even as it remains a valuable instrument for evaluation and codification of knowledge. Fine-tuning should no longer be perceived as a weakness in planning, but rather as an effective way of responding to change. And while donors are answerable to their domestic constituencies and need to enroll continued support for development by demonstrating the impact of their individual forms of assistance, realistic ways of assessing results and successes from collective undertakings must also be found.

The global dimensions

The global dynamics influencing capacity development appear throughout this book. Some can greatly undercut capacity development efforts – the international mobility of highly skilled workers, for example, while contributing to better international flows of knowledge and the formation of international research and technology clusters, erodes talent pools in some countries and regions. The underprovision of global public goods can wipe out years of capacity development efforts, as shown by the HIV/AIDS pandemic.

Other global trends have diverse implications. The explosive growth in information and communication technology (ICT) is spinning powerful social and economic networks, and radically improving the exchange of information. Trade alignments shift constantly, with institutional and social conditions playing an important role in determining whether, and to what extent, a country reaps potential benefits. More trade agreements and policies based on human development could encourage capacity creation, retention and utilization.

A new aid architecture is also emerging. The Millennium Declaration, including the MDGs, offers a framework for development endorsed by virtually all countries. Such a pledge needs to be backed by resources: the estimated cost of achieving the MDGs is placed at US $100 to $120 billion a year, less than .5 percent of global GDP. To put this amount in perspective, military spending in the world is about $800 billion a year, while agricultural subsidies in OECD countries amount to $327 billion, and total expenditures on alcohol and cigarettes in Europe are more than $150 billion (Jahan, 2003). It is time to shine the spotlight on donor countries over the issue of political will.

With a strong global consensus and the financial resources to fulfill the MDGs, the question then becomes, "Where do we begin?" If national leaders and the international community are serious on this common commitment, they will recognize that building lasting local and national capacities can pave the way for achieving the MDGs, and herald a future of sustainable growth.

10 DEFAULT PRINCIPLES FOR CAPACITY DEVELOPMENT

01 Don't rush

Capacity development is a long-term process. It eludes delivery pressures, quick fixes and the search for short-term results.

02 Respect the value system and foster self-esteem

The imposition of alien values can undermine confidence. Capacity development builds upon respect and self-esteem.

03 Scan locally and globally; reinvent locally

There are no blueprints. Capacity development draws upon voluntary learning, with genuine commitment and interest. Knowledge cannot be transferred; it needs to be acquired.

04 Challenge mindsets and power differentials

Capacity development is not power neutral, and challenging mindsets and vested interests is difficult. Frank dialogue and a collective culture of transparency are essential steps.

05 Think and act in terms of sustainable capacity outcomes

Capacity is at the core of development; any course of action needs to promote this end. Responsible leaders will inspire their institutions and societies to work accordingly.

06 Establish positive incentives

Motives and incentives need to be aligned with the objective of capacity development, including through governance systems that respect fundamental rights. Public sector employment is one particular area where distortions throw up major obstacles.

07 Integrate external inputs into national priorities, processes and systems

External inputs need to correspond to real demand and be flexible enough to respond to national needs and agendas. Where national systems are not strong enough, they should be reformed and strengthened, not bypassed.

08 Build on existing capacities rather than creating new ones

This implies the primary use of national expertise, resuscitation and strengthening of national institutions, as well as protection of social and cultural capital.

09 Stay engaged under difficult circumstances

The weaker the capacity, the greater the need. Low capacities are not an argument for withdrawal or for driving external agendas. People should not be held hostage to irresponsible governance.

10 Remain accountable to ultimate beneficiaries

Any responsible government is answerable to its people, and should foster transparency as the foremost instrument of public accountability. Where governance is unsatisfactory it is even more important to anchor development firmly in stakeholder participation and to maintain pressure points for an inclusive accountability system.

PART A

CAPACITY DEVELOPMENT IN PRACTICE: ISSUES, POTENTIALS AND CRITICAL CONSIDERATIONS

Introduction

Since examples are often better than precepts, the first half of this book highlights key considerations for identifying good cases of capacity development. Each of the four chapters brings together a cluster of issues that capacity development sceptics frequently debate. The book does not aim to persuade them, but instead sets out to demonstrate that developing sustainable, indigenous capacities is a process without a blueprint, driven by learning and advancement based on particular circumstances and experiences. Part A will address some of the main challenges, as summarized below.

Chapter 1 discusses the basics of capacity development and defines the parameters of ownership, presenting an endogenous process with implications for national ownership. It also explores some of the hindrances, starting with the aid relationship, which has long dominated the development discussion and has, in many ways, influenced national efforts for better or worse. Other topics include mindsets, vested interests and power differentials, which militate against the development of lasting indigenous capacities, deter meaningful dialogue and erode confidence and trust. National ownership needs to be the default setting for capacity development. Key issues include:

- What are pivotal entry points for societal change? For what and for whom are capacities needed?

- What are the limits of ownership, a concept with many interpretations and present in different agendas?

- How can mindsets and vested interests that are distorting a partnership be dealt with? How can complexities that overburden national institutions be reduced?

- How can trust, dialogue, commitment and self-confidence be built?

- How can development in difficult situations or failed states be fostered?

- What signposts are relevant for capacity development?

Chapter 2 explores the potentials and implications for integrating external cooperation into national priorities, systems and processes. Integration has consequences for programming, implementation, and monitoring and evaluation, while also impacting the broader policy dialogue and the management of external cooperation. The chapter examines the interface between countries and their partners, starting with the policy discussions that shape aid relationships, conditionality and selectivity. Key issues include:

- Can conditionality be conducive to capacity development?

- What is the most effective way to define roles and responsibilities between national authorities and their external partners for policy dialogue, programming, implementation and monitoring?

- Are there clear opportunities for integrating external aid into national systems and processes?

- What are the steps in assessing capacity and monitoring its development?

- How can stakeholders ensure accountability to the ultimate beneficiaries of development efforts?

Chapter 3 focuses on some of the most persistent problems in development. One of them is the long-lasting myth that experts or consultants are a free good. With the world's notions and practices of knowledge acquisition rapidly changing, the presence of expatriate experts in aid recipient countries needs to be re-evaluated. This chapter also looks into how governance and public service incentive systems can strengthen government institutions and enable them to support national processes and private-sector development. Long-standing dilemmas involving project management units and individual salary compensation schemes are assessed. Key issues include:

- What is needed to attract and retain the right people for critical positions?

- How can demotivation due to different work conditions and remuneration packages be addressed?

- What are ways to move from dispersed incentive schemes to aligned and rationalized incentives?

- Are there better approaches to navigating effectiveness and suitability, as well as dealing with parallel structures, such as project implementation units?

- How can brain drain be turned into "brain gain"?

Chapter 4 addresses the challenges of capacity development at three levels: individual, institutional and societal. It offers insights on individual skills development with a focus on education. Institution building and strengthening are emphasized as fundamental in charting a development course. On the societal level, the roles of social capital, civic engagement and self-esteem in empowering individuals and societies are revisited. In addition, the chapter explores global trends with implications for development, examining emerging global knowledge networks and the implications of enhanced mobility. Key issues include:

- What are promising ways to enhance human skills?

- How can institutions for effective service delivery be strengthened?

- How can contributions be made to the protection and nurturing of social capital and societal capacity?

- How can capacities be expanded to benefit from a more globalized world?

This book is not intended to be a how-to manual. Its goal is to be as concrete and specific as possible in proposing options, as well as in exploring some issues that in the past were deemed too complex or controversial to address. Perhaps its most important contribution to the dialogue on capacity development will be Part B, the second half. Through a collection of case studies chronicling effective examples and practical experiences, it affirms the diverse ways in which people can transform their lives by building upon their own creativity and resourcefulness.

1 Capacity development basics

Capacity development is an all-encompassing term that requires explanation and a sharper focus. Fundamentally, it is a broad goal achieved over time.[1] Yet it is not synonymous with socioeconomic development, even though developing capacities to conceive and carry out relevant tasks is crucial to the advancement of living standards.

Another term, often used interchangeably with capacity development, is capacity building. The former is more comprehensive, however, connoting the initial stage of creating and building capacities, as well as the subsequent use and retention of such capacities. There is nothing wrong with capacity building, but it is not sufficient in and of itself, because capacity exists within an environment: labour market trends, institutional governance and other local conditions are all factors that influence it for better or worse. While capacity development may not be the perfect designation for this highly nuanced, multilayered process, at the very least it ventures beyond the first step of building or creating. In many cases, this first step has proved to be the easiest to take on a long, difficult and often frustrating road.

The following chapter begins by establishing capacity development as an endogenous process and exploring two questions: capacities "for what?" and "for whom?" Some fundamental core capacities will be looked into, followed by a discussion on important starting points. Since national ownership and accountability have always been key to sustainable development, this chapter shows how they form an integral part of the default setting for capacity development. As well, every country is a case in itself, with its own peculiarities that require customized solutions. Particular challenges will arise in the form of mindsets, vested interests, power and special development circumstances.

---

[1] Capacity development as an objective corresponds to the goal of people wanting to learn and increase their options and choices. This applies similarly to institutions and societies as a whole. Capacity development is also an approach and a process in development, a means by which individuals, institutions and societies are empowered to make choices and chart their own development course. Finally, the far-reaching nature of capacity development not only makes it an objective, an approach, a process and a means, but also an outcome.

1.1 CAPACITY DEVELOPMENT AS AN ENDOGENOUS PROCESS

> *Learning a musical instrument involves many stages in a long and continuous journey. The road to success is one that nobody but the student can walk on. It leads through trial and error, lots of exercises, dissonance and gradual achievement. The student could benefit from listening to the teacher play beautifully once in a while. But if the teacher takes over, it is likely that the student will feel inferior and lose confidence and motivation. Learning to produce harmonious music requires motivation, perseverance and determination.*

Learning is the key ingredient in human progress, helping people grow and become capable of more sophisticated undertakings. There is, however, a limit to what an individual or organization can achieve through informal learning. A functioning society requires "the ability of people, institutions and societies to perform functions, solve problems, and set and achieve objectives" (UNDP, 2002a).

This is a concise, straightforward, definition of capacity development.[2] But how does it happen?

It is voluntary. Capacity development stems from one's motivation and desire to do things and do them well. Learning anything more demanding requires determination and perseverance to eventually get things right. In schools, incentives such as academic honours and scholarships play an important role in prompting students to learn more and reap rewards. On the other hand, perverse incentives can dwarf or undermine interest. In all likelihood, a student who is consistently told that others are smarter or do much better will become discouraged.

It takes time. Building and developing sustainable capacities is a decades-long endeavour. Training individuals takes years if all stages of education are included, while bringing an organization to the brink of self-sufficiency may take much more than a one- or even five-year budget. Major systemic or societal changes may call for generations. Nevertheless, countries tend to operate on a short-term horizon, as encouraged by regular, democratic elections. Similarly, external cooperation is seldom designed to cover more than five years, and often less. Actual budgets are virtually all determined on an annual basis – an inherent contradiction that remains unresolved.

It is case specific. Every brain uses a different set of faculties and notions to apprehend the world. What is meaningful to one person might not be saying much to another. And Cartesian logic, while essential for some, may be a riddle for others. To succeed, pedagogy must use multiple means to reach people with very different ways of learning.

---

[2] There is a wide range of definitions and conceptual considerations emphasizing one aspect of capacity development or the other. The proposed definition used in *Capacity for Development: New Solutions to Old Problems,* edited by Sakiko Fukuda-Parr, Carlos Lopes and Khalid Malik, seems to capture the essence of what the concept entails.

It is based on existing capacity. Each generation learns from the preceding ones, with language, values, culture and customs serving as strong determining factors for any individual. Learning the Tamil or Amharic languages would be a major challenge to someone who grew up speaking German or Portuguese, while a Western ear may find it hard to follow, or even appreciate, Japanese opera.

It is dynamic. Life and societies are constantly changing, requiring adaptability and flexibility. Today's capacities build upon those established in the past, but also have to be continuously upgraded to respond to evolving needs and opportunities. Since entirely new capacities have to be developed around emerging technologies, the capacity to absorb and manage change itself is now recognized as a critical skill.

Capacity for whom?

The first and basic unit of capacity is the individual, in whom skills and knowledge are vested. The role of education, especially primary education, is crucial. With capacities shifting over time, a solid and appropriate primary education provides the platform for higher levels as well as the acquisition of needed skills and specialities.

A particular area of importance in terms of education has become science and technology: countries that fail to understand this condemn their peoples to a relative, if not absolute, decline in their standard of living. The age of the Internet offers an alternative access to knowledge, but only for those able to take advantage of it. By the end of 2000, more than 400 million people could log onto the Web, a dramatic increase from the less than 20 million users in 1995. More than 20 million Web sites had been set up, a staggering number considering that in mid-1993, fewer than 200 existed. The cost per average unit of universal data transmission also declined from \$150,000 in 1970 to only \$0.12 in 1999 (UNDP, 2001a, p. 31). Unfortunately, the benefits of the information superhighway are seldom available to those most in need of them. As well, for some disciplines, learning without a teacher and structured follow-up is not viable.

The second level of capacity involves institutions, a term with different connotations: it can refer to the act of instituting something; a specific organization or establishment funded for a particular purpose; the building where such an organization is situated; or an established custom, law or relationship in a society or community. Institutions provide the framework for individual capacities to connect and achieve goals beyond the capability of one or even a few people. They also offer continuity and act as repositories of knowledge and experience, reducing dependency on single individuals, while enabling access to accumulated knowledge.

A recent study emphasizes that "within organizations, capacities exist among individuals and groups, and within the organization as a whole. Individuals possess knowledge, skills and attitudes that reflect their experience and training. When individuals share these things with colleagues and they become embedded in group norms and processes, it can be said that they become part of the group's capacity. And when individual and group capacities become widely shared among the organization's members and incorporated into management systems and culture, they become organizational capacities" (Silva et al., 2003).

Institutions and organizations established in response to demand or need are the ones likely to function more efficiently. Their mandates are usually clear, and they are held accountable by end-users, who are often members of their governing structures. They are also likely to be funded adequately so that they can perform their designated tasks, while attracting and retaining staff motivated by the relevancy and visibility of their work.

In other cases, institutions may have lost their original purpose, failing to evolve and adapt to changing circumstances. In some developing countries, for example, institutions have been set up at the suggestion of and with initial funding from diverse external partners, but do not satisfy prioritized needs and are not sufficiently supported after the termination of external funding.

Just as individuals make up institutions and organizations, whose impact is greater than the sum of their individual contributions, institutions and organizations come together to form networks. Their achievements of these often outweigh the total output of their members. This process tends to be spontaneous, but could be deliberately pursued for specific goals.

The third level of capacity is that of a society as a whole, and especially of a country and its governance. A society brings together all segments of the population through numerous groups and networks. It provides an ethos that largely determines the value system within which people and the economy function – embracing elements such as trust, honesty or concern for the poor, or conversely corruption and greed. These patterns in turn shape a society's vision and strategies.

The importance of this level of capacity was not fully appreciated until quite recently. Capacity development efforts focused mainly on individual skills and institutions, tacitly assuming that other factors – usually described as externalities or an enabling environment – would sort themselves out. But experience has shown that externalities such as corruption, governance systems or conflict-prone attitudes are extremely resilient to change and have impeded – and even brought down – many capacity development initiatives.

All three levels of capacity are equally important and mutually interdependent (see figure 1.1.1), as, for example, a functioning judicial system illustrates. For this kind of institution to fulfill its purpose, it needs skilful and capable judges, attorneys, court reporters and other individuals. It must be bound by laws and

FIGURE 1.1.1: THE CAPACITY DEVELOPMENT LAYERS

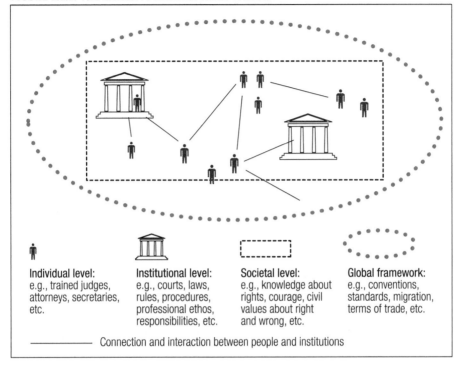

Individual level:
e.g., trained judges, attorneys, secretaries, etc.

Institutional level:
e.g., courts, laws, rules, procedures, professional ethos, responsibilities, etc.

Societal level:
e.g., knowledge about rights, courage, civil values about right and wrong, etc.

Global framework:
e.g., conventions, standards, migration, terms of trade, etc.

——————— Connection and interaction between people and institutions

well-established principles and procedures. Ultimately, the judiciary's success is anchored in a society comprised of people who share values of right and wrong, who know about their rights, and who take the liberty to exercise and defend them. In sum: if one level of capacity is valued more than the others, efforts become skewed and inefficient (UNDP, 2002a).

Across the board, the state's role in governance – encompassing functions such as implementing policies and the rule of law, and improving socioeconomic conditions – is fundamental to expanding capacities, creating more opportunities and sustaining growth. Any vision of societies managing their own destiny needs to include a well-functioning state. Thus, this book contends that bypassing the state, even when the legitimacy of its leadership is questionable, is not a viable course of action. Development cooperation initiatives, under all circumstances, must involve the state and assign it responsibilities.

Capacity for what?

The broad concept of capacity development is easy to grasp, but the reality of specific capacities – their definition and context – is complex and more elusive. For

TABLE 1.1.1: SOME FUNDAMENTAL CAPACITIES

10 KEY CAPACITIES[3]	CORE CAPACITIES[4]
1. To set objectives 2. To develop strategies 3. To draw up action plans 4. To develop and implement appropriate policies 5. To develop regulatory and legal frameworks 6. To build and manage partnerships 7. To foster an enabling environment for civil society, especially the private sector 8. To mobilize and manage resources 9. To implement action plans 10. To monitor progress	• To be guided by key values and a sense of purpose • To define and analyse their environment and their own place in the greater scheme of things • To define the issues and reach working agreements on purposes or mandates • To manage and resolve conflicts • To formulate strategies • To plan, and act on those plans • To acquire and mobilize resources • To learn new skills and approaches on a continuous basis • To build supporting relationships with other parties • To assess performance and make adjustments • To meet new challenges proactively, by adjusting agendas, approaches and strategies

quite some time, the understanding of capacity was influenced by the engineering world. It was felt that technical and scientific skills were exclusive to given fields, such as water management, energy generation, health systems, accounting and social security systems. The transfer of that knowledge required particular processes (Morgan, 2002) – a vertical, sector-specific approach.

Less attention has been paid to areas where horizontal efforts could transform external support for capacity development into more effective and far-reaching impacts. These are cross-cutting and pertain to development strategy and management: they include policy formulation, assessment of policy options, social and economic research for programming future development outlays, systems analysis and management, monitoring, review and feedback mechanisms, and performance auditing. Some of these fall under the rubric of "good governance" – in recent years there has been growing appreciation and external support for this. Others are more accurately described as aspects of good development management.

Table 1.1.1 lists two sets of capacities drawn up by different researchers. On the left are ten key capacities critical to the achievement of the MDGs, which were identified in a recent UNDP analysis (Browne, 2002). On the right, Lavergne and Saxby present a similar list of "core capacities" that represent what could be expected from a highly developed individual, organization or society that "can be considered as empowered and capable of molding its own destiny – not because it is self-sufficient or autonomous, but because it is highly competent in managing its environment" (Lavergne and Saxby, 2001).

There seems to be an acknowledgement that these capacities are crucial for pursuing development, and that all of them are underpinned by fundamental abilities. The

[3] Browne, 2002.
[4] Lavergne and Saxby, 2001.

formulation of policies and strategies, for instance, calls for more than a structured mind and writing skills. First, it requires a vision of the ultimate goal. Then it demands a whole range of capabilities and mechanisms relating to leadership, engagement and dialogue. Knowledge of the stakeholders and the management of a meaningful process including large groups of people are important, as are the facilities to table tricky issues, negotiate, mediate between divergent interests and manage forms of conflict resolution.

The core capacity to plan requires analysis, along with the ability to envision and develop scenarios, assess implications and prioritize. The capacity to act on plans or implement strategies demands a whole range of managerial skills. All of these are premised on essential capacities relating to self-esteem, creativity and values.

These examples illustrate that important entry points for capacity development exist not only in relation to core capacities, but also in many substantive areas and across different sectoral processes. Schools of thought and many experiences have collected around issues such as self-esteem, education and training, lifelong learning, stakeholder analysis, process facilitation, large group processes, voice mechanisms, listening, motivations/incentives, management, results-based management, change management, knowledge management, ICT and connectivity, leadership development and many more, some of which are discussed in this book. Effective capacity development will need to draw on this wealth of existing wisdom and practices, and open creatively to disciplines that usually have not been on the screen of development.

KEY POINTS

 Capacity development is an endogenous process that takes place in every society on the individual, organizational and societal levels. It can be supported or distorted through external intervention.

 Capacity development is voluntary, requiring motivation; takes time and is not amenable to delivery pressures; is case specific and resistant to blueprints; is based on existing capacity and grows from there; and is dynamic and open to adaptation.

 Bypassing the state, even when the legitimacy of its leadership is questionable, is not a viable course of action. Development cooperation initiatives, under all circumstances, must involve the state and assign it responsibilities.

Key capacities include competencies that permit individuals, organizations or societies to mold their own destiny – such as the ability to set objectives, strategize, plan and implement those plans. They also comprise the establishment of regulatory frameworks, empowerment of civil society, partnership building, sound management and monitoring of results.

 There are underlying capacities that lead to development effectiveness, including self-esteem, listening, facilitating change, leadership development and knowledge networking.

REFERENCES PART B

➲ **BHUTAN** *A National Vision Guides Progress and Technical Cooperation (p. 174)*

➲ **CHINA** *Investing in Pharmaceutical Research Capacity to Compete Globally (p. 198)*

➲ **ECUADOR** *National Dialogue Rallies Consensus on Sustainable Development (p. 205)*

➲ **HONDURAS** *Democracy Trust Backs National Consensus Amidst Volatile Politics (p. 229)*

➲ **MONGOLIA AND MOROCCO** *MicroStart Backs Business Plans of Leaders with Vision (p. 255)*

➲ **RWANDA** *Ubudehe Collective Community Action Holds Hope for Rebuilding a Shattered Society (p. 275)*

➲ **AFRICA** *Afrique en Création Supports Cultural Expression and Exchange (p. 313)*

1.2 OWNERSHIP

> *"The New Partnership for Africa's Development seeks to build on and cel-*
> *ebrate the achievements of the past, as well as reflect on the lessons*
> *learned through painful experience, so as to establish a partnership that*
> *is both credible and capable of implementation. In doing so, the chal-*
> *lenge is for the peoples and governments of Africa to understand that*
> *development is a process of empowerment and self-reliance. Accordingly,*
> *Africans must not be wards of benevolent guardians; rather they must be*
> *the architects of their own sustained upliftment" (NEPAD, 2001).*

> *"Assistance should provide Singapore with jobs through industries and*
> *not make us dependent on perpetual injection of aid. I warned our workers,*
> *'The world does not owe us a living. We cannot live by the begging bowl.'"*

> *—Lee Kuan Yew on traditional technical cooperation to Singapore (Lee, 2000b).*

Capacity development is tainted by the perception that often initiatives are externally introduced or funded. This in turn has created a need to understand the central role ownership plays in successful development experiments. There is broad agreement among aid analysts that a lack of ownership on the recipient side has been a major reason for the failure of many projects, including the structural adjustment programmes supported by the international financial institutions (Devarajan et al., 2001). There is less agreement on what is meant by the term ownership itself, however.

A group of "wise people", who reviewed development cooperation with Tanzania, have quoted some typical donor opinions, such as, "Ownership exists when they do what we want them to do, but they do so voluntarily," or, "We have to pressure the local government to take ownership" (Helleiner et al., 1995). Donors[5] often see themselves as bearers of a deeper insight into what is good for the recipient, and in this context recipient ownership will simply mean that the government counterpart realizes what is best for his country. The recipients, on the other hand, see ownership as a question of government command and control over resources and policies.

The term ownership is often misleading, since it is borrowed from the realm of law and is used in a very subjective and abstract context. To avoid misunderstandings, it is useful to define its scope and meaning, both in terms of *what* is being owned, and by *whom*. A Swedish International Development Agency (Sida) study (Edgren, 2003) referred to ownership as "the exercise of control and command over development activities. A country or an organization within a country can be said to 'own' its development programme when it is committed to it and able to translate

---

[5] In the text, the designation "donors" is more commonly used than the now preferred terms of "contributors" or even "external partners". Donor identifies a specific role and set of actors, which is not the case with the others, hence the selective use of partner or contributor when the text refers to broader roles and agents.

its commitment into effective action. This definition incorporates institutional dimensions such as the control of both input and output resources, political ones such as commitment, and behavioural ones such as an observed ability to achieve results." The study tracks the evolution of the debate surrounding development approaches, which first insisted on priority setting, moved to an emphasis on commitment and political will, and finally has ended up with ownership.[6]

This gives rise to the question: is ownership just a powerful metaphor, a fashion to be replaced soon by yet another development round? Certainly the principle cannot be meaningfully used without further definition. It "should not be taken lightly, it has to be defined and qualified for specific situations" (Edgren, 2003), with consideration for its different aspects.

These begin with the *ownership of ideas and strategies.* There is no limit to the number of partners who can share this, and its transfer from one to the other simply takes place through persuasion, based on the qualities of the proposed idea. When a dialogue partner chooses a particular concept from among many competing ones, his or her ownership will not be in question, provided that the choice is free and voluntary. The greater the pressure from donors or other stakeholders in favour of a choice, however, the larger the risk becomes that the decision maker will later disown it.

Second, one can talk about *ownership of processes.* This aspect is particularly important for the implementation of capacity development projects, as it is most often defined in behavioural terms – who took the initiative, wrote the terms of reference, designed a project element and so on. When the donor is seen to control a process too much, it is deemed "donor-driven". If the final outcome is positive, the recipient may eventually assume some responsibility for it, but if it is a failure, it belongs to the donor.

Third, ownership is naturally related to *resources.* Development cooperation entails a variety of resource contributions – from political ones that create space for the project, to financial, human and technological inputs. Recipient governments or institutions that make big contributions of their own are seen to be more committed and as having a greater sense of ownership of a project than those who make only marginal offerings. This aspect is particularly important from the point of view of sustainability, which will be dealt with further on.

Fourth, there is the *ownership of outcomes.* Quite often, the results of an activity are claimed by many if they are successful, but attributed to others if they are deemed a failure. Attribution is a serious concern, creating accountability problems for overall outcomes, especially in cases of negative impact.

---

[6] An interesting definition of ownership has been proposed (United Nations University, 2003): "However the concept of ownership has been used in so many contexts in recent years that its operational usefulness has diminished considerably as a result. In this volume, ownership will be taken to mean that governments have internalized reforms to such extent that they are prepared to defend them before their domestic constituencies."

These aspects of ownership still focus mainly on central governments, and do not satisfy requirements for wider participation. It is also necessary to introduce a dimension of "national ownership" or – when ownership does not extend to a truly national scope – to define the specific stakeholder interests. Who are the forces that expect to benefit from an initiative, and who are those that can be expected to resist it? There is no benchmarking for such analysis, so it will have to be case specific.[7] But the outcome will tell something about the prospect for a genuine and deep-rooted ownership sensibility.

To complicate the picture even further, ownership is a dynamic concept with a tendency to change over time, even during a normal project or programme. In too many cases, projects have been launched by donors in spite of a lukewarm response from the recipients, in the belief that a stronger sense of ownership will emerge along with the positive results. Yet a strong indication of the recipient's commitment is needed even before a project begins; as it moves forward, built-in incentives can encourage beneficiaries and/or the government to take over. Incentives can be related, for instance, to control of service delivery, resource mobilization or the use of advanced technology. Across the board, financial sustainability is critical, albeit often ignored (Catterson and Lindahl, 1999).

When ownership is low or questionable at the outset of a development partnership, a specific element of risk enters the picture. A donor agency may regard the experience of working in a difficult country as worth the risk, for example, but it is unwise to have too many high-risk projects at the same time in a given project portfolio. Some donors have a policy of balancing risky projects with low recipient ownership with projects that have a high degree of recipient commitment. More often, however, donors still shun the latter, because they are close to the recipient's core priorities and, therefore, likely to be implemented even without external contributions. Yet if development cooperation is to produce results, it will have to be fashioned around the recipients' requirements, even at the expense of other concerns.

In fact, all actors involved one way or the other in a particular development activity can, at different stages, claim ownership, which goes against the common use of the word as referring to appropriation by a specific set of actors. This underscores the need to demonstrate that there are various interpretations of the same concept, and to generate demand for a more specific, less general, identification of the real interests linked to each interpretation.

A stakeholder analysis can help in pinpointing these. Every project or programme that involves resource transfers is supported and opposed by numerous pressures, sometimes called stakeholder interests. Some of these are based on positive expectations, opening room for favourable collaborations, while others

---

[7] The World Bank, for instance, in the definition of ownership formulated for the Comprehensive Development Framework, attaches particular significance to the participation in decision-making of the top political leadership and representative institutions like parliaments (World Bank, 2001). Other donor development agencies suggest that civil society organizations and local communities should be involved in the process as a requirement for establishing national ownership.

Box 1.2.1: Owner and stakeholder interests

Indirect winners and losers in a proposed bridge project

	Intended winners	Intended losers	Unintended winners	Unintended losers
Recipient side	Central and local governments	None	Illegal loggers	Forest dwellers, ferry owners, small traders at ferry points, alternative users of aid allocation
Donor side	Aid constituencies	None	Equipment suppliers Donor agency officials	Environmental NGOs
Intermediaries	None	None	Consultants Experts	None

A schematic picture of the layout of indirect stakeholder interests is given below for the case of building a bridge over a river. The bridge will be of direct benefit to industry, agricultural producers and transporters on either side, but will lead to reduced business for ferry owners and traders operating around the ferry berths. It is assumed that local government and communities will not be able or willing to fund the bridge unless foreign aid money covers most of the costs.

This configuration indicates that the project will have strong support on the recipient side among local governments and communities, but that it may face resistance from people and enterprises depending on existing ferry services. The unintended negative consequences in terms of illegal logging may also spark opposition from environmental groups. On the donor side, the aid constituencies expect to benefit, and so do supplier interests.

To draw conclusions from this analysis regarding expected recipient ownership, it will be necessary to estimate the degree of support that the project will have among direct beneficiaries, local governments and communities. Such an analysis has to go deep into the strength of commitment among different actors, and also consider alternative users of the aid allocation, i.e., those who would have benefited from the money had it not been used for the bridge.

Source: Singh, 2002.

---

lead to rejection of a particular project. Shekhar Singh (2002) has elaborated a scheme for stakeholder analysis that identifies direct and indirect involvement, as well as intended and unintended winners and losers (see box 1.2.1). Different interests may appear on the donor side as well as among the institutions, communities and popular groups in the recipient country. They can also be found among the many development industry intermediaries likely to be affected, i.e., consultancy firms, non-governmental orgaizations (NGOs), suppliers of equipment, etc. (Banerjee et al., 2002).

Stakeholder analysis is useful to examine the vested interests that may steer a project away from intended objectives. Suppliers, for example, may sway project design through persuasive arguments for heavier use of consultants and equipment.

Illegal loggers may influence a decision to choose a location closer to the logging sites. Corrupt officials on the recipient side may support a redirection of a project, while politicians may wish to redirect anything that enhances their standing among their voters. All kinds of actors affect development projects by overloading them with local staff and prolonging them beyond the point where there is no value added (Banerjee et al., 2002).

Projects and programmes that go on for long periods need to be checked against these positions, which flourish through clients who depend on the patronage of the officials and enterprises involved. At times, it can be difficult to terminate an activity that has attracted strong lobbying among intended as well as unintended beneficiaries (Catterson and Lindahl, 1999).

KEY POINTS

 With lack of ownership a major reason for the failure of many development programmes, it is essential that development interventions be broadly owned, starting with the initial idea and continuing in terms of responsibility for the process, control over resources, and commitment to and acceptance of all outcomes.

 Ownership is a powerful metaphor that can easily fade, becoming just the latest fashion unless it is understood in its complexity, specificity and nuances.

 Salesmanship does not foster ownership. If something is sold that is not really wanted, it may distort the allocation of energies, at best becoming an investment with very significant opportunity costs. Distinguishing between ownership of ideas and strategies, processes, resources and outcomes minimizes the blurring of initial intentions.

 Proper stakeholder analysis is a crucial step in determining who has a legitimate interest in an intervention, identifying intended and unintended beneficiaries as well as those who are negatively affected.

1.3 LEADERSHIP

An owner is not necessarily a leader, who must possess certain skills, personal commitment and the ability to carry out concrete action. From the highest national authorities to those at community levels, leaders are most effective when they are inclusive and proactive, and ensure allocation of adequate domestic resources. Leaders make transformation happen because they have the courage to take risks, expand implementation, overcome obstacles and empower others.

The relationship between capacity development and leadership is a fundamental one: fostering leadership protects individual, institutional and societal capacity investments. Lack of powerful and responsible leadership can destroy decades of patient nurturing of human skills or developing institutions. It can confuse ownership claims considerably, and open the door for a multitude of heterogeneous interests and demands. In other cases, influential but regressive leaders have actually used all the techniques and knowledge available to degrade their institutions or societies. They have also twisted ownership to suit their own agendas, gearing it towards a culture of entitlement or excessive nationalism that is detrimental to capacity development.

Given the impact of leadership, it is not surprising that complaints about poor examples of it have been topical at least since ancient Greece. For the modern world, a crisis of confidence over the issue has been unfolding since the 18th century, when Enlightenment philosophers such as Rousseau and Voltaire claimed that people could control their destiny through the application of reason. This thinking generated two common viewpoints: belief in progress and in the "perfectibility" of humans. The picture was rosy. However, a hundred years later, Sigmund Freud and then Max Weber challenged these assumptions. Freud theorized that beneath the surface of the rational mind was the unconscious, which he supposed was responsible for a fair proportion of human behaviour. Weber explored the limits of reason, calling it the most destructive force operating in institutions, where he dubbed it technical rationality – that is, rationality without morality.

This analysis subsequently cropped up in the most important Western leadership theories of the 20th century, which can be divided into four categories: those influenced by Max Weber, which are primarily anti-bureaucratic and premised on individual strength; the notion of traits, from which one can derive the qualities of weaknesses and differences; empathy, which grew out of style theory, and looks at different kinds of relationships between leaders and their followers; and finally the concept of context, which set the stage for needing to know which skills to use in various circumstances. These theories influenced ways of looking at leadership for decades, until they confronted the wave of new technology, which has transformed access to information, globalized ideas and eroded central authority.

FIGURE 1.3.1: LEADERSHIP MATTERS

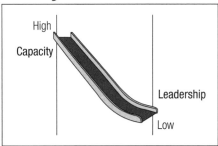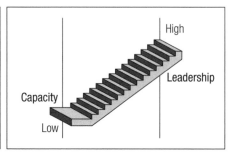

Currently, the field of leadership development emphasizes strengthening individual and team effectiveness, as well as institutions, and is based on principles and practices derived from ground-breaking research in psychology and neurology over the last five to ten years. Leadership, from the post-modern perspective, is a conscious process, starting with clarity about one's own personal goals, how these fit with the overall mission of an organization, and how systems and people must work together. Studies show that successful leadership results in enhanced understanding, improved working relationships, and greater collective effectiveness among working teams and their partners.

Since people with overlapping goals have a better sense of how parts of the system fit together, good leaders build upon relationships and trust, mobilizing energy in a way that is sustainable, fosters ownership and generates commitment. They must be able to manage themselves in stressful and complex environments, and at the same time "read" other people, empathize with their needs and get the job done. They need to know what inhibits effective individual and team performance and what to do in response. The bottom line is that strong capacity with poor leadership can cause an organization or country to stumble. But even with low capacities, strong and positive leadership can bring about progress (see figure 1.3.1).

An important set of competencies for effective management and leadership seem to be those associated with what has been called emotional intelligence (UNDP, 2002). Based on this concept, Daniel Goleman, Richard Boyatzis, Annie McKee and Fran Johnston have collaborated to develop a framework and practices that lead to profound positive change in individuals and organizations. Their model identifies four emotional intelligence "factors" – self-awareness, self-management, social awareness and relationship skills – which encompass competencies related to leadership. The researchers emphasize that everyone can develop these capabilities and improve their performance at work. Key to the process is helping people understand why they should change, what they should change into, how it will benefit both them and the institution, and how it directly impacts results.

Studies indicate that emotional intelligence is twice as important as technical knowledge and IQ combined for today's leaders, and as much as four times as important in terms of overall organizational success. A study of 15 global companies attributes 85-90 per cent of leadership success to emotional intelligence (Goleman, 2002). Yet this revelation is still debatable. UNDP has been experimenting with this knowledge in its HIV/AIDS programme (see box 1.3.1). The main findings point to the need for leaders to be capable of listening and dialoguing (see box 1.3.2). This is true for any level of leadership: community, civil society, private sector, local governance and all the way to the national arena.

In the context of this book, leadership should aim at transformation, where the most important element is the expansion of people's choices. For this, a critical prerequisite is democratic governance – a notion clearly demonstrated by scenario-building exercises in conflict prone societies.

In 2000, UNDP commissioned studies of three civic scenario-building projects: Mont Fleur in South Africa, Destino in Colombia and Visión in Guatemala. Essentially, scenarios are projections of alternative pathways into the future that explore dynamic interactions between the social, cultural, technological, political and economic forces operating within a given context (such as a local community or a nation). Scenarios help highlight opportunities and risks inherent in specific strategic issues; sharing them begins a process of reawakening people's interest in actively shaping their future and taking charge of their socioeconomic and political destiny. Scenario-building[8] works through a moderated process of dialogue and exploration by participant groups, whose composition is key. Participants should be potential future leaders, and they should be diverse and outstanding representatives of society as a whole.

---

[8] Scenario-building resources:
- UNDP has embarked on major scenario-building partnerships through its Regional Bureaux for Africa and for Latin America and the Caribbean
  (www.undp.org/rblac/scenarios/DialogueExperiences/index.html; or www.africanfutures.net).
- Generon, one of UNDP's many partners, has been the facilitator of an array of civic scenario dialogues, including the South African Mont Fleur project
  (www.generonconsulting.com/Publications/UNDPDocument.pdf).
- The Society for Organizational Learning is a global learning community with close ties to the Organizational Learning Center of the Massachusetts Institute of Technology (www.solonline.org/).
- Global Business Network is a premier scenario-thinking resource network (www.gbn.org/).
- Kenya at the Crossroads: Scenarios for Our Future, a joint initiative of The Society for International Development and the Institute of Economic Affairs (www.kenyascenarios.org).

Box 1.3.1: HIV/AIDS Leadership Development Programme methodology

The HIV/AIDS epidemic is pushing global communities to look deeper, ask tough questions, explore new perspectives, and challenge the status quo. HIV/AIDS is a profoundly human phenomenon, forcing us to deal with a host of sensitive issues related to sex and death. It is demanding that we become better leaders and strategists, more accountable, and at the most basic level, more compassionate.

UNDP's Leadership Development Programme is providing individuals, communities, institutions and even whole societies with an unusual opportunity to explore strengths and weaknesses, individual and societal motivations, hopes and dreams, plans and commitments in the area of HIV/AIDS. The methodology is simple: bring together key change agents and influential community members; offer them the opportunity to perceive and respond to the epidemic in a deeper and more systematic way; invest in developing their ability to be compelling, innovative leaders; and expand their capacity to coordinate and manage large-scale, multisectoral HIV/AIDS programmes. The Leadership Development Program is tailored specifically to the needs and challenges of each country in which it has been established.

Programme participants

Between 70 and 150 key leaders are identified and asked to take part in each country programme. They include members of the government, civil society, NGOs, the private sector, the United Nations and UNDP.

Leadership development seminars

Country programmes typically consist of three separate four-day seminars held over approximately nine months. Each seminar includes individual leadership development activities as well as group work related to strategy implementation and goal achievement. In between sessions, reflection groups, peer coaching and action-learning projects reinforce and extend the work.

Change agent training

A central aspect is identifying and further cultivating the local capacity to lead HIV/AIDS programmes. Therefore, eight to ten remarkable individuals in each country are identified to develop their skills and capacities as transformational change agents. They are trained to act as expert resource persons in the programme seminars, assisting in the facilitation of large and small groups. They also act as mentors or coaches to initiate and sustain the workshop participants' in the action-learning projects, and meet regularly with participants in teams to provide guidance, support and encouragement.

The Leadership Development Programme contributes to the following outcomes:

- Increased capacity for more effective and strategic leadership in response to HIV/AIDS

- Strengthened institutional capacity and collaboration of leaders at all levels and across sectors in responding in a strategic and coordinated manner (government, NGOs, civil society, the media and the private sector)

- Increased attention to and deeper understanding of the fundamental causes and drivers that fuel the epidemic, including the impact of HIV/AIDS on human development and poverty reduction, and cross-cutting issues such as gender and human rights

- Strengthened capacity for national and local level planning and implementation of HIV/AIDS initiatives

- Greater capacity of key community group leaders to support and scale-up the response to HIV/AIDS at the local level

Source: UNDP, 2002f.

Box 1.3.2: Listening to people

It can be stated, with practically no qualification, that people in general do not know how to listen. They have ears that hear very well, but seldom have they acquired the necessary aural skills, which would allow those ears to be used effectively for what is called "listening".

In general, people feel that concentration while listening is a greater problem than concentration during any other form of personal communication. This turns out to be true. When we listen, we ask our brain to receive words at an extremely slow pace compared with its capabilities. When we listen, therefore, we continue thinking at high speed while the spoken words arrive at low speed. To phrase it another way, we can listen and still have some spare time for thinking. The use, or misuse, of this spare thinking time holds the answer as to how well a person can concentrate on the spoken word.

Good listeners regularly engage in four mental activities, each geared to the oral discourse and taking place concurrently. All four are neatly coordinated when listening works best, with good listeners tending to direct a maximum amount of thought to the message being received, leaving a minimum amount of time for mental excursions on sidetracks leading away from the talker's thought:

1. The listener thinks ahead of the talker, trying to anticipate what the oral discourse is leading to and what conclusions will be drawn from the words spoken at the moment.

2. The listener weighs the evidence used by the talker to support the points that he makes. "Is this evidence valid?" the listener asks himself. "Is it the complete evidence?"

3. Periodically, the listener reviews and mentally summarizes the points of the talk completed thus far.

4. Throughout the talk, the listener "listens between the lines" in search of meaning that is not necessarily put into spoken words. He pays attention to nonverbal communication (facial expressions, gestures, tone of voice) to see if it adds meaning to the spoken words. He asks himself, "Is the talker purposely skirting some area of the subject? Why is he doing so?"

Listening ability is affected by our emotions. Figuratively, we reach up and mentally turn off what we do not want to hear. On the other hand, when someone says what we especially want to hear, we open our ears wide, accepting everything – truths, half-truths or fiction. In organizations and institutions, there may be many avenues through which management can send messages downward, and very few for movement of information upward. Bad listeners complicate the process, because people do not talk freely and the flow of communication is seldom set in motion.

Source: Nichols and Stevens, 1999.

KEY POINTS

The relationship between capacity development and leadership is a fundamental one: fostering leadership protects individual, institutional and societal capacity investments. Poor leaders can set efforts back by decades, and twist ownership to suit their own agendas, gearing it towards a culture of entitlement or excessive nationalism that is detrimental to capacity development.

A successful leadership style results in enhanced understanding, improved relationships, and greater collective effectiveness among working teams and their partners. Since people with overlapping goals have a better sense of how parts of the system fit together, good leaders build upon relationships and trust, mobilizing energy in a way that is sustainable, fosters ownership and generates commitment.

Important management and leadership competencies seem to be those associated with emotional intelligence, along with the ability to listen and dialogue.

REFERENCES PART B

➲ **BHUTAN** *A National Vision Guides Progress and Technical Cooperation (p. 174)*
➲ **CHINA** *Exposure Visit for Officials Facilitates Profound Policy Change (p. 196)*
➲ **ESTONIA** *Tiger Leap Brings the Benefits of ICT to Everyone (p. 217)*
➲ **JORDAN** *A Non-Threatening Approach to Interdisciplinary Collaboration (p. 243)*
➲ **MALAYSIA** *Raising the Capacity of Marginalized Groups to Facilitate Class Mobility (p. 252)*
➲ **MOZAMBIQUE** *Effective Budget Support for Post-Flood Reconstruction (p. 264)*
➲ **UKRAINE** *Leadership Transforms Awareness and Roles in the Fight Against HIV/AIDS (p. 304)*

1.4 MINDSETS, VESTED INTERESTS AND POWER

> *"They come with their hypothesis, their analytical framework and their reasoning. Once they set their premises, you can't get out of their logic. There is nothing to do... It is better to follow their reasoning and see what we can get out of it, even if we don't believe in it."*

> *"Once the expert sent by the donors has spoken, there is nothing else to add. He has an irrefutable logic. He has the coherence and the weight behind his arguments. He relies on scientific truths. He takes advantage of the technological setup to implement his ideas. But we know within ourselves that his truth is not complete, that he ignores lots of things, that he can be wrong.... The expert can't listen to us; or rather, he listens but does not understand. He is not intellectually and emotionally prepared to question what he is supposed to bring us" (Niang, 2002).*

The two quotes above are stereotypical, yet they reflect a profound dilemma. Where different worlds of knowledge, ways of thinking and arguing, culture and values meet, mutual understanding may not follow. People see and interpret the world through their own eyes and from their own vantage point. Interests motivate action that may well not be aligned with a common development objective, and perceptions breed mistrust and cynicism that stand in the way. What is most problematic is that these issues are highly sensitive, making them difficult to address.

Yet it is crucial to do so in any discussion about transformation and capacity development. Mindsets and personalities often dictate the success or failure of communication and collaboration. They can create influential virtual realities determining how people, institutions and societies behave. As well, language, culture and concepts convey notions, which harden over time into mindsets. For instance, the language of development is full of metaphors of hierarchy and inequality: aid, assistance, developed, developing world, donor, recipients, etc. (Ribeiro, 2002).

Being a donor connotes an act of goodwill, altruism and charity, rather than self-interest. It also implies, nevertheless, some kind of superiority, having something to give that others do not have. This logic extends to reinforcement of beliefs about developing countries having inadequate institutional or individual capacity; or the belief that these countries are insincere and uninterested in their own development. Examples of weak capacity and lack of commitment are cited commonly within the development community. But concepts such as time, efficiency or corruption have an array of connotations. What may be genuine elements of cultural diversity are easily understood as what is wrong, rather than what is different.

FIGURE 1.4.1: VICIOUS CYCLE OF EMPOWERMENT

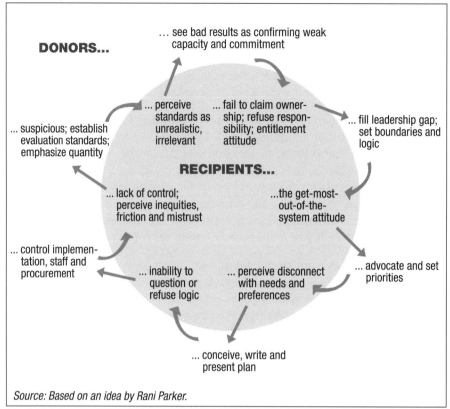

Source: Based on an idea by Rani Parker.

The overly confident posture of many expatriate experts is often mirrored by a widespread lack of self-esteem on the recipient side. Intended beneficiaries, conditioned to view aid as an act of benevolence, tend to be reluctant in questioning its rationale or whether it is used efficiently, regarding it mainly as free or cheap money. In addition, the impeccable logic of expert advice is unquestionable, especially when it imposes systems of managing resources that may be too heavy to control. Accountability has continued to look upwards, while communities in despair express apathy, or simply state what they think the questioner wants to hear (Niang, 2002; Singh, 2002). Local or other government officials who initiate community participation are often disempowered themselves.

Many development thinkers and practitioners talk in terms of "us and them". This division is not necessarily perceived as between expatriates and nationals. There is often an alignment between the interests of external partners and the national elite. Such an alignment is both part cause and part result of a homogeneity of education, aspirations and values, which leads to uniformity of

FIGURE 1.4.2: VIRTUOUS CYCLE OF EMPOWERMENT

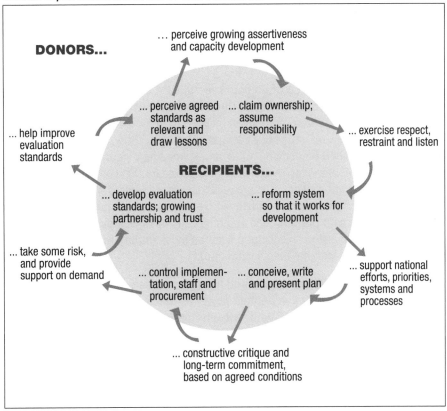

Box 1.4.1: Who is the stakeholder?

↳ Who has a stake in a given issue, intervention, etc.?

↳ Who is likely to benefit? How?

↳ Who loses, directly or indirectly?

↳ What are the expectations associated with the issue or activity?

↳ What effort and resources are people willing to commit to or not?

↳ What other interests may conflict or align with the initiative?

↳ Are there potential conflicts or coalitions?

↳ What does a stakeholder think about other stakeholders?

↳ Who else is a stakeholder, i.e., how else may they be affected or where do they have another interest?

↳ Which group does a stakeholder belong to: gender, age, class/caste (socio-historic dimension), ethnicity, rich/poor (socioeconomic dimension)?

↳ How does the issue or initiative impact on men's and women's roles and responsibilities?

language, concepts and perceptions.[9] Despite a tremendous wealth of goodwill, intention and the right rhetoric, these mindsets often remain within known beliefs and myths. A vicious cycle of domination and disempowerment results, undermining the quest for real partnership (see figure 1.4.1). A virtuous cycle of empowerment would require quite different attitudes from both sides (see figure 1.4.2).

The vested interests who often help keep this cycle spinning can be found on all sides of a development partnership. These are stakeholders who benefit from the current paradigm and therefore are most inclined to resist change, often proving to be a significant drain on capacity development efforts. They may steer a project away from its intended objectives, for example, keeping it going even as the need and demand for its services diminishes or disappears. In reality, projects rarely close until their funding dries up, a process that vested interests are adept at preventing! Where public money is involved, regular and transparent reporting of results, combined with performance auditing, can and does indicate where change is required. The discussion on corruption, as the most virulent form of vested interests, provides more insights (see section 3.6).

Compounding the dilemmas created through mindsets and vested interests is power. Max Weber (1977) even defined power as the capacity to make people do things they do not want to do.[10] While there is nothing wrong with legitimate forms of it, the prevailing norm is still based on unequal relationships, between governments and their citizens, donors and recipients, the elite and the underprivileged.

The poor often have an instinctive comprehension of this, experiencing despair over local elites who may be acting out of self-interest and for illegitimate ends. Yet donors still often fail to appreciate that national civil society is not a homogeneous whole, with vast differences in terms of age, class, caste, ethnicity, and most importantly, gender. Many groups do not have a seat at the table, because opening up to them could question rules that benefit those in charge. In spite of the well-accepted rhetoric of participation and empowerment, power differentials ensure that most development relationships are unidirectional, as well as marked by deep mistrust and exclusion.

This issue, with its potential to profoundly shake the status quo, is seldom discussed directly and candidly. Most analysts take refuge in examples and analogies, because they do not want to rock the boat. For transformation to take place, however, it may be time to acknowledge that a real discussion about power, as it gravitates around access, distribution and prioritization of resources, is central to making progress, especially in terms of ownership and the appropriation of development results.

---

[9] This influences decision-making, e.g., village elders working by consensus in Asia and Africa. A related document is "Getting Better Government for Poverty Reduction: So What's the Problem?" This summary note by Sue Unsworth was circulated by the Development Assistance Committee Network on Good Governance and Capacity Development, also known as GOVNET
(www.oecd.org/oecd/pages/home/displaygeneral/0,3380,EN-about-64-2-no-no-no-no,00.html). Another example can be found in contrasting the word "donor" in reference to self with "recipient" in reference to the developing country.
[10] For further reflections on power, see Ribeiro, 2002.

Table 1.4.1, while far from comprehensive, highlights some of the types of interests, motivations and incentives that come into play in development cooperation.

A dynamic for change

Despite the often firm cast of mindsets, vested interests and power differentials, there is scope for addressing them directly, especially if there is determination to do so at the highest political level. This process will most likely consider the following:

- There should be an initial acknowledgement of the current architecture of interests.

- Stakeholder analysis (see section 1.2 and box 1.4.1) can be particularly helpful for specific interventions, yielding a growing understanding of where the overall difficulties and opportunities are.

- Measures that help simplify an overly complex and fragmented set of relations and influences can be introduced. In the aid relationship, this could mean the reduction of space for closed-curtain dialogue and encouragement of more transparent forms of negotiating.

- Forums for policy dialogue – such as the consultative group or round table, PRSP, or other planning and review processes – provide an opportunity for more genuine debate. It may be preferable to consolidate and build on such mechanisms. But sometimes it is better to create independent processes that are less locked into established dynamics.

- Promotion of harmonization measures may enable convergence around national priorities, processes and systems.

- Information relevant to the different stakeholders should be accessible to all. This includes addressing very down-to-earth issues such as using local languages, eliminating technical jargon, and distilling critical information in concise and digestible formats.

- Opening up space for dialogue may encounter resistance, but it will be difficult for any party to argue that public participation and transparency are not the way to go. Freedom of expression, an active media, opposition and pressure groups, as well as a functioning judicial system comprise a conducive framework for vibrant civil society participation.

TABLE 1.4.1: MOTIVATIONS, INTERESTS AND INCENTIVES

Across all constituencies in development cooperation, there may be a basic motivation to contribute to improving people's lives, but other motivations, interests and incentives can lead to distortions.

RECIPIENTS	DEVELOPMENT INDUSTRY	DONORS
Political constituencies • Bringing in donor dollars is politically savvy • Aid money is used to dish out patronage	**Development industry** • Effective capacity development may actually render the industry redundant or create new/different consulting opportunities	**Audit bureaus** • Reporting to parliament **Legislatures** • Votes, taxpayer concerns
Civil service • Working with various donor agencies is a learning experience • Prestige and perks – computers, vehicles, salaries in dollars, foreign trips, etc. • Demoralization due to comparing differentials	**Consultants** • Career prospects: livelihood, status, not having to work in "structured" surroundings; often better pay than full-time jobs in the development sector • Northern citizens often can afford/are provided very lavish lifestyles in southern countries	**Foreign ministry** • Political and trade interests **Private companies (goods, equipment and logistics suppliers)** • Business opportunities • Philanthropy is good for business
Private contractors and goods/equipment suppliers • Business opportunity • Job protection for unions • Rent-seeking can continue under politically patronizing regimes	**Consultancy firms** • Organizational survival, development contracts are getting larger and more attractive • Useful parallel cash flow mechanism for consultancy firms to hedge against corporate sector downturns. More "protected" market often due to tied aid	**Average taxpayer** • Concern for tax dollars • Concern about corruption, mismanagement in recipient countries **Donor agencies** • Rules on procurement, confidentiality of payments, etc. • Insecurity of some staff within donor agencies who fear redundancy in a new regime • Disbursal pressures • Employment
Southern NGOs • Civil society frustration with state failure • Opportunities for accessing available finance • Potential for international travel, etc.	**Universities/research institutions** • Initiators of ideas • Many universities encourage faculty to get consulting work to cover salaries and overheads • Source of revenue	**Northern NGOs** • Expectations of specific constituencies at home (greens, women's groups, churches, etc.) • Compete with southern NGOs
Elite and middle class • Aspirations are more aligned with their counterparts in northern countries than with the poor in their own countries, creating a "natural" bias in their decisions • Personal enrichment		

KEY POINTS

 Mindsets and vested interests, coupled with power differentials, can breed mistrust and scepticism. These highly sensitive issues are difficult to address.

 In the end, mindsets may be the most pervasive determinants for success or failure, fueling either a vicious cycle of domination and disempowerment, or offering hope for transformation.

 Vested interests may extract a high toll from capacity development efforts. A common example is the perpetuation of projects long after the need for them has passed.

 In spite of the well-accepted rhetoric of participation and empowerment, power differentials ensure that many development relationships are unidirectional, as well as marked by profound mistrust and exclusion. It may be time to acknowledge that a real discussion about power, as it gravitates around access, distribution and prioritization of resources, is central to making progress, especially in terms of ownership and the appropriation of development results.

 A dynamic for change may include: acknowledging the architecture of current interests; analysing stakeholders; setting up measures to simplify overly complex relationships; establishing clear rules of engagement; promoting participation by civil society; and favoring processes and consultations that allow discourse on divergent perspectives.

REFERENCES PART B

➲ **EGYPT** *A Confident Community Learns to Manage Its Environment (p. 208)*
➲ **GUATEMALA** *Coordination and Flexibility Help Civil Society Broker Trust After War (p. 223)*
➲ **JORDAN** *A Non-Threatening Approach to Interdisciplinary Collaboration (p. 243)*
➲ **RWANDA** *Ubudehe Collective Community Action Holds Hope for Rebuilding a Shattered Society (p. 275)*
➲ **SOUTH AFRICA** *Women Analyse the Budget, and Parliament Heeds the Gaps (p. 284)*
➲ **UKRAINE** *Leadership Transforms Awareness and Roles in the Fight Against HIV/AIDS (p. 304)*

1.5 DIFFICULT DEVELOPMENT CONTEXTS

Crisis has many faces, with conditions differing in their nature and impact. Yet these situations all aggravate capacity development dilemmas. Examples include: capital flight or brain drain; the loss of decades of development efforts in Southern Africa due to HIV/AIDS; domination of one ethnic or religious group over others; domestic and cross-border conflict; terrorism; an absence of credible conflict resolution mechanisms; corrupt judicial sectors; poor policy environments for rich natural resource bases; uneven access to political decision-making between urban and rural areas; natural disasters; expenditures heavily favouring the military over social investments; and repression that precludes the free exchange of ideas.

It may at times be useful to cluster countries with fundamentally similar problems. Classifications that have been used include: low-income countries under stress (LICUS)[11], poor performers or fragile states, countries with a low human development index (HDI), nations with a negative GDP, armed conflict, low levels of democracy, corruption and HIV/AIDS prevalence. However, classifying difficult development contexts is prone to subjectivity and, in terms of capacity development, offers little motivation for transformation. Instead, there is the risk of generating a deceptive view of a particular country or reality.

Pre-crisis, crisis and post-crisis stages have their own needs in terms of capacity development. These are specific to individual situations and require a tailored analysis and response, with a threshold in determining the most promising course of action. In a country without basic institutional capacity, it may not be possible to work through existing mechanisms. For instance, if the most straightforward forms of accountability are lacking, budget support may not make sense. In cases where authorities are responsible and responsive to their own people, it is more likely that external partners will work with them.

While operational responses may vary, capacity development principles are nonetheless universal. They should be upheld wherever possible, despite the difficulties encountered along the way. Weakened societies in particular need capacity development if they are not to be abandoned in a downward spiral of illiteracy, poor health and loss of hope. The arguments that follow review some of the default principles.

Distinguishing between short-term emergency and transitional needs, and long-term requirements and opportunities, is essential. But the bridge over the relief-development gap is a persistent challenge. Those working in relief are familiar with the dilemma that sets in when short-term emergency support becomes a long-term institution because of the dependencies created. At all points along the way, interventions need to consider ways to strengthen potential agents of longer term transformation.

---

[11] A World Bank designation.

In building these alliances for change, it is essential to understand what is at stake for whom. A bias towards the marginalized, women, poor people and minorities is justifiable, whereas arrogant leadership breeding mistrust and resistance is not. Not all value systems are acceptable. For example, female genital mutilation or honour killings are violations of human rights. Another issue is the overpowering presence of aid agencies in complex emergencies, which often makes local leaders look weak and powerless. Local people may end up begging rather than dealing with their own legitimate authorities. In some cases, to counteract these tendencies, scenario-building exercises have been used to develop trust and confidence (see section 1.3).

In the most difficult crises, individual wisdom and survival strategies prevail. However, much of this knowledge is tacit and may not be easily shared or codified. During reconstruction, despite a probable willingness to make use of what has been learned, hurdles arise, including limited access to ICT and related skills development. Yet it remains essential that people select, digest and adapt knowledge in order to apply it to improving their lives.

Frequently, vested interests and power differentials exacerbate difficult development situations. Some leaders are able to muster support through patronage, coercion and other means of dominance. A meaningful engagement requires paying careful attention to these interests and power games. Open challenges are rarely a viable option; hence, there is a need to initiate dialogue around less sensitive issues, gradually building up to more complex ones. To ensure conflict prone power structures are not further reinforced, it may be advisable to establish new forums, such as village committees (Pillay, 2003). The presence of external agents can, if handled carefully, protect such space for dialogue.

The immediate needs of the day should not eliminate possibilities for capacity development. Opportunities can be seized early on – for example, displaced populations may be more accessible for various kinds of basic and civic education. In some countries, vocational, entrepreneurial and professional training schemes have been useful during their transition to independence (Angola, Mozambique and South Africa are examples). More generally, the critical role of women and education in development is well established, while a low level of education among young men is said to be a high risk factor in prompting conflict. "Each year of education reduces the risk of conflict by around 20 per cent" (Collier et al., 2001).

In numerous cases, those who have benefited from education and training during exile have become the backbone of new post-conflict leadership. Cases in point are the educational support provided to the African National Congress in South Africa, or the Canadian scholarship programme that assisted 11 of the ministers in Chile's first post-Pinochet government (OECD/DAC, 2001). Pillay argues that the challenge is "to break the vicious cycle through a bridging effort to kick-start development, targeting technical cooperation programmes to strengthen capacity in a manner that would enable the delivery of assistance to address those constraints that are of most critical importance to a reversal of the deterioration of economic and developmental conditions" (Pillay, 2003). He suggests that while any response needs to encapsulate the *sui generis* needs of a given situation, the main interventions should emphasize sustainable conflict resolution, the rule of law and justice, anti-corruption measures, the strengthening of local institutions, economic diversification and employment, youth employment, delivery of services, and HIV/AIDS prevention and control.

There is little hope for change after any crisis if coercion, violence, torture, patronage and corruption destroy civic engagement, with those who may be able to challenge the existing power and vision retreating from public life in frustration or leaving their countries in disgust. The most fundamental incentives for capacity development are personal security and the rule of law, because potential change agents need a degree of predictability to ensure that engaging in the public arena or the private sector can be worth their efforts. In the most difficult environments, it may be possible to improve incentives at first only on the local level. However, if a country wants to permanently escape destitution and poverty, determined and responsible national leadership is a prerequisite.

Processes and systems for planning, implementation and monitoring need to be inclusive and integrated into national systems. It has often been suggested that the international community should in effect take over "failed states" for a period, in order to guarantee the delivery of basic services, restore order and maintain good governance. A role for parallel service structures in the areas of health and education has recently been suggested.[12] Yet the dilemma is fundamentally the same as for project implementation units (see section 2.4). Apart from the philosophical and political considerations, there are often high risks associated with vested interests in such parallel systems. However, efforts to improve basic service delivery, particularly in education and health, remain less sensitive than human rights and governance reforms, and can have a critical long-term effect on national capacity.

There is frequently a temptation in fragile environments to fill leadership gaps, which may undercut local capacity and initiative.[13] The challenge is therefore to identify and work with change agents within society and government, and to nurture social capital wherever it exists. This requires sensitivity and ingenuity, as well as cooperation with NGOs, civil society organizations, private sector institutions and local authorities. Area development schemes provide a planning and management framework and have been used with considerable success in numerous conflicts. They allow different external agents to support local ownership in a coherent

---

[12] The World Bank has proposed the establishment of independent service authorities for LICUS as quasi-autonomous agencies that could function in a manner similar to that of the independent revenue authorities set up in institutionally weak environments (World Bank, 2002; OECD/DAC, 2002).

[13] In *Eroding Local Capacity*, Juma and Suhrke (2003) provide an analysis of international humanitarian action in Eastern Africa and its effects on local capacities for dealing with crisis situations.

and coordinated way, with an initial focus on reinforcing the capacities of local governments and traditional institutions. Such entities can then plan and manage relevant development activities, becoming the nucleus for transformation at the regional and national levels.

When crises result from or give rise to governments that are less committed, more corrupt or indifferent to the plight of the poor, aid flows tend to decrease. External partners typically tighten conditionalities, take control of vital functions, or in some cases disengage altogether. As a result, citizens of these countries are "doubly damned". It is essential to stay engaged for the sake of these people, which often means working with the government to promote accountability in areas such as revenue collection, rebuilding and maintenance of basic infrastructure, and basic social service delivery. This also allows for longer term sustainability and entry points to influence policy and other decisions. The donor community regularly overwhelms crisis countries for a year or so and then moves on, abandoning them just when the long-term agenda needs to be tackled. For capacity development to have any chance at taking off, it is critical that donors continue to be involved.

Fragile countries are prone to a host of agendas and interests, yet external agents often do not understand these, so two-way consultation with local communities is essential. Communities may undergo rapid flux and evolution in the aftermath of a conflict, for instance, when refugees return. Fine-tuning or reorienting projects should not be seen as a flaw or weakness in planning, but rather as a virtue in terms of needs being acknowledged. In addition, the political landscape needs to be recognized as a key determinant of whether a country's situation will improve. Reinforcement of parliamentary processes, voice and accountability systems, space for an inclusive and professional cadre for the justice and security sectors, support to alliances of the poor, civic education, and the promotion of human rights all contribute to a future of greater stability.

Whenever a crisis prevails, there is a broad spectrum of potential responses, along with a danger that everybody may pick and choose what is considered relevant. Donors inadvertently end up targeting the same sectors, while neglecting others that offer less political mileage and visibility. This is particularly evident where there is a lack of leadership. But even in these situations, development partners still need to be accountable to beneficiaries. External agents must be willing to accept coordination, which implies an agent with the ability to assume such responsibility as well as the willingness of development partners. Ideally, an emerging national institution plays the coordination role, as was the case in Afghanistan with the Afghanistan Assistance Coordination Authority (AACA).

Where a national framework is not in place, emerging external agents should pool their resources in a temporary arrangement, perhaps in a country level agency. It can serve as a clearinghouse and local broker, and should offer a high degree of flexibility, competent staff and credible autonomy.

KEY POINTS

Crisis has many faces that can aggravate capacity development dilemmas. While operational responses vary, capacity development principles are universal. They should be upheld whenever possible, despite difficulties encountered along the way.

Donors need to remain engaged in difficult development contexts. Immediate needs should not completely overshadow possible openings for capacity development and sustainability. The presence of external agents can, if handled carefully, provide a space for dialogue and building trust.

During reconstruction, hurdles to gaining knowledge arise, despite a willingness to make use of it. In some places, area-based programmes and scenario-building exercises have been successful in addressing reconstruction issues. Social service delivery can provide a less contentious entry point, allowing continued engagement for short- and long-term impacts.

In the most difficult situations, where a government is no longer functioning, external agents should be willing to accept coordination by a national institution or temporarily pool their resources in an appropriate local agency.

REFERENCES PART B

➲ *AFGHANISTAN* Local Capacity Grows Amidst Conflict and Collapse of Central Authority (p. 171)

➲ *CAMBODIA* Decentralization Lays a Foundation for Reconstruction and Governance (p. 190)

➲ *EAST TIMOR* Volunteers Ease the Transition Between War and Reconstruction (p. 202)

➲ *ECUADOR* National Dialogue Rallies Consensus on Sustainable Development (p. 205)

➲ *GUATEMALA* Coordination and Flexibility Help Civil Society Broker Trust After War (p. 223)

➲ *RWANDA* Ubudehe Collective Community Action Holds Hope for Rebuilding a Shattered Society (p. 275)

➲ *YEMEN* PRSP Preparation Paves the Way for Inclusive Policy-Making (p. 310)

2 Integrating external cooperation into national systems and processes

Defining capacity development as essentially an endogenous process has fundamental implications for external cooperation,[1] which this chapter explores by discussing the aid relationship[2] and the different stages of the programming cycle from a capacity perspective. It underscores the essential need for integrating development assistance into national priorities, systems and processes, following the default principle of grounding capacity development firmly within national ownership.

All over the world, external cooperation plays a disproportionately dominant role. Donors with their 63,000 projects dispense goodwill, priorities, interests and constraints – often leading to confusion and inefficiency. It is no surprise that this scenario is particularly acute in the weakest and poorest countries, the ones lacking enough vision, political self-confidence and professional expertise to follow their own path. By contrast, countries with a clear agenda tend to have a consistent and coherent set of policies, and are more likely to take charge and use their capacities to the fullest.

---

[1] There are broader factors such as debt burdens, the effects of structural adjustment and chronic trade deficits that are decisively hampering capacity development. Please refer to section 4.4.

[2] We are using the established terms "aid" and "donor-recipient". These do not reflect the complexity of the relationship. In effect, the donor is also a receiving partner, including in terms of large amounts of the resources, and vice versa. Despite their limitations, these phrases convey the nature of the relationship and help avoid terminological confusion.

2.1 THE AID RELATIONSHIP: BEYOND CONDITIONALITY

"Sustainable development...must be locally owned. The role of external partners is to help strengthen capacities in developing partner countries to meet those demanding, integrated requirements for sustainable development, guided by the conditions and commitments in each country. To give substance to our belief in local ownership and partnership we must use channels and methods of co-operation that do not undermine those values.... In a partnership, development co-operation does not try to do things for developing countries and their people, but with them.... Paternalistic approaches have no place in this framework. In a true partnership, local actors should progressively take the lead while external partners back their efforts to assume greater responsibility for their own development"[3] (OECD, 1996).

FIGURE 2.1.1:
THE AID RELATIONSHIP AND PROGRAMMING CYCLE

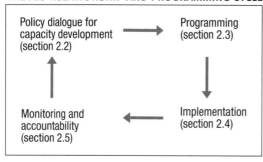

Since the aid relationship can significantly sway the outcome of development cooperation, it is useful to examine some of the ways in which it influences capacity development. Based on the simple notion that every aid transaction has a donor and a recipient, this relationship is driven by two sets of motives, objectives and expectations that may coincide or differ. These comprise a framework that cannot be said to rest upon a level playing field. Figure 2.1.1 generically summarizes the programming cycle familiar to all practitioners in development cooperation.

When the aid relationship works, it is characterized by strong correspondence between the objectives of the parties, either broadly, as when the two commit to the same strategy, or more narrowly, such as when there is agreement on specific operational goals. Even when the parties converge on some issues, however, they may be pursuing different interests, which in due course may spark tensions and threaten a common understanding. One side may be more interested in commercial or geopolitical aspects than in development, for example. Hence, from the very beginning, the two parties must be clear about sharing basic objectives with regard to *what* is supposed to be achieved.

---

[3] This quote was taken from the landmark report *Shaping the 21st Century: The Contribution of Development Co-operation*, which was endorsed by the OECD Ministerial Council in 1996 (www.oecd.org/search97cgi/stc.htm).

It seems superfluous to say that partners should share the *how* as well. But here is a dimension where foreign aid has gone seriously wrong over more than four decades. The Pearson Commission, reporting to the World Bank President as long ago as 1969, stressed that the aid relationship was to be based on mutual respect for rights and obligations, and stated, "The formation and execution of development policy must ultimately be the responsibility of the recipient alone, but the donors have a right to be heard and to be informed of major events and discussions" (Commission on International Development, 1969). Yet as the volume of official development assistance (ODA) transfers increased, along with impatience over slow implementation and poor outcomes in countries providing the funds, donor involvement and control expanded greatly, dipping into aspects from strategy formulation to actual implementation.

Donor dominance has been most common in poor countries with low development management capacity, with a few exceptions (Bhutan, Bolivia, Botswana, Cape Verde, Egypt, Ethiopia, India, Jordan and Vietnam, at least during certain periods in the last two decades). But on the whole, aid relationships have degenerated into paternalism, especially as many of the poorest countries have run into economic recession and huge debt problems. Consensus is now emerging that these donor-driven, patronizing approaches have been a major factor fueling the poor outcomes of development cooperation.

As a result, it has become necessary to reinvent the aid relationship, based on the original principles as well as current realities. The latter include the vast number of new stakeholders outside central governments (such as local governments, NGOs, community groups and the private sector). Many of these actors, who formerly belonged to the recipient side, now serve as donors in their own right – international and domestic NGOs and foundations, for instance, routinely provide inputs into projects or programmes. Changes like these imply the need for a more sophisticated approach than the old give-and-take. While the concept of partnership is one attempt to move forward, it does not quite capture the complex interactions between all the different actors. More often, a thorough stakeholder analysis is required.

Today's aid relationships are also no longer as exclusive as they used to be. In countries with quantities of external resources that are more than what they can effectively manage, donors often find it easy to cooperate among themselves, rather than through a recipient government aid coordinator. This structure offers possibilities for closer coordination, although there are "gang-up" risks, including intimidation or even marginalization of national agents. These risks are particularly acute when donor representatives are technically more experienced and better informed than national counterparts. By its very nature, the aid relationship is asymmetric, and it takes some very deliberate measures to counterbalance the advantages of the fund providers.

The configuration of various donors working with an individual recipient country remains significant, as are the donor group dynamics with the institutions of the host government. These may vary considerably between countries, even though most of the donor participants are the same, as studies of aid management and coordination in different African countries have revealed in terms of responses to problems of low absorptive capacity. The European Centre for Development Policy Management (ECDPM), for instance, reports that in Uganda and Tanzania, donors are going out of their way to help the recipient governments find ways of integrating all external aid flows into their budgets, while in Mali the tendency has been for each donor to try to protect its own projects in a manner that undermines integration (Baser and Morgan, 2002; Danielson et al., 2002; OECD/DAC, 1998).

Through a series of case studies, the ECDPM report determines that the aid relationship is an important factor in creating preconditions for developing capacity. There is no general lesson that can be drawn, because each national situation has its own potential and drawbacks. But the report makes clear that a small group of like-minded aid managers, donors and recipients can achieve better results through integrated aid management.

For their part, recipient governments can start shifting aid relationships in their favour by trying out new methods with those interested and then developing a general policy based on evaluations. Where a substantial group of donors finds it possible to collaborate under new conditions, it should be reasonable to expect others to eventually follow.

From conditionality to agreed conditions

There is a fine but very important line between agreed conditions that define the way development partners cooperate, and conditionalities that are imposed from the dominant partner (see box 2.1.1). It makes or breaks ownership. As Joseph Stiglitz put it:

> "Conditionality and borrower ownership can be contrasted by posing the question: If the country owns a reform program, why is conditionality needed?" (Stiglitz, 1998).

Imposing change from the outside (aside from the risk of being inadequate) is as likely to engender resistance as it is to facilitate progress. It also undermines incentives to acquire analytic capacities and then erodes recipients' confidence in their ability to use them. Instead of involving large segments of society in a process of discussing change – thereby altering ways of thinking – conditionality merely reinforces traditional asymmetric relationships and fails to empower those who could serve as catalysts for transformation. In some cases, it openly demonstrates their weakness.

After the Cold War dominated aid culture that characterized the 1960s and 1970s, there was the rise of a top-down conditionality approach promoted by the Washington consensus in the 1980s and 1990s.[4] There were numerous cases where a government in dire need of money signed structural adjustment loans with the International Monetary Fund (IMF) and the World Bank that were conditional on certain policy measures. In reality, the government lacked the capacity to implement these, did not believe in them, and hoped in the end it would not have to adopt them. The implicit lack of ownership in this arrangement explains many of the now well-documented negative outcomes of these reform programmes (Devarajan et. al, 2001).

The weight of these conditions has again fallen mostly on poorer countries, those with the most limited ability to satisfy them. A majority are in Africa, but can be found in other regions as well. Driven into a "conditionality trap" by heavy debt burdens and cash-strapped states, these countries struggle to satisfy steep demands even as these further undercut their already weak capacities. The perversity of this incentive structure is underscored by the fact that countries with more capacities, such as Brazil, Indonesia and Turkey, face less conditionality. They can avoid the trap, maintaining their own national sovereignty, simply because they are strong enough to do so.

One reason why so many structural adjustment programmes have failed is that they were designed without sufficient understanding of the situations faced by individual nations. Although the way conditionality is applied does not offer the ultimate test for the achievement of intended objectives, the approach does stumble into a credibility problem related to its lack of knowledge. This has caused the World Bank, which has admitted it has radically overestimated its own power for encouraging reform in poor policy environments (Santiso, 2002), to replace structural adjustment programmes with a more focused poverty reduction agenda.[5]

Developing countries themselves collectively agreed to implement national poverty reduction strategies at the World Summit for Social Development, held in Copenhagen in 1995. Yet they are now also being asked to sign up for PRSPs, which have been introduced by the Bretton Woods institutions to move towards more country-owned, poverty-oriented strategies. The catch: despite all good intentions, the PRSPs do not necessarily work like that, in part because of the limited choices available to developing countries. There is also the danger that, without sufficient trust and open dialogue, the papers can be seen as yet another donor requirement rather than a genuine shift in modalities. PRSP preparation can still be driven by the desire to obtain continued concessional assistance, as some recent cases have shown, rather than desired development objectives.

---

[4] Parallel to that, significant efforts were being made to overcome the traditional view of development as being measured solely by macroeconomic performance.

[5] The World Bank's founding charter prohibits it from taking into account political factors in aid programmes. But these principles have been surpassed by events. When the World Bank lends money, it usually also produces ideas guiding its usage (Rist et al., 1999; Stern, 1997).

Box 2.1.1: Conditionality, PRSPs and the MDGs

It is hard to find a measurement of performance that can replace conditionality. David Dollar and Paul Colliers' original argument for rewarding good results was a splash warmly welcomed by donors concerned with lack of progress. But the more one looks closely into the argument, the more questionable it becomes.

The principle of rewarding good performers first confronts the fact that the majority of countries are in the middle ground between good and bad (World Bank, 1998). And the weaker the capacity, the greater the need for support. Donors can try to skirt the issue by being "selective" – namely, providing assistance only to the good performers. But this can easily become an avoidance technique, a form of conditionality wrapped in more favourable public relations.

The more different actors and interests get involved in laying down their own selectivity or conditionality, the more difficult it becomes for the host government to piece together a coherent strategy that is accepted by the electorate and the donors. Does this mean money should be injected into corrupt or hopeless governments? The answer is no. There is a need, however, to work with complexity, rather than retreating into one-size-fits-all conditions, and selecting recipients "we like" because they mirror "our own views and strategies".

Poverty reduction strategy papers

A step in the direction of flexibility is the PRSP, introduced to offer heavily indebted poor countries (HIPC) debt relief under the HIPC initiative of the IMF and World Bank. Member countries prepare the papers through a participatory process involving domestic stakeholders as well as external development partners, including the Bank and the Fund. Updated every three years with annual progress reports, PRSPs map out a country's macroeconomic, structural, and social policies and programmes over a three-year or longer horizon to promote broad-based growth and reduce poverty, as well as to secure

external financing. Interim PRSPs (I-PRSPs) summarize the current knowledge and analysis of a country's poverty situation, describe the existing poverty reduction strategy, and lay out the process for producing a fully developed PRSP in a participatory fashion. For over 70 of the poorest countries, PRSPs are becoming the main framework for attracting donor support.

The World Bank and the IMF view PRSPs as a policy compact based on mutual commitment to poverty reduction and policy reforms. Instead of conditionalities, the compact is shaped by jointly determined objectives and directions, implying there should be little (if any) need for imposing conditions, especially those, such as economic stability, that have not proven to guarantee poverty reduction. By building an approach around dialogue, the World Bank and the IMF are trying to infuse the lender-borrower relationship with new meaning, and instill greater trust and commitment. Developing countries can assert their leadership over the PRSP or similar strategies and negotiate a foundation for a mutual partnership. Donors can be much more flexible in what constitutes an adequate poverty reduction framework, PRSP or a national equivalent.

Yet despite representing a step forward, PRSPs still risk being associated with poverty-related conditionality, which can be regarded as superimposed onto an expanded list of economic conditionalities. Once countries formulate PRSPs, they are required to reflect these priorities in their national budgets, a process monitored through annual reviews. If PRSPs become simply another layer of compliance for debt relief or concessional lending, they will do little to build national capacities or motivate efforts to develop.

The Millennium Declaration

As outcome indicators, the MDGs may become the key that turns the conditionality dilemma into an opportunity, measuring progress without a specific prescription on how to achieve it. Policy choice remains a critical factor for success, but since there are different routes to the same target, the MDGs do not specify any particular one. Instead, national actors need to engage in a broad discussion to select nationally relevant objectives that combine ambition with feasibility. These can then shape a realistic framework consistent with current capacity constraints as well as geared to short- and long-term capacity development. Since it is possible to measure progress against the goals, MDG monitoring can then become a powerful tool for holding national decision makers as well as the international community accountable for delivering on their promises.

For capacity development, an important aspect of the MDGs is that they offer a long-term perspective, in contrast to conditionality, which focused on short-term performance, typically between one to three years. Both donors and recipients need to increase their time horizon to the longer term as an essential ingredient of a new ODA incentive structure. With nearly all the countries of the world having signed onto the Millennium Declaration, with its consensus on mutual accountability between North and South, a strong impetus in this direction is now emerging.

The Millennium Declaration was the culmination of a series of world conferences and international agreements over the last few decades. In addition to the MDGs, it calls for good governance, conflict prevention, human rights and sustainability, and is premised on fundamental values such as freedom, equality, solidarity, tolerance, respect for nature and shared responsibility.

Guided by the Declaration, the Third UN Conference on the Least Developed Countries in Brussels later agreed on an elaborate Programme of Action for the first decade of the millennium, with a strong emphasis on capacity development in critical areas. These included fostering people-centred policy, good governance, human and institutional capacities, productive capacities and trade; reducing vulnerability; and mobilizing financial resources. This was followed by the International Conference on Financing for Development in Monterrey, Mexico, where the development community obtained major new commitments linked to progress towards the MDGs. The World Summit on Sustainable Development in Johannesburg further crafted a common framework on achieving progress in the areas of water, energy, health, agriculture and biodiversity (WEHAB). It also formally endorsed the MDGs as a framework for sustainable development.

Is there any way out of this dilemma? One thing is certain: the success of ODA depends on it. And hope for progress has come in the form of the MDGs, which represent a new framework for development policies and capacity development. As a compact between donor and developing countries, with an emphasis on national determination of targets and development routes, the goals provide a fresh platform for positive incentives and mutually agreed conditions. They also offer a long-term approach, with 2015 as the finish line.

If the PRSPs can incorporate these principles, they will be able to serve as country-specific programme strategies to achieve the MDGs. Since the PRSP design puts stakeholder consultation and participation at the centre of defining national priorities and actions, PRSP countries have a tremendous opportunity to reclaim ownership of their development processes. And even in cases where governments are not committed to the MDGs, other societal forces can exert pressure to make authorities more responsive.

KEY POINTS

The aid relationship, which is by its very nature asymmetrical, has a significant influence on the outcomes of development cooperation and in particular the prospects for capacity development. A solid aid relationship is characterized by high correspondence between the objectives and agreed conditions of donors and recipients.

For their part, recipient governments can start shifting aid relationships in their favour by trying out new methods with those interested and then developing a general policy based on evaluations. Where a substantial group of donors finds it possible to collaborate under new conditions, it should be reasonable to expect others to eventually follow.

Although the way conditionality is applied does not offer the ultimate test for the achievement of intended objectives, the approach does demonstrate a credibility problem, often linked to lack of knowledge of a country's situation. Tailoring targets to country circumstances is the best way to design a realistic framework consistent with current capacity constraints, and geared to short- and long-term capacity development needs.

If national strategies, including PRSPs are country-driven, results-oriented, comprehensive, prioritized, partnership-oriented and based on a long-term perspective, they will contribute to attaining nationally customized MDGs. Since the PRSP assigns a central role to stakeholder consultation and participation, developing countries have a tremendous opportunity to reclaim ownership of their development processes.

REFERENCES PART B

➲ **ECUADOR** *National Dialogue Rallies Consensus on Sustainable Development (p. 205)*
➲ **ESTONIA** *Tiger Leap Brings the Benefits of ICT to Everyone (p. 217)*
➲ **LAOS** *A Team Approach Aligned to the Local Decision-Making Style (p. 246)*
➲ **MOZAMBIQUE** *Effective Budget Support for Post-Flood Reconstruction (p. 264)*
➲ **TANZANIA** *Independent Monitoring Holds a Government and Its Partners to Account (p. 292)*
➲ **TANZANIA** *Twinning Institutions with Trust and Equity (p. 295)*
➲ **SOUTH-EAST EUROPE** *A Virtual Meeting Place for Education Reformers (p. 322)*

2.2 POLICY DIALOGUE FOR CAPACITY DEVELOPMENT

It might appear self-evident that every country would embrace and articulate a policy framework conducive to developing capacities. However, this is not the case. Policy and politics are closely related, and swayed by associated choices and sensitivities. For policy dialogue to lend itself to transformation, capacity development objectives and outcomes need both to be on the domestic agenda and appear in negotiations between national authorities and donors.

Dialogue is a critical instrument for establishing the sense of ownership that produces successful outcomes, appearing in three forms: *partnership dialogue* between donors and a recipient government; *donor dialogue* between donors; and *social dialogue* between the government and civil society. All of these are premised on the understanding that conditions impinging on programmes undertaken within a partnership can be of various types, some more technical and administrative, others more policy related. When dialogue is not effective or does not take place, and policies differ from the government's own values or strategies, ownership and development outcomes suffer. While a good overall partnership creates some leeway for bridging such differences, this lasts only up to a point. If several donors are supporting policy conditionalities led by the international financial institutions, for example, even individual partnerships may erode (Edgren, 2003).

To the extent that external partners contribute to a country's development, it is reasonable to allow them to comment on and even contribute to policy debates. However, this process cannot substitute for an ongoing national policy dialogue. Without this, there have been instances where recipient governments were more open to consultations with donors than to their national constituencies. According to a Kenyan researcher,[6] this dynamic has led to entire ministries being organized around donor priorities rather than national imperatives.

This emphasis on external expertise can quickly subsume the important qualifications of local actors – even though they possess a far better grasp of the sociology and the politics of the country. It is ironic that for many recipient countries, dependence on outsiders to accomplish planning tasks began at their independence! These countries have never drawn up a development plan or strategy without external assistance; they have never envisaged their future development without external support. Over the years, this dependency has produced an attitude among national leaders that is inimical to seeking endogenous answers, and development processes have become inextricably reliant on aid. Instead of activities flowing from an internal policy framework and related set of goals shaped by dialogue and owned by the host country, they tend to start – and finish – at the project level, where the external partner has traditionally felt most comfortable, as it permits greater control and financial accountability.

---

[6] From a presentation at the International Roundtable on Capacity Development in December 2001 at Turin, Italy (http://capacity.undp.org/roundtables).

Box 2.2.1: National development forums

The Programme of Action from the Third United Nations Conference on the Least Developed Countries referred explicitly to the issue of national development forums in the following paragraphs:

99. The implementation and follow-up of the Programme of Action at the national level are of primary importance. The LDC Governments should undertake this task within their respective national development framework and poverty eradication strategy, including, where they exist, PRSPs, CCAs and UNDAF, and with the involvement of civil society, including the private sector, on the basis of a broad-based inclusive dialogue. The development partners should support agreed objectives and policies designed by LDCs on the basis of the Programme of Action and existing national development and cooperation frameworks. On the basis of each LDC's commitment to these long-term policy frameworks and plans, development partners commit to extend adequate support for their implementation, including financial and technical support.

100. In some LDCs, national arrangements are already in place for broad-based and inclusive dialogue on development issues and policies. These forums are critical to ensuring genuine consensus and national ownership of national programmes of action and need to be fully supported. Other LDCs should follow this example by developing such national forums. The National Preparatory Committees set up for the preparations for the Conference with the participation of representatives from the public sector and the civil society, including the private sector, should be incorporated into these forums. The national forums, working in close collaboration with development partners, could provide a platform for regular and systematic follow-up and monitoring of the implementation of commitments by individual LDCs and their development partners at the national level, as well as providing inputs to follow-up at the global, regional, sub-regional and sectoral levels.

101. Success of LDCs in implementing this Programme of Action at the national level will depend *inter alia* on effective human, institutional and technical capacity relating to policy developments, monitoring of implementation and co-ordination. The UN Resident Coordinator system and the country teams, as well country-level representatives of the Bretton Woods Institutions, and other bilateral and multilateral donors and other development partners are encouraged to collaborate with and provide support to the national development forums.

Source: Programme of Action for the Least Developed Countries, adopted by the Third United Nations Conference on the Least Developed Countries, Brussels, 20 May 2001 (A/CONF 191/11).

By contrast, in a partnership based on common values and grounded in dialogue, where both sides want the same result, policy conditionality does not represent major obstacles, and the decision on which policy measure to use becomes a rather technical question. It is only where values and strategic visions differ that conditionality may hinder efforts, either to the point of breaking off negotiations, or by driving borrowing governments to embrace policies they do not believe in.

Within a country, dialogue can be critical in resolving policy disagreements, so it is a capacity that itself is an important form of social and organizational capital. Often, differences arise in the national context simply because reforms bring advantages to some groups while disadvantaging others. Acceptance is more likely if there is an effort to form consensus, a sense of equity and fairness, and a feeling of ownership derived from participation. Numerous examples have already shown the importance of consensus in macroeconomic stability, for example. On the other hand, a decision to, say, eliminate food or agricultural subsidies, particularly if it is imposed from the outside through an agreement between the ruling party and an international agency, is not likely to meet widespread support.

In other cases, countries that have not employed dialogue processes and developed consistent, nationally owned strategies and policies end up torn between a multitude of competing and overlapping development frameworks, which in turn prevents them from concentrating their capacities effectively and assuming leadership. To the extent possible, there should be only one nationally developed and owned development framework, be it a PRSP or an equivalent national strategy. National authorities will then be in a better position to insist on alignment of development cooperation and to reject propositions that run counter to national objectives. They will also be able to more clearly determine whether their policies and institutional framework will facilitate sustainable capacity development, on a scale necessary to support implementation.

In terms of dialogue between cooperation partners, it is critical to level the playing field by addressing the problem of asymmetry of information. Partners naturally have different sources of information, some of which may be hidden in order to gain tactical advantages in negotiations. Host country representatives may keep to themselves what they have been offered by several donors, in order to play one against the other. Likewise, donors are often cautious in making a long-term commitment. Sometimes they do not even inform the host country of the actual costs of their contributions in kind. All of these information gaps increase transaction costs, mostly because they lead to decisions based on insufficient data and short-term considerations.

Most policy dialogue in the past has been structured around consultative groups and round tables, facilitated by the World Bank and UNDP respectively. Slowly, nationally owned processes are replacing externally led arrangements like these. Even some LDCs are beginning to take charge by establishing national development forums (see box 2.2.1). These and other aid coordination reforms might take into account the following considerations:

- *The government leads:* The government needs to assume control, shaping the agenda, schedules and desired outcomes. This may include subcontracting of certain tasks if it eases the burden.

- *In-country venue:* The forum should preferably take place in the country, rather than Paris or Geneva. This not only sends a clear ownership signal, but also allows more involvement of national stakeholders.

Box 2.2.2 A framework for donor cooperation

A donor's assistance is shaped by an institutional framework for its relations with the partner government and other donors, as well as by its own internal rules and culture. An OECD/DAC paper sets out nine guiding principles for providing more coordinated and effective assistance. The paper also describes specific good practices donors may adopt for developing the overall framework for donor-partner relations, donor-donor coordination and individual donor systems.

👆 **Guiding principles**

1. Donors should support country-owned, country-led poverty reduction strategies, or equivalent national frameworks, and base their programming on the needs and priorities identified in these.

2. Development assistance should be provided in ways that build, and do not inadvertently undermine, partner countries' sustainable capacity to develop, implement and account for these policies to their people and legislature.

3. Coordination of donor practices enhances the effectiveness of aid, particularly for aid dependent countries. Aid coordination should, whenever possible, be led by partner governments.

4. Reliance on partner government systems, where these provide reasonable assurance that cooperation resources are used for agreed purposes, is likely to enhance achievement of sustainable improvements in government performance.

5. Partner countries and donors have a shared interest in ensuring that public funds are used appropriately.

6. Donors should work closely with partner countries to address weaknesses in institutional capacity or other constraints that prevent reasonable assurance on use of cooperation resources.

7. The development of appropriate partner country systems will often be a medium-term process. Until donors can rely on these, they should simplify and harmonize their own procedures to reduce the burden placed on partner countries.

8. No single approach is suitable for all countries. The manner in which harmonization is implemented needs to be adapted to local circumstances and institutional capacities.

9. Assistance to empower civil society and support effective organizations representing the private sector also can enhance improvements in partner government performance.

Donor-partner relationships

- Set out the objectives and operations of individual country programmes and make these widely available
- Multi-year programming of aid
- Use common performance indicators
- Build a common framework for aid cooperation
- Provide full information on aid flows

Donor-donor relationships

- Consult with partner governments
- Coherent communication with a partner government
- Share information
- Explicit agreement on roles
- Burdens on partners can be reduced by standardizing sys-

Individual donor systems

- Create top level advocates of harmonization
- Encourage initiatives in partnership and joint working by country offices
- Decentralize decision-making
- Ensure programme managers' awareness of the degree of flexibility
- Manage staff to create the right environment for them to behave collaboratively and flexibly

• Support leadership in aid coordination by partner governments	tems and procedures	• Set transparent performance standards
• A common conditionality framework	• Share examples of common procedures	• Be open to assessments of aid management performance
• Compatibility of commitments and disbursements with partner government cycles	• Global common procedures only in certain circumstances	• Review procedural requirements regularly
• Budget support review integrated into partner government review processes		• Review legal framework
• An open process for managing any concerns		• Ensure coherence between the various agencies of an individual donor
• Clear rules for any suspension of aid		

Source: The full paper is available at www.oecd.org/dc/donorpractices.

Box 2.2.3: Project aid, programmatic approaches and budget support

The development community has been experimenting with aid modalities that can be grouped into three clusters: project aid, programmatic or sector-wide approaches, and budget support.

Project aid

Project aid has long been the target of severe criticism as: being costly and often unsustainable; leading to duplication; poorly connected to intra- and inter-sectoral concerns and the macro level; frequently not corresponding to local priorities; easily dominated by donors and expatriate personnel; and overwhelming local capacities needed to manage fragmented interventions and donor relations.

Particularly during the era of centralized development planning, planning ministries attempted to lay down rules for externally assisted projects so that they would conform to planning priorities. This was also the principle behind Uganda's attempt in 1997 to confine project proposals to the activities listed in its Poverty Eradication Action Plan (Balihuta et al., 2002). Such general rules tend to be ineffective, however, unless they are backed by discretionary examination by a strong planning or finance authority. Uganda had this capacity, which explains why the strategy was at least partially successful; China, Brazil and India with their well-equipped central governments can claim similar achievements. Vietnam also has a government that attaches high importance to leading the identification and implementation of development projects. But its Ministry of Plan Implementation does not have the administrative scope to keep sector ministries from accepting donor-driven aid projects unless counterpart contributions are excessive (Vanarkadie et al., 2000).

Discretionary bureaucratic screening helps to weed out blatant cases of unnecessary and unsustainable projects, but it does not automatically instill the feeling of ownership required for a truly country-driven mode of operation. As explained earlier, ownership grows from stakeholder interest and from participation of all affected parties in identification and implementation of a project. When all participants feel accountable for the outcome to the beneficiaries, local ownership is ensured.

This process requires dialogue, which rests upon listening (see box 1.3.2). Although some expatriate experts may pretend they know the country's needs even better than its representatives, a sensitive donor should take a step back at the point of decision on project design, and invite discussion as well as stakeholder consultation on all the options and possible consequences. Since donors are often under pressure to show results in terms of disbursements and action on the ground, initiatives for allowing such time-consuming sensitivity will therefore have to come from the highest echelons in the donor agencies.

There has been some discussion on the extent to which execution modalities influence the sense of domestic ownership. For instance, UNDP's shift from agency execution to national execution (NEX) was approved by its Executive Board as an important step towards domestic ownership. The feedback from recipients has been mixed. Countries with sufficient managerial capacity to take over all aspects of project implementation have welcomed NEX as an opportunity for domestic control. Where administrative capacity is lower, as in many African countries, NEX has been seen as a lot of paperwork for rather small projects, and in many cases recipients have favoured direct execution by country offices (UNDP, 2002b).

Programmatic or sector-wide approaches:

A sector-wide approach, more commonly known as SWAP, is a framework of cooperation adopted by a group of donor agencies and NGOs in partnership with a recipient government. The multilateral nature of a SWAP provides the host government (usually represented by a sector ministry) more flexibility in implementing a programme that is widely endorsed. In principle, the donors support the programme as a whole and do not insist that their individual contributions be directed to a specific activity. As much as possible, external resources are managed together with contribu-

tions from the domestic budget, and a ministry's rules and regulations apply to the use of all resources as well as to reports and audits. In some SWAPs, a group of donors agree to pool their resources in so-called baskets (see ECDPM passage below). In other cases, donors contribute their funds to a sector programme through parallel financing, where they maintain a separate account.

The sector-wide approach also reduces bureaucracy and transaction costs by eliminating the plethora of project implementation units, special accounts, procedural requirements and donor review missions that bedevil so many government departments in sectors that are popular with donors (education, health, roads, agriculture, etc.). Under the SWAP setup, the recipient government, through a ministry, formulates its own programme before donors are invited to offer support. Donor coordination is managed by the designated ministry through joint donor meetings and programme reviews, giving top ministry officials more control. In some cases, however, ministry officials find themselves "outgunned" by the heavy expertise provided by donors for the programme reviews, which overshadows the opinions of domestic stakeholders and users, and in the process demonstrates that strong political leadership is not enough for building locally owned sector programmes (Reinikka, 2001).

Pooling arrangements can be quite complex and cumbersome when rules are negotiated on a case-by-case basis, accommodating the particular needs of all participating agents. Increased transaction costs may result. For similar reasons, the research seems to show that pooling can put additional pressure on already weak capacities. Although the goal of SWAPs may be to increase ownership, the result can sometimes be the opposite, especially when large numbers of technical assistants effectively take control.

Budget Support

In its purest form, budget support consists of grant money provided to the recipient's exchequer or central bank to cover an expected shortfall in the government budget. It offers maximum flexibility, completely blending with other government revenue. This form of aid, which identifies the donor with the government's whole expenditure programme, rather than with a specific sector or project, is justified by low absorptive capacity. It is certainly less complicated, and more focused and potentially cost-effective.

Budget support is commonly used to provide financial assistance to a government that needs aid in a fast-disbursing and flexible form (Justice, 2001), often related to a couple of different situations:

- The country acutely needs financial resources, but its capacity for managing new projects is very limited. It is deemed capable of expanding ongoing development activities without straining that capacity.

- The country has a demonstrated capacity for managing development programmes, but it has been hit by a temporary financial shortfall. A one-off infusion of budget funds will enable the government's return to its development path.

The first case is one where capacity development may not be furthered by additional project aid – the country being incapable of absorbing more external resources. Usually, this situation will occur in countries that are heavily dependent on project aid. On the other hand, further development and growth is possible by expanding current activities, which makes an argument for increasing aid transfers. The second case concerns countries that have capacity for managing development programmes, and mainly applies to temporary financial relief.

Budget support is not a new form of aid. As a political subsidy, it is older than any other aid form in history. Practised in recent times in small island economies in the South Pacific, for instance, it has become increasingly common in Africa for several reasons. First, the structural adjustment drive has created the space for international financial institutions to move into reform-related packages that include budget support. Second, bilateral donors have realized that there are very narrow limits to the quantity of project aid that some of the poorest countries can effectively manage. Third, the expansion of programme lending and debt relief has advanced public expenditure reviews as an effective instrument for scrutinizing the development performance of borrowers. It is now possible to track the use of budget resources quite closely, to ensure that additional money is used for development purposes and not for buying military hardware, for example. Of course, this analysis presupposes detailed income and expenditure data and the use of rather sophisticated models for predicting financial outcomes (Fozzard, 2001; Devarajan and Swaroop, 1998; IMF, 2001).

From the point of view of capacity development, budget support is more country-driven than project aid. At the same time, since it is based on policy conditions rather than on the implementation of specific activities, it makes countries more vulnerable to donor pressure. For a recipient government to be fully in charge of this modality, it must have both effective management systems and a very good database. Whether budget support will lead to more capacity development depends entirely on the priorities of the government.

The use of budget support and other similar transfers, such as balance of payment support or debt relief, is becoming increasingly frequent, with growing awareness among donors about the transaction costs of aid transfers being closely connected to verified activities and reports. When different sources of finance are available to a government, they will to some extent be fungible, no matter how closely expenditure is tied to a given activity or procurement item (Devarajan and Swaroop, 1998). A high degree of fungibility makes it less rational for a donor to link a contribution to a project.

Box 2.2.4: ECDPM research on pooling arrangements

Pooling of technical assistance, especially for sector-wide assistance, is one aspect of the donor harmonization debate. Pooling is defined as a collective action among international development organizations and a government to share or transfer resources for meeting policy objectives defined by the country.

Research entitled "Harmonising the Provision of Technical Assistance: Finding the Right Balance and Avoiding the New Religion" was carried out by the ECDPM. It included country cases in Botswana, Ethiopia, Mali, Mozambique, Tanzania and Uganda, as well as interviews with most of the European bilateral donors and some international development organizations outside Europe.

The study found that while the number of technical assistance pooling schemes in operation is small, it is increasing in most of the countries surveyed. On the basis of this limited survey, the following conclusions were drawn, which should be tested as experience increases.

In the countries examined, five interrelated factors appeared to shape the use and performance of technical assistance pooling:

1. The policies and organizational context within the country: most governments still encouraged the use of multiple funding channels within sector programmes that could be used to fund both pooled and coordinated technical assistance.

2. Much of the behaviour within the international funding community to do with technical assistance pooling was influenced by three interconnected factors: policy and procedural restrictions, strategies and the pattern of organizational incentives.

3. A key factor that helped the shift to pooling was the structure and management of the broader aid relationship between a government and donors. Relationships that generated an enabling environment for

pooling – a culture of collaboration – set the stage at the sector, programme and project levels.

4. Relationships within the international funding community in a particular country also shape the use and effectiveness of pooling.

5. The design and management of sector programme support is the immediate context for a good deal of pooling. Much as in the broader aid relationship itself, sector mechanisms are a form of collective action.

The following reforms and improvements would encourage more pooling:

1. The scope for pooling depends to a large degree on participants rethinking the means and ends of technical assistance.

2. There remains a need to develop better frameworks for assessing capacity building. Coming up with an effective approach to organizational analysis seems to be one of the missing links in making technical assistance pooling more effective.

3. The crafting of strategies frequently has to balance detailed, upfront preparation and more incremental approaches to learning by doing.

4. A decision to proceed with technical assistance pooling needs to be accompanied by a clear idea about the organizational support required for its success.

5. The harmonization of procedures is a success factor for pooling.

6. Many of the potential opportunities for pooling and procedural harmonization depend upon the willingness of external partners to work within the national administrative, financial and legal systems.

7. The need for improved monitoring and evaluation raises the issue of the trade-offs among different approaches to pooling. Under pooling arrangements, the "controller" roles of technical assistance will

likely diminish as national governments take charge of technical assistance to support their own interests.

8. There is a need to accelerate the leisurely pace of the organizational reform of international funding agencies. The shift to greater collaboration and pooling, including that of technical assistance, has implications for their structure and functioning.

9. The research suggests that pooled technical assistance is not a decisive innovation, but as part of a broader set of combined reforms, it can make a useful contribution. It is important, however, to assess the conditions in a country before deciding on the appropriateness of pooling or its form.

Source: www.ecdpm.org/en/pubs/technical assistance_case_studies.htm.

- *Continued dialogue:* In many countries, consultative groups and round tables have developed from annual meetings into a process.

- *Stakeholder participation:* Interest groups are associated with transparency and accountability (see section 1.2).

- *Frankness and trust:* The number of participants and the duration of the proceedings do not measure a forum's value. The quality of the debate and deliberations are more important. A move towards constructive engagement requires attention to process, including facilitation, group dynamics and conflict resolution (see section 1.4).

Applying to policy dialogue the default principle of grounding capacity development in ownership is the best guarantee for consistency. Through reforms like those above, it becomes possible in fact to protect and encourage ownership while increasing the quality of the dialogue.

Since the choice of aid modalities has increasingly become an issue, and in particular the trend away from project aid to pooling arrangements and budget transfers, policy dialogue needs to be open and upfront about the options (see box 2.2.3 and 2.2.4). While the factors that promote or undermine ownership may have been sufficiently examined in the case of project aid, more flexible forms of programme aid present a picture that is rather blurred. Such alternatives as general budget support or SWAPs should offer a straighter road to local ownership than project aid, with its more complex management structure, which is easily pre-empted by the donor. But evidence from the budget support and education sector programmes in Tanzania and the health sector programme in Uganda indicates that the flexibility provided through money transfer is often progressively circumscribed by a series of informal arrangements by which donors are keeping a closer check on where the money goes. These arrangements can be throwbacks to earlier generations of project aid, may prevent programmes from reducing transaction costs, and may threaten national ownership – debate over the issue is honing sharper understanding of the ownership of resources.

From a capacity point of view, there is a clear case for applying policy dialogue to the integration of all aid inputs into national priorities and processes. Where a government does not fully represent its population or management systems do not meet minimum standards, budget support may not be feasible, but may still be a good starting point for exploring options and mutually agreeable conditions. The appropriateness of various modalities is ultimately a question of choice and fit, with a reasonable expectation for more flexibility on the donor side. Care needs to be taken that the problems of project aid are not inadvertently imported into the new arrangements.

Overall, policy dialogue could benefit from greater donor flexibility, which rests at the heart of current efforts for harmonizing and simplifying donor practices. Development agencies, with all good intentions, have invented a jungle of rules, procedures and requirements that impose high transaction costs on developing countries and strain weak capacities, including to carry out meaningful discussions on national priorities. It is like the spell of the sorcerer's apprentice: the invented systems are now difficult to get rid of or even modify.

Instead, there needs to be a consistent understanding that the primary goal is convergence and dialogue around national priorities. This shifts the onus of flexibility to donors, implying that the way to do business may differ significantly from one country to another. Piecemeal alignments among groups of donors otherwise can throw up obstacles to real harmonization.

So far, multilateral development banks, OECD/DAC members, the European Union and UN agencies have pledged to make greater efforts to coordinate their activities, while the international momentum reflected at the Rome High-Level Forum on Harmonization offers a platform for developing countries to renegotiate and rationalize their aid systems. The good practice papers developed by the OECD/DAC task force on donor practices present a concrete and potentially powerful entry point for some new forms of policy dialogue to begin[7] (see box 2.2.2).

---

[7] Participants in the DAC task force on donor practices included: Bangladesh, Bolivia, Cambodia, Egypt, Senegal, Guatemala, Kenya, Kyrgyz Republic, Mali, Morocco, Mozambique, South Pacific Forum, Romania, Tanzania, Uganda and Vietnam. The work received top political endorsement in February 2003 at the High-Level Forum on Harmonization in Rome. In the *Rome Declaration,* participants committed themselves to pursuing local solutions, simplifying and harmonizing around national systems, reducing transaction costs and promoting capacity development.

KEY POINTS

 Policy dialogue with donors is not a replacement for policy dialogue with domestic constituencies. To be conducive to transformation, policy dialogue, both domestic and between recipients and donors, needs to explicitly focus on capacity issues.

 Countries should insist on the primacy of one single development framework, whether a PRSP, a national development plan or the equivalent, to which there is broad national commitment. This requires the capacity to reconcile different perspectives on policies.

 National development forums are replacing consultative groups and round tables, both arrangements led by external parties. Important factors are the country-led nature of the forums, along with serious efforts to improve frankness and trust among partners.

 From a capacity point of view, there is a clear case for the integration of aid inputs into national priorities and processes. This should be the starting place for exploring options even in cases where capacities are weak. However, the appropriateness of various aid modalities is ultimately a question of choice and fit.

 Since individual donor country programmes can undermine genuine dialogue and add complexity to aid management, the current momentum around harmonization of donor practices offers a major opportunity for aid system reforms conducive to increasing national ownership and capacity. Country-level harmonization, naturally specific to each reality, differs from standardization across donor groups. At the core of the harmonization debate, however, is nothing less than a shift of the onus of flexibility from developing countries to their external partners.

REFERENCES PART B

➲ **BOLIVIA** *Citizens Exercise Their Right to Be Involved in the Aid System (p. 177)*
➲ **ETHIOPIA** *A PRSP Encounters the Constraints and Promises of Participation (p. 220)*
➲ **GUATEMALA** *Coordination and Flexibility Help Civil Society Broker Trust After War (p. 223)*
➲ **HONDURAS** *Democracy Trust Backs National Consensus Amidst Volatile Politics (p. 229)*
➲ **SOUTH AFRICA** *Poor People Fight for Their Space Through Organized Fora (p. 281)*
➲ **SUDAN** *Future Search Technique Creates a Vision for Peace (p. 286)*
➲ **TANZANIA** *Independent Monitoring Holds a Government and Its Partners to Account (p. 292)*

2.3 PROGRAMMING EXTERNAL COOPERATION

> *"The challenge is not in drafting an excellent technical document but rather in facilitating the participation of the relevant stakeholders and ensuring the full exchange of relevant information. Through this process, a design emerges that is the product of the intellect, knowledge and ingenuity of the participating persons. The process is also a starting point for ownership and sustainability. Any draft of a project document thus needs to emerge from the process and should not be prepared as a substitute for the process."*

> *- UNDP Programming Manual* [8]

Programming development activities is a strategic part of governance and a domestic exercise for transforming a broad national vision into concrete actions. Nevertheless, the reality for a number of countries is that without external resources, development ambitions would have to be severely curtailed, forcing hard choices on priorities and use of scarce local resources. And while recipient governments can technically refuse offers of extrabudgetary external cooperation that do not fit their priorities, few of them want to turn down these opportunities, even when they contradict national development strategies.

In many cases as well, it remains easier to agree on operational objectives than policies. As a result, policy controversies are swept under the carpet when projects are approved. There may also be a failure to pay full respect to national procedures for the selection and approval of priorities and related budgetary allotments. The common practice whereby major flows of external cooperation bypass these mechanisms, including parliamentary scrutiny, is undemocratic, potentially diverts national resources to non- or lower priority activities, and obscures the true cost of development efforts.

Programming generally starts with a diagnosis that includes needs assessments, sector studies, environmental and gender analyses, financial accountability and other inputs. In any serious effort to develop a reform programme, capacity assessments are an important first step. They provide baseline information to measure progress and performance, as well as the identification of strengths and weaknesses, gaps and challenges. Although needs assessments tend to be done regularly, they are seldom systemic or initiated by national entities – capacity self-assessments may provide a preferable alternative (see box 2.3.1).

Even if the entire range of issues required by a systemic analysis cannot be included, asking hard questions sets the right tone for internal discussion. An example of a useful tool for this process is UNDP's Country Assessment in Accountability and Transparency, also known as CONTACT. It provides a set of

---

[8] For more information, see www.undp.org/bdp/pm/.

generic guidelines formulated to assist governments in conducting self-assessments of their financial management and anti-corruption systems. The UN Task Force on Harmonization and Standardization has endorsed CONTACT, particularly for its ability to assess public financial management systems.[9]

Overall, programming still suffers from a number of common problems detrimental to lasting results. One is the prepackaging of ideas, a tendency that can exclude alternative and perhaps more adaptable and home-grown solutions to a development problem. Another is overambition and unrealistic assumptions about change. Rome and Beijing were not build overnight; democracy is a construct of several centuries. Benchmarking needs to be realistic, and informed by historic and social processes. What matters are the ultimate results, and while definitions of outputs and activities may be desirable, these can become the cause for rigidities that force a programme to lose touch with emerging realities. Whenever possible, governments should try scenario-building or similar approaches to encourage debate among national entities as a means for determining future directions. Scenario-building is particularly suited for countries under special development circumstances.

It is unfortunate that current incentive structures for the development industry are heavily stacked in favor of quantity over quality. An emphasis on quantity can make sense in the private sector, where most activities are centred on projects involving factories, services or other enterprises, each assessed on its ability to produce goods or services. In the public sector, the same applies, but with two important distinctions: first, the quantity and quality of output is frequently difficult to measure (profitability and competition are not present when services are free or not-for-profit); second, interventions may be manifold – literally hundreds – in support of one single undertaking.

For example, enhanced agricultural performance may require a countrywide combination of actions such as fixing appropriate farm gate prices, securing land tenure, selecting appropriate cropping, improving seed and implements, and providing credit and access to markets through better infrastructure. What then are the benchmarks for agricultural success? Higher outputs may be a factor, but are they sustainable? Or is the fertility of the soil more important? Do all farmers benefit, or only those with larger farms and capital assets? Has food security been enhanced for the country and its region? And so on. Isolated implementation of any of the aspects mentioned above can lead to suboptimal performance or failure.

Yet virtually every donor has its individual requirement checklist for a Country Programme or a similar document. This describes donor inputs, and is invariably followed by more detailed documents specifying a wide range of processes and targets. These come in all shapes and sizes, guiding work such as setting up a small health clinic, funding vocational training, building a feeder road, establishing rural cooperatives, reinforcing the judiciary system or establishing a university. Most

---

[9] More information is available at www.undp.org/governance/contact_cdrom.htm.

Box 2.3.1: Capacity assessment

What is capacity self-assessment?

A capacity assessment is triggered by a policy decision of some sort – such as the need to improve the delivery of a particular government service, to downsize the cost of government or to strengthen the legislative process. A capacity self-assessment determines the present status of capacity needs and priorities – it identifies what capacities are present and where capacity is lacking. It also measures the magnitude of the capacity gaps. By identifying these gaps, countries can then develop a plan of action for overcoming them. This method recognizes the fact that capacity needs will change over time and that assessment has to be ongoing.

How can one go about it?

- State the issue that needs to be addressed and how to approach it
- Identify and engage a broad set of stakeholders
- Note what is already known about capacity building needs within the country
- Identify the key capacity constraints
- Develop an action plan for building and sustaining capacity

----

What are the approaches, tools and techniques for capacity assessments?

Assessing capacity at the individual level refers to the process of changing attitudes and behaviours – imparting knowledge and developing skills while maximizing the benefits of participation, knowledge exchange and ownership.

- *Job requirements and skill levels:* Are jobs correctly defined and are the required skills available?

- *Training/retraining:* Is the appropriate learning taking place?

- *Career progression:* Are individuals able to advance and develop professionally?

- *Accountability/ethics:* Is responsibility effectively delegated and are individuals held accountable?

- *Access to information:* Is there adequate access to needed information?

- *Personal/professional networking:* Are individuals in contact and exchanging knowledge with appropriate peers?

- *Performance/conduct:* Is performance effectively measured?

- *Incentives/security:* Are these sufficient to promote excellence?

- *Values, integrity and attitudes:* Are these in place and maintained?

- *Morale and motivation:* Are these adequately maintained?

- *Work redeployment and job sharing:* Are there alternatives to the existing arrangements?

- *Interrelationships and teamwork:* Do individuals interact effectively and form functional teams?

- *Interdependencies:* Are there appropriate levels of interdependence?

- *Communication skills:* Are these effective?

Assessing capacity at the institutional level focuses on overall organizational performance and capabilities, as well as the ability of an organization to adapt to change. It aims to develop the institution as a total system, including individuals, groups and the organization itself:

- *Mission and strategy assessment:* Do the institutions have clearly defined and understood missions and mandates?

- *Culture/structure/competencies assessment:* Are the institutions effectively structured and managed?

- *Process assessment:* Do institutional processes such as planning, quality management, and monitoring and evaluation work effectively?

- *Human resources assessment:* Are the human resources adequate, sufficiently skilled and appropriately deployed?

- *Financial resources assessment:* Are financial resources managed effectively and allocated appropriately to enable effective operation?

- *Information resources assessment:* Is required information available and effectively distributed and managed?

- *Infrastructure assessment:* Are material requirements such as buildings, offices, vehicles and computers allocated appropriately and managed effectively?

Assessing capacity at the societal level emphasizes the overall policy framework in which individuals and organizations operate and interact with the external environment, as well as the formal and informal relationships of institutions.

- *Systems or policy framework assessment:* What are the strengths, weaknesses, opportunities and threats (SWOT) according to the socio-political, government/public sector, economic/technological and physical environment factors?

- *Legal/regulatory assessment:* Is the appropriate legislation in place and are these laws effectively enforced? (These may be both formal and informal, such as cultural mores.)

- *Management/accountability framework assessment:* Are institutional responsibilities clearly defined and are responsible institutions held publicly accountable?

- *Policy framework assessment:* Is the overall policy environment favourable?

- *Economic framework assessment:* Do markets function effectively and efficiently?

- *Systems-level resource assessment:* Are the required human, financial and information resources available? (These may be in national or local governments, the private sector, and civil society, including NGOs.)

- *Processes and relationships assessment:* Do the different institutions and processes interact and work together effectively? (This includes national and local government, the private sector and civil society.)

What are critical considerations to make capacity assessment work?

Key principles that should guide the capacity development process during the assessment stage:

- Building on existing capacities to ensure national ownership, leadership and policy commitment

- Adopting a holistic approach to capacity development

- Utilizing existing coordination mechanisms and structures where appropriate

- Promoting comprehensive participation

- Adjusting capacity development programmes for local needs

- Adopting a long-term approach within the broader development context through coordination and linkage with ongoing efforts, and integration with other development initiatives

Source: Adapted from UNDP-GEF, 2001; UNDP, 1998.

Box 2.3.2: Good practices for country analytic work and preparation of projects and programmes

1. Guiding principles

- A partner government should be fully involved in donor-supported country analytical work and preparation of donor operations where national ownership is critical for analytical or operational effectiveness.

- A partner government's systems should be used where they provide the quality of analysis required. Where capacity is insufficient, donors should undertake the analysis in ways that help build capacity.

- Where reliance cannot be placed on partner systems, donors should seek to harmonize their country analytic work and activity preparation in ways that minimize the burden on the partner government.

- Harmonization of analysis should not mean a single source of policy advice.

2. Good practices

a) Development of analytic tools

- Donors should make available their diagnostic toolkits to other agencies, partner governments and other interested groups.

- Donors should collaborate with each other and with partner countries to establish what new diagnostic tools are needed, how to develop them and how to rationalize the existing stock.

- In any further development and rationalization of diagnostic tools, donors should give priority to: reducing unnecessary overlaps, particularly for analysis of systems and capacity, and reorienting the application of tools towards capacity development. A systematic follow-up should be included in the design of each tool, to monitor how governments and donors are managing its application. Tanzania's Poverty Monitoring System is an example of a rationalization of diagnostic tools at a country level.

- Donors should enable partner countries to participate in further development and rationalization of diagnostic tools.

b) Application of diagnostic tools

- Donors should aim to rely on analytic work produced by partner governments and by other donors.

- Under partner government leadership, donors should collectively help plan the key analytic work to be done in the next time period.

- Donors should undertake analytic work jointly or rely on the work of the partner country or other donors. Where this is not possible, they should coordinate their work and missions with donors and the partner government, planning similar analytic tasks to lessen the burdens on partner officials.

- Donors managing analytic work in a partner country should have clear and appropriate contact points in the partner government.

- Where the analytic work is cross-cutting, the government contact points should be from all the departments most affected.

- In helping plan the supply of data and analysis, donors should work closely with government departments that use it, as well as with the technical producers (e.g., statistical offices).

- Donors should promote common analytic work on sector policy and programming as the basis for donor-supported operations in a sector.

- Donors should use partner country expertise in teams for analytical work, as far as possible, to build national analytic capacity.

- In multi-donor analytic work, the optimal team size should be determined by function and task rather than donor representation.

c) Dissemination and use of analytic work in development of policy

- All analytic work should be shared to the fullest extent, observing individual participating donors' policies and the prior agreement reached with the partner country.

- Where partner countries have public "right to information" laws, donors should respect and promote the right of public access to analytic work under these laws.

- Donors should ensure that all their documents are put into accessible and readable form, with simple, clear concepts and language.
- Donors should ensure wide electronic distribution of analytic documents by maintaining online libraries.
- Distribution lists for study reports (including to sub-national levels of government) should be included in reports and terms of reference.
- Print runs for analytic work important to partner countries should be set generously, with copies widely available within the country.
- For particularly important work, "popular versions" should be issued to build widespread understanding, including through media coverage.
- Donors should support partner policy formulation based on empirical evidence.
- Strategy documents should acknowledge the supporting analytic studies.
- Training seminars focused on the results of important work should be available to members of a country's legislature and other policy makers to whom it is relevant.

d) Specific work to prepare donor-supported operations

- Donors should ensure consistency of a possible operation with any programming framework agreed with a partner government. If it is not consistent, or where no such framework is in place, they should consult partner governments on the consistency with the national poverty reduction strategy or equivalent framework.
- Donors should promote a shared understanding of each other's approaches to project preparation by adopting a common terminology for the stages of the project cycle. Where possible, this should be based on a partner government's terminology.
- Donors should build flexibility into their procedures to enable the use of the project notes, logical framework and financing proposals of a partner government or other donor. This should include flexibility on formats and labels.
- Donors should seek opportunities in project design for involving partner countries in a way that develops their capacity to undertake such work.
- Where donors use a results framework to identify possible activities, they should do so jointly with the partner government and other agencies in order to achieve a shared understanding of problems and solutions.

Source: OECD (www.oecd.org/dac/donorpractices).

projects are run by a discrete accounting entity, with clearly delineated management structures, implementation responsibilities and legal obligations. Log frames have provided a tool "to ensure consistency among objectives, outputs, activities and inputs, to identify important risks or assumptions, and to ensure the intervention is likely to achieve measurable results."[10] In developing programmes and project documents it is, however, essential to keep open space for iteration, learning and readjustment.

Project documents are supposed to be drawn up in collaboration with representatives of the host country and through close consultation with the relevant stakeholders (see box 2.3.2). But in fact, a consultant often undertakes this task, given that the procedure places a significant demand on usually hard-pressed government officials. This is evidence of the fact that programming is still dominated by an attitude of just getting the job done, which is legitimate, but the real

---

[10] As defined in the UNDP Programming Manual (www.undp.org/bdp/pm/).

challenge is to embark on a meaningful process that engenders participation and ownership while establishing a basis for sustainable results and capacity development. Programme or project documents serve not only as the prime reference for implementation and monitoring, but also should consider such sustainability aspects as the financial basis and institutional context for continued progress in the post-project period.

KEY POINTS

 Development programming, which plots the transformation of ideas and goals into concrete actions, is first of all a national government's strategic responsibility.

 External partners must respect national procedures for the selection and approval of priorities and related budgetary allotments, while host countries must be prepared to refuse offers of extra-budgetary external cooperation that fit poorly with national development strategies.

 There is scope for countries to shape and use country analytic work, and for rationalizing related tools and processes. Capacity assessments, particularly those that are self-generated, need to be integrated into analysis and programming from the beginning, in order to address difficult questions relating to sustainability and incentives.

 It is not enough to concentrate on the merits of individual projects; the entirety of a programme must be kept under review and projects assessed against that larger background. It is in the interest of host countries and their external partners alike to move actively towards integrated or programmatic approaches, so as to underpin national ownership and focus attention and action on the achievement of major development goals.

 Any improvements in the area of programming have to take into account lessons learned from the fragmentation produced by donor Country Programmes, project documents under the log frame approach, and the dominant role sometimes played by the development industry. The challenge is not an excellent document, but a meaningful process and real ownership by the respective stakeholders.

2.4 IMPLEMENTING EXTERNAL COOPERATION

While countries normally establish rules and regulations for programme and project implementation, multiple processes introduced by donors may run counter to these, yielding parallel and competing systems and requirements, and diffusing relevant capacities. Execution may be the responsibility of national institutions, but the reality often looks different, with the development industry continuing to play a strong role to the detriment of national ownership and capacity. Even NEX has in many cases led to parallel NEX units staffed by nationals but handling implementation according to UN rather than national rules.

Whether within an established public sector framework or one set up explicitly for a specific project, effective implementation depends upon sound management.[11] Lines of responsibility and accountability should be clear and in accordance with legislated and established practice. If these are weak or lack transparency, steps should be taken to strengthen them rather than automatically setting up parallel mechanisms.

Implementation also needs to be well linked to higher level oversight and ultimately accountable to parliament or the equivalent. Oversight bodies track progress, and ensure that activities are being efficiently executed, objectives remain valid and frameworks appropriate. They also play a role in addressing interdependencies, both horizontal as well as vertical micro-macro linkages. While management can and must ensure that the appropriate authorities are aware of the collateral effects of related decisions, oversight bodies need to be visible for bottlenecks, and accessible in particular for the legitimate concerns of national staff, who may find themselves overwhelmed by foreign expertise.

Once a funding agreement is reached with donors, funds should be available to and managed by the responsible national institution, following agreed procedures for accountability and auditing. At this point, a fund manager's sense of ownership depends, to a great extent, on budget authority. Where funds are committed for reasonable time periods and managers have the ability to use them within government rules and the stipulations of the aid agreement, they can be expected to take personal responsibility for results in a way they would not do if the donor was the real decision maker (Edgren, 2003). A particular constraint recipient countries face relates to delayed disbursements, which cause frustration, erode trust and provoke cascading inefficiencies.

The issue of financial and institutional sustainability beyond the period of external funding must be pursued during implementation; responsible management must make this a priority. It is vital that provision be made for future funding, whether in the form of recurrent government budgets or user fees and other direct

---

[11] Management is key to asserting ownership. A distinction can be made between management and implementation: management entails making strategic decisions on how the resources shall be deployed, while implementation means carrying out what is contained in the project document.

income. The history of development is littered with examples of appropriately established institutions that have foundered due to a lack of subsequent resources.

Daily choices on sub-contracting and procurement that are more or less conducive to capacity development also fall within the scope of management. For instance, contracting consultants, national or international, requires careful selection, including factors beyond technical know-how, such as language, cultural sensitivity and interpersonal skills. Terms of reference need to be explicit on what is expected, not only technically, but also in terms of effectively sharing knowledge and skills with national staff. Managers should not hesitate to solicit regular feedback from national staff about the relevance, usefulness and quality of services provided, much along the lines of the mini-evaluations common in workshops and training.

Project or programme implementation units

Project or programme implementation units (PIUs) present a major dilemma. While some commentators declare that they have a negative impact on capacity, practitioners tend to see them as inevitable (while not necessarily disagreeing about the potential for negative impact). It has been well established that such units are often fast, convenient executing entities when juxtaposed with lethargic, cumbersome, uncoordinated government equivalents. Where donor funding for specific projects is large, they are useful as a mechanism to cope with increased workloads. And by providing the opportunity for outsourcing potentially complicated transactional processes, they prevent the burgeoning of bureaucracies, especially around aid flows, following the logic of lean public institutions. Donor-assisted projects have their own momentum, and PIUs allow for rapid procurement and disbursements, and cleaner implementation.

The impact on capacity, however, can be quite another story. As parallel structures, PIUs can usher a host of vague outcomes.[12] Project implementation that bypasses existing institutions misses opportunities for capacity development, increases fragmentation and distorts incentives (Hilderbrand, 2002). Parallel entities actually tend to undermine established structures and chains of command, and typically divert scarce skilled human resources from mainstream administration. Often, when seen through a capacity lens, parallel implementation structures appear to be odd imports. A Chilean researcher stated that PIUs become mini-ministries, with well-paid staff, fancy training possibilities and superior equipment, making other government staff jealous (Banerjee et al., 2002).

Some key drawbacks to parallel implementation structures include:

- "Fast-tracking" may not necessarily be compatible with institutional learning.

---

[12] The issue was discussed in some depth during the Second Reforming Technical Cooperation Roundtable, held in Turin in December 2001 (http://capacity.undp.org/rountables/index.html) and in a number of UNDP knowledge networks. A UNDP practice note on PIUs is under preparation.

- PIUs can be used as a cop-out for fundamental reforms.

- Parallel arrangements introduce perverse incentives.[13]

- Powerful PIUs may drive a development agenda and impose prescriptions on how a government should work.

Arguments for or against PIUs are not quite cut and dried, however, because evaluation evidence alone does not provide a clear verdict. Under certain circumstances, such units can be fine-tuned to meet stated capacity objectives. PIUs have been more capacity friendly, for example, in situations where they have been berthed within ministries or departments (or even within a harmonization mechanism anchored by one donor), rather than when used as stand-alone structures.[14] More positive experiences have also been reported from "organic" PIUs. For instance, in the Philippines, they are headed and staffed by a significant number of nationals. The use of foundations (some backed by the government) may twin the advantages of capacity development with outsourcing.

One can also make the argument that donor harmonization should apply to PIUs. There may not be a real justification for a multitude of units. A more permanent, nationally managed, unified service structure for project execution may offer significant economies of scale.

But in the larger scheme, the fundamental dilemma remains: the problem of draining capacity away from legitimate institutions. And it is clear that the use of PIUs, or PIU-like structures, is more widespread than commonly admitted. Working groups, financing and contracting units, reform councils and coordination centres are all often thinly disguised PIUs. In the Kyrgyz Republic (Cukrowski, 2002), for example, the Public Administration Reform Working Group functions like a PIU, without calling itself one. Many other actors in the development arena have also found creative ways of disguising PIUs with different names and attributions. It is easy to detect them, though, through their funding arrangements. Artificial labeling cannot hide the fact that they would not survive without project money.

Countries that are firmly in control over their development stand a greater change of employing PIUs with little risk of undermining ownership, while benefiting from efficiency gains. Yet countries with weak capacities face a fundamentally different situation, one where the risk of overwhelming national entities is very high. In these cases, working through national priorities, systems and processes may be cumbersome and challenging, but it should still be the default setting. Particularly in the LDCs, PIU type arrangements should be the rare and well-justified exception, with a clear exit strategy. "Gap-filling without shame"

---

[13] This is extensively discussed in the following chapter.
[14] Brazil offers an interesting case, because integration has been practiced for many years. As the country gained strength in managing development processes, the National Execution Unit was transferred back to UN agencies in an arrangement that corresponds to subcontracting. Despite the negative capacity connotations of PIUs, it is possible to use certain PIU models that have consistently demonstrated better capacity outcomes.

(Berg et al., 1993), i.e., placing technical assistants into line functions, will in many cases be the preferable option. Box 2.4.1 summarizes a number of critical considerations, while the issue of PIUs and incentive schemes is further discussed in section 3.3.

Box 2.4.1: Gap-filling – separating ideology from reality

Conventional wisdom in discussing the reform of the aid system is that gap-filling undermines capacity development, and that there are virtually no circumstances under which it should be considered a viable option. Yet these assumptions can in some cases be challenged.

There are a number of countries today where severe capacity shortages, especially in government services, are unlikely to be relieved for at least a generation. In these situations, the conundrum is sometimes as dramatic as either agreeing to fill line positions or allowing government services to collapse into chaos. Even when the need is this clear, however, experience suggests a number of areas require reflection before moving into gap-filling, such as:

- *Ownership:* Where is the demand for gap-filling – on the side of a developing country government or donors?

- *Institutional capacity:* Is the government able to define needs and manage support once it has been provided? Is the existing capacity adequate to manage the institutional requirements of the country? And is the absorptive capacity sufficient to ensure proper accountability?

- *Public service reform:* Is a reform programme underway to look at system-wide constraints in order to make government service more attractive over the longer run?

- *Capacity assessment:* To what extent has there been an assessment of available skills in key sectors and plans developed to address the shortages?

- *Critical and strategic areas:* Are the posts to be filled absolutely critical for the functioning of government?

- *Training programmes:* Are there parallel programmes to train staff to compensate for the shortfall in skills over the longer term?

- *Integration into the system:* Are posts filled by expatriates part of the government establishment or supernumerary? Do expatriates report to local managers or to project authorities who are not part of the government service and may themselves be expatriates?

- *Alternatives:* Has the government discussed or developed plans to lure back diasporas? Are alternative and cheaper sources of qualified staff being tapped?

Conclusions

The challenge is not to insist on advisory assistance over gap-filling, but to match the needs of the situation with the mechanism most likely to facilitate the realization of national development objectives. As developing countries take more leadership in defining development assistance, they may choose to use gap-filling in selected and strategically important areas. To refuse to respect a well-considered decision of this nature would be a return to the old paradigm of "the expert knows best". That being said, gap-filling is not an approach to be used lightly and, most importantly, not in a way that would undermine existing local capacity.

Source: Baser, Hauck and Land: www.capacity.undp.org/cases/insights/index.html.

KEY POINTS

 Execution is the responsibility of national institutions. Management and oversight require clear delineation of responsibility and relationships, as well as accountability.

 Management skills are an important dimension of implementation. They help ensure quality oversight, proper systems for disbursements, analysis of financial sustainability and respect for cross-sectoral linkages. It is the responsibility of programme management on all levels to make strategic and daily choices that favour capacity development.

 For countries firmly in the driver's seat, parallel implementation structures may present little risk of hampering ownership, while providing major efficiency gains. The situation is fundamentally different in countries with weak capacities, where the risk of undermining national entities is very high. Particularly in the LDCs, PIUs should be the rare exception, with clearly defined exit strategies.

 Although working through national priorities, systems and processes may be cumbersome and challenging, it should still be the default setting. Integrating external expertise through direct gap-filling "without shame" is preferable to parallel institutions.

REFERENCES PART B

➲ **ESTONIA** *The Innovative Use of Foundations to Implement National Policies (p. 214)*
➲ **JORDAN** *A Non-Threatening Approach to Interdisciplinary Collaboration (p. 243)*
➲ **LAOS** *A Team Approach Aligned to the Local Decision-Making Style (p. 246)*
➲ **MONGOLIA AND MOROCCO** *MicroStart Backs Business Plans of Leaders with Vision (p. 255)*
➲ **MOZAMBIQUE** *Effective Budget Support for Post-Flood Reconstruction (p. 264)*
➲ **AFRICA** *Private Sector Growth Begins with Better Managers (p. 316)*
➲ **WEST AFRICA** *Harvesting a New Rice Through South-South Cooperation (p. 328)*

2.5 MONITORING: ACCOUNTABILITY VERSUS CONTROL

"The customer is always right."

"Satisfaction guaranteed or your money back."

Companies in the service industry have institutionalized customer service concepts, such as the ones quoted above, to boost their bottom line. The formula has worked because mature businesses recognize that quality service, building trust, accepting client feedback and establishing mutual accountability all attract and keep customers. Development accountability is not supposed to be much more complicated than this.

Accountability is linked to a performance record: the use of public funds needs to be justified. To this end, bilateral and multilateral donors have to put in place reporting systems with requirements largely falling under two areas: financial and programmatic accountability. The latter is normally approached through monitoring and evaluation.

Currently, discussions on financial and programmatic accountability do not focus on capacity development. Yet there are three ways in which accountability arrangements may actually undercut capacity development efforts:

- Project implementation can become an objective in its own right, pursued regardless of collateral dimensions and possible damage to aspects such as capacity.

- When separated from national management systems, project and programme accountability may service external constituencies at the expense of more organic forms of accountability.

- Disparate accountability standards and monitoring and evaluation formats have created a massive enterprise of recipient country data collection and information management, which is poorly connected to end results.

These characteristics may provoke a perverse cycle: to respond to weak national capacities, parallel accountability structures are put in place, which themselves lead to a further weakening of capacity.

Key accountability features

Development agencies – as an integral part of their programmes – should support host country arrangements for public accountability. Among the foremost instruments is transparency, which allows stakeholders to monitor and apply pressure. To encourage transparency, accessible public information needs to include financial appropriation, recruitment, actual expenditures, operational target setting, outreach efforts, past service delivery, managerial performance assessment, and client feedback and complaints (Hauge, 2002). Information about positive experiences and success stories can be as important as monitoring of failure and misconduct.

Systematic feedback from ultimate beneficiaries of development and from those responsible for development activities also helps ensure appropriate responses. As one observer states, no large famine has ever occurred in societies characterized by democracy and freedom of expression (Sen, 1999). Public service managers who depend upon client feedback and approval to obtain their share of public resources (as well as for their performance appraisal and remuneration) appreciate the significance of customer service and suggestion boxes. These are common practices in large corporations.

Other ways to ensure accountability include voice mechanisms, such as client scorecards, user satisfaction surveys, public hearings, public postings of accounts and ombudsperson offices. Whatever the imperfections of such mechanisms, "at the end of the day, it is better to have approximate information about important issues rather than to have precise data on those that may be irrelevant to human development" (Hauge, 2002).

Full integration into national structures and systems applies to accountability too. Donors should support established national procedures, while additional capacity is allowed to emerge from within national institutions. Reliance on national capacities may in the short term entail lowering the bar on accountability standards: this does not mean that there will be no standards, but rather that there will be a common set of minimum requirements, based on international standards. In addition, the introduction of ICT can bring major benefits: improving accuracy, reducing transaction costs, simplifying priority setting, and enhancing resource allocation and tracking. Ultimately, all partners can input into the same systems, file requests, follow disbursements and monitor target outputs online.[15]

Abandoning the quest for individual attribution is essential for a nationally integrated accountability system to function. It is true that donors themselves are answerable to their domestic constituencies: if they cannot show what is done with their taxpayers' money, they have a credibility problem. On the other hand, true commitment to human development outcomes is incompatible with individual attribution. Human development is holistic and changes are wrought by many stakeholders. Consequently, the very act of trying to connect a particular outcome to a specific external input becomes inappropriate and removed from a more complex reality. It is essential that the development community move from micro-management and unilateral control to performance measurement and mutual accountability based on agreed standards and collective results, for example, in monitoring the achievement of the MDGs with outcome indicators.

---

[15] UNDP, for instance, has been supporting the establishment of such systems in countries as diverse as Egypt, Fiji, Nepal and Syria.

An increasingly important instrument for monitoring and evaluation of public policy is the public expenditure review (PER), already one of the most popular macroeconomic instruments available (see box 2.5.1). By comparing expenditure to outcomes and development targets, PERs show the relationship between resource allocations and results. Another popular trend has been the widespread adoption of the results-based management approach. Integrating this into national

---

Box 2.5.1: Public expenditure reviews

Joint reviews of public expenditure data by representatives of donor and recipient countries have been common for many years, particularly in connection with IMF Article IV consultations. Structural adjustment, debt relief and balance of payment support have in fact driven the interest in the PER. More recently, this mechanism has proven to be one of the best ways to track social expenditure against competing priorities, and donors have increasingly come to rely upon it. In a number of African countries (particularly Ethiopia, Ghana, Mozambique, Tanzania and Uganda), the PER has emerged as a major instrument for reviewing development strategies, despite data weaknesses.

PERs are useful for several purposes. A World Bank guideline (Pradhan, 1996) identifies six main purposes:

1. Analysis of aggregate levels of spending and their macroeconomic significance

2. Monitoring of allocations to programmes and sectors with respect to maximizing welfare

3. Monitoring of the complementarities and divisions of roles between public and private sectors

4. Analysis of the impact of expenditure patterns on the poor

5. Monitoring of input mixes, e.g., capital/recurrent expenditure and sector distribution

6. Examining whether the incentive structure is conducive to fiscal discipline and to allocation and technical efficiency

This is a much broader perspective than earlier expenditure reviews, which were narrowly focused on the budget machinery and on inputs rather than outcomes. Moreover, the earlier reviews did not involve the government in an active role but were donor-driven (Schick, 1998). The PER tries to assess the relevance and effectiveness of all expenditure with respect to the development strategy, and to suggest changes in resource allocations based on registered outcomes.

The PER also provides opportunities for much more detailed analysis of expenditure structures as well as outcomes. Departmental budget allocations are often difficult to relate to programme objectives and indicators of success, but by trying to match inputs and outputs, the PER helps bring the two closer to each other. By using a more participatory approach, the present generation of PERs has supported policy analysis both at central and sector levels, and has given finance managers incentives to see their performance in relation to policies and programme outcomes rather than merely in terms of financial discipline. The PER has been used as well for reviewing inter-departmental poverty programmes, often involving many different budget items managed by various ministries.

Another result of the interest in PERs is that transparency and data quality are being improved, and accountability questions have been raised, including in relation to users and stakeholders. Since the reviews cover virtually all government expenditure, including external resources, the final word on them should come from the legislative bodies responsible for approving the overall budget, rather than from donors, technical agencies or even individual ministries (Foster and Fozzard, 2000).

Source: capacity.org, issue 17, April 2003.

planning systems can be quite powerful, and developing countries should have a keen interest in institutionalizing it.

In general, good donor practices on reporting and monitoring in line with capacity requirements can be summarized as follows (OECD/DAC, 2003):

- "Donors should work with partners to rely and build on partner countries' reporting and monitoring systems.

- "Where partner systems do not provide appropriate information, donors should work with partner countries to improve them according to a nationally led and clearly defined national strategy for developing and strengthening these systems.

- "Donors should avoid creating parallel reporting and monitoring systems that undermine the sustainable capacity of partner countries to provide quality information that meets their own requirements.

- "Donors co-financing a discrete set of activities – project, sector, or budget support – should work towards agreeing, in consultation with partner countries, on common formats, content and frequency for a single periodic report that meets the needs of all partners. The reports should cover all of the activities in the defined area, and meet the information needs of key stakeholders in the country as well as individual donors.

- "In addition to alignment with government systems, and co-ordination among donors, donors should seek to simplify, whenever possible, their own reporting requirements in order to help alleviate the burden on partner government systems.

- "Donors should seek to reduce the number of donor missions and reviews while ensuring that they meet the learning and accountability needs of both partner countries and donors."

What should not get lost in the discussion on accountability is that monitoring and evaluation are primarily mechanisms for learning and adjusting to evolving conditions, and a valuable tool for codifying knowledge.[16] The process is an essential part of development management in any given country, as well as highly useful for exchanging comparative experience across borders. It is vital that evaluation reports, rather than collecting dust on shelves and filling up disk drives, find their way back into strategizing, decision-making, and achieving better and more sustainable development results.

---

[16] Evaluation results can be used in three main ways:
- *Direct use* occurs when a decision maker acts on the basis of an evaluation report's conclusions and recommendations.
- *Indirect use* occurs when an evaluation report is just one of many sources of information used by a manager to prepare a position on a specific topic.
- *Symbolic use* occurs when the impression is given that evaluation results are accepted or being used in decision-making when, in fact, they are not.

KEY POINTS

 Accountability to ultimate beneficiaries by both national governments and donors is essential. Transparency is the foremost instrument of public accountability, not just with respect to financial resources, but also with regard to institutional management practices, planning and actual service delivery.

 Issues of attribution have spoiled the development debate for decades. Donors are answerable to their domestic constituencies; however, it is important to find realistic ways of associating results and success with collective undertakings.

 With the expansion of various forms of programme aid, PERs are rapidly becoming an important instrument for monitoring and evaluation of public policy.

 Donors must follow established national accounting, reporting and assessment processes and systems, while the capacity for monitoring and evaluation needs to be allowed to emerge from within national institutions. Recipient countries should integrate results-based management into national mechanisms for development management.

 Monitoring and evaluation are primary tools for learning and adjusting to evolving conditions, while also codifying knowledge that is essential for accountability systems and informed development choices.

REFERENCES PART B

⊃ **BOLIVIA** *Citizens Exercise Their Right to Be Involved in the Aid System (p. 177)*
⊃ **BRAZIL** *How Participatory Budget-Making Can Improve the Quality of Life (p. 183)*
⊃ **CAMBODIA** *Decentralization Lays Foundation for Reconstruction and Governance (p. 190)*
⊃ **INDIA** *Public Hearings Arrest Corruption in Rajasthan (p. 234)*
⊃ **THE PHILIPPINES** *Civil Society Puts a Watch on Public Spending (p. 270)*
⊃ **SOUTH AFRICA** *Women Analyse the Budget, and Parliament Heeds the Gaps (p. 284)*
⊃ **TANZANIA** *Independent Monitoring Holds a Government and Its Partners to Account (p. 292)*

3 *From perverse to positive incentives*

Human beings are driven not only by directives, but also by objectives, values, expectations and emotions. Even dictates from government or moral authorities may be ignored unless they are connected with rewards for compliance or sanctions for non-compliance. While many people are motivated by the hope of improving the welfare of society or other collective goals, most also need incentives in the form of individual rewards, like wages, job security, occupational and social status, and a whole range of fringe benefits connected with employment or a political position.

Incentives can motivate not only individuals, but also collective actors, such as enterprises, government departments or agencies, academic institutions and civic groups. Nationwide aspirations may take forms such as the desire for victory or the dream of a "grand nation". In many cases, motivation revolves around power, with individuals or organizations prepared to forgo some material benefits to gain more influence and a stronger long-term position.

For its part, the state is obligated to set up an incentive structure to "motivate its employees by providing security, honor, stability, civility and fulfillment" (Mkandawire, 2002). Creating optimal conditions for a civil service or other public institutions to function rests upon both material and moral incentives, such as "catching up", nation-building, charity, military superiority, economic development and cultural affinity. However, moral incentives cannot flourish in cultures of rampant greed and self-interest (Mkandawire, 2002).

This chapter explores the different incentive systems driving development cooperation – some support capacity development, while others do not. Of particular concern are incentives that were originally intended to produce a positive effect, but which have become serious obstacles to development. The following pages discuss the implications of these perverse incentives,[1] and examine how they block sustainability; promote the use of external resources rather than more cost-effective domestic ones; discourage local initiatives; and, at least indirectly, stimulate brain drain.

---

[1] The Collins English Dictionary defines perverse as "deliberately deviating from what is regarded as normal, good and proper; persistently holding to what is wrong, wayward or contrary; obstinate".

3.1 INCENTIVES AND DEVELOPMENT COOPERATION

The development experience of the past half-century has taught just how difficult it is to bring about changes simply through the imposition of control and direction. It has also demonstrated that what encourages people to change is often a very complex and abstract mixture of objectives and expectations, with some elements of concern for society at large, but with a heavy emphasis on individual rewards.

On the recipient side of a development partnership, many agents (administrators, consultants, academics and organization officials) are strongly attracted to the benefits that projects may bring to their society. Involving users and beneficiaries in the planning and implementation of projects can harness this tendency. But one also cannot expect implementing agents to forgo the essentials of livelihood simply for the sake of the greater good. They may have alternative avenues for making a living, and if their involvement in a project is necessary for its success they have to be paid competitive salaries.

On the donors' side, development cooperation depends on the interest of constituencies, as well as of political leaders, in transferring resources, whether they are gathered through taxes or voluntary donations. It also depends on administrators and intermediaries using this money for the agreed purposes. Since legislative and executive powers in donor countries cannot personally supervise each operation, a system of incentives and disincentives that takes into account factors such as global labour markets, and public and private sector roles must be put in place. The incentives should compel those who are entrusted with aid money to do their best to ensure it is used for agreed purposes.

Perverse incentives

Countries dependent on development cooperation are more exposed to the pull of external incentives, which are often based on legitimate intentions that confront complex realities on the ground. For instance, when all donors in a country simultaneously strive to satisfy their individual agendas, the total outcome is likely to turn out poorly. Each may want to produce visible and positive results, which generates reasons for agents on all sides of a partnership to associate achievements with the donor's inputs. This distorts efforts to build sustainable mainstream capacity by spawning fragmented development efforts, as well as parallel organizations, processes and structures.

These kinds of perverse incentives thrive on objectives and constraints on both sides of a partnership. Donors usually believe the best course for transformation is to establish well-functioning units, reporting and resource flows. However, all these ingredients may disrupt the normal routines of the recipient.

For instance, disbursement pressure is one of the strongest perverse incentives, making administrators on both sides sacrifice quality in order to spend as much money as possible in the shortest possible time. In countries where corruption is widespread and managerial skills are scarce, development projects are often doomed from the start.

Commercial objectives also distort development efforts. When selling as many goods and services from the donor country as possible is a mandatory part of resource transfers, commercial incentives enter the picture even though they are not the primary goal. Studies show that on average, goods and services bought with this kind of tied aid are at least 15 per cent more expensive than they would be if they were purchased on untied terms (Development Initiatives, 2000). But this is not the only cost of tying. By distorting the whole price structure of large development projects, tied aid leads to the use of more capital-intensive technology and to discrimination against domestic skills in favor of imported ones (see box 3.1.1).

Political and strategic considerations remain well-known producers of perverse incentives. While development actors are eager to claim that development assistance is primarily guided by development objectives, the reality is that politics often gets in the way. This has led to more aid funds being given to countries with mixed development results, rather than to those with successful growth and equity (World Bank, 1998). The effect of such trends generates what market analysts call "moral hazard" – one is not rewarded for achieving good development. This problem crops up consistently in the international financial institutions' experiences with structural adjustment.

On the recipient side, there is usually great eagerness for quick approvals and large disbursements of external funding, with very few recipient governments saying "no" to offers of development finance, even when they are aware that the quality of the offer is questionable or that the donor's objectives differ from their own. Perverse incentives arise as governments play for time, hoping eventually to be able to divert the resources to undertakings of higher national priority.

Finally, development cooperation itself has developed an opaque and unwieldy working culture over just 50 years of existence. It is difficult to imagine alternatives, although one can perhaps make a comparison with the Marshall Plan after World War II, or with the budget support provided by the European Commission for depressed regions in Europe. This stark contrast clearly reveals what a behemoth the international community has created for managing a relatively modest resource flow, with hundreds of aid agencies, rules, regulations, missions, procedures, reporting formats and incentives of all kinds. Reform of development cooperation will not get far without changing this apparatus, and in particular the perverse incentive systems that are woven throughout it. These include the vested interests in professional institutions, consultancy firms and procurement agents,

---

Box 3.1.1: OECD/DAC position on tied aid

In April 2001, OECD/DAC agreed to untie "to the largest extent possible" aid to LDCs from January 2002. Although this agreement still does not include all developing countries, it is an acknowledgement that tied aid devalues and undermines development assistance.

The DAC argues that this recommendation represents a concrete signal of its commitment to the reform of aid practices, and will contribute to broader efforts to increase the effectiveness of aid as well as strengthening the ownership and responsibility of partner countries. Under the recommendation, aid loans and grants covering a wide range of financial and project support (such as capital equipment, sector assistance and import support) will be open to international competition and no longer reserved for suppliers in the donor country.

According to the DAC, this will offer better value for money, both for taxpayers in donor countries, and for recipient countries. It estimates tied aid to cost on average of between 20-25 per cent more than if the goods or services in question were procured through international competition. The agreement will also help recipient countries shape more efficient and rational public procurement capacities.

Total bilateral aid to the LDCs currently stands at around $8 billion (some 17 per cent of the total). The recommendation now unties about $5 billion of that sum. DAC members have been invited to continue to provide untied ODA in areas not covered by the recommendation when they already do so, and to study the possibilities of extending untied aid in other areas and to other developing countries.

Source: OECD.

---

all of whom work closely with both donor and recipient governments, often inspiring choices that favour unsustainable capacity options (see section 1.4).

Positive incentives

In order to create a policy environment that supports capacity development, incentive systems have to be turned around, starting with the issue of cost. A fundamental problem with the whole development cooperation industry is that so few of the goods and services it provides have a visible price tag, which tells the user how much money the service requires from the provider, or what the user has to sacrifice to get it. Even if both sides know all the sums, the recipient is very seldom aware of the possible alternative uses of the money. Eliminating perverse incentives is to a large extent a question of introducing more price consciousnesses among users, as well as among providers and intermediaries (Berg et al., 1993; Ajayi et al., 2002).

If significant incentive changes can be envisaged, it becomes necessary to begin spreading knowledge about good practices more widely and determining their replicability. There is a need for knowledge networks involving practitioners from developing countries to have a serious discussion about how the aid relationship can become more demand-driven, and how incentives can be based on integration rather than fragmentation of government organizations. One of the major issues is the balance between rewarding the good performers and catering to the requirements of the needy. It is a delicate one, and there is no simple answer. Yet one thing is clear: strong political leadership is required among recipient countries. Redirecting the aid industry is a task that cannot be accomplished without the insistence of host governments.

KEY POINTS

 Development cooperation is subject to incentives and disincentives. For transformation to take place, there is a need first to acknowledge the role positive or perverse incentives play.

 Each donor may want to be closely associated with positive results in a country, which encourages agents on all sides of a partnership to associate success with the donor's inputs. This distorts initiatives to build sustainable mainstream capacity by fragmenting development efforts, and spurring the growth of parallel organizations, processes and structures.

 In order to create a supportive policy environment for capacity development, the incentive systems have to be turned around. Experience shows that political leadership gives strong signals to those who manage development cooperation; these leaders could urge the adoption of a more flexible approach to incentives. However, redirecting the aid industry is also a task that cannot be accomplished without the insistence of host governments.

REFERENCES PART B

➲ **AFGHANISTAN** *Local Capacity Grows Amidst Conflict and Collapse of Central Authority (p. 171)*
➲ **BRAZIL** *Bolsa Escola Helps Mothers Send Children to School (p. 180)*
➲ **EGYPT** *Governorate Human Development Reports Provide Analysis at the Community Level (p. 211)*
➲ **INDIA** *Citizen Report Cards to Improve Public Service Performance (p. 232)*
➲ **TANZANIA** *From "Top-Ups" to Sustainable Incentives for Civil Servants (p. 289)*
➲ **AFRICA** *Private Sector Growth Begins with Better Managers (p. 316)*

3.2 GOVERNANCE SYSTEMS

Because capacity development refers to the competencies that permit individuals, organizations or societies to shape their own destiny, it is linked directly to governance. The governance system that is most conducive to capacity development is one that offers the positive incentives that arise from inclusive democracy and protection of human rights, supported by the rule of law, strong judicial institutions, a free press and a vibrant civil society. It is characterized by effective, transparent and accountable public administration, with decentralization where required, and mutually respectful and beneficial partnerships with the private sector, NGOs and external development partners. Capacity development thus rests upon more than the basics of good governance and efficient performance; it calls for humane governance, which encompasses good governance but is also sensitive to equity.

The connections between humane governance and capacity development begin with inclusive democracy, which is not only about elections, but about the opportunity for all people to participate, at every level, in the political process – whether that involves setting priorities, or formulating and implementing development strategies. This form of governance is not about the might of the majority, but about the right of the minority. It is therefore essential to capacity development, with its emphasis on the ability to set objectives, and form and implement plans and strategies. Inclusive democracy also involves a political structure that is sensitive to national interests as well as open and accountable to people – other prerequisites for capacity development.

None of this is possible, of course, if people's basic human rights are not guaranteed. A rights-based approach to development stresses several factors that sustain capacity development. First, people who have no access or have not benefited from development have a right to claim delivery. Second, duty holders are clearly identified. In traditional development, the implication is that nobody can be held responsible if it does not happen. And in fact, the government (one major duty holder) often faults other actors or issues for non-delivery. But under the rights-based approach, duty holders are accountable and people can take them to court. Public litigation in India over the failure of the government to provide school for children is a case in point. This has been possible only because basic education is regarded as a human right in India.

A third point is that the rights-based approach stresses the process as much as the final outcomes. For example, two countries – A and B – might have reduced their population growth rate from four per cent to two per cent. In development as usual, which emphasizes outcomes over process, both countries have been equally successful. But from a rights-based perspective, if country A's achievement is through incentive mechanisms, while country B's is through coercion, then the process used in country B is not acceptable.

For human rights to mean more than just lofty principles, they must be consistently supported by the rule of law and a proper legal system. Without these, neither incentive mechanisms nor external interventions for capacity development will bear the desired results. Judicial and legal reform can involve improving the structure and administration of courts and law enforcement, training judges and lawyers in human rights principles, and ensuring an independent judiciary and equal access to justice by all.

Aside from the law, a free press and an energetic civil society serve as watchdogs to deepen inclusive democracy, bolster support for the protection of human rights, and further check the misuse of incentive mechanisms, which encompass monetary aspects, forms of recognition of individual and institutional efforts, and external interventions. Both the media and civil society can also play a critical role in initiating broad-based debates and dialogues on various issues related to capacity development. Lack of awareness and knowledge, as well as internalization of human rights principles, particularly among marginalized groups, is probably one of the greatest obstacles to the realization of human rights through development. In addition, the media and other civil society organizations can sensitize policy makers to their international obligations and support calls for the development of baseline indicators.

Perhaps the most critical form of support for capacity development is an efficient, transparent and accountable public administration, partly because a significant portion of all development work takes place in this system. More importantly, public administration influences the overall framework for developing capacities – including through policies, strategies and institutions. An efficient system can help identify, without any bias, the degree and locations of capacity gaps; develop strategies to overcome them, both in terms of incentive and recognition mechanisms; and make sure that these are properly implemented and monitored.

Overall, ensuring good governance that carries capacity development forward should take five elements into account:

- Capacity does not lie in just formal systems or governments, but also in informal systems, and in commu nities and civil society. National entities have a better understanding of the realities on the ground, while external partners do not necessarily have better capacities.

- There are advantages in promoting a sufficiently decentralized public administration system with robust and effective local governments, so that the issue of capacity development can be addressed both at macro and micro levels.

- There are benefits from solid alliances among various development actors – governments, the private sector, civil society and external development partners.

- A viable mechanism for learning from and replicating the experiences of communities, NGOs and the private sector is needed.

- External agents should act as catalysts.

In the end, the state plays a crucial role in whether a country can adopt a nation-wide rights-based approach to development. The extent to which human rights are protected in a country will not only depend upon the nature of a government, but also on the strength of its laws, the quality of its governing institutions, the voice of its civil society and the macroeconomic policies that have been put in place.

KEY POINTS

Governance systems are directly responsible for establishing an environment where positive incentives can prevail. This begins with inclusive democracy and a rights-based approach to development.

Neither incentive mechanisms nor external interventions for capacity development will bear results unless there is the rule of law and a proper legal system. A free press and a vibrant civil society serve as watchdogs to deepen inclusive democracy, bolster support for the protection of human rights and further check the misuse of incentive mechanisms.

The role of the state remains crucial to the adoption of a nation-wide rights-based approach to development.

REFERENCES PART B

⮕ **BOLIVIA** *Citizens Exercise Their Right to Be Involved in the Aid System (p. 177)*
⮕ **BRAZIL** *How Participatory Budget-Making Can Improve the Quality of Life (p. 183)*
⮕ **ESTONIA** *The Innovative Use of Foundations to Implement National Policies (p. 214)*
⮕ **HONDURAS** *Democracy Trust Backs National Consensus Amidst Volatile Politics (p. 229)*
⮕ **SOLOMON ISLANDS** *Connectivity Is the Option for Remote Islanders (p. 278)*
⮕ **TURKEY** *City Dwellers Transform Municipal Governance (p. 298)*
⮕ **UGANDA** *Developing the Capacity for Decentralization and Local Governance (p. 300)*
⮕ **YEMEN** *PRSP Preparation Paves the Way for Inclusive Policy-Making (p. 310)*

3.3 PUBLIC SERVICE INCENTIVES

> *"A request from a provincial governor in Mozambique for $50,000 to recruit 100 additional teachers was rejected for lack of budgetary resources. Meanwhile, an expatriate consultant could be provided for $150,000 since this expert's salary was not in the national budget."* [2]

A factor often forgotten is the novelty of civil service in a number of developing countries (Mkandawire, 2002). The rudiments of civil service can be traced only to the last period of colonial rule, when civil services were often confined to law-and-order functions, with some later expanded to take care of fiscal activities. In the decades after independence, when they were seen as a modernizing force, civil services were often protected from major disruption. But eventually, the size and efficiency of the state began straining at the imperatives of fiscal discipline; the rolling back of bureaucratic apparatuses dominated most of the development literature in the 1980s and 1990s. At the same time, through structural adjustment programmes, a wave of public service reforms made it necessary to examine the issue of capacity.

Today, countries such as Bhutan, Botswana, Brazil, Cape Verde, Costa Rica, Mauritius, Singapore and Tunisia can claim levels of public service efficiency comparable to industrialized countries. But by and large, most public service experiments have struggled to reconcile modernization, efficient service delivery and sustainable capacity. In this process, incentives have played an important role – often a negative one. The incentive structures of public administration in most developing countries are known for their counterproductive effects on staff morale and efficiency, even apart from the poor outcomes they produce when incentives become mixed in associations with donor agencies. In many of the poorest countries, the general salary level of public servants is too low to support a family, which forces the employee to moonlight, or indulge in corrupt practices, and reduces his or her ability and motivation to deliver a good day's work.

This scenario of slow desperation took root in the 1970s, when many governments, particularly in Africa and Latin America, used the public sector to counter high levels of unemployment. Government structures expanded very rapidly, ignoring the issue of overstaffing, which has negative incentives of its own. During the 1980s, when structural adjustment, the debt crisis and a stagnating world economy slashed government revenues, it wasn't long before a veritable disaster struck the civil services of countries that were most affected. Many African governments reacted by freezing nominal wages in spite of runaway inflation. Civil servants experienced a very dramatic cut in real incomes, which in many cases forced them below the poverty line. Large staff reductions followed: in Africa and Latin America by one-third on average, in Asia by almost twice that amount

---

[2] Mentioned by a former Mozambique Finance Minister at the Reforming Technical Cooperation Round Table in Geneva, 16-17 July 2001.

(Schiavo-Campo et al., 1997; Colclough, 1991). This had devastating consequences for the quality of public service delivery in the poorest countries.

Additional problems arose from the far-reaching compression of salary differentials that took place at the same time, particularly in Africa. This was due partly
to political considerations, and partly to the techniques used for salary revisions.
By the 1990s, professionals and managers were earning salaries just barely higher than those of support staff. Many departed for the private sector or to countries
that offered better pay. Skilled professionals such as doctors and engineers used
their civil service positions for private purposes, and an over-reliance grew on outsourcing as opposed to developing capacity within government institutions. By
the early 1990s, something needed to be done. Most countries resorted to
"decompression" as a corrective measure (Schiavo-Campo et al., 1997).

While they are critical, levels of remuneration are not the only incentives for
civil servants. It is also important how recruitment is undertaken and what criteria
determine promotion. Staff motivation is higher when salary scales, recruitment
and promotion are generally regarded as fair. It is arguable that, at least up to a
point, low salaries are more likely to be accepted in a system that is commonly
regarded as equitable. Such cases are rare, however, and most studies of public
administration in the LDCs mention nepotism in recruitment and promotions, and
little delegation of authority. Hardly anybody proposes any innovation, since the
chances of promotion depend on avoiding mistakes rather than on taking initiatives, particularly in organizations demoralized by salary cuts and downsizing.

When incentive structures like these cross the ones offered by donors, the
outcome can be highly counterproductive. The donors want to produce visible
results in the shortest possible time, and they are not going to wait for the public
administration to develop the capacity to deliver them. Various forms of bypass
organizations spring up, like project management units that attract the most competent and enterprising members of the civil service (see section 2.4).
Department heads and other key personnel are given incentives like training, study
tours and vehicles to pay special attention to donor-funded projects. Short-term
consultancies circumvent rigid civil service salary and employment rules, and
sometimes are offered simply to curry favour with higher officials.

These practices frequently drain the civil service of its best personnel and divert
the interest of the remaining staff from their main duties to the possibilities of having
access to aid-funded perks. In the case of the fortunate few who have been recruited
to work for the donors or special units, their motivation is more often to perpetuate
their new employment arrangements rather than to complete their tasks and return
to their own government (Godfrey, 2000). Where foreign aid is a major source of funding, the effects can be disastrous, leaving only the ruins of public service units
in-between well-staffed and well-equipped project offices (see box 3.3.1).

In many countries, local agreements have been made between donors not to offer salaries, travel or meeting allowances above certain ceilings. The closer the ceilings are to government pay standards, the less distorting they will be in terms of the government maintaining its staff.[3] But while pay ceilings stabilize incentive structures and make them more predictable, they do not solve the fundamental problem: staff who are fully or partially paid for by donors owe their allegiance to their paymaster and will often see the future of their careers as lying outside the civil service.

Another unfortunate impact of donor-funded salary incentives is that the civil service loses interest in reforming itself in terms of salaries and organization of work. Those who have gained access to salary supplements will no longer be pushing this agenda, and ministers and leading civil service administrators will confront resistance to plans calling for the government budget to shoulder full responsibility for costs otherwise funded by donors.

Yet since pay reform can be essential for sustainable capacity development, it must be considered, and include the entire civil service. Successful efforts tend to be based upon some commonly accepted principles, such as:

- Full-time employees who perform the tasks required by their positions should earn decent incomes.

- Equal pay should be provided for equal work performed under comparable conditions, for women and men, regardless of the source of funding.

- Pay differentials should be sufficient to ensure recruitment of staff who are competent to carry out the managerial, professional and technical tasks required to deliver services.

- Recruitment, tenure and promotion should be transparent, and based on merit determined by commonly accepted criteria.

The points below are attempts to delineate a sequence, from the most preferable to the least preferable courses of action for dealing with incentive schemes. Sensible solutions need to be tailored to the context.

- Nationally led schemes are preferable to donor-led solutions.

- The donor community, including multilateral partners, should not shy away from funding such schemes through pooling resources, ideally through the national budget.

- When this is not feasible, governments should be encouraged to lead, while possibly outsourcing the pooling arrangement.

---

[3] See the case of Tanzania as reported by Philip Courtnadge in an e-discussion on incentives (www.capacity.undp.org/project-docs/index.html).

Box 3.3.1: Donor-funded ad hoc schemes

The pressure from donors to launch large and complex development projects in poor countries with a low capacity for project management is the driving factor behind the introduction of special salary supplements for civil servants and separate administrative units for managing project implementation. Rather than adjusting the project to the existing implementation capacity, donors provide additional funding for creating temporary capacity in the form of the units and salaries. These arrangements are supposed to be ad hoc measures to overcome initial capacity problems, but they have a tendency to become both big and permanent, and in the poorest countries they distort the incentive systems and the management structure of the government as a whole.

Purposes of incentive schemes

Special arrangements and incentives from donors are most often motivated by their interest in being associated with progress in the programmes funded by their aid. More rarely do their objectives relate to the macro policy environment, such as aiming for a better general utilization of human resources. The most common justifications for these special arrangements are:

1. The capacity at institutional as well as individual levels is too low to permit line ministries or agencies to implement the new project at the same time as they perform their mainstream functions.

2. The general pay level in the civil service is too low to sustain the workers, leading to poor attendance and productivity. In extreme cases, the government claims it is unable to pay the workers any remuneration at all.

3. The salary differentials for skills, responsibility, etc., are too small to bring about the additional effort required for implementing the project.

4. Rigidities in the civil service contract rules and career systems make it difficult to respond quickly and effectively to rapidly changing requirements.

The instruments

The following are the most common instruments used for special arrangements:

1. *Subsistence payment:* The donor gives food or pays full wages to public employees engaged in a project. This is common where the government claims an inability to pay basic wages and salaries to its own employees.

2. *Salary supplements:* As the implementation of the donor-funded project entails additional efforts by civil servants, the donor feels justified in paying salary inducements to some or all of the officials involved. The donor takes no financial responsibility for making any such payments beyond the project period.

3. *Training and study tours:* Technical cooperation projects often provide generous grants for travel and training.

4. *Consultancies and non-government employment:* Donors will offer well-paid consultancies and project posts outside the government establishment. Civil servants are often well placed to compete for these jobs.

The practice of setting up special implementation units usually goes together with salary and recruitment inducements. The units often hire their senior officials from the line ministries of the government, thereby undermining capacity at the core. Because of their higher salary levels, they can also attract professionals from the private sector or NGOs. Often run jointly by the government and the donor and with better access to external resources and high-level government leaders, the special project units operate more freely than government units. Many regularly bypass established structures in order to ensure the funding agency rapid implementation.

Problems caused by special incentive schemes

The difficulties flowing from these arrangements are well known. Paying the salaries of public servants generally leads to a lack of government ownership of the programme. The employees as well as the public see the whole activity as being driven by the donor, and the government's interest in taking over financial responsibility may disappear.

Possible paths towards a solution

To find a sustainable solution to the incentives problem, the development partners will first have to address two fundamental deficiencies:

1. *Civil service incentive structure:* It is impossible to build a rational incentive scheme on the basis of a civil service structure that provides insufficient incentives for work and sometimes even contains disincentives for undertaking very important development tasks. The principles of a general salary reform must at least be envisioned, even if the reform is not already decided on in detail. If this is the case, temporary solutions for individual departments can be designed as steps towards a more universal reform.

2. *Integration of external contributions:* The donors will have to reduce their ambitions for visibility and provide contributions on a collective rather than individual basis. There are ways to organize special units that are less separate from mainstream operations in a ministry or agency. Even a partial integration of the unit in the regular work as a whole would reduce the degree of separation. From the very beginning, a clear exit strategy should be part of the agreement with the donor, providing an incentive for unit officials to achieve eventual integration.

Implementation

Since the problems of special units and incentive schemes are caused by several interlocking factors, only comprehensive approaches involving both donors and recipients can begin to address them. These require broad coalitions and partnerships that are not dependent upon the odd donor or government department that breaks the mold. It is also not realistic to expect instant and widespread support. In some cases, mandates prevent donor agencies from joining SWAPs or pooling resources. Both at the international and national levels, therefore, the effort should be to build coalitions of partners who are convinced that the current system will have to be reformed. Once the coalition starts to work, it is likely that new members will join and that the impact will build momentum.

Source: Gus Edgren discussion paper prepared for UNDP, 2003.

- Where government does not take the lead, for instance in conflict or post-crisis situations, a collective approach negotiated and coordinated by donors and relevant national stakeholders may be a possible solution.

- In cases where a national anchor cannot be found or constructed, collective harmonized solutions are preferable to a multitude of different schemes, e.g., from UN agencies, international financial institutions and bilateral donors.

- Anarchic incentive schemes in cash or kind are the least preferable avenue and should be ruled out as a "no-go" option.

- An exit strategy is absolutely indispensable, regardless of the option selected.

KEY POINTS

 The novelty of civil service explains its dilemmas in a number of countries. Long before they could establish strong traditions, public services in most developing countries have faced the undermining of their capacity through low remuneration, skewed recruitment and promotion criteria, the compression of salary differentials and downsizing.

 Motivated by the need to ensure quick delivery of projects, donors provide additional incentives in the form of salary supplements, travel and meeting allowances. Yet these practices drain the public service of its most able employees and reduce the motivation for a comprehensive reform of public administration.

 While there are no quick solutions for civil service reforms, there is a general need for harmonized approaches, preferably led by national agents, and optimally integrated in the national budget. For credibility and sustainability, an exit strategy is essential.

REFERENCES PART B

⮑ **BHUTAN** *A National Vision Guides Progress and Technical Cooperation (p. 174)*
⮑ **GUINEA BISSAU** *Building a Research Institution in an Inhospitable Environment (p. 226)*
⮑ **MALAWI** *Facing Capacity Erosion in the Public Sector (p. 249)*
⮑ **TANZANIA** *From "Top-Ups" to Sustainable Incentives for Civil Servants (p. 289)*
⮑ **UGANDA** *Developing the Capacity for Decentralization and Local Governance (p. 300)*
⮑ **EASTERN EUROPE** *IPF Initiative Facilitates Research and Curbs Brain Drain (p. 319)*
⮑ **WEST AFRICA** *Action Research Teaches Problem Solving on the Job (p. 325)*

3.4 EXPERTS, CONSULTANTS AND ADVISORY SERVICES

Mamadou migrates to Europe with the hope of finding a job. As the prospects of getting something meaningful become more elusive, he hangs around in trendy disco clubs, in the hope of making useful acquaintances. And he does! He starts dancing with people he just met. Before long, he has expanded his list of dancing friends significantly. But he cannot avoid more and more questions about what he does for a living or where he comes from, and so on. He decides to sell the idea that he is a witch doctor, given that his newfound friends are obviously mesmerized by exotic cultures. It works! He is asked to give consultations and advice, and bit by bit this becomes big business. After making good money, Mamadou goes to his hometown on a well-deserved holiday. Intrigued by his big spending habits, Mamadou's family wants to know what work does he do in Europe. Mamadou cannot reveal the full truth. It would be hard for people to understand or accept. But he can tell them how he sees it: I am an expert!

This story makes a caricature of the traditional expert, someone who knows more about a subject just because he or she comes from a specific region. That is enough to pay, no questions asked, big money for advice – even though sometimes the advice might just be invented. While most experts do not reflect the caricature, their widespread use for technical cooperation projects has to be seriously questioned (Berg et al., 1993).

Government agencies offered the use of technical cooperation personnel are often not given the choice between spending a certain sum of money for hiring an expert or for other purposes, such as acquiring domestic expertise or investing in staff training. Experts are provided on a take-it-or-leave-it basis. Faced with what seems to be a free good, a government official wants to have as many foreign experts as possible.

The actual opportunity costs, however, are considerably higher even than what may be steep local costs for providing the foreign expert with support staff, offices, telephones, etc. Imported experts extract their own price when they undermine national capacities by working through parallel structures, distorting local labour markets and drawing away scarce local capacities. If the expatriates are supposed to do something that is actually needed, they will replace domestic expertise that would otherwise have been hired.[4] Even in some of the poorest countries, there is often individual competence available, either in the private sector or in the diaspora, a resource that could be utilized at a fraction of the cost of using expatriates.

Are there any alternatives to this bypassing of domestic resources and squandering of external ones? The answer is obviously yes – one only needs to look at

---

[4] If not, their contribution will be in addition to what would have been achieved without the aid project, but both ownership and sustainability would be very doubtful. It is nevertheless important to acknowledge that there are genuine gap-filling needs in countries leaving crisis or post-conflict situations.

the private sector or successful developing countries who have understood that existing national capacity can only be retained if the principles that create incentives for expatriates are considered for the nationals. However, the same principles do not mean the same package of incentives. Transnational corporations such as accounting or consulting firms do attract the best local talent. But PriceWaterhouseCoopers, Ernst & Young and Accenture do not offer identical salaries in Switzerland and Zambia. They follow the local labour market and craft incentives around it to return and attract capacity. Likewise, UN system agencies do not pay their locally recruited staff the same wage as in New York, Geneva or Vienna. An elaborate system of local employers' comparators is used for each country, in order to guarantee that the labour market is taken into consideration. Together with career and moral incentives, this package is supposed to attract the best local talent.

Any agenda for reforming technical cooperation should also clearly give high priority to establishing more competition-based incentives to maximize the efficient use of external experts. Donors allowing consultants and experts from the recipient country to compete with their own nationals and consultancy firms have taken a step in this direction. While the impact of such measures has, so far, been fairly limited, a burgeoning consultancy sector has taken root in some developing countries and receives large amounts of technical cooperation. This in itself represents a significant boost for national capacity, at the individual level and in some cases even at the institutional one.

Many donors, however, continue to see *their* consultants and experts as spearheads of their own capacity, offering a unique two-way combination of salesmanship for national technology, and feedback on economic and social conditions in the host country. In fact, a major reason for giving bilateral aid is precisely to promote technical, commercial and cultural links. Kanbur and Sandler may be right in not expecting a quick endorsement of their proposal for pooling ODA (Kanbur and Sandler, 1999). It is true that the momentum on reforming development assistance is linked to the perception that the world has changed, and there is a need for more cost-effectiveness in the use of all public funds, including ODA. What is less clear is whether an essential issue is adjusting the ways funds are accounted for and disbursed. It may be far more important to look into conceptual changes in the manner in which areas such as technical cooperation operate.

Any reconsideration of technical cooperation must first acknowledge the fundamental impacts of knowledge networking on today's world. Steve Denning (Denning, 2002) has delved into this issue, identifying 12 aspects that have shaken the view of expert advice:

1. Knowledge sharing has become central (it is not wise to opt out).

2. Knowledge sharing is voluntary (it is based on wanting to learn).

3. Local knowledge is the foundation (advice in one context can be unwise in another).

4. Knowing "who" is strategic (personal connections drive the process).

5. Learning takes time (it needs to be processed through internalization and experience).

6. Learning from knowledge requires autonomy and background (the combination of local and cosmopolitan knowledge makes teams successful).

7. Capacity needs tacit knowledge (we need to know how to act).

8. Unlearning is part of societal transformation (sometimes people need to unlearn what they think is the way of doing things).

9. A group uses tacit knowledge better (for transformation, more is needed than individual contributions).

10. Knowledge cannot be transferred (it has to be learned, adapted and reinvented in a different context).

11. Knowledge is non-linear (paradigms constantly change).

12. Sharing knowledge is hard (as it requires changing of mindsets, systems and processes).

Only once these aspects are recognized does it become possible to address many of the dilemmas posed by the myth of the "free" expert. As a start, the following menu of options can be considered:

- *Costing of technical cooperation incorporated within national budget systems:* In India, the central government charges state governments for the cost of external assistance – a mechanism that is the equivalent of a soft loan. Charging the full costs of technical cooperation to the users is probably the most effective way of exploding the myth of experts as a free good. Budgeting should reveal the actual costs of all inputs, and user agencies might be debited all or some of the costs of the activity funded by an external agent. If several sources of funds could be posted, competitive bidding can even be added to the scheme.

- *Independent oversight mechanisms:* All of the points above can be integrated in more holistic approaches to technical cooperation rationalization, including better programming and oversight mechanisms that veto or approve requests following a "rules of engagement" list. Such a list would look into dimensions that favour the use of the most cost-effective solutions, respectful of prevailing local market conditions. Sometimes an expatriate professional is the best option. But that should be obvious to all.

- *Greater use of local consultants* (OECD/DAC, 1991; Berg et al., 1993): All parties endorse this one, and enormous progress has been made in the use of local consultants, whenever appropriate and available.

- *Greater use of short-term advisors and coaching models:* After OECD/DAC's endorsement of this principle in 1991 and its inclusion in UNDP's Rethinking Technical Cooperation study, this approach has become standard doctrine (OECD/DAC, 1991; Berg et al., 1993). It in turn will create space for better and more frequent use of local talent.

- *Time-bound gap-filling:* The model developed by the African Management Services Company (AMSCO) and extensively practised by countries such as China is very attractive. Expatriates are used for line functions provided they are paired with the eventual job holders for a predetermined period, usually quite short. This encourages learning without the perversity of long-term or undefined arrangements. However, it is important to complement the gap-filling with the right incentives for the ultimate takers of the job (see box 2.4.1).

- *Use of volunteers:* Building up space for voluntary action, including through national/international volunteer assignments, is an important way to improve the effectiveness of technical cooperation. Voluntary action not only promotes more cost-effective solutions, but also can build civic engagement and social cohesion. This can be particularly valuable in special development situations, where the need for external input may be urgent and clearly defined, such as in countries devastated by HIV/AIDS, conflict and other forms of crisis (see box 3.4.1).

Box 3.4.1: Volunteers – experts with a touch

At the core of international development cooperation is the pressing need to address poverty, both its root causes as well as its manifestations. In almost all societies, the most basic value is people helping people and, in the process, helping themselves. People aid one another in countless ways – from participating in burial societies to patrolling streets to make them safe; from replacing roofs on houses after a storm to providing community care for people with HIV/AIDS.

Voluntary mutual aid or self-help is typically an important safety net for the poor. Extreme poverty can even be expressed in terms of situations where a poor person or household has no friends or neighbours to turn to for mitigating risks and coping with the effects of shocks. Research from the World Bank shows that increases in the incidences of people working

together have the greatest proportional impact on the poverty of the poorest. It also points to the positive contribution of voluntary action to social cohesion, especially in conflict and post-conflict situations. Organized volunteers offer new skills while working closely with local people to build on their own aspirations.

In any discourse about local ownership, development practitioners would be well served in opening up the debate to cover all forms of voluntary involvement. No nationwide immunization or illiteracy campaign or low-cost housing programme has fully succeeded without massive voluntary participation on the part of local people.

In the North, the spirit of volunteerism is now extolled and increasingly measured, but in developing countries the tendency is to refer to local voluntary action as "contributions in kind" – what people have to provide at local level to earn the right to donor "largesse". There is less recognition of such action as building on the deep-rooted traditions of people helping one another and strengthening democratic governance. Without addressing this blind spot – clearly identified in the title of a recent United Nations Volunteers (UNV) publication, *Below the Waterline of Public Visibility* – the task of making significant headway towards the 2015 MDG of reducing poverty levels by half will be much more difficult.

In both industrialized and developing countries, volunteer groups make substantial contributions to human development through their own as well as collaborative actions. Solidarity, building on beneficiaries' own initiatives, equality, mutual trust and confidence are among the key principles guiding their work, which is also firmly rooted in the notion that capacity development is a local process, with technical cooperation serving mainly to provide an external stimulation.

Volunteers can work on policy or institutional growth, and also support organizational development and the sharing of skills. These services build links not only between individuals, but also between institutions in both the North and South, bringing out a desire to share and learn. Serving alongside others in a community increases the chances of skills development and tends to contrast with the lack of emphasis given to this aspect in many other forms of technical cooperation.

It also helps to reduce the power imbalances for which technical cooperation is often criticized. The limited financial benefits accruing to volunteer organizations and the detailed participatory research carried out by the best of them before making placements mean there is more likely to be a shared agenda. Long-term partnerships are encouraged, and there is less of a possibility of technical cooperation being a condition for the host agency.

Even when the volunteer returns home, the learning and sharing continues, contributing towards global solidarity and understanding. Many organizations managing volunteer placements encourage serving and returned volunteers to convey what they learned to their own communities. In part, this helps ground the debate in the donor countries more firmly in the realities of the South, and lends momentum to organizations in the North advocating equitable global policies.

Some of the necessary reforms for technical cooperation also apply to volunteering. There is, for example, room for improvement in the identification of appropriate areas for volunteer involvement, including the balance between capacity building and service delivery, the link with wider national and donor agendas, and the need for monitoring and evaluation. Yet the overall potential and need for volunteering remains clear. As a form of collaborative action that supports civil society and good governance, both critical factors in tackling poverty, and as an approach to technical cooperation, there is much that can be learned from it.

Source: UNV and Voluntary Services Overseas (VSO)

- *Institutional twinning:* Enabling institutions to gain access on a systematic and continuing basis to know-how accumulated in another institution is a standard practice in the corporate world. Nevertheless, in the public sector, efforts to pair institutions continue to be rare. Although twinning has long been used as an effective mechanism to avoid the transitional expert-counterpart model, it can develop perverse incentives as well. The design of the arrangement is critical to setting up the right incentives (OECD/DAC, 1991; Berg et al., 1993).

- *Use of non-resident nationals:* A number of technical institutions in Bangladesh, for example, are now benefiting from the technical know-how of non-resident nationals (see section 3.7).

KEY POINTS

 Experts are never free. Their costs have to be known, budgeted, transparently handled and compared with alternatives. Donors should provide space for more innovative and cost-effective approaches.

 The agenda for reforming incentives has to give priority to market-based lessons for retaining talent and respecting prevailing labour market conditions, while avoiding the erosion of capacity.

 Even when new approaches to technical cooperation are allowed or introduced, it is important to understand the role of knowledge sharing. This creates a completely different setting for the use of expertise.

 Greater use of short-term advisors, coaching models and local consultants; institutional twinning; time-bound gap-filling; costing of technical cooperation incorporated within national budget systems; the use of volunteers and independent oversight mechanisms are modalities consistent with positive incentives.

 The provision of volunteers offers a cost-effective and less intrusive modality that may be particularly valuable in special development situations where the need for external input may be urgent and clearly defined, such as in countries devastated by HIV/AIDS, conflict and other forms of crisis.

REFERENCES PART B

⮑ **CAMBODIA** *Angkor Wat Combines Conservation with Community Participation and Innovative Development (p. 186)*
⮑ **EAST TIMOR** *Volunteers Ease the Transition Between War and Reconstruction (p. 202)*
⮑ **THE PHILIPPINES** *Accenture's Strategy to Attract and Retain Local Talent (p. 267)*
⮑ **AFRICA** *Afrique en Création Supports Cultural Expression and Exchange (p. 313)*
⮑ **AFRICA** *Private Sector Growth Begins with Better Managers (p. 316)*
⮑ **SOUTH-EAST EUROPE** *A Virtual Meeting Place for Education Reformers (p. 322)*
⮑ **WEST AFRICA** *Harvesting a New Rice Through South-South Cooperation (p. 328)*
⮑ **GLOBAL** *Training Moves in New Directions Thanks to ICT (p. 334)*

3.5 PROCUREMENT

Procurement of goods and services is more closely linked to capacity development incentives than it first appears. It deals with contracting consultancy
services, employing longer term expertise under project funding and securing
non-personnel related items. Normally, it entails managing the selection process,
understanding price and cost, setting up contract modalities, applying total quality
management principles, accommodating legal considerations, and measuring and
evaluating performance. If a national agent does not possess a strong and transparent
procurement policy, they will most likely not be in a position to make strategic decisions, manage the various parties' expectations, and ensure a procurement modality
guaranteeing cost-effective expertise. Quite often, this situation drives donors to
adopt their own procedures. But opportunities are then lost, because procurement
can be used to attract and use talent that otherwise would not be accessible, and variations between procurement and other accountability rules can be understood and
inserted within a strategy that promotes capacity development.

On its part, the World Bank defines five basic concerns that govern its procurement policies:[5]

1. To ensure that goods and services needed to carry out a project are procured with due attention to economy and efficiency

2. To ensure that the loan is used to buy only those goods and services
   needed to carry out the project

3. To give all qualified bidders from the Bank's member countries an equal
   opportunity to compete for bank-financed contracts

4. To encourage development of local contractors and manufacturers in borrowing countries

5. To ensure that the procurement process is transparent

With some 40,000 contracts awarded each year by the World Bank alone, it is
imperative to have in place clear accountability systems for procurement across the
world of international development. The most important procurement tasks – including
analysing legal and organizational frameworks, assessing the impact of international agreements, conducting oversight and monitoring, and seeking ways to
reduce corruption – all feed into capacity efforts that development agencies are eager
to fund. However, it is also essential to take a hard look at unintended incentives
that undermine capacity development through the disguise of good procurement.

A key factor often hampering the development of procurement capacity itself
is that countries are overwhelmed with complex procedures. The complicated
procurement regimes of large development agencies are commonly designed in

---

[5] See project procurement notes for the International Bank for Reconstruction and Development (IBRD)
and the International Development Association (IDA) (www.worldbank.org/html/opr/procure/index.htm).

deference to bidding by national entities from donor countries for capacity development projects funded by these governments. In this case, an international policy to ensure transparency has a lateral effect of preventing local talent from competing. Data on procurement reveals that at least half of all aid money goes back to donor countries (Banerjee et al., 2002), a trend exacerbated by tying aid. Some development agencies even tender technical cooperation contracts (Banerjee et al., 2002) with reservations for their nationals (as for most European aid contracts, which are now the largest source of funding for most LDCs).

Under the two-tier tendering process, large single tenders are bifurcated (such as a technical bid and a financial bid, or as a local component and an international component). A certain "unspoken guarantee" exists among expatriate consulting firms in Southern countries that there is a reasonable chance of success for them in these bifurcated bids. They compete fiercely for the expertise component, yet the very fact that there is a form of conditionality allows unhealthy practices to creep in. Procurement, as has been shown in many cases, is one of the largest sources of corruption and big monetary kickbacks, and can even involve rigging of tender boxes and violent clashes between opposing groups.

A particular problem encountered with the two-tier process is the proliferation of external consultants irrespective of their core competence. Let's say a world-renowned bilateral linguistic and cultural agency – also an active player in the consultancy market – is bidding for contracts in the health, water and sanitation sectors. In a country where English language skills are not widespread, the organization knows it can produce well-crafted reports, which give it an advantage over most local consulting firms, despite the fact that it has no expertise in the subject area. It also helps that both its top management as well as the top management on the multilateral technical cooperation side socialize informally. But should linguistic or cultural comfort factors for external partners be deciding factors?

Window dressing is also an anomalous outcome of two-tier tendering. Local consultants bring in well-known external consultants to improve their chances of bagging contracts. Window dressing can also be used in reverse, when nationals are associated with external bidders as a token presence. Sometimes in the project formulation, several elaborate processes take place to demonstrate the participation of nationals, even though civil servants or other local agents may scarcely contribute a thought!

Another practice arises in the assignment of relative weights in deciding bids. Bid criteria often emphasize the need for experience (sometimes specifying variations such as "cross-cultural experience") as opposed to criteria of competence such as education and management skills. This skews consulting opportunities away from local firms that are just starting out. High weighting age to experience can be used to eliminate women and new players with innovative ideas, for example, leading to the adoption of outdated capacity development approaches.

Last but not least is the issue of where tenders and vacancies are advertised. Announcements of contracts are very often shared through word-of-mouth or offered as "invitation only" consultations. A well-connected network among donors ensures that a host of consulting and even full-time openings are advertised on each other's notice boards and not much elsewhere. In other words, a host of genuine non-merit entry barriers exist to discourage the participation of national development industry aspirants, undermining transparency requirements.

All of these factors contribute to the existence of a guild system that is informal, but powerfully connected. This has to be reversed, by simplifying government bureaucracy on the side of both donors and recipients of assistance to improve transparency, and by ensuring procurement policies address the requirements of capacity development. In the process, one eliminates "gatekeepers" who are in a position to exact tolls from users; reduces the number of steps required to gain approvals and payments for goods and services; and clarifies regulations to ease business transactions. There is also a need for minimizing areas of discretion, publishing clear guidelines on exercising it, and making accessible procurement manuals to departments in charge of oversight functions.

KEY POINTS

 Procurement transparency is central for the establishment of a culture of accountability and cost-effectiveness. Organizations involved in huge numbers of contracts need streamlined procedures.

 Procedures that are complex and include certain requirements from donors tend to overwhelm countries and local agents with limited capacity or exposure to sophisticated procurement policies.

 It is essential to take a hard look at unintended incentives that undermine capacity development through the guise of good procurement, including the way tenders are advertised and processed.

 Procurement policies among donors as well as recipients should explicitly address the requirements for capacity development. The best overall course of action is to adhere to institutional standards that are transparent and simplified, and minimize areas of discretion.

REFERENCES PART B

- ➲ **CAMBODIA** *Decentralization Lays a Foundation for Reconstruction and Governance (p. 190)*
- ➲ **MOROCCO** *Clear Decisions on Telecommunications Power Economic Growth (p. 258)*
- ➲ **THE PHILIPPINES** *Civil Society Puts a Watch on Public Spending (p. 270)*
- ➲ **VENEZUELA** *The Oil Industry Flourishes, Along with National Capacities to Serve It (p. 307)*
- ➲ **GLOBAL** *Corporate Social Responsibility at the Body Shop (p. 331)*

3.6 CORRUPTION

Corruption is the misuse of public power, office or authority for private benefit – through bribery, extortion, influence peddling, nepotism, fraud, speed money or embezzlement. Although corruption is often considered a sin of government and public servants, it also bedevils the private sector (UNDP, 1999).

Depending on a society's economic and political institutions, incentives and opportunities for corruption vary. This partly explains why it manifests differently around the world, although there are two broad types: petty and grand. Petty corruption is found where public servants who may be grossly underpaid depend on small kickbacks from the public to feed their families. Grand corruption typically involves high officials who make decisions on large public contracts.

The amount of corruption in a country's political system relates to the interplay of several factors. Low levels are typically found when institutional mechanisms prevent, detect and penalize wrongdoing; the nature of government activity provides relatively few opportunities; and society holds the practice in contempt. Economic opportunities are plentiful, and while state officials are highly accessible to interest groups, corruption is controllable because many competing interests, including critics, have access to the elites. People and firms have alternatives to dishonest officials and recourse against those who try to exploit them.

High levels of corruption flourish where institutional mechanisms to combat it are weak or not used; extensive government control and regulation of economic resources provide ample opportunities; and it is already so predominant that it is accepted and tolerated. An entrenched political elite dominates and exploits economic possibilities, manipulating valuable political contacts in return for personal gains. There are few checks on official manipulation or alternative outlets for exploited interests and groups. In some cases, officials given the job of dealing with corruption are the worst problem.

The trans-border nature of corruption adds another dimension, as national integrity is threatened by external factors that local officials may find harder to contain. Globalization has created many more opportunities – organized crime, for example, has taken advantage of the explosive development of global communications to evade effective law enforcement. Although developing countries need to combat this scourge, international conventions and treaties can also contribute by harmonizing national laws and forming a basis for mutual legal assistance.

Consequences of corruption for capacity development

Corruption costs the developing world billions of dollars every year, debasing human rights, siphoning off resources, degrading the environment and derailing development, including capacity development. It can drive conflict in and between nations, and destroy confidence in democracy and the legitimacy of governments. Where corruption is endemic, the consequences are disproportionately and cruelly borne by the poor, who have no resources to compete with those able and willing to pay bribes.

In developing countries and transition economies, particularly in the LDCs, past structural adjustment programmes aimed at generating growth and external viability have instead effectively lowered per capita income and real wages, ultimately deepening poverty. Many members of the civil service have been forced to resort to corrupt activities for economic survival. As corruption spreads, it spins into a vicious cycle: even when there are signs of positive economic performance, there is fear that prospects for development could easily be wiped out. The lack of integrity in emerging political and administrative systems becomes one of the most serious disincentives for the mobilization of domestic private savings and investment, and economic and political reforms end up being undermined.

Unfortunately, the process of economic, political and social change currently taking place in many LDCs, mostly in Africa, gives additional impetus for corrupt practices. Particularly for countries in crisis or periods of transition, opportunities for corruption grow when one set of rules has broken down, but another has not yet been institutionalized.

Determining causes and opportunities for corruption

Corruption is principally a governance issue, reflecting a failure of institutions. Weak institutions cannot supply a framework for competitive processes or effectively link the political and economic arenas. When democratic governance institutions and systems crumble, it becomes hard to implement and enforce laws and policies that ensure accountability and transparency, and corruption arises as a natural, organic response. It becomes entrenched when institutions designed to govern relationships between citizens and the state are routinely used instead for the personal enrichment of public officials and the provision of benefits to the corrupt (Rose-Ackerman, 1997). This is often the case when public officials have wide authority, little accountability and perverse incentives, or when they become accountable to informal rather than formal forms of regulation.

For civil servants, the reward structure within the state administration has traditionally been seen as one of the key determinants in the evolution of corruption. If officials are paid wages comparable to those available for similar duties in the private sector, and are compensated according to performance, the potential gains from engaging in corruption may not be large enough in relative terms to make it worth the risk. If, instead, officials in the public sector are paid wages well below those for similar duties in the private sector, then the opportunities for corruption may become the principal reason for choosing the public sector post (Goudie and Stasavage, 1997). This scenario threatens capacity development, as the incentive is perverse from the very beginning. Individuals simply will have no motivation to participate in institutional development or transformation.

Dealing with the corruption dilemma

In order to preserve and develop capacity, it is essential to fight corruption. Since government alone cannot hope to tackle it without the active support and involvement of its citizens, a successful campaign demands the full participation of all sections of society, including civil society and the business community. And while international actions can help, the struggle to contain corruption at the national level is essentially a domestic responsibility. External actors, including donors, can assist this process, but for it to be effective and enduring it must be locally owned, devised and driven (see box 3.6.1).

There is no one model to fight corruption, but generally efforts that make the most impact are comprehensive and participatory. They also start with strong political commitment, which distinguishes between superficial reforms and those backing real and sustainable change. Ideally, reforms should focus on incentives for prevention and on changing systems, rather than on indulging in witch-hunts. It is essential to evaluate historical and cultural sensitivities, understand existing vulnerabilities, and build supportive state structures that promote good governance and reduce poverty as a fundamental basis for change.

A developing country that is serious about fighting corruption may need to establish new institutions or strengthen existing ones to carry out some specific anti-corruption functions. One option is the creation of an independent anti-corruption commission, which has broad investigative capabilities (including arrest, detention, search and seizure) and prosecutorial powers, as well as a public education mandate. Such a commission must be genuinely independent of the country's rulers, but subject to the rule of law, or it risks becoming a force for repression in its own right. It must also have committed high-level political backing; political and operational independence to investigate even the top sections of government; adequate powers to access documentation and to question witnesses; and leadership of the highest integrity.

However, the creation of independent anti-corruption commissions is not the only solution to the corruption problem. Alarmingly, most countries recently embarking on anti-corruption campaigns have focused solely on the creation or strengthening of such an institution, as it appears to be a "quick fix". There are actually

---

Box 3.6.1 Jan sunwais – citizen involvement in oversight

The *jan sunwais* (public hearings) in India are a good example of citizen involvement in oversight. Essentially, they involve a public audit of development expenditure conducted by village residents. There are four objectives: transparency, the accountability of officials, the redress of grievances, and the legitimization of the process of social or public audits.

A *jan sunwais* begins with a demand from the citizens of the *panchayat* (a rural local government unit) to obtain copies of bills, vouchers and muster rolls of expenditures. When this information is obtained, it is organized and prepared so it can be understood by all. A date is set and announced for the hearing, where the records will be read out and placed before the people for verification, while an eminent set of outsiders functions as a panel to ensure that the proceedings run smoothly. Everyone who has been concerned or involved with the work is invited, including the government and elected representatives. After the reading of the records, people are invited to testify and other participants are free to corroborate or dispute what is being said. At the end of the day, the findings are compiled, including any irregularities, and the panel comments on them. Residents of the village can then assess what action needs to be taken, and who will be responsible for it.

This example is quite inspiring, as it began as an experiment in a remote village that ended up spearheading a national campaign on the right to information. For the first time, local accountability emerged from the confines of an intellectual debate and was defined by the poor as something related to their survival. The campaign slogan became: "The right to know; the right to live." The impact of public hearings, which are now taking place across the country, has been dramatic. Local heads of public offices and bureaucrats have been forced to attend, and when faced with proof of corruption, several have offered a public apology and returned stolen money. Apart from the effect this has had in the concerned panchayats, the fear of potential public exposure now deters the kinds of brazen dishonesty that were far more common in the recent past.

Source: Roy and Dey, 2001.

---

very few examples of successful independent anti-corruption commissions. Often cited are the experiences of the Hong Kong Independent Commission Against Corruption (ICAC), the Singapore Corrupt Practices Investigations Bureau (CIPB) and the Botswana Directorate for Economic Crime and Corruption (DCEC). Yet these models are generally not replicable due to the specific context in which they operate (and the particular history of their evolution). For a commission to function effectively, it requires tailoring to local circumstances, sustained governmental support, a coherent strategy and organizational capacity,[6] along with significant human, technical and financial resources.

Most often, independent commissions form just one pillar of a larger reform package that needs to be anchored in a comprehensive governance programme, one that seeks to identify activities most prone to corruption and reviews both substantive law and administrative procedures to reduce vulnerabilities. Other oversight mechanisms that may need to be strengthened include institutions such as the Office of the Auditor-General, the Office of the Ombudsperson and the Office of the Contractor General (or National Tender Board). Reforms also need to

---

[6] "Are Independent Corruption Agencies an Effective Solution to the Corruption Problem?" Paper presented at the 9th International Anti-Corruption Conference by the Corruption and Anti-Corruption Strategies Research Project funded by DFID, October 1999 (unpublished).

examine the role of an Elections Commission in guaranteeing an independent and impartial review of the electoral process, and must curb the corrupting influence that money has over many democratic processes, partly by reducing the costs of elections and restricting expenditures.

Stronger legislative mechanisms for accountability, such as a Public Accounts Committee, can ensure public access to oversight proceedings, while in order to investigate corruption cases reported by oversight and watchdog groups, governments can improve the capacity and integrity of the police force. Sound financial management practices should feature timely and efficient accounting systems along with punctual, professional reviews by internal and independent auditors (Pope, 2000). Finally, countries need to restore integrity in their judiciary, instilling accountability without eroding the judiciary's essential independence.

Alongside all of these reforms, it is also necessary to build the capacity of civil society, including the media, to serve as independent watchdog bodies. They play an important part in raising public awareness about the seriousness of corruption, which is crucial to the fight against it, and in developing an engaged and informed public that can insist on good governance. Governments need to ensure that responsible citizens can highlight instances of corruption without fear of reprisals, and that the media can report freely on issues that help hold relevant individuals and institutions accountable. In general, any reform process should inspire broad ownership, with partnerships between government and civil society for collective action that is participatory and built on consensus.

Another crucial component in the fight against corruption is the private sector, especially given its increasing role in providing essential goods and services, many of which have for generations been the preserve of government agencies. Improved corporate governance is a powerful tool (Pope, 2000) for reinforcing rules not just by written regulations, but also by the moral standards of business ethics and by responsible corporate behaviour. Corporate governance strongly depends on the institutional development of a country – which can be a great challenge in developing countries where institutions are weak. But it is critical not only to staunch corruption but also to reinforce the values of the rule of law, transparency and fairness,[7] and to transform corruption into an unacceptable action.

Efforts to improve corporate governance include guarantees of transparency in all corporate transactions, encompassing accounting, auditing and purchasing procedures. The development of a set of business standards demonstrates, in independently verifiable ways, a commitment to integrity. Corporate codes of conduct may also have some positive influence, depending on the degree to which they are "embedded" or part of the corporate culture – the key determinant in adherence to a code appears to be training, monitoring and enforcement activities (Pope, 2000). Finally, the members of the banking community and others play a significant

---

[7] *Corporate Governance: An Antidote to Corruption.* Report of the Centre for International Private Enterprise workshop at the 10th International Anti-Corruption Conference in Prague, October 2001

role in establishing mechanisms (including those enforceable through international obligations) to record transactions accurately and curb money-laundering, which could in some cases facilitate the return to developing countries of funds looted by corrupt leaders.

The international community is another source of support for initiatives against corruption, particularly those that strengthen national and local capacity building by devising homegrown solutions through participatory processes. Precisely because international organizations are in a position to share knowledge, resources and expertise gathered from around the globe, they can assist with innovative methodologies that analyse the nature and extent of corruption, and assess the effectiveness of particular reforms. They can also facilitate access to information communications technology, which offers rigorous diagnostic, empirical analysis and monitoring tools. These in turn enhance national capacities to transform information management systems as an integral part of institutional reforms.

International organizations in particular have a critical responsibility to support the ratification and implementation of global and regional treaties that address the supply and demand of bribery and corruption, as well as provide the impetus for international cooperation. Transparency International, a global coalition of NGOs that has mobilized the world's attention to fight corruption, is an important civil society partner in this effort; more can now be done within developing countries to strengthen independent civil society voices there. International networks can also help foster mutual legal assistance arrangements and the development of anti-corruption conventions for the African and Asian regions. Of great importance will be the work of the United Nations in putting in place a Global Convention on Corruption, which will aim to criminalize all forms of it. Monitoring will become vital for consistency and cooperation at the global, regional and national levels.

KEY POINTS

 Capacity development requires an active stand against corruption, with efforts focusing on prevention through fostering positive values, creating a culture of professionalism and meritocracy within institutions, improving transparency and disclosure, and building external accountability

 Reform needs to be anchored in a comprehensive governance programme, one that seeks to identify activities most prone to corruption and reviews both substantive law and administrative procedures to reduce vulnerabilities. Countries should implement comprehensive anti-corruption legislation, improve the capacity and integrity of the police force, and instill accountability in their judiciary without eroding its essential independence.

 Accountability mechanisms such as reporting and follow-up systems should be enforced to monitor bureaucratic performance. The reform of public programmes and procedures should be supported by independent investigators and prosecutors, and broad ownership of reforms should be established to create partnerships between government and civil society for collective action that is participatory and built on consensus.

 Transparency in information and knowledge helps eliminate the immunity enjoyed by high public officials. ICT tools enhance national capacities to transform information management systems as an integral part of institutional reforms.

 Channels for effective complaint making or whistle blowing should be developed.

REFERENCES PART B

➲ **BHUTAN** *A National Vision Guides Progress and Technical Cooperation (p. 174)*
➲ **BOLIVIA** *Citizens Exercise Their Right to Be Involved in the Aid System (p. 177)*
➲ **BRAZIL** *How Participatory Budget-Making Can Improve the Quality of Life (p. 183)*
➲ **INDIA** *Public Hearings Arrest Corruption in Rajasthan (p. 234)*
➲ **MOZAMBIQUE** *Bringing Back Justice, Law and Order Tests Long-Term Commitment (p. 261)*
➲ **THE PHILIPPINES** *Civil Society Puts a Watch on Public Spending (p. 270)*
➲ **SOUTH AFRICA** *Poor People Fight for Their Space Through Organized Fora (p. 281)*

3.7 BRAIN DRAIN

Contrary to perceptions, global migration is not as widespread as it looks. Today, 175 million people reside in countries other than the one of their birth, about three per cent of the world's population. Although the number of migrants has doubled since 1975, the more developed regions gained only an estimated net 2.3 million migrants per year, or nearly 12 million over the period 1995-2000. An important percentage of migrants stay in their regions, while, perhaps contrary to general impressions, the flows of migrants go both ways between industrial and developing countries.

One of the most publicized impacts of the current migration flows is the flight of human capital, otherwise known as brain drain, which adversely affects capacity development. Often, students from poor countries study in the West only to remain there after graduation rather than returning home. Even many who have been trained in the developing countries are attracted to industrialized countries by higher salaries and more promising job prospects. Institution building efforts are seriously undermined where this exodus of qualified people reaches significant proportions.

Dimensions of the problem

The phenomenon of highly educated professionals from developing countries working in industrialized economies, particularly the United States, gathered steam in the 1960s and has become increasingly common during the last 40 years. An IMF study based on 1990 data showed that a very large percentage of professionals with tertiary education from certain developing countries were working in OECD member states. Particularly high percentages of professionals came from small countries in the Caribbean, Central America and Africa. Even some larger Asian nations such as Iran, the Philippines, the Republic of Korea and Taiwan have suffered significant brain drain, although their percentages have been lower. Figure 3.7.1 lists countries whose numbers of highly educated nationals resident in OECD states was estimated to cross 15 per cent in 1990.

These figures cannot be interpreted as a straight measure of the drainage of human resources from the poor countries, nor of the loss that these countries have suffered in terms of education investment. A number of professionals covered by this data were still engaged in higher studies in their host countries. Moreover, a large portion of the total number received their tertiary education in their countries of residence rather than in their countries of origin, with the investment financed by their families and to some extent by the host countries.

Migration of skilled and professional people to countries with higher salary levels and better working conditions is an age-old survival strategy for poor countries, including many of those that are now industrialized. One member of the family

FIGURE 3.7.1: PERCENTAGE OF NATIONALS IN INDUSTRIALIZED COUNTRIES WITH TERTIARY EDUCATION

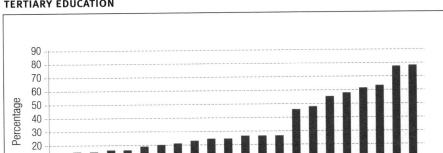

Source: Carrington & Detraglache, 1998. (Because of data compatibility problems, the estimates are given as ranges.)

Box 3.7.1: Migration in the IT industry

During the period 1964-1986, 58.5 per cent of graduates in computer science from one branch of the Indian Institute of Technology, IIT Madras, migrated abroad. And this was before the global demand for skilled IT workers kicked into high gear. Since then, the United States has increased its cap for software engineers from India to 195,000, while Germany is seeking 20,000, Japan 10,000 over the next three years, Ireland 32,000 by 2005, France 10,000, Italy 8,000 and the Republic of Korea another 10,000. Other countries, such as Belgium, Iran, Singapore, Spain and Syria, have also shown an interest in importing Indian talent, although without indicating precise figures. When the total supply of IT engineering graduates is just over 90,000 per annum, it is clearly going to be a major problem for India to retain its best and brightest.

In a major study in South Africa, brain drain, estimated to involve 200-300 highly trained IT specialists per year, was cited as the most common cause of local skills shortages. It was suggested that international employers see South Africa as a "soft target", given the poor performance of the rand, the crime statistics, the quantity of IT skills available, and the consequent mobility of educated individuals. In Pakistan, while there appears to be a mismatch in terms of the quality of personnel being supplied by educational institutions and what is required by software companies, there is at the same time a significant movement of skilled workers to the international market. The best students leave immediately after graduation or as soon as they fulfil visa requirements. Other quality students are absorbed by local industry, but soon leave for international markets after gaining the relevant experience. The large numbers that are left behind are not acceptable to software houses.

Brain drain has an impact even in the industrialized countries that seek to reap its benefits. Many organizations representing professional workers, such as the Software Professionals Political Action Committee (SOFTPAC) in the United States, stress that the main reason for employers favouring immigrants is that they accept much lower wages. These groups suggest that training and retraining the existing domestic workforce could overcome many of the skills shortages.

Source: ILO, 2001.

may be selected to go abroad and receive an education, so that he or she can later support the family with remittances or in other ways. These migratory flows can be positive, not only for the migrants, but for the societies they come from, contributing a steady flow of income and opening new horizons. But in recent decades, migratory flows have increased sharply in certain professions because of active recruitment by firms and institutions in developed countries, where the growth of knowledge industries is outpacing the supply of graduates with the appropriate education.

Recruitment has focused on certain professions that are of key importance for development both in sending and receiving countries. For example, it is estimated that there are more African scientists and engineers working in the United States than in the whole of Africa. Close to half of all medical doctors trained in Africa depart to work abroad (Ndulu, forthcoming). Nurses are leaving the Philippines at a rate of more than 3,000 a year to work in the Gulf or the United States. The most recent phenomenon is the surge in recruitment of computer science graduates by Canada, Germany, Japan, the United States and other industrialized countries, which have eased their visa restrictions on immigrants with those qualifications (see box 3.7.1). In India, a very large proportion of these graduates are now opting to work in the industrialized world (ILO, 2001).

While the driving forces behind these migration flows are higher income opportunities and better conditions of work, other incentives are equally important. In the countries of origin, facilities for work are unattractive, and recruitment is corrupt and nepotistic. Salaries are low, not only compared to overseas, but they are very often insufficient to support a family. Despite the market-driven widening in the 1990s that followed the compression of civil service salary structures during the 1970s and 1980s, financial as well as political obstacles in many countries have hobbled the restoration of professional salaries to levels that could be considered reasonable (Schiavo-Campo, et al., 1997).

Possible remedies

Brain drain is caused by several interlocking factors, and there is no single remedy that will deal with all of them at once. Measures will have to be directed at both the demand and supply sides of the labour market, and all actors involved must try and replace the current defeatist attitude to market forces with one built on the belief that those same forces can be turned around to work for "brain gain", i.e., for recovering the losses caused by brain drain and for developing sustainable capacity for poverty reduction. The current debate about brain drain has suggested the following list of remedies:

- *Upgrading the quality and status of public services:* As mentioned above (see section 3.3), the professional quality of civil services is mostly low in countries suffering from brain drain. Officials are poorly paid and their working environment is inadequate for producing good results. Better material incentives are required for recruitment of competent staff, along with an institutional environment that attracts and stimulates them. When higher professional standards are attained, qualified staff will be prepared to work for the public services even though salary levels are lower than in industrialized countries.

- *Raising the standards of tertiary education:* One reason why many bright students leave their countries to study abroad is that the universities in their countries are ill-equipped, poorly staffed and do not uphold certifiable academic standards. Degrees even from national universities may not be recognized unless supported by patronage or bribes. Governments must recognize this problem as a crucial obstacle to sustainable capacity development and reform tertiary education to introduce more effective teaching methods and up-to-date curricula, as well as acceptable and impartial standards for certification. International and regional cooperation with other universities may help establish standards that will make it unnecessary for students to seek their basic academic education abroad (Ndulu, forthcoming).

- *Making better use of existing national capacity:* While institutional capacity may be low in the public sector, underutilized individual capacities often exist in civil society and the private sector. These can be better tapped if monopolies for professional work are eased – for instance, in health, education and law – and small enterprise is allowed to compete on equal terms with government and large international firms in the domestic consultancy market.

- *Restricting the use of technical cooperation to where it is needed:* The prevailing incentive structure favours using expatriate technical cooperation personnel even in situations where local expertise is available. There are cases where over-reliance on technical cooperation appears to have crowded out domestic expertise, thereby encouraging brain drain (Banerjee et al., 2002).

- *Bonding of university graduates to national service:* Several countries have in the past imposed a bond on students who graduate from government-funded programmes, obliging them to hold a government job for a certain number of years after graduation. In view of the vast pay differences between domestic government jobs and the alternatives offered by industrialized countries, bonding is not an effective method to restrain international migration. However, if like a loan, the bond can be redeemed, for instance by a private employer who wants to recruit the graduate before the end of the bonded period, it becomes more attractive.

- *Immigration restrictions in receiving countries:* During recent decades, restrictions on immigration from developing world countries have become a major obstacle to the international mobility of labor. This also applies to skilled and professional people, with occasional exceptions for those occupational areas where immigration is considered a means to cover an acute shortage of human resources.

- *"Brain gain":* Returning migrants bring back foreign education, valuable management experience, increased ties to foreign research institutions and access to global networks (see box 3.7.2). Professionals in the diaspora could be seen as an untapped resource whose expertise is freely accessible via the Internet. Reverse flows of income in the form of remittances can be channeled towards development, including capacity development (see box 3.7.3 and table 3.7.1).

Box 3.7.2: Facilitating the return of skilled migrants

As carriers of capital, technology and entrepreneurship, skilled migrants can contribute to the development of their native communities, so organizations like UNDP and IOM have initiated programmes seeking to facilitate their return (permanent, temporary or even virtual). While permanent return might be hard to achieve, since developing countries cannot offer comparable salaries and infrastructures, temporary and virtual repatriation can go far in employing expatriate knowledge and skills.

UNDP's TOKTEN programme

UNDP's TOKTEN (Transfer of Knowledge Through Expatriate Nationals) programmes help qualified expatriates return to work in their countries on specific projects on a volunteer basis. TOKTEN consultants perform tasks that are otherwise done by expensive international consultants who have less knowledge of the country's social and cultural context. Thus, transfer of knowledge occurs at a much lower cost (often with savings of 50-70 per cent) and at greater speed (the motivation of TOKTEN experts naturally is very high). In virtually all cases, networks are created and follow-up takes place.

TOKTEN missions last between three weeks and three months. Institutions in developing countries send their requests to national TOKTEN committees, who search in a knowledge network for candidates. While consultants forego professional fees for their services, they receive a daily allowance at applicable United Nations rates and are reimbursed for the cost of travel from their country of residence. In addition, while on mission they receive medical insurance.

Programs like TOKTEN are most successful when they are supported by an active diaspora organization (as in the Colombian Network of Researchers and Engineers Abroad, also known as Caldas). The TOKTEN programme in the West Bank and Gaza strip was introduced as a part of UNDP's Programme of Assistance to the Palestinian People (PAPP) in January 1995. Both these experiences are significant demonstrations of the advantages of mobilizing nationals abroad, who would have otherwise encountered difficulties in reinserting themselves because of prevailing conflicts. TOKTEN has also been successfully applied under other circumstances, including post-independence and in efforts to offer investment opportunities.

UNV manages TOKTEN for UNDP, along with another important programme, UN International Short-Term Advisory Resources (UNISTAR). The latter focuses on private sector related inputs whereas the former is more traditionally oriented towards the public sector. UNISTAR also mobilizes retirees and pro-bono expertise from private corporations for short-term assignments.

IOM's Return of Qualified Nationals programmes

IOMs Return of Qualified Nationals programmes are directed towards short- and long-term return, including permanent repatriation. They are implemented in three stages: pre-departure, transportation and post arrival, and consist of recruitment, job placement, transport and limited employment support. The Return of Qualified African Nationals (RQAN) initiative focuses on returning Africans to home countries where their expertise is in high demand. The programme is carried out through recruitment missions in Europe and North America, and in several placement missions in Africa. In the 1990s, RQAN was directed at permanent repatriation of refugees.

The objective of the Return of Qualified Afghanis (RQA) programme is to assist the active engagement of skilled Afghans living abroad in the reconstruction, capacity-building and development process of Afghanistan. IOM, in coordination with the Afghan Interim Administration, the provincial authorities, and local and international organizations in Afghanistan, is working to identify sectors critical to the country's reconstruction and sustainable development where expatriates expertise is most urgently needed. The initial focus on such priorities will help construct the infrastructure necessary to eventually encourage a larger scale return, and contribute to the long-term stability and development of Afghanistan. So far, about 300 Afghanis have gone back and more than 4,000 have registered to do so. Under the project, 500 entrepreneurs will be awarded grants to open their own businesses, with the aim of generating additional employment opportunities for the local workforce and returnees.

Source: UNV, IOM.

The concept of the diaspora as a "brain bank" from which knowledge can be borrowed by people in the country of origin is not new, but the development of the Internet has inspired fresh and very promising applications during the last ten years. Knowledge networks, built to connect expatriate professionals with their country of origin and to promote the exchange of skills and knowledge, have emerged all over the world, particularly in countries with large immigrant populations such as the United States. The motivation for joining the networks is usually a combination of national solidarity and interest in keeping informed. Diaspora networks can be important channels for knowledge transfers through what the International Organization for Migration (IOM) calls "virtual return migration" as opposed to physical travel. They may also have the effect of enhancing self-confidence and credibility within the home country, which has been the case with a number of networks set up by expatriate Indians (Kapur, 2001).

Mercy Brown has identified 41 knowledge networks related to expatriates from 30 different countries, most of them in the middle or higher income bracket (Brown, n.d.). According to Brown, in order for these networks to be successful, an effective system must facilitate the exchange of information. This can be backed by an incentive scheme that ensures the continued commitment of members to the network and ultimately its sustainability. Support from governments and other institutions in the home country are also key in generating projects and activities.

Box 3.7.3: Remittances

The increasing social and economic importance of remittances is drawing national and international attention. In 1998, the global total was $52.4 billion, as much as the net ODA of $52 billion in that year (Kapur, 2001). In Albania, remittances are equivalent to 150 per cent of the value of the country's exports; for Greece, India and Morocco, they equal about 20 percent of exports. In 1999, 70 percent of China's $50 billion in foreign direct investment (FDI) came from ethnic Chinese abroad. There are, however, cases like Sri Lanka, where skilled immigrants are not remitting. That is why actively encouraging return flows in terms of investment and remittances is important in order to capture the potential benefit, and further apply it towards development.

Mexico's 3-for-1 programme

In July 2001, the Mexican government announced a "godfather programme" that encourages Mexican-Americans to invest in Mexico. In the state of Zacatecas, for example, which depends heavily on remittances, each dollar contributed by a migrant or hometown association in the United States for community development projects, such as paving streets, is matched with three additional dollars, one each from the federal, state and local governments. This 3-for-1 approach improves infrastructure, but does not create jobs. However, under a new initiative, the state government and the Inter-American Development Bank provide infrastructure support and financing for returned migrants who invest their remittances in job-creating enterprises.

TABLE 3.7.1: COUNTRIES WHOSE REMITTANCES FROM ABROAD MAKE UP 10 PERCENT OR MORE OF THEIR GDP

	Country	Workers' remittances 2000 (in millions US$)		
		Total	As % of GDP	Per capita
1	Jordan	1,664[b]	22.5	339
2	Samoa	45[c]	18.7	282
3	Yemen	1,288	15.1	70
4	Albania	531	14.1	169
5	El Salvador	1,751	13.3	279
6	Cape Verde	72[a]	13.2	169
7	Nicaragua	320	13.2	63
8	Bosnia and Herzegovina	549	12.9	138
9	Jamaica	789	10.9	306
10	Ecuador	1,317	9.6	104

Source: International Migration Report 2002.   a - Data refer to 1998; b - Data refer to 1999; c - Data refer to 1999

While in a few rare cases outflows of highly skilled workers can have positive technological and social effects, mainly through the use of their expertise virtually or through their return, much more needs to be done in order to turn the situation into one that benefits the majority of the developing world. Development programmes and migration policies tackling the problem of scarce national capacities need to work hand in hand on ways to strengthen existing capacities and turn the drain into gain. Particularly for countries that are extremely vulnerable to the negative effects of brain drain, there is a need to expand national abilities to monitor, evaluate and respond to the emigration of the highly skilled as well as to stimulate and assist return migration. Over the long term, policies promoting economic development and addressing labour market incentives are the best response. These can include shaping opportunities for innovation and high-tech entrepreneurial activities, which will draw highly skilled workers home and retain those who would otherwise leave.

KEY POINTS

 Combating brain drain, which erodes capacity development, requires putting in place measures for reducing the push factors causing people to leave their countries, as well as for encouraging them to return.

 Reverse flows of income and investments are the strongest link between migrants to their communities.

 Brain drain is caused by several interlocking factors, and there is no single remedy that will deal with all of them at once. Measures will have to be directed at both the demand and supply sides of the labour market, through policies promoting economic development and addressing employment incentives, as well as policy dialogues between sending and receiving countries.

 Particularly for countries that are extremely vulnerable to the negative effects of brain drain, there is a need to expand national abilities to monitor, evaluate and respond to the emigration of the highly skilled as well as to stimulate and assist return migration.

REFERENCES PART B

➲ **CHINA** *Investing in Pharmaceutical Research Capacity to Compete Globally (p. 198)*
➲ **GUINEA BISSAU** *Building a Research Institution in an Inhospitable Environment (p. 226)*
➲ **THE PHILIPPINES** *Accenture's Strategy to Attract and Retain Local Talent (p. 267)*
➲ **SUDAN** *Future Search Technique Creates a Vision for Peace (p. 286)*
➲ **EASTERN EUROPE** *IPF Initiative Facilitates Research and Curbs Brain Drain (p. 319)*
➲ **GLOBAL** *Training Moves in New Directions Thanks to ICT (p. 334)*

4 Re-examining the layers of capacity development

Offering practical advice on what needs to be done to develop capacity is often not enough – it remains equally important to re-examine the "givens", touching upon basic issues such as education, institution building or the level of civic engagement. This chapter delves into these, while deconstructing the three overlapping layers that comprise effective capacity development. It concludes with some insights on the relationship between capacity development and the evolving global development agenda, which has been invigorated by the Millennium Declaration and the MDGs, as well as by the debate at the International Conference on Financing for Development.

Any current discussion about transformation as the engine of development should refer to an important new direction in sociology: the relationship between subjects and external observation (Corcuff, 2002). The so-called social-constructiveness approach tries to venture beyond the traditional oppositions between objective and subjective, collective and individual. It examines social reality as a whole, produced by construction, rather than treating society and its elements as data, and takes into account historical roles that individuals and institutions play, one by one as well as collectively.

> "Like a game of chess, any action taken in an independent relationship represents a move on the social chessboard, which inevitably triggers a counter move by another individual (in reality, on the social chessboard, many counter-moves are made by many individuals), limiting the first player's freedom of movement. Society is therefore perceived as the shifting and fluctuating fabric of multiple, reciprocal, dependent relationships that bind individuals to each other" (Corcuff, 2002).

As commonly occurs with development projects, an expatriate advisor and the project beneficiaries fail on both sides to perceive all the links between decisions and choices, as individual knowledge and appreciation of facts is conditioned by each person's mindset. So the more the full array of perceptions can be brought into a structured process, the greater the chances that a genuine transformation will take root. Discourse and practice will find a fertile common ground if tacit knowledge is respected and unintended consequences minimized. For that to happen, there is a need for flexibility and openness.

Let's say an NGO activist promotes the introduction of a constitutional amendment to protect access to land in a particular region for migratory people. The region is the only one that offers possibilities for crop cultivation in the entire country, so any threat to small farms will jeopardize livelihoods and increase poverty. Although this was not the NGO's original intention, if it is not considered, there may be dramatic consequences. These can be avoided only through a more encompassing analysis.

Fortunately, today's development agenda is evolving in a holistic direction. After a period where plans and planning were challenged, they are back, but with techniques that are more innovative and respectful of flexibility. There are new opportunities to insert capacity concerns into the strategic planning debate, ensuring sustainability. This can be done even though capacity development yields returns over the long term, whereas strategic planning often focuses on immediate results.

4.1 HUMAN RESOURCE DEVELOPMENT

In every society, the basic unit of capacity is the individual, in whom skills and knowledge are vested. "In the capability concept, the focus is on the functioning that a person can or cannot achieve, given the opportunities he or she has. Functioning refers to various things a person can do or be, such as living long, being healthy, being well nourished, mixing well with others in the community and so on…. The capability approach concentrates on functioning information, supplemented by considering, where possible, the options a person had but did not choose to use. For example, a rich and healthy person who becomes ill nourished through fasting can be distinguished from a person who is forced into malnutrition through lack of means or as a result of suffering from a parasitic disease" (UNDP, 1997).

To exercise his or her capabilities to the fullest, an individual requires choices. This underscores the need for empowering those who don't have them, regardless of the reasons for a given distribution of power. There are three levels where this empowerment can take place: individual, local and community, and state or country (Lopes, 2002).

Empowerment of individuals begins with education and skills enhancement, which offer the chance of securing employment and a better standard of living – in other words, the expansion of individual options.[1] In the developing world, wages have been estimated to increase tenfold with each additional year of schooling (Summers, 1992). The impact spreads outward from there, as skilled human capital strengthens production processes and fuels economic growth. "Human development stresses the need to invest in human capabilities and then ensure that those capabilities are used for the benefit of all" (UNDP, 1993).

Education is also intrinsically valuable, as it contributes to the cognitive development of human beings, expands their knowledge, and provides them with confidence and self-esteem so that they can, to paraphrase Adam Smith, "interact in public without shame". For this reason, while education might not be the most cost-effective approach under certain circumstances, it is clearly an end in itself (Lopes, 2002).

Over the years, the vast analytical and empirical work done in the area of education has presented some widely accepted conclusions, which have important policy implications, particularly for human resource development. These are generic, and must be adjusted and prioritized to specific circumstances. They do not always lead to win-win situations, yielding painful trade-offs in many cases.

It is now generally acknowledged that primary education is a basic human right; universal access by 2015 is one of the MDGs. Primary education provides people with basic literacy and numeracy, which are essential for further skills

---

[1] Selim Jahan has provided an important input for this section.

development and thus the basis of human capital formation. Compared to other levels of education, the rate of return from primary schooling appears to accrue over a longer period (ILO, 2001).

But today, there are more than 113 million children in the developing world who are out of school. Furthermore, in countries such as Cambodia, Ethiopia, Guatemala and Nicaragua, half of those enrolled do not complete grade five. Even in developed countries like Ireland, the United Kingdom and the United States, one in every five adults is functionally illiterate. In Poland, Portugal and Slovenia, four out of every ten adults do not reach functional literacy (UNDP, 2002d).

Strikingly, in all countries, irrespective of income levels, both the private and social rates of return are highest for primary education. In terms of private return, the figures are 27 per cent for primary, 17 per cent for secondary and 19 per cent for tertiary, and in terms of social rate of return, 19 per cent for primary, 13 per cent for secondary and 11 per cent for tertiary (Psacharopoulos and Patrinos, 2002). In low-income countries, the social rate of return at 21 per cent for primary education is higher than the 17 per cent in middle-income countries and 13 per cent in higher income countries.

This highlights the urgency of universal primary education, yet at the current rate of progress, it is unlikely to be reached by 2015 in 57 countries (UNESCO, 2002). However, the world has made a commitment to strive in this direction, through the MDGs, so any longer term vision for human resource development, policies and resources must be geared towards achieving it.

If primary education is fundamental to cognitive development, secondary education is essential for skill formation, as many researchers have argued (Colclough and Lewin, 1993; ILO, 2001). Its importance has increased as countries have embarked on export-orientation to capitalize on globalization and meet the challenges of the network age. In particular, secondary education in science and technology can make a difference, as examples from Hong Kong (China, SAR), the Republic of Korea and Taiwan (a province of China) show. But even in 1998, for countries for which data were available, nearly 20 developing countries had a net enrolment rate of less than 15 per cent at the secondary level (UNDP, 2002d). In 2000, nearly 212 million secondary school age boys and girls were out of school (UNDP, 2001a).

Tertiary education is crucial for highly specialized skills, for technology development, and for expanding the frontiers of knowledge. University education creates highly skilled individuals who reap larger incomes: the private real rate of return to higher education has been found to be more than 10 per cent in countries like Denmark, France, Sweden, the United Kingdom and the United States (OECD, 2002). But it is also at the heart of creating national capacity to generate jobs, to adapt technology to the country's needs and to manage the risks of technological change – benefits that touch all of society. These capacities have grown exponentially in countries where tertiary enrolment has soared – as happened in the Republic of Korea, where the net tertiary enrolment ratio more than quadrupled in less than 20 years, from 16 per cent in 1980 to 68 percent in 1996.

In today's world, both secondary and tertiary education have to meet the demands of high technology in particular – some researchers now argue that the contents and modus operandi of the education system at every level, including the primary one, must be recast in this direction (UNDP, 2001a). Some trends and issues under discussion include:

- *Computer penetration and school enrolment:* In Eastern and Western Europe, computer penetration has been found to be a major determinant for school enrolment. But even in those regions, significant variations exist. For example, in 1997-1998, while there were more than 140 primary school students per computer in Portugal, there were less than 10 in France (ILO, 2001). The availability of computers may become a major factor for attracting students to schools in other places, in which case most of the developing world is lagging behind, despite significant advances in countries such as Brazil, Costa Rica and Malaysia.

- *Digital literacy and digitalization of literacy:* Through computerization of schools and school-nets, a few developing countries have established broad Internet access for schools through nationwide networks, among them Chile, Thailand and South Africa.[2]

- *Digital literacy of teachers:* While digital literacy of teachers is critical, spending on teachers' training even in OECD countries is only one part of the scant one to two per cent of the overall education budget spent on ICT. The European Union's Council of Ministers endorsed a strategy of achieving 100 per cent connectivity in school systems by 2001 – with all teachers trained in the technologies by 2002 (ILO, 2001). But this issue still poses a major challenge for developing countries, even though countries like Malaysia have made good progress.

- *Action-learning:* Action-learning has become a powerful tool to train people who have potential but little experience, particularly where accelerated development of leaders is a national priority. It helps organizations ensure that participants can relate what they have learned in the classroom to the issues they face in the workforce. This approach generally guarantees that an investment in leadership or any other form of capacity building has an immediate effect (see box 4.1.1).

- *Virtual universities:* These have emerged as a powerful instrument in teachers' training, distance learning through agricultural extension, and

---

[2] The Enlaces Project in Chile has linked 5,000 basic and secondary schools to its network. Thailand has developed the first widely available free-access network for education in Southeast Asia. The South African School Net (School-NetSA) is an interesting example for its structure and partnerships (UNDP, 2001a).

Box 4.1.1: Action-learning: South Africa's experience

Many organizations spend enormous sums on educating high-potential employees through in-house training programmes or university degrees. Typically, training programmes challenge individual and organizational mindsets, aiming to inspire a healthy dissonance between current and desired functioning. They expose participants to global best practices and research, build high-level problem-solving ability and stimulate challenging debates.

Yet many graduates leave their jobs soon after completing their degrees, and many in-house training programmes fail to produce any significant change in the organization. Frequently, employees do not connect these management development initiatives to the overall business strategy in their organizations, so that training becomes a one-time event rather than a process of capacity building for individual and organizational growth.

As a result, in South Africa, many multinationals, including General Electric, Boeing, ABB and Johnson & Johnson, along with local companies such as Standard Bank, Nedcor and Sasol, are taking a more strategic and holistic approach. These organizations are increasingly employing blended learning, where a variety of learning processes are combined to develop a range of competencies directly tied to organizational strategies.

One particular tool is called action-learning, where students, through guided reflection, tackle real business problems and develop the conceptual understanding necessary to solve them. Action-learning normally takes place among project teams, and the business problems chosen need to meet specific criteria. These include having an appropriate degree of complexity, cross-functionality and operational or strategic importance. While academic input

and other types of learning are not excluded, action-learning sticks closely to real-time scenarios, generalizes understanding for use in other situations and institutionalizes learning to ensure that it generates change.

Action-learning generally involves five key elements:

- The active involvement and support of senior management

- Participants working in teams on real issues and exploring new strategic opportunities

- Action research and learning focused on internal and external organizational experiences and thinking that can help resolve issues

- Leadership development through teamwork and coaching

- Follow-up on issues and leadership development, thus enhancing positive results and ensuring that learning is greater than the rate of change

As a philosophy, action-learning is based on the belief and practice that some of the best solutions can and should come from fellow employees. Many of the organizations that use this strategy have a high respect for their employees and believe that learning often comes from openly sharing experiences, which in turn encourages reflection and practical application.

These organizations now realize that knowledge, with an emphasis on "actionable knowledge", is an asset for competitive advantage. The past focus on individual development and learning has been replaced with the view that individual learning should contribute clearly to a stronger organization.

Source: Business Day, *Johannesburg/Cape Town, 25 September 2002.*

Box 4.1.2: HIV/AIDS and conflict

There is a twofold intersection with HIV/AIDS: both the impact of HIV/AIDS on the educational sector and the use of education to confront the phenomenon. On the first front, the evidence is clear – the epidemic is wreaking havoc on enrolment, teachers and resources, deeply undercutting overall capacity. Because of HIV/AIDS, by 2010, the primary school age population will be reduced by 24 per cent in Zimbabwe, 21 per cent in Zambia, 14 per cent in Kenya and 12 per cent in Uganda (World Bank, 2002). An estimated 860,000 children lost their teachers to AIDS in Sub-Saharan Africa in 1999 alone (UNESCO, 2002). Policies and resources are needed to keep education systems in the hardest hit countries functioning, even as they offer one of the best hopes for delivering important messages about cures and prevention, and building awareness that will prompt people to demand that more effective policies be put in place. It has been estimated that costs for achieving universal primary education related to HIV/AIDS in Sub-Saharan Africa now top $975 million (UNESCO, 2002).

Conflict has also extracted a heavy toll on education. During the 1990s, so many complex humanitarian emergencies sprung up that they began to seem commonplace, and by 2001, there were an estimated 15 million refugees in the world. The total number of internally displaced people in 2001 was estimated to be at least 25 million (UNHCR, 2001). This dilemma poses an acute need for education in emergencies: in 2000 alone, UNHCR supported the education of some 850,000 children at primary level and 63,000 young people at secondary level. Education has been described as probably the best tool for defusing many of the problems perpetuating crises. Systems set up for emergencies should offer flexibility in terms of physical infrastructure, facilities, teachers and curricula; draw upon significant community participation; and enjoy strong international support both in terms of resources and institutional back-ups.

the development of other professional skills. In the United States, the average yearly cost per student for virtual universities has been found to be $350, compared to $12,500 for a traditional school (ILO, 2001). An institution like the University of South Africa (UNISA), with a long tradition of distance education and more than 140,000 students, can become a major asset way beyond national borders.

- *Research and development:* In OECD countries, 2.3 per cent of GNP is spent on research and development, and nearly 3,000 people per million are scientists and engineers in this field. In comparison, Latin America and the Caribbean spend only 0.6 per cent of GNP here; in South Asia, only 158 people per million are research and development scientists and engineers (UNDP, 2002d). To garner benefits from technology, the educational systems of the developing world must turn their sights in this direction. Hong Kong (China, SAR), the Republic of Korea, Singapore and Taiwan (a province of China) have proven the value of this strategy.

Across all forms of education, higher returns consistently come from investing in access for women. Each additional year of schooling has been found to increase female wages by 15 to 20 per cent and reduce female fertility by about 5 to 10 per cent. For each additional year for a mother, child mortality drops up to 10 per cent

(World Bank, 1993). The overall rate of return for women's education at 10 per cent is higher than that of men at 9 per cent. In secondary education, women's rate of return is 18 per cent compared to 14 per cent for men (Psacharopoulos and Patrinos, 2002).

In most developed countries, two additional issues are hotly debated: quality and public versus private education. On the first, the consensus is now that quantity is not enough; countries should strive to achieve a higher quality as well. Low quality has several adverse impacts. First, it disturbs the flow of education – poor quality secondary education leads to meagre completion rates and then minimal university enrolments. Second, it produces low-quality skills. Third, it crimps the potential for taking advantage of technological opportunities. Improving quality requires paying equal attention to the "software", such as curricula and teachers, and the "hardware", for example, buildings and equipment. It may include revamping curricular content, resources for better infrastructure, more teachers, enhanced teacher training, better use of information and communications technology, and more flexibility in higher education for keeping education and career options open.

On the public versus private education debate, it is important to recognize two facts. First, private education may be complimentary to public education, but not a substitute for a good public education. Second, private education in many societies has turned education into a luxury commodity, even at the primary level, and has contributed to further inequalities and social polarization (Jahan, 1997). Privatization by itself does not guarantee efficiency or quality, and it does not, in many cases, ensure equity. However, it is widely used for on-the-job training by the private sector, and may be appropriate for higher education, as has been the case in the Republic of Korea. By the early 1990s, private institutions there accounted for 81 per cent of enrolments in university education. Today, spending on private education is equivalent to 2.5 per cent of GDP (UNDP, 2001a). But the country also channels most public education resources to the primary level, and is more selective about the mix of private and public funds for higher education.

In the overall context of human resource development, educational policies should target three important issues: resources, teachers and the labour market. Across most of the developing world, public education expenditure still represents less than 5 per cent of GNP and less than 20 per cent of government expenditure (World Bank, 2001). In poorer countries, the situation is even worse. But in low-income countries, the social rate of return to primary education is 21 per cent – significantly higher than the expected rate of four per cent from a power plant (Psacharopoulos and Patrinos, 2002; Summers, 1992). And the resource requirements are not that great. In the early 1990s, estimates calculated that an additional $4 to $6 billion per year could achieve the goal of universal primary education within ten years (UNDP, 1994).

Ensuring completion and quality of education also rests upon well-trained teachers, who in turn need proper incentive structures, better environments and enhanced facilities. To reflect the demands of the labour market, education systems as a whole must carefully tailor outputs to reflect these and acknowledge the dynamics of a rapidly changing world. A lack of links to other areas such as action-learning, training and enterprise development will only continue to encourage brain drain (see section 3.7) and actually erode capacities.

Two particular additional factors that arose in the 1990s, HIV/AIDS and armed conflicts, are worth mentioning because of their significant impacts on education and human resource development (see box 4.1.2). And one overall observation may be pertinent. Regardless of the context of education, there is no leapfrogging here, unlike in technology. However, if a sound educational structure is built gradually upon a strong foundation, it will eventually allow a society to leapfrog in other critical areas.

KEY POINTS

 Capacity development starts with education. Ensuring universal primary education for all is the foundation, offering basic literacy and numeracy. The secondary level should serve as the framework for skills development, particularly emphasizing science, engineering and technology. Tertiary education should be linked to the labour market demands of the network age, stressing research and development and ensuring flexible options for participants.

 At all levels of education, investing in women and girls offers significant social returns. Equal attention should be paid to "software", such as curricula and teachers, and "hardware", for example, buildings and equipment. Quality must be emphasized as much as quantity.

 There is a need to strike a balance between private and public education. Good public education at the primary and secondary level cannot be replaced by private education, which serves a greater purpose at the tertiary level and for action-learning initiatives.

 Education in countries hard hit by HIV/AIDS or conflict is critical, but it must reflect the realities of both phenomena. With HIV/AIDS, the dampening effects on education must be addressed to keep the system going, even as it is being used to help staunch the epidemic by spreading awareness.

4.2 INSTITUTION BUILDING

Capacity and institution building have often been treated as synonymous. Even though the new understanding of capacity development is broader and more complex, institution building – the second level of capacity development – remains an essential component. It is important to underline that institutions are more than organizations. They encompass rules, norms and behaviours accepted by a group of people. However, development has tended to focus on institutions from an organizational point of view, differentiating the capacity of individuals from that of institutions more than it should. While institutions grow out of sustainable individual capacities, ignoring group behaviour in the end undermines efforts to support this growth.

Management and institutions

Institution building is to a considerable extent about improving management. Paradoxically, the importance of quality management for institutional success has not generally been emphasized or even recognized in developing countries, and development cooperation itself has largely ignored evolving work on management issues. Recently, however, this direction has begun to shift, and development professionals are turning to management literature for ideas about how to improve institutional performance. Yet a certain uneasiness remains. In a recent compilation done by *The Economist* (Hindle, 2002), it is clear that part of the problem resides with the plethora of theories and approaches marketed by management specialists, who have created a big business. The level of commercialism has often intimidated development specialists, who assume management concepts will be difficult to grasp and use.

But lessons from management research are extremely useful. Modern theories and practices have been characterized by a pendulum movement between the work of Frederick Taylor, the creator of scientific management, and more humane views. Synthesizing these two schools is today's challenge, and many business leaders have done this successfully.

Essentially, Taylorism is centered on output productivity, measuring time and results, and leaving little room for individual initiative and imagination, let alone differentiation and diversity. Although today we know management is not about turning people into robots, the drive for measurement and results is still present. At the same time, authors like Peter Senge and Peter Drucker, who introduced learning and cultural dimensions, have insisted on the need for relying on instinct and judgment as much as economic reasoning. There is a growing understanding that empowered individuals are more productive, and organizations in fact need to have a fundamental belief in them.

There is no single approach to running a company or organization, and there are no blueprints for good management: institutions, the individuals within them, and their contexts vary widely, requiring different management styles and strategies for each situation. But there are some fundamentals, identified by studies of good institutional performance in developing countries and drawing on management literature. One of these is that managers of successful institutions find ways to invoke strong dedication among staff to the institution and its work, and they demand and reward good performance.

A study on good governmental performance in the state of Ceará in northeast Brazil (Tendler, 1997) demonstrated that the importance of worker commitment in productivity improvements and other aspects of institutional performance applies equally to government. The research uncovered better performance than might have been expected, given the history and the context – the study included rural health workers, business extension to small firms, a public works programme and agricultural extension. The high performance was largely connected to the unusual dedication that workers showed for their jobs. The state government had created a strong sense of "calling" around the programmes and workers by a public screening process for applicants, public information campaigns, worker orientation and open praise for the programmes' successes. Commitment also stemmed from the way work was organized, which included allowing workers to do a range of different tasks in response to the needs of their clients. It gave them some discretion in choosing and performing their work. Publicly accessible details about what they were supposed to be doing and the requirement of customizing for clients provided checks and accountability.

Merilee Grindle looked at a number of developing country institutional cases that included both good and poor performers. Drawing on organizational culture literature, she concluded that the identification of a mission for the institution and a "mystique" about the value of the work were key elements behind a high-performing institution, and that the presence and strength of such a culture separated the good from the poor performers. Furthermore, management was critical in making organizational culture develop, not only by identifying the mission, but by fostering its internalization and mystique, along with the dedication of the workers. Good managers supported this approach and acted on a clear and consistent message that performance mattered (Grindle, 1997). Several features of their management style were relatively consistent: fairly open, non-hierarchical styles for interacting with staff; encouragement of participation in decision-making and problem-solving; efforts to insulate the institution from disruptive elements in its environment; and consistent efforts to reward employees for high performance (see section 1.3).

Tendler and Grindle both emphasize a very positive approach to management, which they maintain can find ways to cultivate workers' dedication and create organizations where performance is expected and rewarded (Grindle,

1997). This seems familiar and reasonable and perhaps not surprising: it is widely practiced in private firms in Northern countries. Yet it is at considerable odds with how management questions have been approached within development coopera-tion. Discussion of governance in developing countries, at least in the past 20 years, has emphasized persistent problems with private interests taking prece-dence over the public good, clienteles, patronage, corruption, mismanagement and a general failure to deliver. In response, management approaches advocated for developing countries have been oriented towards downsizing, control and reduc-tion in discretion. Yet both the management literature as well as experience in developing countries indicates that more attention needs to be paid to approach-es that not only try to reduce problems but are designed to breed success.

Integrating an entrepreneurial spirit into public institutions

Osborne and Gaebler argue that a set of basic rules should guide management within governments. They should: 1) steer, not row ("it is not government's obli-gation to provide services, but to see that they're provided"); 2) empower communities to solve their own problems rather than simply delivering services; 3) encourage competition rather than monopolies; 4) be driven by missions, rather than rules; 5) be results-oriented by funding outcomes rather than inputs; 6) meet the needs of the customer, not the bureaucracy; 7) concentrate on earn-ing money rather than spending it; 8) invest in preventing problems rather than curing crises; 9) decentralize authority; and 10) solve problems by influencing market forces rather than creating public programmes (Osborne and Gaebler, 1992).

But as Osborne and Gaebler also point out, markets are only half the answer. Impersonal, unforgiving and inequitable, they must be coupled with "the warmth and caring of families and neighbourhoods and communities" (Osborne and Gaebler, 1992). In other words, entrepreneurial governments need to embrace both markets and communities as they begin to shift away from administrative bureaucracies.

They need to become more strategic as well. There are two main parties involved in formulating strategies, and the challenge is to bring the two together:

- *Decision developers:* groups of professionally and technically experienced individuals whose role is usually advisory. Most of these organizations are nationally or locally based, but there are external players such as international banks, multinational aid agencies, bilateral donors and international NGOs. They are responsible for reflecting and coordinating the needs and aspirations of the full range of legitimate interest groups.

- *Decision takers:* central and local governments, politicians and members of the boards of large national and multinational companies. They bear the ultimate responsibility for decisions and their impact.

In turn, building stronger institutional frameworks requires:

- The establishment of multi-stakeholder structures. These need to operate over a longer term as a basis for exploration, development and normative clarification of both the values and the procedures that will be brought to bear in decision-making.

- The provision of facilitated workshops, which can be instrumental for reaching decisions. It should be kept in mind that they are a means to find decisions, not to pre-determine them.

- The pursuit of full or at least partial consensus, which is integral to most strategy decisions. It serves as a valuable basis for agreement and for building understanding, trust and commitment.

- The development of guidelines for negotiation, which helps ensure that stakeholders are consulted on target setting, and that proper risk analysis is conducted and taken into account.

A good example of how to employ these principles for capacity development is process consultation (see box 4.2.1 and figure 4.2.1); various organizations have identified similar techniques to enhance participation and improve organizational standards. While there needs to be a bottom-line understanding that institutions grow organically and mirror society, they can also use management experience and knowledge sharing to support sustainable capacity development.

Box 4.2.1: Process consultation

An important addition to the development professional's arsenal is process consultation. Used successfully first in private corporations as well as in the military, this form of management consultation aims at initiating and sustaining a process of change and continuous learning for systemic improvement.

The role of the process consultant differs significantly from that of the typical business or technical expert. Instead of simply analysing the client's situation and prescribing a course of action, the process consultant engages the organization in a step-by-step design and implementation of its own organizational learning and change process. Unlike the alternative expert approach – which imposes new roles and relationships, and runs the risk that directives will not be understood entirely and therefore will not be accepted – process consultation provides space for

change with hierarchy and power suspended. It confers mutual respect on all participants, through developing the collective understanding of how the system works and how it might be transformed. Through genuine dialogue, process consultation places the responsibility for change upon the members of the organization themselves, and secures their ownership for the best proposals.

In this way, process consultation provides principles that could guide the overall course of development assistance and effective technical cooperation. It could also help sustain evolution of the public management systems in developing countries. Here, the first step forward is the identification and empowerment of the client. The acknowledgement of the interests and perspectives of all participants is essential, because ownership is a key performance criterion of progress. The role of the consultant is not that of an advocate but of a leader coaching communication and debate for mutually desired and accepted change, without dependency on external agencies. An internal consulting unit can serve as an established steering committee, while the external consultants provides guidance and training (UNDP, 1996).

One approach to process consultation is the future search methodology, used all over the world in businesses, nonprofits and communities to maximize their capacity for action. Diverse groups of stakeholders representing an entire system explore together the past, present and future; identify shared values; and commit to action plans. Their purpose is to agree on a desired future for the whole system, i.e., the community, organization, etc. This diverges from traditional organizational development meetings, which tend to diagnose gaps between intentions and reality, and prescribe actions to close the gaps by training, on the assumption that people don't know how to do what they claim they want to do. By contrast, future search meetings do not provide people with management models, because the idea is not to strive to reduce complexity to a few issues, to resolve disagreements or to solve long-standing problems. Future search does not judge current practices as good or bad.

Instead, by allowing participants with different backgrounds and diverse agendas to engage in open dialogue, it achieves levels of integration unreachable by other means. Once participants discover new forms of cooperation, they use time, energy and resources profitably. Future search meetings bridge barriers of culture, class, age, gender, ethnicity, power, status and hierarchy by bringing people together as peers working on tasks of mutual concern. The process breaks peoples' tendencies to follow old patterns and repeat mistakes. Instead of trying to change the world or each other, people change the conditions under which they interact.

FIGURE 4.2.1:
THE CYCLE OF PROCESS CONSULTATION

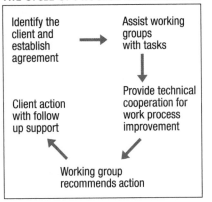

Knowledge networks

No discussion about institution building can be complete in today's world without reference to knowledge networks, also called communities of practice or thematic groups. These have rapidly become an essential way for institutions to tap the flow of global information with high-tech tools, and they have revolutionized how organizations around the world approach learning and share knowledge.

Knowledge networks open opportunities for improving the efficiency and value of technical cooperation, and capacity development in particular. They shrink space and time for learning, span borders and institutional affiliations, and are more closely driven by actual demand than other forms of knowledge sharing. For organizations and governments, they can mean the ability to keep abreast of a world in constant change, where new knowledge routinely emerges to guide the use of resources, the fostering of team building and the management of complex matrix relationships.

Of special value are South-South communities. While sharing experiences and disseminating knowledge, they also merge indigenous knowledge and production systems with modern modalities, and reduce the cost of expertise in some cases to virtual referrals and free informal advice (Denning, 2002).

KEY POINTS

 For a long time, institution building in the context of development did not take into consideration essential developments in the private sector and management science. This gap has now been recognized, and management literature is being explored in the development arena.

 Management has evolved from a mechanistic hierarchy towards a belief in the value of individuals, whose empowerment and participation improves productivity. The building of institutions should take such lessons into account, while recognizing there is no single way to run a business or an organization. Respect for diversity is key to drawing upon all potential capacities.

 Knowledge networks have rapidly become an essential way for institutions to access the flow of global information with high-tech tools. Other important trends include the role of process consulting, and strategy formulation with participatory techniques, such as future search.

REFERENCES PART B

⮥ **EGYPT** *Governorate Human Development Reports Provide Analysis at the Community Level (p. 211)*
⮥ **GUINEA BISSAU** *Building a Research Institution in an Inhospitable Environment (p. 226)*
⮥ **JORDAN** *Diving Club Evolves into Influential Actor on Coastal Management (p. 240)*
⮥ **MONGOLIA AND MOROCCO** *MicroStart Backs Business Plans of Leaders with Vision (p. 255)*
⮥ **MOZAMBIQUE** *Bringing Back Justice, Law and Order Tests Long-Term Commitment (p. 261)*
⮥ **THE PHILIPPINES** *The Long Road to Reliable Agricultural Statistics (p. 272)*
⮥ **TANZANIA** *Twinning Institutions with Trust and Equity (p. 295)*
⮥ **VENEZUELA** *The Oil Industry Flourishes, Along with National Capacities to Serve It (p. 307)*
⮥ **AFRICA** *Private Sector Growth Begins with Better Managers (p. 316)*

4.3 CIVIC ENGAGEMENT

> *"If we agree to the idea that now, and especially in the future, information and public opinion are vectors that can produce as many political effects as the vote of citizens, the shaping of judgement clearly becomes a democratic issue. From now on, the interaction of individuals is both multiplied and de-localized. Belonging to communities that have diverse interests is no longer determined by proximity or local demographic density. Through transportation and telecommunications, we are involved in an increasing number of diverse relationships, as members of abstract communities or of communities whose spatial configurations no longer coincide or offer enduring stability"* (Bellanger, 2002).

UNDP's *Human Development Report* defines civic engagement "as a process, not an event, that closely involves people in the economic, social, cultural and political processes that affect their lives" (UNDP, 1993). As development practitioners become more interested in informal ties between people as well as social capital,[3] the role of civic engagement has moved to the centre of development debates. In the capacity development discussion, the third layer of capacity, the societal level, is fundamentally dependent on civic engagement.

This, however, does not reduce the societal level to civic engagement alone. Society brings together all segments of a population, embracing numerous groups and networks. It provides an ethos that largely determines the value system within which people and the economy function. Elements such as trust, honesty and concern for poor people – or conversely corruption and greed – derive from this prevailing ethos; clearly, they significantly influence the direction and performance of development efforts, and the course of civic engagement.

Putnam (et al., 1992) demonstrated the centrality of values and civic institutions in the transformation of Italian society. More than the institutions traditionally associated with economic growth and modernization of the state, it was the attitudes and networks of Italian citizens that contributed to what the country is today. Putnam insisted on the long-term nature of civic engagement, and described how a value system is constructed on historical grounds. The lessons from Italy are valid elsewhere and define what civic engagement is: people's involvement in decision-making, solicitation of their contributions to development interventions, and shared benefits.

According to UNDP (2002e), civic engagement promotes:

- The growth of community life and the capacity of groups to improve their own welfare through the political, economic, cultural and moral resources of the state

---

[3] Social capital has been defined as those aspects of social organization, including networks, norms and social thrust, that facilitate coordination and cooperation for mutual benefit (Putnam et al., 1992).

- Specific styles of interaction that place a premium on flexibility, adapt-ability, collaboration, accountability and problem solving

- More accurate and representative information about local needs

- A diversity of civil society interests and views that ensure the state is not held captive by a few groups

- Adoption of interventions in accordance with people's needs

- Mobilization of local skills and resources

- State accountability

- Creation of institutional bases that reduce the cost of access for various social groups in development interventions

- National ownership, by broadening the base of conscious stakeholders who have the chance to raise their voices

- Trust between donors and the recipient government, and more impor-tantly, between national authorities and end-users.

Civic engagement is therefore a way of reinforcing the importance of "how to do" development as opposed to "what to do" (see section 1.1).

A new agenda for capacity development has to understand the real roles of the state and civil society, beyond the rhetoric of participation. For a long time, civic engagement has been perceived as a debate about obligations and rights; it has since evolved into an understanding of the roles individuals perform collec-tively within a structure for the public good. A civic culture embraces as much the seeking of collective privileges as the submission to authority, and each facet counts (Bellanger, 2002).

Local and community-based institutions' promotion of civic engagement has contributed greatly to the legitimization of NGOs, and lies at the centre of empowerment discussions on issues from self-help income-generating activities to democratic political participation. At the same time, traditional institutions based on cultural and religious customs have a long history at the forefront of protecting social capital.

The state itself can facilitate or hamper civic engagement, determining whether information flows, decision-making processes and accountability systems are friendly to citizens at large. Yet "sovereignty resides ultimately in the citizenry…their engagement is about the right to define the public good, to determine the policies by which they will seek that good, and to reform or replace those institutions that no longer serve" (Korten, 1998). This squarely positions civic engagement in the realm of politics, demonstrating that more than any other governance entry point, civic engagement is the source of transformation. The process is valued as much as the product, starting with the recognition of individuals (through birth certificates, registrations of all sorts, etc.) and access to education, so as to initiate forms of socialization that will boost civic engagement (Bellanger, 2002).

Based on findings from successful experiments, civic engagement can be promoted through the following activities:

- Inclusion of non-state actors in development initiatives to enhance ownership and participatory governance

- Promotion of information-sharing strategies to increase countries' knowledge capital as well as sensitize public authorities to produce appropriate information resources

- Building capacity for citizens to play informed roles, and expand their political engagement and space

- Use of civic oversight as a reservoir of political, economic, cultural and moral resources to check the accountability and transparency of state institutions

While civic engagement is key for transformation, as well as one of several primary areas that require a policy response in developing capacity, it needs to be scaled up. In the past, civic engagement initiatives have remained mostly at the local and community levels. This has been important, but their impact is rarely felt on the state or national fronts, where they have the potential to make a difference in terms of prompting internal policy dialogue, setting major priorities, and ensuring transparency and accountability (Malik and Wagle, 2002).

Another aspect that must be addressed has less to do with processes, and more to do with mindsets. The quality and extent of civic engagement stems directly from self-confidence and self-esteem, as the following quotation makes clear:

> *"I have something to give, you need it and I am generous enough to give it to you. If you don't use it well, it is because you are a failure – your people are corrupt and your institutions are weak."* [4]

When people have a strong sense of themselves, such a statement is intolerable. But when asymmetries in power, money and knowledge fray the individual and social fabric, people draw back from the belief that they can make any kind of difference, throwing up a barrier to capacity development on the most basic level. Since the forms of power that benefit from the status quo, often aligned through similar backgrounds, aspirations and mindsets, rarely delve into this issue, it needs to be routinely incorporated in the design and implementation of civic engagement policies and activities.

---

[4] An expression used by Rani Parker in the contributions to the Reforming Technical Cooperation for Capacity Development initiative.

KEY POINTS

The third layer of capacity development, the societal level, recognizes a key role for the state. For public goods to be ensured, the state has an indispensable governance role, while civic engagement is an indispensable contributor.

Civic engagement initiatives have frequently taken place among communities. These now need to be scaled up to have an impact at the macro-level, where civic engagement can make a difference in terms of prompting internal policy dialogue, setting major priorities, and ensuring transparency and accountability.

Confidence and self-esteem have to be recognized as a factor in the design and implementation of civic engagement policies and activities.

REFERENCES PART B

➲ **EGYPT** *A Confident Community Learns to Manage Its Environment (p. 208)*
➲ **ETHIOPIA** *A PRSP Encounters the Constraints and Promises of Participation (p. 220)*
➲ **GUATEMALA** *Coordination and Flexibility Help Civil Society Broker Trust After War (p. 223)*
➲ **INDIA** *Citizen Report Cards to Improve Public Service Performance (p. 232)*
➲ **JORDAN** *Diving Club Evolves into Influential Actor on Coastal Management (p. 240)*
➲ **THE PHILIPPINES** *Civil Society Puts a Watch on Public Spending (p. 270)*
➲ **SOUTH AFRICA** *Poor People Fight for Their Space Through Organized Fora (p. 281)*
➲ **SUDAN** *Future Search Technique Creates a Vision for Peace (p. 286)*
➲ **AFRICA** *Afrique en Création Supports Cultural Expression and Exchange (p. 313)*

4.4 THE GLOBAL DIMENSION

"Two things tend to happen: your economy grows and your politics shrink.... The Golden Straitjacket narrows the political and economic choices of those in power to relatively tight parameters. That is why it is increasingly difficult these days to find any real differences between ruling and opposition parties in those countries that have put on the Golden Straitjacket. Once your country puts on the Golden Straitjacket, its political choices get reduced to Pepsi or Coke – to slight nuance of policy, slight alterations in design to account for local traditions, some loosening here or there, but never any major deviation from the core golden rules" (Crook, 2001).

The purpose of this section is not to present an essay on globalization, nor to attempt any comprehensive chronicle of all the global facets that influence and characterize the debate on capacity development. The intention is solely to identify the major trends that need to be considered, and touch upon how they relate to capacity development. Each one briefly presented below offers challenges and/or opportunities. Tackled with sophistication they can be powerful enablers for transformation, but they require, nevertheless, concerted common action.

Aid architecture and financing for development

Addressing the asymmetry in aid relations, caused by the fact that the providers and not the receivers finance development interventions, means strengthening the voice of recipient countries in aid policy debates. A Southern parallel to the OECD/DAC could pave the way for balancing the relationship. The South also needs a more coordinated and sophisticated capacity to conduct development aid negotiations. Currently, its voice manifests itself mostly in large world conferences and their preparatory processes. Although this is laudable, it is not enough. Somehow, it may also be too much, as these conferences appear to be losing momentum. In many forums, the Group of 77 and China as well as other arrangements for collective negotiation lack the teeth that OECD/DAC members have. Governments of the South often find themselves debating without proper preparation – a particularly acute problem in trade talks.

Despite these hurdles, recent agreements, cemented at the International Conference on Financing for Development, have set forth a clear global agenda on development assistance for the coming years.[5] The leading actions include:

- Mobilizing domestic financial resources for development

- Mobilizing international resources for development, including foreign direct investment and other private flows

---

[5] For more information on the International Conference on Financing for Development, see www.un.org/esa/ffd.

- Agreeing on international trade as an engine for development

- Increasing international financial and technical cooperation for development

- Addressing systemic issues, such as enhancing the coherence and consistency of the international monetary, financial and trading systems in support of development

The Monterrey consensus also includes a set of recommendations on technical cooperation, such as: harmonizing and simplifying procedures, untying aid, enhancing the absorptive capacity and financial management in recipient countries, supporting ownership, leveraging ODA, strengthening triangular cooperation (South-South with North input), and improving the targeting of aid to the poor along with coordination and measurement of results. This agenda could not be clearer in its support for capacity development. It is a critical one as well for moving forward on the MDGs, which for the first time offer a global partnership involving shared responsibility for development, internationally agreed outcome targets and choices on policies to achieve them.

Trade and investment

Globalization has the potential to advance human development around the world through economic growth. International trade can expand markets, facilitate competition, disseminate knowledge, increase exposure to new technology and generate employment. But liberalizing and increasing trade does not always have a necessary correlation to human development. Institutional, political and social conditions play an important role in determining to what extent a country reaps the potential benefits (Rodrik, 2001).

A global trade system cannot deliver desirable human development outcomes unless all players have the capacity to negotiate and extract these benefits. Currently, developed countries enjoy vastly superior bargaining power and expertise. Developing countries, on the other hand, struggle not only with a deficit of the capacity to implement trade obligations, but also with negotiating favourable trade agreements to start with. Without strengthening these capacities, poorer countries face even further marginalization. Building them is also important for improving and maintaining the legitimacy of the World Trade Organization (WTO), because the system's credibility rests upon a minimum level of confidence.

Developing countries, particularly the LDCs, urgently need to coordinate their efforts on trade-related capacity, become more proactive in developing collective positions, oppose unfavourable agendas and use trade to their advantage. They should draw from the expertise of the plethora of NGOs and civil society organizations working on these issues, while traditionally overlooked national universities can assume a greater role.

Most developing countries also gain less from trade than industrial countries because they lack mechanisms to cope with the vulnerabilities induced by liberalization. Market access may be important for developing countries to begin to compete on an equal basis, but it is hardly enough. A recent study published by UNDP advocates four key principles:

- Trade is a means to an end — not an end in itself.

- Trade rules should allow for diversity in national institutions and standards.

- Countries should have the right to protect their institutions and development priorities.

- No country has the right to impose its institutional preferences on others.

A human development oriented trade regime would give governments the space to design policies that embody these principles (UNDP, 2003).

Migration

The liberalized movement of goods, services and capital is not matched in terms of people. However, migration is an unavoidable issue for the future. When it snatches away a country's most skilled workers, it impedes capacity development.

The international mobility of the highly skilled contributes to better international flows of knowledge and the formation of international research and technology clusters. Additional benefits are found in the greater opportunities for job matches: on the one hand, employers are able to find unique skill sets, while on the other hand, workers can locate more interesting and lucrative jobs. From a global point of view, international competition for scarce human resources could have a positive net effect on incentives for individual human capital investments. The benefits to host countries seem even more obvious, as illustrated by the example of the United States and other OECD countries, who are fiercely competing for the world's best brains (see section 3.7).

The social and economic impact of brain drain in sending countries, however, is by no means all positive, even though there are cases of brain drain turning into "brain gain". The crucial importance of human capital with respect to institutional capacity development presents a major concern, particularly for countries with a small talent pool. In the end, the consequences may be more inimical to these institutions than to human resource development (Kapur, 2001).

HIV/AIDS

The underprovision of global public goods can negatively affect years of development efforts. This is the case with HIV/AIDS, which has, in a short period, decimated capacities in many countries, killing teachers, doctors and nurses, and disproportionately striking the most productive portion of the work force, those between 25-40 years old. The links between public health, particularly epidemiology, and economic impact are now better understood than before. In order to facilitate closer connections between domestic policy-making and international cooperation, it is important that civil society organizations become more systematically involved in helping fill the gaps left by the inability of markets and governments to provide public goods (Kaul and Ryu, 2001).

No other area of development suffers from inaction or inadequate action more than HIV/AIDS. The devastating effects it has on capacity can shake the fundamentals that this book defends. Countries where capacity in key functions has been wiped out might be obligated to go the capacity substitution route, bringing in expatriates to serve in line functions until the health system can be stabilized. Several countries in Southern Africa might be close to this threshold.

The spread of the disease is affected by a variety of factors, most of which are behavioural rather than medical, and which lie outside the purview of health ministries (Chen et al., 2001). HIV/AIDS prevalence is fanned by lack of information and education, trade and migration, poverty, air and water pollution, and poor food security. The interconnectedness of these issues demonstrates the need to move HIV/AIDS to the realm of development policy formulation, yet recent efforts to increase funding for staunching the disease fell short of reaching the target set by the UN Secretary-General of $7-10 billion per year. Although levels of awareness have increased considerably, the world has not yet awoken to the truly enormous devastation of HIV/AIDS. Only realism, strong leadership and candidness will allow countries to transform the pandemic into a controllable dimension of their development.

Information and communication technology and the digital divide

ICT is key to globalization, and, as such, it is an integral part of the longer debate on potential benefits and risks. The levels and pace of global flows of physical and intangible assets have been dramatically enhanced by the ability to connect vast networks of individuals across geographic boundaries, at negligible cost. However, because of the digital divide between industrialized and developing nations, there is a concern that ICT will reinforce the advantages of the developed countries and perpetuate the disadvantages of the developing countries.

As well, while ICT enables unprecedented collection, storage and access to explicit knowledge, much knowledge remains tacit. Tacit knowledge is embodied in individuals and institutions and – unlike explicit knowledge – is hard to codify and transmit. This is where ICT-enabled knowledge networks and communities of practice come into play, facilitating knowledge sharing and developing capacity (Fukuda-Parr and Hill, 2002).

The real benefits of ICT lie not in the provision of technology per se, but rather in its application to create powerful social and economic networks that radically improve information exchange. Directly targeted towards specific development objectives through the right policies and practical applications, ICT can be a powerful enabler of development, and capacity development in particular, increasing the effectiveness and reach of interventions and lowering the costs of service delivery.

ICT can be applied to a full range of activities, from personal use to business and government. Its flexibility allows for tailored solutions to meet diverse needs. Impervious to geographic boundaries, it brings remote communities into global networks and transcends cultural barriers, while challenging current policy, and legal and regulatory structures within and between nations.

The "digital" and "virtual" nature of many ICT products and services allows for low costs. Replication of content is virtually free, regardless of its volume, and the price of distribution and communication is near zero. The power to store, retrieve, sort, filter, distribute and share information can lead to substantial efficiency gains in production, distribution and markets, with barriers to entry significantly lowered, and competition increased.

Higher efficiency and decreased costs can prompt the creation of new products, services and distribution channels within traditional industries, as well as innovative management models. The elimination of the need for intermediaries makes it possible for users to acquire products and services directly from the original provider. Learning can improve in quality and accessibility – distance education can be a particularly successful model where affordability and geography are real barriers to access. Scientific research networks can help empower indigenous research and development programmes. Virtual research groups, composed of interconnected specialists in far-flung parts of the world, allow for the sharing of databases, the circulation and discussion of papers, the organization of conferences and collaborative research. A proliferation of such collaborations is occurring both between the North and South and among countries of the South themselves.

Another rapidly growing area is the delivery of technical and vocational training. Because ICT can facilitate sophisticated and customized performance simulation at a low cost, many organizations and vocational training facilities are employing it to train workers in an array of functions, from health care to IT services to education. There are also significant opportunities for enhancing education administration, since data repositories and networks allow for collaborative development of curricula, more cost-effective procurement of educational materials, more efficiently scheduled staff and student time, and more closely monitored student performance.

Recent experience shows that countries that have employed ICT to help reach their development goals, rather than just to position their economies in the global market, have increased exports and built national capacity (UNDP, 2001b). In contrast, those countries that have failed to integrate development imperatives into their national ICT vision have produced narrowly defined ICT initiatives that do not fully address development issues. While it is imperative to use ICT to strike a competitive stance in the global economy, an explicit focus on ICT in pursuit of development goals clearly allows countries to achieve a wider diffusion of benefits.

KEY POINTS

 Global trends influencing capacity development include new aid architectures and financing for development, trade and investment negotiations, migration challenges, the HIV/AIDS pandemic and the digital divide. These can constitute a positive or negative force for capacity.

 For the first time, the MDGs offer a global partnership involving shared responsibility for development, internationally agreed outcome targets and choices on policies to achieve them.

 The liberalization of trade does not necessarily result in human development. Institutional and social conditions play an important role in determining whether a country reaps the potential rewards. Developing countries face a capacity deficit in terms of negotiating trade agreements and implementing trade obligations, which necessitates building their capabilities. A human development oriented trade regime could enhance the capacity of developing countries to benefit.

 From a global point of view, the international mobility of the highly skilled contributes to better international flows of knowledge and the formation of international research and technology clusters. However, the brain drain that results has a harsh social and economic impact particularly for countries with a small talent pool, even though under some circumstances, brain drain can be turned into "brain gain".

The under-provision of global public goods can wipe out years of capacity development efforts, as illustrated by the HIV/AIDS pandemic.

 The real benefits of ICT lie not in the provision of technology per se, but rather in its application to create powerful social and economic networks that radically improve information exchange.

Bibliography

Ajayi, S. Ibi, and Afeikhena Jerome. 2002. "Opportunity Costs and Effective Markets." *Development Policy Journal,* 2, 23-45. New York: UNDP.

Balihuta, Arsene, et al. 2002. "Uganda: Driving Technical Cooperation for National Capacity Development." In *Developing Capacity Through Technical Cooperation: Country Experiences,* edited by Stephen Browne. New York/London: UNDP/Earthscan.

Banerjee, Niloy, Leonel Valdiva and Mildred Mkandla. 2002. "Is the Development Industry Ready for Change?" *Development Policy Journal,* 2, 131-159. New York: UNDP.

Baser, Heather, and Peter Morgan. 2002. "Harmonizing the Provision of Technical Assistance: Finding the Right Balance and Avoiding the New Religion." ECDPM Discussion Paper, 36. Maastricht: ECDPM (www.ecdpm.org/Web_ECDPM/Web/Content/Navigation.nsf/index.htm).

Bellanger, Helene. 2002. *Le civisme.* Paris: Autrement.

Berg, Elliot, and the United Nations Development Programme (UNDP). 1993. *Rethinking Technical Cooperation: Reforms for Capacity Building in Africa.* New York: UNDP and Development Alternatives International.

Brown, Mercy. n.d. "Using the Intellectual Diaspora to Reverse the Brain Drain: Some Useful Examples." Cape Town: University of Cape Town (www.uneca.org/eca_resources/conference_reports_and_other_documents/brain_drain/word_documents/brown.doc).

Browne, Stephen. 2002. "Introduction: Rethinking Capacity Development for Today's Challenges." In *Developing Capacity Through Technical Cooperation: Country Experiences,* edited by Stephen Browne. New York/London: UNDP/Earthscan.

Campilan, Dindo, and Matilde Somarriba Chang. 2003. "Using and Benefiting from Evaluation." Guest contribution to the Web-based publication capacity.org (www.capacity.org). Maastricht: ECDPM.

Carrington, W. J., and E. Detragiache. 1998. "How Big is the Brain Drain?" IMF Working Paper, 98/102. Washington, D.C.: IMF.

Catterson, Julie, and Claes Lindahl. 1999. *The Sustainability Enigma – Aid Dependence and the Phasing Out of Projects. The Case of Swedish Aid to Tanzania.* Stockholm: Almqvist & Wiksell International and EGDI.

Chen, L. C., T. G. Evans and R. A. Cash. 2001. "Health as a Global Public Good." In *Global Public Goods: Taking the Concept Forward,* edited by Michael Faust, Katell Le Goulven, Inge Kaul, Grace Ryu and Mirjam Schnupf. New York: UNDP Office of Development Studies.

Colclough, C. 1991. "Wage Flexibility in Sub-Saharan Africa: Trends and Explanations." In *Towards Social Adjustment: Labour Market Issues in Structural Adjustment,* edited by G. Standing and V. Tokman. Geneva: ILO.

Colclough, C. and K. M. Lewin. 1993. "Educating All the Children: Strategies for Primary Schooling in the South." Oxford: Clarendon Press.

Collier, Paul, and Anke Hoeffler. 2001. *Greed and Grievance in Civil War.* Washington, D.C.: World Bank

Commission on International Development. 1969. *Partners in Development: Report of the Commission on International Development.* New York: Praeger Publishers.

Corcuff, Philippe. 2002. *Les Nouvelles Sociologies.* Paris: Nathan.

Crook, Clive. 2001. "Globalisation and Its Critics." In *Globalisation: Making Sense of an Integrated World.* London: *The Economist.*

Cukrowski, Jacek, et al. 2002. "The Kyrgyz Republic: Developing New Capacities in a Post-Transition Country." In *Developing Capacity Through Technical Cooperation: Country Experiences,* edited by Stephen Browne. New York/London: UNDP/Earthscan.

Danielson, Anders, Paul Hoebink and Benedict Mongula. 2002. "Are Donors Ready for Change?" *Development Policy Journal,* 12, 161-179. New York: UNDP.

Denning, Stephen. 2002. "Technical Cooperation and Knowledge Networks." In *Capacity for Development: New Solutions to Old Problems,* edited by Sakiko Fukuda-Parr, Carlos Lopes and Khalid Malik. New York/London: UNDP/Earthscan.

Devarajan, Shantayanan, David R. Dollar and Torgny Holmgren. 2001. *Aid and Reform in Africa: Lessons from Ten Case Studies.* Washington, D.C.: World Bank.

Devarajan, Shantayanan, and Vinaya Swaroop. 1998. "The Implications of Foreign Aid Fungibility for Development Assistance." DC 20433. Washington, D.C.: World Bank.

Development Initiatives. 2000. *The Reality of Aid.* A basic briefing on policies and modalities, edited by Judith Randel and Tony German. London: Earthscan.

Easterly, William. 2001. *The Elusive Quest for Growth: Economist's Adventures and Misadventures in the Tropics.* Cambridge: MIT Press.

Edgren, Gus. 2003. "Donorship, Ownership and Partnership. Issues Arising From Four Sida Studies of Donor-Recipient Relations." An informal paper.

Ekoko, Francois, and Dennis Benn. 2002. "South-South Cooperation and Capacity Development." In *Developing Capacity Through Technical Cooperation: Country Experiences,* edited by Stephen Browne. New York/London: UNDP/Earthscan.

El-Refaie, Faika, et al. 2002. "Egypt: Building Private Sector Capacity Through Technical Cooperation." In *Developing Capacity Through Technical Cooperation: Country Experiences,* edited by Stephen Browne. New York/London: UNDP/Earthscan.

Erhard, David. 2003. "Pro-Poor Structural Checklist for Private Participation in Infrastructure." In *Infrastructure for Poor People,* edited by Penelope J. Brook and Timothy C. Irwin. Washington, D.C.: World Bank/Public-Private Infrastructure Advisory Facility.

Foster, Mick, and Adrian Fozzard. 2000. "Aid and Public Expenditure: A Guide." Working paper, 141. London: Overseas Development Institute.

Fozzard, Adrian. 2001. "The Basic Budgeting Problem: Approaches to Resource Allocation in the Public Sector and Their Implications for Pro-Poor Budgeting." Working paper, 147. London: Overseas Development Institute.

Fukuda-Parr, Sakiko, and Ruth Hill. 2002. "The Network Age: Creating New Models of Technical Cooperation." In *Capacity for Development: New Solutions to Old Problems,* edited by Sakiko Fukuda-Parr, Carlos Lopes and Khalid Malik. New York/London: UNDP/Earthscan.

Godfrey, Martin, et al. 2000. "Technical Assistance and Capacity Development in an Aid-Dependent Economy: The Experience of Cambodia." Working paper, 15. Phnom Penh: Cambodia Development Resource Institute.

Goleman, Daniel, Annie McKee and Richard E. Boyatzis. 2002. *Primal Leadership: Realizing the Power of Emotional Intelligence.* Boston: Harvard Business School Press.

Goudie, A., and D. Stasavage. 1997. "Corruption: The Issues." OECD Development Centre Technical Paper, 122. Paris: OECD.

Gray Molina, George, and Gonzalo Chavez et al. 2002. "Bolivia: The Political Context of Capacity Development." In *Developing Capacity Through Technical Cooperation: Country Experiences,* edited by Stephen Browne. New York/London: UNDP/Earthscan.

Grindle, Merilee. 1997. "The Good Government Imperative – Human Resources, Organizations, and Institutions." In *Getting Good Government: Capacity Building in the Public Sectors of Developing Countries.* Harvard Institute for International Development. Cambridge: Harvard University Press.

Hauge, Arild. 2002. "Accountability – to What End?" *Development Policy Journal, 2,* 73-94. New York: UNDP.

Helleiner, Gerald K., et al. 1995. *Report of the Group of Independent Advisers on Development Cooperation Issues Between Tanzania and Its Aid Donors.* Copenhagen: Royal Danish Ministry of Foreign Affairs.

Hilderbrand, Mary E. 2002. "Overview: Meeting the Capacity Development Challenge: Lessons for Improving Technical Cooperation." In *Developing Capacity Through Technical Cooperation: Country Experiences,* edited by Stephen Browne. New York/London: UNDP/Earthscan.

Hindle, Tim. 2000. *Guide to Management Ideas.* London: *The Economist.*

Illo, Jeanne Frances I., et al. 2002. "Philippines: Bringing Civil Society into Capacity Development." In *Developing Capacity Through Technical Cooperation: Country Experiences,* edited by Stephen Browne. New York/London: UNDP/Earthscan

International Labour Organization (ILO). 2001. "Life at Work in the Information Economy." *World Employment Report 2001.* Geneva: ILO.

International Monetary Fund (IMF). 2001. "Tracking of Poverty-Reducing Public Spending in Heavily Indebted Poor Countries (HIPCs)." Washington, D.C.: IMF.

Jahan, Selim. 1997. "Education for All in the Ten Most Populous Countries: The Issue of Private and Public Provisioning." Paper presented at the seminar Education for All in the Ten Most Populous Countries. New Delhi: UNESCO.

———. 2003. "Financing Millennium Development Goals." Paper prepared for the international seminar Staying Poor: Chronic Poverty and Development Policy. New York: UNDP.

Justice, G. 2001. "Moving to Budget Support." Report from the OECD Task Force on Donor Practices. Paris: OECD.

Kanbur, Ravi, and Todd Sandler, 1999. "The Future of Development Assistance: Common Pools and International Public Goods." ODC Policy Essay 25. Washington, D.C.: Overseas Development Council.

Kapur, Davesh. 2001. "Diasporas and Technology Transfer." Background paper for the *Human Development Report 2001.* New York: UNDP.

Kaul, Inge, and Grace Ryu. 2001. "Global Public Policy Partnerships: Seen Through the Lens of Global Public Goods." In *Global Public Goods: Taking the Concept Forward,* edited by Michael Faust, Katell Le Goulven, Inge Kaul, Grace Ryu and Mirjam Schnupf. New York: UNDP Office of Development Studies.

Korten, David. 1998. "When Corporations Rule the World: An Interview with David Korten." In *Corporations Are Going to Get Your Mama,* edited by Kevin Danaher. Common Courage Press.

Lavergne, Réal, and John Saxby. 2001. "Capacity Development: Vision and Implications." Capacity Development Occasional Paper Series, 3 (January). Ottawa: CIDA.

Lee, Kuan Yew. 2000a. *The Singapore Story.* Abridged version. Singapore: Federal Publications.

———. 2000b. *From Third World to First: The Singapore Story 1965-2000.* Singapore: Singapore Press Holdings.

Lopes, Carlos. 2002a. "Should We Mind the Gap?" In *Capacity for Development: New Solutions to Old Problems,* edited by Sakiko Fukuda-Parr, Carlos Lopes and Khalid Malik. New York/London: UNDP/Earthscan.

Lopes, Carlos. 2003. "Does the New Development Agenda Encapsulate Real Policy Dialogue?" In *Dialogue in Pursuit of Development,* edited by Jan Olsson and Lennart Wohlgemoth. Stockholm: EGDI.

————. 2002b. "Sustainable Development: Meeting the Challenges of the Millennium." *Choices* (August). New York: UNDP.

Malik, Khalid, and Swarnim Wagle. 2002. "Civic Engagement and Development: Introducing the Issues." In *Capacity for Development: New Solutions to Old Problems,* edited by Sakiko Fukuda-Parr, Carlos Lopes and Khalid Malik. New York/London: UNDP/Earthscan.

Malloch Brown, Mark. 2002. "Meeting the Millennium Challenge: A Strategy for Helping Achieve the UN MDGs." Speech at a policy dialogue on the Millennium Development Goals jointly organized by UNDP and the German government. Berlin (www.undp.org/dpa/statements/administ/2002/june/27jun02.html).

Mkandawire, Thandika. 2002. "Incentives, Governance and Capacity Development in Africa." In *Capacity for Development: New Solutions to Old Problems,* edited by Sakiko Fukuda-Parr, Carlos Lopes and Khalid Malik. New York/London: UNDP/Earthscan.

Morgan, Peter. 2002. "Technical Assistance: Correcting the Precedents." *Development Policy Journal, 2,* 1-22. New York: UNDP.

Ndulu, Benno J. Forthcoming. "Human Capital Flight: Stratification, Globalization and the Challenges to Tertiary Education in Africa." Washington, D.C.: World Bank.

New Partnership for Africa's Development (NEPAD). 2001. "The New Partnership for Africa's Development" (www.avmedia.at/nepad/indexgb.html).

Niang, Cheikh Ibrahima. 2002. "Le coté des pays en développement." Project document for Reforming Technical Cooperation for Capacity Development. New York: UNDP.

Nichols, Ralph, and Leonard Stevens. 1999. "Listening to People." In *Harvard Business Review on Effective Communication.* Boston: Harvard Business School Press.

Organisation for Economic Co-operation and Development/Development Assistance Committee (OECD/DAC). 1991. *Principles for New Orientations in Technical Cooperation.* Paris: OECD.

————. 1996. *Shaping the 21st Century: The Contribution of Development Co-operation.* Paris: OECD.

————. 1998. "Improving the Effectiveness of Aid Systems: The Case of Mali." Conference room paper. Paris: OECD.

————. 2001a. "Poor Performers: Working for Development in Difficult Partnerships." Background paper, 2001:26 (November). Paris: OECD.

————. 2001b. "Poor Performers: Working for Development in Difficult Partnerships." Background paper, 2001:32 (December). Paris: OECD.

————. 2002. "Education at a Glance." *OECD Indicators 2002*. Paris: OECD

Osborne, David and Tedd A. Gaebler. 1992. *Reinventing Government: How the Entrepreneurial Spirit Is Transforming the Public Sector*. Cambridge: Perseus Publishing.

Pillay, Rajeev. 2003. "Halting the Downward Spiral: Returning Countries with Special Development Needs to Sustainable Growth and Development." UNDP background paper. New York: UNDP.

Pope, Jeremy. 2000. *Transparency International Source Book 2000: Confronting Corruption – The Elements of a National Integrity System*. Berlin: Transparency International.

Pradhan, Sanja. 1996. "Evaluating Public Spending: A Framework for Public Expenditure Reviews." World Bank Discussion Papers, 323. Washington, D.C.: World Bank.

Pratt, Brian. 2002. "Volunteerism and Capacity Development." *Development Policy Journal, 2*, 95-117. New York: UNDP.

Psacharopoulos, George, and Harry Anthony Patrinos. 2002. "Returns to Investment in Education: A Further Update." World Bank Policy Research Working Paper, 2881. Washington, D.C.: World Bank.

Putnam, Robert D., Robert Leonardi and Raffaella Y. Nanetti. 1992. *Making Democracy Work: Civic Traditions in Modern Italy*. Princeton: Princeton University Press.

Quah, Jon S. T. 1999. "Comparing Anti-Corruption Measures in Asian Countries." Centre for Advanced Studies Research Paper Series, 13. Singapore: National University of Singapore.

Reinikka, Ritva. 2001. "Recovery in Service Delivery: Evidence from Schools and Health Centres." In *Uganda's Recovery: The Role of Farms, Firms, and Government,* edited by Ritva Reinikka and Paul Collier. World Bank Regional and Sectoral Studies. Washington, D.C.: World Bank.

Ribeiro, Gustavo Lins. 2002. "Power, Networks and Ideology in the Field of Development." In *Capacity for Development: New Solutions to Old Problems,* edited by Sakiko Fukuda-Parr, Carlos Lopes and Khalid Malik. New York/London: UNDP/Earthscan.

Rist, Gilbert, et al. 1999. *The History of Development: From Western Origins to Global Faith*. London/New York: Zed Books Ltd.

Rodrik, Dani. 2001. "The Global Governance of Trade As If Development Really Mattered." Background paper for the Trade and Sustainable Human Development Project. New York: UNDP.

Rose-Ackerman, Susan. 1997. "Corruption and Good Governance." UNDP Discussion Paper, 7/97. New York: UNDP.

Roy, Aruna, and Nikhil Dey, MKSS Rajasthan. 2001. "The Right to Information: Facilitating People's Participation and State Accountability." Paper presented at the Asia Pacific Regional Workshop at the 10th International Anti-Corruption Conference. Prague.

Santiso, Carlos. 2002. "Governance, Conditionality and the Reform of Multilateral Development Finance: The Role of the Group of Eight." In the report *G8 Governance*. Baltimore: Johns Hopkins University.

Schiavo-Campo, S., Giulio de Tommaso and Amitabha Mukherje. 1997. "Government Employment and Pay in Global Perspective: A Selective Synthesis of International Facts, Policies and Experience." World Bank Governance Working Paper, 895. Washington, D.C.: World Bank.

Schick, Allen. 1998. "Why Most Developing Countries Should Not Try New Zealand's Reforms." *The World Bank Research Observer,* 13 (1), 123-131. Washington, D.C.: World Bank.

Sen, Amartya Kumar. 1999. *Development As Freedom.* New York/Toronto: Alfred A. Knopf/Random House of Canada Limited.

Silva, Jose de Souza, and Albina Maestsry Boza. 2003. "The Basics of Organizational Capacity Development." Guest contribution to the Web-based publication capacity.org, *17* (www.capacity.org). Maastricht: ECDPM.

Singh, Shekhar. 2002. "Technical Cooperation and Stakeholder Ownership." *Development Policy Journal,* 2, 47-71. New York: UNDP.

Smith, Warrick. 2003. " Regulating Infrastructure for the Poor: Regulatory System Design." In *Infrastructure for the Poor People,* edited by Penelope J. Brook and Timothy C. Irwin. Washington, D.C.: World Bank/Public-Private Infrastructure Advisory Facility.

Sobhan, Rehman, and Debapriya Bhattacharya, et al. 2002. "Bangladesh: Applying Technical Cooperation to Health and Financial Reform." In *Developing Capacity Through Technical Cooperation: Country Experiences,* edited by Stephen Browne. New York/London: UNDP/Earthscan.

Stern, Nicholas. 1997. "The World Bank as 'Intellectual Actor'." In *The World Bank: Its First Half Century,* vol. II, edited by Davesh Kapur, John Lewis and Richard Webb. Washington, D.C.: Brookings Institution.

Stiglitz, Joseph. 1998. *Assessing Aid: What Works, What Doesn't, and Why?* World Bank Policy Research Report. Washington, D.C.: World Bank and Oxford University Press.

————. 1999. "Scan Globally, Reinvent Locally: Knowledge Infrastructure and the Localization of Knowledge." Keynote address at the First Global Development Network Conference. Bonn.

Summers, Lawrence. 1992. "Investing in All the People." Policy Research Working Paper, 405. Washington, D.C.: World Bank.

Tendler, Judith. 1997. *Good Government in the Tropics.* Baltimore: Johns Hopkins University Press

United Nations. 2000. *Role of UNDP in Crisis and Post-Crisis Situations.* New York: United Nations.

United Nations Development Programme (UNDP). 1993. *Human Development Report: People's Participation.* New York: Oxford University Press.

———. 1994. *Human Development Report: New Dimensions of Human Security.* New York: Oxford University Press.

———. 1996. *Systemic Improvement of Public Sector Management: Process Consultation.* New York: UNDP Management Development Programme.

———. 1997. *Human Development Report: Human Development to Eradicate Poverty.* New York: Oxford University Press.

———. 1998. *Capacity Assessment and Development.* Technical Advisory Paper, 3. New York: UNDP Management Development and Governance Programme.

———. 1999. "Fighting Corruption to Improve Governance." Corporate position paper. New York: UNDP.

———. 2001a. *Human Development Report: Making New Technology Work for Human Development.* New York: Oxford University Press.

———. 2001b. "Creating a Development Dynamic. Final Report of the Digital Opportunity Initiative." New York: UNDP/Accenture/Markle Foundation.

———. 2002a. *Capacity for Development: New Solutions to Old Problems.* Edited by Sakiko Fukuda-Parr, Carlos Lopes and Khalid Malik. New York/London: UNDP/Earthscan.

———. 2002b. *Development Effectiveness.* Review of evaluative evidence. New York: UNDP.

———. 2002c. *Developing Capacity Through Technical Cooperation: Country Experiences.* Edited by Stephen Browne. New York/London: UNDP/Earthscan.

———. 2002d. *Human Development Report: Deepening Democracy in a Fragmented World.* New York: Oxford University Press.

———. 2002e. "Civic Engagement." *Essentials,* 8 (October). New York: UNDP Evaluation Office.

———. 2002f. "Developing Capacity of Leaders to Successfully Respond to HIV/AIDS: Leadership Development Programme." New York: UNDP.

———. 2003. *Making Global Trade Work for People.* New York/London: UNDP/Earthscan.

United Nations Development Programme–Global Environment Facility (UNDP-GEF). *Capacity Development Initiative.* New York: UNDP.

United Nations Educational, Scientific and Cultural Organization (UNESCO). 2002. *Education for All. Global Monitoring Report: Is the World on Track?* Paris: UNESCO.

United Nations High Commissioner for Refugees (UNHCR). 2001. *Survey of Refugees and Internally Displaced People in the World.* Geneva: UNHCR.

United Nations University. 2003. *Reforming Africa's Institutions: Ownership, Incentives and Capabilities.* Edited by Steve Kayizzi-Mugerwa. Tokyo/New York: United Nations University Press.

Vanarkadie, B., V. T. Boi and T. D. Tien. 2000. "National Ownership in an Emerging Partnership Context: Review of Technical Cooperation in Vietnam." Hanoi: UNDP.

Weber, Max. 1977. "Sociologia de la Dominación." In *Economia y sociedad,* 695-1117. Mexico City: Fondo de Cultura Economica.

World Bank. 2001. "Comprehensive Development Framework. Meeting the Promise? Early Experience and Emerging Issues." CDF Secretariat. Washington, D.C.: World Bank.

———. 2002. "Low-Income Countries Under Stress." Draft discussion paper (6 March). Washington, D.C.: World Bank.

PART B

A CASEBOOK OF EXPERIENCES AND LESSONS

Introduction

The following section collects 56 case histories from across the world that offer evidence and inspiration on how capacity development works. Telling a story about practical experiences is perhaps the most powerful way to prove a point.[1] It enhances the understanding of issues and concepts still widely considered to be poorly defined. Stories can show us what "capacity" looks like and how to nurture it. They can tell us how to know when it does and does not exist. And sometimes they can give us valuable insights into remedying capacity gaps in one situation by learning from another.

Each case history featured here profiles an innovative experience that relates to the issues and arguments presented in the first part of this book. While a number of the cases emphasize one particular theme, others touch upon several subjects. For instance, "Decentralization Starts with Assessing Current Capacities" provides a practical look at the ownership and commitment issues discussed in chapter one. "Public Hearings Arrest Corruption in Rajasthan," which describes the public auditing of development projects, is relevant to the deliberation on corruption in chapter three as well as the issue of self-esteem and civic engagement debated in chapter four. A list of relevant cases follows each subsection in the chapters.

The cases cover experiences in specific countries and regions, as well as a range of actors, including governments, civil society, NGOs, the private sector and

---

[1] Stephen Denning. 2002. "Technical Cooperation and Knowledge Networks." In *Capacity for Development: New Solutions to Old Problems,* edited by Sakiko Fukuda-Parr, Carlos Lopes and Khalid Malik. New York/London: UNDP/Earthscan.

research institutions. Some deal with macro-level processes, others highlight micro-level innovations within communities or organizations. As individual cases are relevant illustrations of several arguments, a thematic classification was not feasible. They are thus presented in alphabetical order, with the respective country at the beginnng of the title. Some regional and global experiences are grouped together at the end.

Each case is divided into four sections:

> *In a Nutshell:* Briefly introduces how the case relates to arguments presented in this book
>
> *The Story:* Describes the background, rational, actors and processes, as well as key considerations
>
> *Results and Critical Factors:* Summarizes the main achievements and the factors behind them
>
> *Further Information:* Provides related references, Web sites and contact details

As individual experiences, case histories tend to be specific to their context, presenting lessons for other situations mainly through some degree of abstraction. To expect them to cover every conceivable empirical nuance would be unreasonable, so they do not pretend to be comprehensive or methodologically rigorous. For most of the cases, key protagonists who had first-hand experience contributed primary material. They do not promise recipes for future success, but offer knowledge that perhaps can be reconceived and shared in other places.

⮑ AFGHANISTAN:
LOCAL CAPACITY GROWS AMIDST CONFLICT AND COLLAPSE OF CENTRAL AUTHORITY

In a Nutshell

By redirecting development assistance to local levels, capacity development can continue even amidst prolonged warfare and the collapse of a government. This was the case in Afghanistan in the 1990s, when external support could not be provided in the traditional manner through an established central authority. So UNDP began working with communities and supporting civil society organizations providing critical services.

Staying engaged instead of disassociating from a difficult country may be considered a virtue in itself. More significantly in this example, keeping essential services going – such as health care and the provision of water and sanitation – helped lay the foundations for eventual post-conflict reconstruction.

The Story

During the 1990s, UNDP progressively expanded its work in Afghanistan within zones of intermittent peace. Projects began as stand-alone efforts with diverse goals, but attempted to meet many different local needs. Overarching programmes focused on providing food security through sustainable crop production and livestock development, strengthening the self-help capacities of rural communities and disabled people, and rebuilding urban communities.

NGOs served initially as the primary vehicle for delivering humanitarian and development assistance, as well as for providing ad hoc social services, but efforts were also made to enlist beneficiaries in programme decisions affecting their communities. By the mid-1990s, community organizations had become the most vital channel for project work.

At a 1996 international forum in Ashkabad, a consensus emerged on the purposes and methodology of providing outside assistance to Afghanistan. Peace-keeping was an overall objective, supported by a long-term approach that integrated humanitarian, rehabilitation, development and human rights efforts – all vital to addressing community concerns and supporting Afghan civil society. This agreement led to the establishment of the Poverty Eradication and Community Empowerment (PEACE) Initiative in 1997. It consolidated five projects into a single programme, boosting the impact of each through close coordination and unified management. The approach was based on the assumption that there is a positive correlation between peace-building and conflict prevention on the one hand, and poverty alleviation, community empowerment and improved governance on the other.

The programme derived from the logic of the situation on the ground in Afghanistan, where social and economic structures were in ruins, and government institutions had collapsed. Action at the community level offered the best possible response to local needs and enhanced prospects for addressing some of the most difficult issues – deteriorating infrastructure and social services, poor food security, gender discrimination, environmental decline and the exploding cultivation of opium poppies. Engaging directly with communities and civil society offered them a chance to help themselves. Over the course of the PEACE Initiative, more than 2,100 community organizations, farmers' groups and cooperative associations were established or reactivated.

In recognition of the importance of capacity development, considerable effort was devoted to training community workers and the communities at large. Community mobilization demanded extensive preparation to establish the programme as well as continuous attention and follow-up. About 8,000 community members learned to work through *shura* development committees to consult stakeholders and identify community needs. In turn, the programme bolstered the committees with infrastructure and social service projects as well as credit and income generation schemes. Different credit systems supported these activities, encouraged community initiatives and assisted vulnerable groups. The creation of revolving funds became a corollary to community empowerment, reflecting the need to open investment opportunities in a cash-poor environment.

Results and Critical Factors

Developing the institutional capacities of civil society and community organizations in Afghanistan resulted not only in improved infrastructure and service delivery, but also in the establishment of a network of viable local institutions to take the lead in post-conflict development. A number of important lessons emerged:

- When there is a collapse of delivery systems and infrastructure, decentralized service delivery is likely to work better than unified, national service delivery.

- Economic development or small-scale projects undertaken at the village level do not by themselves lead to development. Projects have to be part of a process that changes the community environment and people's lives. Such a transformation can only be achieved by steadily building up community and village institutions.

- Community intervention implies working with existing social structures and power relationships. Individual members of the community who are better off can more easily take advantage of opportunities. Initiatives do not necessarily reach the poor and most vulnerable, while NGOs – and other implementing partners – can, if not managed carefully, easily weaken links with communities, and complicate programme and staff management.

- No community can make a valid contribution to decision-making unless it also controls resources to implement those decisions. As local institutions mature – and assets grow – they tend to work more independently of the sponsoring project and act in what they perceive to be their best interest. This became evident in Afghanistan when 160 communities embarked on independent activities, and 225 approached other aid agencies for support.

- Rehabilitation activities cannot be conducted in a total political vacuum. A working rapport must be established with the de facto authorities.

Further information

Bernt Bernander, et al. 1999. *A Thematic Evaluation of UNDP's PEACE Initiative in Afghanistan*. A draft paper. Stockholm: Stockholm Group for Development Studies.

Bernt Bernander. 2002. *Community Empowerment in Afghanistan: A Review of the UNDP Experience in the 1990s*. New York: UNDP.

Poverty Eradication and Community Empowerment (PEACE) Initiative (www.pcpafg.org/Organizations/undp/).

Organisation for Economic Co-operation and Development/Development Assistance Committee (OECD/DAC). 1997. *Conflict, Peace and Development Cooperation*. Paris: OECD.

Brief summary of UNDP in Afghanistan (www.undp.org/afghanistan/undpafghanistan.html).

➲ BHUTAN:
A NATIONAL VISION GUIDES PROGRESS AND TECHNICAL COOPERATION

In a Nutshell

In 1958, Bhutan was among the world's least developed countries. A visit by the Indian Prime Minister in that year, however, marked the beginning of modernization. The vision was clear: to embrace those forms of contemporary life essential for the functioning of a modern state, while retaining those aspects of Bhutan's traditional culture that make the country unique.

The first priority since then has been to build human resources and related institutional capacities. Over the years, Bhutan has made great strides in developing a strong system of governance and public administration, as well as establishing firm social and economic infrastructures. Credit for this remarkable transformation can be attributed to the sustained determination of Bhutan's leaders, the ongoing support of India and other countries and organizations, and the insistence on recognizing the importance of preserving identity, cultural traditions and values.

The Story

In 1958, Bhutan, a small Himalayan country the size of Switzerland cradled between China and India, was among the least developed countries on the planet. With a subsistence economy, most people lived in isolated homesteads, cultivating small family plots and bartering any surplus. There was no industry and foreign trade was minimal. Tourism did not exist; only a handful of foreigners had ever been allowed to visit the country. There were no schools, aside from those offering religious education to a small number of boys aspiring to become Buddhist monks. Literacy was confined to children from elite families educated in India. Western medicine and hospitals had not yet appeared.

The extremely rugged terrain posed an enormous challenge to any infrastructure development. There was not a single paved road, and other physical infrastructure was almost entirely lacking. Electricity was provided by small diesel generators in only a few places. With no telephone system, a network of radio sets connected the more important administrative centres. Governance was rudimentary – the country became an absolute monarchy early in the 20th century, having evolved from a feudal system of regional chieftains. The government's main preoccupations were law and order, and tax collection.

In 1958, the Indian Prime Minister was invited to pay an official visit to Bhutan. The trip was historic, marking the first attempt by the leadership of Bhutan to align itself with either of its neighbours. It also reflected a decision to embark on a path of development and modernization. Since that time, Bhutan has remained true to a vision of setting up a contemporary state while protecting its traditional culture.

The first priority was the building of human resources and related institutional capacities to undertake the many tasks required by a modern society and economy – technical cooperation in support of these goals took priority, and Bhutan found in India a partner that understood and supported this approach.

In the 1960s, formal education began, first at primary and subsequently at secondary and tertiary levels. Since the need to fill key government posts with Bhutanese was paramount, all post-secondary education and training was explicitly geared to providing the requisite knowledge and skills. Subsequently, human resources and institutional development linked to priority nation-building tasks became the principal focus of Bhutan's negotiations for external cooperation for many years.

The Bhutanese monarchs were also determined to minimize corruption. From the beginning, the Bhutan Civil Service has been consciously modeled on that of Singapore. Civil servants are selected through a rigorous, merit-based process, paid well and expected to perform efficiently; any proven corrupt behaviour is punished severely.

As a direct result of the vision and policies pursued by Bhutan's leaders and the support received from India, Bhutan became a member of the United Nations in 1971. By that time, Bhutanese occupied most of the important government posts in Bhutan. Since then, other partners – notably the UN family – have joined the country in its modernization efforts, but always subject to the overarching vision of Bhutan's leaders and the priorities of its government, sketched out in detailed five-year plans that are conscientiously implemented. There have been several instances when Bhutan rejected offers of technical and capital cooperation because these were not consonant with its plans and policies.

Today, it is clear that Bhutan has made great strides in nearly every area over the past decades, working from a base of strong and responsible macroeconomic management that has made a progressive social agenda a reality. Metalled roads and digital telecommunications now connect all the main population centres. The national airline links the country to its neighbours and Thailand. All except the most remote corners have access to education and medical institutions. The quality of these establishments is improving steadily, while services remain free and increasingly are provided by Bhutanese personnel.

A number of hydroelectric plants, largely run by Bhutanese engineers and technicians, generate electricity as well as foreign earnings from the export of surplus power to India. A flourishing private sector has grown, encouraged by government policies and reliable banking, insurance and legal services. The per capita income of Bhutan is among the highest in South Asia, even as the country is noted for exemplary preservation of its natural environment. Small and efficient, the government commands respect for the calibre and integrity of its personnel, and gradually, the absolute monarchy is evolving into a constitutional monarchy.

Such achievements have not been at the expense of Bhutan's traditional values and culture. Inevitably, change has come through exposure to outside ideas. Yet the government has tried to soften the impact. Bhutanese sent abroad for study and training have been assured of challenging and relatively well-paid jobs on their return. As a result, there has been virtually no brain drain. The number of tourists permitted to visit the country each year also remains limited, while concerted efforts to showcase and preserve popular traditions inculcates pride in Bhutanese identity.

Results and Critical Factors

The remarkable transformation of the Kingdom of Bhutan can be attributed to the following factors:

- The vision and sustained determination of its leaders, the present King and his father, to bring the country out of self-imposed isolation and to modernize

- The focus given to the development of human resources, the careful matching of education and training to needs, and the sustained commitment of resources in these directions

- The emphasis on a small, professional and motivated civil service, able to attract and retain the country's top talent in pursuit of the realization of its development goals

- The insistence on recognizing the importance of identity and of preserving cultural traditions and values

- The far-sighted and sustained support of the government of India, as well as the assistance provided by other countries and organizations over the last 30 years

Bhutan has taken full advantage of the external support that has been generously offered, without deviating from the path it chose to follow a mere four decades ago. Through its responsible use of resources and demonstration of results, it has been able to secure sustained cooperation from its partners, essentially on its terms. The bulk of this has been in the form of grants for technical cooperation, which has allowed capacities to expand without forcing the country to incur a debt burden.

The technical cooperation edifice built between Bhutan and its partners has been constructed on the government being firmly in the driver's seat; sound and clear policies and plans that receive the full backing of partners; low corruption; and a highly qualified, motivated civil service, especially at upper levels. Some capacity problems continue underneath. As each five-year plan becomes more expensive, given Bhutan's expanding development needs, even while ODA has been declining until recently, it is to be hoped that Bhutan will not eventually fall into the debt trap.

Further information

Bhutan's Royal Civil Service Commission (www.rcsc.gov.bt/BCSR.asp).

Government of Bhutan (www.bhutan.gov.bt/rgobdirectory/agenciesbyministry.htm).

Bhutan-India relations, background information (www.bhutannewsonline.com/india_bhutan.html).

United Nations Development Programme (UNDP). *Bhutan Development Cooperation Report 2001* (www.undp.org.bt/DCR2001.pdf).

UNDP Bhutan (www.undp.org.bt).

The authors gratefully acknowledge the contributions of UNDP Bhutan.

➲ BOLIVIA:
CITIZENS EXERCISE THEIR RIGHT TO BE INVOLVED IN THE AID SYSTEM

In a Nutshell

A host of measures – some endogenous, some externally driven – have infused a new era of government in Bolivia, one where the growing strength of citizen voices has put to rest the prior history of poor governance by "cocaine generals". It all began in 1994, when the Bolivian Parliament passed a seminal law on decentralization that devolved basic governance down to the municipal level, while providing for close monitoring by citizens' vigilance committees. Other measures included the streamlined management of aid and technical cooperation, and the 1998 National Dialogue.

The result has been greater citizen involvement in governance and policy-making, which has significantly buttressed the capacity of local institutions and encouraged a burgeoning sense of national ownership of development. Recently, widespread participation in the preparation of the Bolivian PRSP garnered an array of new perspectives on policy issues, leading Bolivia to be dubbed a model country.

The Story

The Law of Popular Participation passed by the Bolivian Senate in 1994 introduced accountability to Bolivia, from the central government down to the local municipalities. It empowers democratically elected municipal councils to design and execute local development policies and programmes, funded by budgetary transfers from the central government. The law also requires that community organizations participate in the formulation of five-year municipal plans that contain social, infrastructure, production and environmental components.

Parallel vigilance committees monitor the municipal councils. They consist of six elected representatives from traditional institutions such as peasant syndicates and neighbourhood associations. Their key function is to ensure that municipal programmes and budgets reflect local priorities. Additionally, they can invoke a legal instrument (called a *denuncia*) against local councils. They may call for regular audits, and, upon detecting corruption, can report it to the national executive, which in turn passes the complaint to a special committee of the Senate. The Senate has the power to suspend funding to the council until the matter is resolved.

The Law of Popular Participation was one of a handful of factors helping Bolivia shift from being a country with a high degree of donor control and a proliferation of expatriate consultants to one where development is now driven by national or local leadership. Particularly since the National Dialogue in 1998 – which brought together most constituencies within the country to discuss development issues – donors and the government have worked constantly to harmonize the large number of donor interventions. To begin with, the current national government reassigned aid management within the executive branch. Under this arrangement, the Ministry of Economy, through the Vice Ministry of Public Investments and External Financing, replaces the Ministry of Planning as the primary agency for all technical cooperation and aid matters.

The legal framework guiding aid and the development of the capacity to manage it is now set by the Executive Power Organization Act and its by-laws. This has put an end to individual meetings with donors, which were overwhelming for the national bureaucracy. The programme on education reform, for example, required eight to ten mission meetings a year, which meant ministry staff spent a great deal of time setting up meetings and receiving missions. The new government policy calls for transmitting country and regional priorities to all international donors. Communication with donors and foreign governments is ongoing, but without the need for frequent meetings.

Donors have welcomed this approach. Under the earlier regime, many felt that the government heeded only the larger agencies. A committee system now ensures that all participate equally and facilitates the flow of information. In general, decision-making abilities within the national government and municipalities have been enhanced.

However, the results are far from perfect, and at best the case can be cited as a work in progress. Donor domination is still evident in a number of areas, such as macroeconomics and social spending. Key development players also wrangle over how to identify the best mechanisms for strengthening municipal institutions, with the government striving continually to define national and field policy actions for municipalities. Currently, the Vice Ministry of Public Investments and External Financing collects demands from departmental and municipal governments, evaluates requests, and eventually files petitions and negotiates with donors.

The National Dialogue was a large step towards boosting citizen participation in setting policy priorities. Yet in 2000, the peasant protests in Cochabamba against the privatization of water resources showed clearly that popular participation in policy-making has only had partial success. Bolivia also continues to face the challenge of matching the devolution of resources with capacity in outlying areas.

Results and Critical Factors

- The Law of Popular Participation has officially recognized the existence and importance of community organizations. It has legally enshrined a role for civil society that aims at a synergy between local government and community groups, while also setting up a watch-dog mechanism whereby people can hold the state accountable.

- Civil society organizations are now formally involved in planning, discussion and negotiation with local government. In the future, the depth of their involvement will depend on the ability of the state to fully embrace a transparent political culture. As recent political events following the national legislative elections in Bolivia indicate, this can be a risky venture, one that needs to be carefully managed to avoid raising false expectations that later collapse in frustration and loss of trust.

- The devolution of funding to the local level has resulted in some municipal council budgets increasing by up to 100 per cent. Municipal councils are also in a position to apply for donor funds, and community organizations have become the most important area for donor investment, mostly in the form of capacity development and support for participatory methods.

- Government and donors have established a level of comfort with the degree of participation and oversight engendered by the National Dialogue. The PRSP formulation was deemed to be a model having been reasonably led by national priorities.

Further information

G. G. Molina, et al. 2002. "Bolivia: The Political Context of Capacity Development." In *Developing Capacity Through Technical Cooperation: Country Experiences,* edited by Stephen Browne (www.undp.org/capacity). New York/London: UNDP/Earthscan.

J. Blackburn. 1999. *Participatory Methods and Local Governance Effectiveness in Bolivia.* Paper presented at the workshop "Strengthening Participation in Local Governance." Institute of Development Studies, University of Sussex, Brighton.

R. McGee. 2000. Workshop on civil society participation in national development programming, Brazil trip report. Institute of Development Studies, University of Sussex, Brighton.

Institute of Development Studies (www.ids.ac.uk/).

The authors gratefully acknowledge the contributions of George Gray Molina.

➲ BRAZIL:
BOLSA ESCOLA HELPS MOTHERS SEND CHILDREN TO SCHOOL

In a Nutshell

Brazil has taken a new route to modifying a subsidy regime in education, with dramatic impacts in terms of school enrolment, attendance and community participation. The government, through its municipalities, offers mothers a stipend for enrolling and keeping their children in school – a modest sum of about $6 per child that is met through a federal tax.

This incentive has inspired strong commitment among parents, and also helps to keep the subsidy from going to the potentially leaky state educational machinery. Crucial to the programme's success has been the broad-based partnership forged between state, municipal and private sector organizations, as well as considerable support across the political spectrum.

The Story

About 11 million Brazilian children aged 6 to 15 live in poverty and achieve little in school. In 2001, to reduce poverty and at the same time boost school enrolments, the Brazilian federal government launched a national initiative guaranteeing an income transfer for disadvantaged families, known as the Bolsa Escola (School Stipend) National Programme. It entails a monthly sum for families with an income that is lower than roughly $30 per person, and whose children in the 6-15 age group are attending primary school.

Bolsa Escola came about as a result of the lessons learned from the pilot Programa de Geração de Renda Minima (Minimum Income Programme), which began in 1997. It also drew upon similar programmes, such as the pioneering Federal District Bolsa Escola implemented in 1994 by Minister Cristovam Buarque, and the experiences of other Brazilian municipalities. With increased budget availability in 2001, Bolsa Escola was able to start offering a continuous source of funds, averaging approximately $505 million per year. The benefits of the programme have been readily apparent, as indicated by the promptness with which the Brazilian Congress has enacted legislation in support of it. For financial year 2002, $600 million was reserved in the federal budget.

Currently, Bolsa Escola is running across nearly all 5,561 Brazilian municipalities. An allowance of $6 is made for each child, with a maximum of $18 per family, and on the condition that children attend a minimum of 85 per cent of classes. Attendance rates are checked every three months by the federal government before the money is released. The children's mothers then take a magnetic card to withdraw the allowance at ATM machines or at bank branches. The decision to entrust the mothers with the administration of these resources came about after a study of social and economic patterns revealed that they are more efficient than fathers in making the best use of the allowance. Despite the small amount, it is nonetheless an extremely important addition to the family income in many economically deprived regions.

Bolsa Escola's success can be attributed to the following:

Financial sustainability: Programme funds are met by a federal tax collected by the banking system. Known as the Fundo de Redução da Pobreza (Poverty Reduction Fund), the tax is guaranteed by federal legislation for the next ten years.

Targeting the poorest: The programme attempts to reach the poorest people by according priority to municipalities presenting the lowest human development indicators, as well as those affected by natural calamities like drought and reporting high rates of violence. It also mobilizes municipalities participating in the Comunidade Solidária – a federal programme that involves the distribution of basic food baskets.

Partnerships and networks: A network of partners supports the initiative, from the federal to municipal levels. They include:

- Ministério da Educação (Ministry of Education): coordinates Bolsa Escola and provides cash income to the beneficiaries or caregivers
- UNDP: contributes to analysis of programme impact on families, communities, schools and students' performance; the development of managerial and monitoring systems; and the establishment of technical cooperation with similar programmes
- Instituto de Pesquisa Econômica Aplicada (Institute of Applied Economic Research): designs and tests programme evaluation
- Unão Nacional dos Dirigentes Municipais de Educação (National Association of Municipal Educational Managers): a key partner in programme implementation and monitoring at municipal level, it provides input to the design of evaluation methodologies as well as strategies and performance indicators
- Municipal authorities: responsible overall for beneficiary selection and programme management at the local level, and contribute to the evaluation process
- Conselhos Municipais de Controle Social (Municipal Social Control Councils): register and select recipients of Bolsa Escola, monitor school attendance and assess local performance.
- Caixa Econômica Federal (Brazilian Savings Bank): makes monthly payments to recipients through its nationwide network of agencies and ATMs

Community participation, social control and after-school activities: To be included in the programme, municipalities are required to select eligible families and supervise the allocation of grants. They are also responsible for running social and educational programmes after school hours and for setting up a Municipal Social Control Council comprised of members of the local community. The involvement of the community in supervision greatly reduces patronage and misuse of funds; to ensure diverse participation, legislation has restricted municipal staff from taking more than half the council seats.

Results and Critical Factors

Bolsa Escola is now recognized, including in a number of manifestos among Brazil's political parties, as playing a fundamental role in retaining children at school and thus democratizing education in Brazil. The programme currently benefits over 5.1 million families and more than 8.42 million children, and has brought over a million children back to school.

Although an extensive evaluation has yet to be completed, some conclusions can be drawn based on preliminary studies conducted by the Secretaria Nacional da Bolsa Escola (National Secretary of Bolsa Escola) in 2002. These suggest that Bolsa Escola is:

- Raising awareness among families of the importance of placing their children in school – leading to extended enrolment

- Improving access to schooling and attendance for those segments of society most affected by lack of formal schooling

- Involving families in the process of educating their children, which fosters positive attitudes towards education among segments of society traditionally excluded from schooling

- Assisting in combating child labour and discouraging the option of living on the streets as a way of life for poor families, thereby reducing exposure of children and adolescents to situations of personal and social risk, particularly those associated with drugs, sex work, violence and crime

- Improving the quality of life and financial status of families with very low per capita incomes, restoring the dignity of excluded segments of the population, and stimulating self-esteem and the hope of a better future for their children

Almost all successful programmes in education draw from some common principles. Bolsa Escola proves what is needed: a high level of political commitment; involvement of the community (and especially parents) in management; assured and sustained funding; the participation of local government; and a high degree of coordination among multiple agencies. In this case, an innovation – turning the subsidy regime around to bypass school machinery and directly reach the beneficiaries – has also proven to be a pillar of Bolsa Escola's accomplishments.

Further information

United Nations Educational, Scientific and Cultural Organisation (UNESCO). 2002. *Education to Confront Poverty* (http://portal.unesco.org/en/ev.php@URL_ID=10422&URL_DO=DO_TOPIC&URL_SEC-TION=201.html).

A. Vawda. n.d. *Brazil: Stipends to Increase School Enrollment and Decrease Child Labor: A Case of Demand-Side Financing.* Human Development Network (www.worldbank.org/education/economicsed/finance/demand/case/brazil/brazil_index.htm).

International Development Research Center (IDRC). *Bolsa-Escola (School Bursary Program): A Public Policy on Minimum Income and Education* (www.idrc.ca/lacro/foro/seminario/caccia_pb.html).

UNDP Newsfront (www.undp.org/dpa/frontpagearchive/2002/may/30mayo2/).

The authors gratefully acknowledge the contributions of Maristela Baioni and Luiza Maria S. dos Santos Carvalho.

BRAZIL:
HOW PARTICIPATORY BUDGET-MAKING CAN IMPROVE THE QUALITY OF LIFE

In a Nutshell

Ten years ago, the Brazilian Municipality of Porto Alegre created an innovative system to manage municipal funds: people join officials and locally elected leaders to decide on investment priorities, actions and public works, and build a participatory budget.

The results demonstrate that community involvement, transparency and accountability can improve the effectiveness of public expenditures. Concrete changes have come to Porto Alegre, along with a revival of the sense of citizenship and the realization that it is possible to actively participate in public affairs. The citizenry of Porto Alegre has acquired a form of democratically management that was dubbed an exemplary urban innovation by the 1996 UN Conference on Human Settlements in Istanbul.

The Story

Public budgeting and accounting in Brazil has been characterized by resource wastage, political clientelism and corruption. In the past, high inflation helped turn municipal budgets into fictitious documents over which citizens had little control. Although inflationary pressures have now eased to some extent, scandals, the misuse of resources and the absence of accountability are still pervasive. Porto Alegre's participatory budget process has sought to remedy this situation by bringing people, officials and locally elected leaders together to debate and consult on investment priorities, actions and public works.

At first, the legacy of inadequate financing, opaque decision-making and simple lack of experience resulted in low participation. But as the municipality recovered its investment capacity through a radical reform of the taxation system, the participatory budget system started taking off. The municipality mobilized resources to respond to popular demands, while community members began seeing tangible improvements in their living conditions. In 1994, some 11,000 people took part in meetings and plenary assemblies – by 1997, the figure was 20,000. Adding the people who attended the many different meetings organized by community associations, more than 50,000 citizens have contributed so far.

Every year, the process involves the municipality organizing two large plenary assemblies in each of the city's 16 regions, along with five thematic groups on the organization of the city and urban development; circulation and transportation; health and social services; education, culture and leisure; and economic development and taxation. The first assembly reviews the investment plans of the former year, ensuring transparency. In the second round, citizens identify their priorities and elect their board members for formulating the new budget. Between these two rounds, additional meetings take place, either in the thematic groups or in the regions, where people articulate their needs. This stage is the most important, as it decentralizes discussion to the neighbourhood level, particularly in poor areas.

A forum of regional and thematic delegates and a board for the participatory budget are then constituted. Selected delegates meet once a month. Their role is to support the board members, to inform the general community about the topics discussed, to hold strategic meetings and to follow up on the investment plans. The board comprises two members and two substitutes elected in each of the regions; two members and two substitutes elected in each of the thematic groups; one representative and one substitute from the Union of Civil Servants; and one representative and one substitute from the Association of Dwellers of Porto Alegre. The government has two representatives who do not have voting rights. Board members are elected for one year and can be re-elected once.

Preparation of the budget and investment strategy begins with government divisions and agencies discussing the options, as well as their costs and feasibility. Board members and delegates then organize debates within the communities. Based on their feedback, the Executive presents to the board a detailed budget proposal including all items of income and expenditure. An investment and work plan is prepared for each region, together with the sector investments that are important for the whole city. At the end of the process, the board approves the investment plan.

The Executive then sends the budget to the City Council, where a complex debate between participatory and representative democracy takes place. It is a naturally tense and difficult relationship, but it has proved to be a positive one.

City Council members discuss the overall budget with the Executive and, together with the board members, present amendments and suggestions for change. Negotiations unfold, resulting in some modifications that do not affect the overall structure of the budget, and the City Council passes a final draft.

Results and Critical Factors

- The participatory budget process demonstrates that participation, transparency and accountability can improve the effectiveness and efficiency of public expenditures. It has been a valuable tool for bringing concrete changes to Porto Alegre, such as almost universal access to water and sanitation; improved roads, drainage and street lighting; doubling of school enrolment and the expansion of primary health care. An influential business journal nominated Porto Alegre as the Brazilian city with the best quality of life for the fourth consecutive year.

- The budget also has served as a tool for profound changes in the political culture of the city, eliminating the traditional practices of corruption and clientelism, and giving new value and meaning to citizen involvement. Today, the people of Porto Alegre have access to information about public investments and are empowered to make decisions affecting their future.

- A notable change in attitudes among technical staff, who are well versed in matters of budgeting and engineering, has also been observed. Through a jump from "techno-bureaucracy to techno-democracy", these staff have changed the way they communicate, trying hard to make themselves understood in simple language. Lively debates have been witnessed between the increasingly assertive delegates and staff over the latter's technical criteria and proposals.

- The participatory budget is neither perfect nor a finished process. It faces problems and issues that require constant attention. However, it offers lessons that are nationally and internationally useful. Many other municipalities have adopted the system, and scholars from different countries have visited the city to learn more about it. There are now more than 70 municipalities implementing participatory budgets in Brazil.

- This experience has also stimulated public reflection and debate about the limits and insufficiencies of representative democracy. In a country like Brazil, where democracy is young, voters' views are usually disregarded or defrauded through frequent political shifts and changes of elected representatives. The compliance of programmes with electoral platforms and policies is often ignored, while citizens have become inured to poor representation.

Further information

L. Avritzer. 1999. *Public Deliberation at the Local Level: Participatory Budgeting in Brazil* (www.ssc.wisc.edu/~wright/avritzer.pdf).

B. De Sousa Santos. 1998. "Participatory Budgeting in Porto Alegre: Towards a Redistributive Democracy." In *Politics and Society*, 26.

J. Motta, and A. Betânia. 2001. *Gestão Democrática em Porto Alegre: dificuldades e oportunidades para avançar uma experiência exitosa* (www.urbared.ungs.edu.ar/portafolios/prescaso3.html).

World Bank. "Porto Alegre, Brazil: Participation in the Budget and Investment Plan." Under case studies on civic engagement in public expenditure management (www.worldbank.org/participation/web/webfiles/cepemcase1.htm).

"The Experience of the Participative Budget in Porto Alegre Brazil." An article featured in MOST Clearing House Best Practices (www.unesco.org/most/southa13.htm).

⮕ CAMBODIA:
ANGKOR WAT COMBINES CONSERVATION WITH COMMUNITY PARTICIPATION AND INNOVATIVE DEVELOPMENT

In a Nutshell

A world heritage site is a global public good. Its conservation, accessibility and the blending of these with local realities can test planning, execution, institutional coordination and commitment. Complex and multiple capacities are called for. In Cambodia, Angkor Wat is especially challenging not only because it is the world's largest temple complex, but also because the site is in a country that has recently emerged from war and has 22,000 inhabitants.

While an international umbrella arrangement remains, Angkor Wat is today primarily managed by the Cambodian Authority for the Protection of the Site and the Development of the Region of Angkor (APSARA), which has with wide-ranging competencies and authority. Together with the local communities and other partners, APSARA moderates the tourist flow, safeguards the complex and manages social transformation in the surrounding area.

The Story

After 20 years of conflict, the signing of the Paris peace agreements in 1991 ushered in a new era in Cambodia. His Majesty King Norodom Sihanouk and the Director-General of UNESCO immediately launched appeals to the international community to safeguard the historical site of Angkor Wat. It had been included on the List of World Heritage in Danger in December 1992, after being systematically looted during the war. By October 1993, an intergovernmental meeting had adopted the Tokyo

Declaration, which created an International Co-ordinating Committee (ICC) for the site, co-chaired by France and Japan. UNESCO provided the secretariat for the ICC, and has since worked to focus international efforts covering not only architectural and archaeological conservation, but also related capacity development and training.

The ICC is staffed by diplomatic nominees from various countries. Given the complexity of coordinating the restoration of a site of such magnitude, a technical wing was also formed to provide scientific advice and evaluate project proposals. A forum for debate as well as exchanges of experience and advice, this ad hoc group of experts guides the ICC on the monuments, defines standards and ensures a level of consistency in the numerous restoration projects. Since 1993, the ICC has coordinated over 100 projects involving some 30 partners (international organizations, universities, private enterprises, NGOs and governments). Each has worked along the lines advocated by the ICC, which, in addition to enforcing highly successful conservation practices, has promoted an approach based on integrating culture and development.

Although the umbrella for Angkor Wat remains international, an early step was to adopt protective national measures and to create the Cambodian Authority for the Protection of the Site and the Development of the Region of Angkor (APSARA). It has wide-ranging authority over any measures taken by national and/or local authorities, with the sole right to grant building permits and destroy unauthorized buildings without compensation. It has also benefited from new financial regulations, which channel roughly 50 per cent of entrance fees in its direction.

Overall, three principles guide restoration work at Angkor Wat.

- It must be done by and for Cambodians.
- A long-term vision requires close links between research and study, and entails investigation and reflection before any work is undertaken.
- There must be a commitment to balancing restoration with the economic and social development of the local communities.

With these in mind, all international projects include training components based on the knowledge offered by the international teams and the resources of Cambodian craftsmen. One initiative supported by Japan in 1993 enabled the training of more than 500 Cambodian archaeologists and architects, 50 of whom were subsequently employed by APSARA and the Cambodian administration, thus ensuring the sustainability of restoration.

Starting in 2003, an International Documentation Centre created by UNESCO will be administered by APSARA, but will continue to benefit from the UN organization's intellectual and scientific contributions. Its mission is to collect, develop and manage all the scientific and technical documents related to the site, keep track of activities, and allow access for researchers, experts and institutions. The centre will also promote the scientific studies needed for future projects.

Today, Angkor Wat receives more and more national and foreign visitors. In 2000, the number of international tourists in Cambodia reached 466,365, a 27 per cent increase over the previous year, and in 2003 the number is expected to jump substantially. With tourism poised to become pivotal to the country's economic development, the Cambodian authorities and the ICC are now considering ways to offer cultural tourism, which includes economic, social, educational, scientific, environmental and ethical considerations along with the involvement of local communities. An overarching strategy to control the tourist flow, safeguard the site and manage social transformation is in the works. One area of critical focus is a job creation strategy. It covers the development of infrastructure; civil and public works; maintenance of facilities; training in tourism services, including for guides and tourist transport operators; and production and marketing of crafts.

With a view to future challenges, the Cambodian government declared an Angkor Development Decade from 2002 to 2012 to step up its struggle against poverty, promote stable economic growth and improve the overall quality of life. This declaration is consistent with a royal decree signed in 1994, which specifically underscores the involvement of local communities and the preservation of their traditional cultures and lifestyles. The Angkor Wat site, with its 22,000 inhabitants, has a unique opportunity to put into practice community participation and innovative development.

Results and Critical Factors

The end of conflict in Cambodia has mobilized the international community and enabled the government to develop an integrated vision and strategy backed by strong political will. This manifests in several ways:

- New legislation for the conservation, management and protection of Angkor Wat as well as coordinated economic development provides a unique framework for conservation and enhancement.

- Endowed with a large and clear mandate over the entire site, APSARA can strategize, plan and implement balanced conservation and development activities.

- The ICC steers all activities on the site, thereby providing invaluable and consistent scientific backing to the government, including on issues related to conservation of monuments, training, tourism, urban development and community participation.

- UNESCO, as the only UN organization whose mandate covers culture, has provided its unique professional expertise, developed over five and a half decades of international activity.

- Strong capacity development components – including creating the ad hoc group of experts, setting up APSARA, training and absorption of locals in their capacity as architects and managers, and maintaining an information resource centre – have all added up to a successful whole.

- The strong political commitment of the Cambodia government and the responsive collaboration of the international community have succeeded not only in establishing effective oversight of Angkor Wat, but also generated an unprecedented learning process that transcends the mere transfer of know-how and skills.

Further information

Authority for the Protection of the Site and the Development of the Region of Angkor (APSARA) (www.autoriteapsara.org/).

United Nations Educational, Scientific and Cultural Organisation (UNESCO). International Co-ordinating Committee for the Safeguarding and Development of the Historic Site of Angkor (http://portal.unesco.org/en/ev.php@URL_ID=10348&URL_DO=DO_TOPIC&URL_SECTION=201.html).

Angkor Wat (www.angkor.com/index.shtml).

The authors gratefully acknowledge the contributions of Galia Saouma-Forero, Senior Progamme Specialist, Cambodia unit, Division of Cultural Heritage, UNESCO.

➲ CAMBODIA:
DECENTRALIZATION LAYS A FOUNDATION FOR RECONSTRUCTION
AND GOVERNANCE

In a Nutshell

In the aftermath of a brutal war, a Cambodian government programme for decentralizing governance is resurrecting local capacities to manage develop-ment funds, while respecting the rule of law, human rights, environmental concerns and so on. Called Seila, the programme has also created a system for funnelling resources from central to local government bodies.

The Seila experience features many potential lessons for countries emerg-ing from conflict, proving that if donors and reconstruction agencies work in the immediate post-conflict stage in a decentralized service delivery mode, this provides the natural launch pad for a decentralized governance structure dur-ing rehabilitation. It also demonstrates that trust-building among stakeholders is a central tenet of capacity development in countries wounded by internal conflict.

The Story

Cambodia was confronted with a large population of refugees and internally dis-placed people at the cessation of hostilities in 1991. Since the resettlement and rehabilitation projects undertaken by the UN Transitional Authority often worked with local communities, a decentralized governance structure was a logical out-come at the end of the transition period. This second phase of rehabilitation included support for the Cambodian government's Seila programme.

Seila, meaning foundation stone, is a collective undertaking of seven ministries. An approach to decentralization built upon participation, empowerment, gender equity and good governance, Seila is a radically new concept in Cambodia, char-acterized as it has been by local and international conflict, a centralized command economy and political structures, and isolation from the international community.

Capacity development for managing development funds at the provincial, commune and village levels is a central activity for Seila, which now works in 17 out of 24 provinces. It has developed participatory planning processes using provincial rural development committees, which link both to the central Seila Task Force and to the district, commune and village level development committees in the outlying areas. An important feature of this structure is that planning originates at the village level and filters upwards to commune, provincial and central levels, with concomitant financial management and accountability at each stage.

Seila covers basic services for poverty alleviation, including the provision of local development funds to cover income-generating activities, agriculture, health, water and sanitation, and education and culture. Since the February 2002 commune council elections, Seila has focused on capacity development for newly elected councils, providing training to all councillors on administration, the local planning process and financial management.

Beginning in 2001, Seila has functioned under Cambodia's Partnership for Local Governance programme, with joint funding from UNDP, the UK Department for International Development (DFID) and the Sida. The programme addresses policy and procedural challenges by refining and testing decentralized systems for planning, financing and managing local development; helping establish institutional arrangements and capacities necessary for both local democracy and development; and assisting the government to address problems related to inadequate or unreliable funds for local authorities to deliver public goods and services.

Partnership for Local Governance incorporates a strong capacity development component. It has supported national agencies to improve aid coordination, execution and supervision, and to translate policies into regulations and systems. At the provincial and commune levels, projects have focused on the new governance functions of elected councils, while facilitating public information and civic awareness campaigns on the roles, obligations and responsibilities of provincial and commune authorities. The programme has also developed, tested and institutionalized participatory planning procedures; set up decentralized financing facilities; and developed local public sector procurement practices and public-private partnerships for infrastructure and service delivery.

Other contributions include: provision of locally managed infrastructure and services; technical and financial contributions to policy statements, drafts for legislation and decrees; the preparation of policy-oriented reports based on the lessons learned (for example, improving local fiscal income and resource mobilization, bettering relations between commune authorities and civil society, and promoting multi-actor arrangements for service delivery); and special-purpose studies on subjects such as how to improve the access of the rural poor to affordable, locally managed, and sustainable public services and infrastructure.

Results and Critical Factors

Seila teaches some important lessons. Some of the toughest challenges have pertained to mindsets – project managers agreed that changing them was often the most difficult task. Some of the programme's main accomplishments have been:

- Formulation and implementation of transitional arrangements to help create departments of local administration at the national and provincial level
- Assisting communes in becoming more efficient and responsive through support for the formulation of the sub-decrees and guidelines on commune development planning, the commune financial management

system, and various operational and accounting guidelines, as well as the development of commune profiles designed to serve as tools both for planning and for determining the poverty index

- Support for the creation of a common curriculum on commune orientation and administration, and the training of commune councils and clerks to empower agents for transformation

- Expansion and development of new partnerships between the programme and national government agencies on the one hand, and between the programme and other donors on the other as a way of mainstreaming Seila and making its achievements more sustainable

Seila rests on four principles: dialogue, clarity, agreement and respect. At the heart of its success is the extensive level of collaboration between the government and its development partners, as well as stakeholders at various levels. All have shared a vision of creating mechanisms that promote transparency, accountability, equity and participation.

Further information

Jan Rudengren, and Joakim Ojendal. 2002. *Learning by Doing – An Analysis of the Seila Experiences in Cambodia.* Stockholm: SPM Consultants.

United Nations Development Programme (UNDP). 2001. *Peace-building from the Ground-Up: A Case Study of UNDP's CARERE Programme in Cambodia 1991-2000.* Emergency Response Division. New York: UNDP.

Yanara Chieng. 2001. A presentation at the Round Table on Reforming Technical Assistance. Turin, 3-7 December.

Background on local development funds in Cambodia (www.uncdf.org/english/consultants/impact/cmb_des.pdf).

The authors gratefully acknowledge the contributions of UNDP Cambodia.

➲ CAMBODIA:
A FRAMEWORK TO ENTER THE ARENA OF WORLD TRADE

In a Nutshell

The integrated framework (IF) is part of a commitment made by developed countries to assist developing countries in capitalizing on trade liberalization opportunities. In Cambodia, six multilateral agencies participate in managing this framework, while also supporting the mainstreaming of the IF initiative into the national poverty reduction strategy.

In 2001, a pilot study of Cambodia's entry into the international trading system was presented at the Fourth Ministerial meeting of the World Trade Organization (WTO), which found it to be among the best examples of the benefits of technical assistance to an LDC. Notable factors behind Cambodia's success include the dynamic leadership and strategic vision of the Ministry of Commerce, along with an overall national reform process grounded in strong country ownership and donor coordination.

The Story

Cambodia depends greatly on a single economic activity: a third of its GDP comes from garment exports alone. Sustaining this rate will be difficult unless Cambodia can join the WTO. Along with the looming end of the Multi-Fibre Agreement regime in 2005, WTO membership is therefore a major incentive driving a broad range of public reforms.

Complying with WTO requirements places heavy demands on a small developing country, because accession is not merely about trade capacity alone, but about capacity development across a range of sectors. For example, in Cambodia there are concerns over whether the judicial system is sufficient, given that qualified people staff only a handful of positions in the legal machinery. Several other areas requiring stronger capabilities include legislative frameworks, valuation procedures, trade policy evaluation and reporting, and assessments of the impact of trade protection.

As a step in the direction of improving its capacity, and supported by six multilateral agencies, the Cambodian government adopted the IF in 2000. Under it, the government opted to pursue a growth-enhancing, pro-poor trade strategy within its overall national poverty reduction strategy. The Ministry of Commerce came forward from the start and clearly demonstrated its intention to take strong leadership and ownership of the trade reform process in Cambodia, a stance that varied from past practices.

Following the signing of a memorandum of understanding with the agencies, the government tabled a study entitled "A Pro-Poor Trade Sector Strategy for Cambodia: A Preliminary Concept Paper." Key elements were then incorporated into the draft

Second Socio-Economic Development Plan and the Cambodia Ten-Year Plan of Action prepared for the Least Developed Countries III Conference. Cambodia also used the conference to further explain the importance of capacity development in trade as a means to enhance poverty alleviation.

Subsequently, the government issued the "Road Map". It outlined three critical actions: (a) strengthening the capacity of the Ministry of Commerce to lead and manage the formulation (and eventually the implementation) of the pro-poor trade sector integration study through broad partnerships with all key trade sector stakeholders and development partners; (b) ensuring solid assessment, targeting and monitoring of poverty reduction in the context of poverty reduction strategy formulation and implementation efforts; and (c) exploring best practice capacity development approaches tailored to the specific circumstances in Cambodia.

Following the presentation of the "Road Map" at a 2002 consultative group meeting, the government and donors agreed to conduct a pilot diagnostic study of Cambodia's integration into the international trading system. The research addressed overall trade policy, facilitation, promotion and supply-side capacity, and included an initial poverty analysis. A matrix of technical cooperation that identified priority needs in relation to trade reforms was appended, providing the entry point for coordination of donor assistance. When the pilot was presented in Doha at the WTO's Fourth Ministerial meeting, delegates applauded Cambodia's integration process as among the best examples of effective technical assistance to an LDC.

A November 2002 publication by the OECD/DAC, "Studies on Donor Practices: Cambodia Case Study", later concluded: "The vast majority of recipients interviewed in government stressed problems in donor practices that fall into the 'lack of ownership' category.... These recipients also complained of their own lack of capacity – in some cases holding donor practices responsible for not allowing them the opportunities to develop their own capacity further. But the ministries of Health, Education and Commerce stood out as exceptions, since the problems they identified were not 'lack of ownership'. In these, firstly, fewer problems were identified. Secondly, problems identified were more to do with coordination among donors or derived from poor budgeting and cash management within government as a whole."

The crux of Cambodia's IF trade reforms involves several instruments for donor coordination, including the technical cooperation matrix and the constitution of a steering committee, chaired by the Ministry of Commerce, with members from government ministries, donor agencies, the business sector and civil society. The overall capacity development agenda itself focuses on several priorities. The first is knowledge acquisition. A core group of eight professionals leading the trade negotiations and integration process is expected to go through an extensive process of learning, with an emphasis on experiences in other countries in the South. These national experts will then work with other government ministries and agencies as well as the business sector and civil society in driving the national response and targeting international support.

A second objective is organizational development. The Ministry of Commerce places great emphasis on not limiting trade reforms strictly to itself, but involving other public institutions. Overall public sector reforms are still at a nascent stage, with ongoing efforts to re-align incentive systems and ensure sustainability. This includes the critical requirement of adopting new forms of work that are less centralized and bureaucratic.

Finally, there is the area of institutional environment and partnerships. The requirement to mainstream a trade reform process in the national poverty reduction strategy has led to the need to address the broader institutional environment within which poverty reduction is unfolding, especially in terms of wider participation. While civil society in Cambodia is still weak, it has nevertheless become increasingly involved in the poverty reduction strategy process and the WTO accession debate. By way of illustration, labour unions in the textile sector are organizing and mobilizing workers for demonstrations. International NGOs play a role as well, by closely scrutinizing labour standards.

Results and Critical Factors

Some key capacity development lessons have emerged from Cambodia's IF experience. These include:

- There is a need for strong leadership. In this case, the Ministry of Commerce drove the trade reform process by shaping a strategic vision – including bridging knowledge gaps and nurturing an institutional change process – and placing it at the core of the national growth strategy.

- It is crucial to set up a nationally driven reform process at the outset (captured in the "Road Map") with country ownership and donor coordination as its main pillars. This should include the establishment of national priorities and partnership coordination instruments (similar to the technical cooperation matrix and the IF steering committee).

- The integration of trade in the national poverty reduction strategy triggers the need to address trade within the broader institutional and global environment, which shapes efforts to reduce poverty and inequality.

- The setting of an ambitious target such as WTO accession in the context of the ongoing national poverty reduction process has led to a spill-over response, in the form of a growing national constituency on trade and poverty.

Further information

Asian Development Bank (ADB). 2001. *Cambodia Financial Sector Blueprint 2001-2010* (www.adb.org/Documents/Reports/CAM_Blueprint/chapoo.pdf).

————. 2000. *Cambodia Country Assessment Strategy* (www.adb.org/Documents/CAPs/CAM/0303.asp).

Cambodia World Trade Organization membership negotiations background (www.wto.org/english/news_e/news03_e/cambodia_membership_16apo3_e.htm#background).

The authors gratefully acknowledge the contributions of UNDP Cambodia.

CHINA:
EXPOSURE VISIT FOR OFFICIALS FACILITATES PROFOUND POLICY CHANGE

In a Nutshell

Capacity development does not necessarily require extensive resources. Much depends on the appropriateness of interventions. In this case, a small grant to fund a carefully coordinated exposure and learning trip for a group of junior functionaries of the Chinese government influenced China's trade and macro-economic policies when, years later, the functionaries rose through the ranks to become important officials.

This short-term project, underpinned by a clear vision and strong commitment on the part of the recipient government, led to lasting and significant impact. It illustrates two aspects critical to projects involving governments: first, anchoring the project at an appropriately senior level; and second, choosing the right instrument of intervention. It also underscores that coordinated exposure by itself can be a significant capacity development initiative.

The Story

In 1980, China had only recently begun opening to the outside world. It had set up a foreign investment/import-export commission under the State Council in 1979, which had just decided to recommend to the Cabinet the creation of a number of special economic zones in China's south-east provinces of Guangdong and Fujian. The Guangdong administration had set forth a preliminary set of regulations for the operation of the zones. However, the central government wanted to gain a broader perspective by learning from the experiences of other countries. Chinese authorities had taken particular note of the successes of neighbours such as Singapore and Malaysia.

Consequently, the government contacted UNDP and UNCTAD about arranging a six-week study tour to educate a team of senior government officials about investment promotion. The leader of the Chinese delegation was the Vice-Minister of the newly created Foreign Investment Commission. A high-level mission from UNCTAD's International Trade Center (ITC) went to Beijing to discuss the project, and to speak about special economic zones.

Subsequently, a government/ITC workshop took place in Beijing to plan the mission and tailor it to the interests of the participants. It focused attention on specific areas and marked them for further investigation. In September, the group left for six countries: Ireland, Malaysia, Mexico, Philippines, Singapore and Sri Lanka.

Participants took part in over 75 meetings, concentrating on issues related to special export zones such as fiscal incentives, physical infrastructure, common infrastructure facilities and services for foreign investors, banking issues and investment promotion. An UNCTAD expert accompanied the group for the duration of the trip, offering independent observations and perspectives. At the end, a debriefing session took place at the ITC in Geneva, followed by a meeting in Beijing with UNDP before the Chinese participants prepared their final mission report.

The continuing discussions during the entire life cycle of the mission ensured clarity of purpose and a comprehensive understanding of the experiences. In Beijing, discussions centred on the formulation of clear recommendations to the government and the initiation of follow-up action, such as the drafting of national legislation.

As it turned out, the delegation leader, Vice-Minister Jiang Zemin, went on to serve as Mayor of Shanghai and then as President of the Peoples' Republic of China, where he became a major proponent of economic reforms. Other than Jiang Zemin, Qin Wenjun is now a member of the Politburo; Lu Zifen established the Xiamen special export zone; Huang Shimin set up the Shenzhen zone and currently heads the Hong Kong–Macao Political Committee; and Wu Jinquan is a member of the Party Central Committee.

Results and Critical Factors
In helping to shape the vision and understanding of future leaders, it may be claimed that this initiative contributed in its own small way to the rapid – almost exemplary – growth that China has demonstrated in recent years, making it a model for the developing world. There were several ingredients contributing to the success of the project.

- The Chinese were fully committed and had a desire to see the initiative prove fruitful, partly because at that time there was no internal consensus within China about the strategy for economic reforms.

- Strong leadership from the Chinese side and selection of the right people to go on the mission was critical.

- The exhaustive meetings between Chinese and UNCTAD/ITC officials to plan and design a carefully targeted programme in terms of countries to visit, agencies to meet and questions and issues to discuss were all critical steps.

- The strategic debriefing and follow-up discussions with UNCTAD in Geneva and UNDP in Beijing helped to crystallize the experience and clarify understanding, as did the facilitation by the international expert in each country and his final report.

- Rigorous internal discussions, process documentation and debriefings ensured that the lessons learned were developed and communicated to those making the decisions. Formal reports were submitted to the State Council and later to the National People's Congress when it debated the legislation prepared by the government for the eventual establishment of China's first special economic zones.

Further information

Ministry of Foreign Trade and Economic Cooperation (MOFTEC), Peoples Republic of China (www.moftec.gov.cn).

The authors gratefully acknowledge the contributions of Bob Boase, UNDP China.

➲ CHINA:
INVESTING IN PHARMACEUTICAL RESEARCH CAPACITY TO COMPETE GLOBALLY

> ### In a Nutshell
>
> The WTO's Trade-Related Aspects of Intellectual Property Rights (TRIPS) Agreement has brought momentous changes to China and its pharmaceutical sector. The country can no longer rely solely on reverse engineering patented medicines for its 1.3 billion people. Further, mortality from chronic diseases such as cancer is rising, the population is ageing and the health needs of the poorest pose an ongoing challenge – all factors that will test China's health science capacity.
>
> This case highlights the response of the Chinese government and scientific community to changing internal and external circumstances, and the actions they have taken to develop capacities for pharmaceutical research and development (R+D). This has included the promotion of collaborations between the government, academia and industry; the facilitation of foreign joint ventures in contract research and manufacturing; and legal and institutional reforms.

The Story

Disease and health trends largely dictate manufacturing as well as research and development priorities in the pharmaceutical and biotechnology sector. Over the past decades, China has been in the midst of an epidemiological transition from an overwhelming infectious diseases burden to a rising incidence of uncommunicable, chronic illnesses.

Already considerable in size, China's pharmaceutical industry is one of the fastest growing in the world. However, research and development investment has been barely 2-4 per cent of revenue, compared to 20 per cent among the multinational pharmaceutical companies that hold the majority of high-value intellectual properties in novel chemical entity discovery. Consequently, 90 per cent of the modern medicines distributed in China is estimated to be reverse engineered. With pharmaceutical product trade liberalization and the WTO's strict patent protection requirements, the Chinese health science industry has no choice but to raise research and development capacity to compete and survive. Government as well as industry initiatives are well underway.

There are a number of promotional efforts by the government to enlarge research capacity through academia and then commercialize the outputs. The Ministry of Science and Technology is spending $600 million over five years to promote biotechnology and genomics research, for example. State and local governments are also a part of the funding channels. The Shanghai Center of Research and Development for New Drugs, for instance, provides assistance and financing for joint ventures and commercializes discoveries in the region. In the arena of genomic chips, companies and universities, with the active encouragement of the government, are racing to develop these building blocks for research and development on new medicines. Collaboration in this area is creating a cluster effect in the form of knowledge-intensive, high-tech industry cropping up around academic institutions.

China has also encouraged joint ventures between research and development entities, and technology- and cash-rich foreign companies. Many of the world's top pharmaceutical firms have already set up manufacturing as well as research and development operations, attracted by a large pool of skilled scientists. Many have trained at world-class universities in the US and Europe, and returned to China with government incentives. Foreign corporations are also eyeing a growing domestic market opening for foreign competition and offering cost advantages. In 2001, $1.8 billion of foreign direct investment as well as domestic public and private financing poured into the pharmaceutical sector.

The dynamics of the global pharmaceutical industry provide China a window of opportunity for capacity development. The international contract manufacturing market is close to $10 billion in size, with an average of $800 million spent over ten years by big pharmaceuticals for every successfully commercialized molecule. Significant cost pressures, coupled with high attrition rates and an acute shortage of specialized labour in biopharma, mean that today's discovery research efforts take place in multiple transnational locations. Contract research forms an integral part of product development efforts as multi-country, multi-centre clinical research is conducted on a global scale.

These global contracts are often based on strict quality conditions that require a regulatory agency's certification for good manufacturing, clinical and even agricultural practice. The conditions are accompanied by on-site training and sometimes a sponsor's investment in clinical facilities and equipment. Despite this expensive outlay, research outsourcing is on the rise, constituting a major financing and capacity-building source for many small- and mid-size research-oriented companies worldwide. The completion of the Human Genome Project, for example, has generated a huge research need for linking the workings of thousands of genes to diseases through functional genomics and proteomics. Many pieces of the research and development puzzle require informatics capability and labour-intensive laboratory work, making outsourcing a necessity. To capitalize on this trend, Chinese institutions are building modern bioinformatics capacity. In addition, since China was one of two Asian countries participating in the International Human Genome Sequencing Consortium, some Chinese research and development institutions have existing collaborative research projects with advanced foreign companies.

Another notable factor driving pharmaceutical capacity development in China is research to unearth the scientific basis of traditional Chinese medicines. The potential value of these can be significant, making research on them a priority among China's research and development entities. In conformity with the international regulatory approval requirements, some Chinese traditional medicines have already been taken through the formal drug discovery and development process, with scientific documentation and modern technologies to investigate their efficacy and safety.

The initiatives described above have evolved based on a widely accepted consensus that it has been necessary to propel competitiveness in knowledge-based industries while the overall Chinese economy has grown. This has been supported by landmark legislation, further accelerating capacity development. Examples include reforming pharmaceutical regulatory requirements in line with international standards; revamping the State Drug Administration; ensuring quality standards for drug safety; providing government incentives for building pharmaceutical and biotechnology capacity; protecting product patents; setting up strong enforcement measures; and deregulating imports and exports and the distribution of pharmaceutical products.

Some argue that these reforms are double-edged in that they remove certain safeguards from the fledging domestic pharmaceutical industry, exposing it to direct competition with powerful global companies. In an environment where regulatory approval of novel drug discovery is becoming increasingly difficult, it is likely that many initiatives will face consolidation. However, the steps currently underway in China to develop capacity will likely allow it to skilfully manage this transition.

Results and Critical Factors

China's experience offers practical insights and realistic approaches to capacity development in the pharmaceutical R&D sector. Critical factors that have contributed to its many achievements include:

- The government's determination not to hide behind reverse engineering but to accept international standards and the rules of the game, combined with competitive pressures acting as a motor for innovation

- Collaboration between the government, academia and industry that has nurtured new scientific, technological and human capacity, enabling China's R&D efforts to leap forward towards the discovery of new molecules for pharmaceuticals and research on unearthing the scientific basis of traditional Chinese medicines

- Multiple government reforms ranging from the regulation of medicines to enforcement of patent protection to pharmaceutical industry liberalization

- A large market, to which the investment capital for R&D and future return on equity is linked (In the past, big markets, like in Brazil, China or India, have stimulated development of pharmaceutical capacity outside the developed world.)

Further information

Feng Cai. 2002. "Risks and Rewards for Pharma in Post-WTO China." In *Pharmaceutical Executive,* April.

Michael Fernandes, and David Miska. 2002. "Strategic Rethink for German Biotechnology." In *Nature Biotechnology,* October.

Jin Ju. 2001. "Life Science and Biotechnology in China." Speech by the head of the Chinese Delegation at the 5th Session of the United Nations Commission on Science and Technology for Development, Geneva.

World Health Organization (WHO). 2002. *Active Ageing, A Policy Framework.* Geneva: WHO.

The authors gratefully acknowledge the contributions of Sunil Chacko, M.D., Science and Conscience Foundation.

⮕ EAST TIMOR:
VOLUNTEERS EASE THE TRANSITION BETWEEN WAR AND RECONSTRUCTION

In a Nutshell

When it broke away from Indonesia, East Timor was left bereft of administrative and technical capacity. Amidst the backdrop of conflict and crisis, UNV made use of volunteers to bridge the gap. This case illustrates two areas where UNV helped build local capacity – in a fisheries project and in civic education – using a mix of skills, knowledge, catalytic technical inputs and innovation. The volunteers themselves were mid-career professionals with a high degree of proficiency.

The case profiles how volunteers can serve as powerful instruments of technical cooperation, more so in situations of post-conflict reconstruction where trust and human interaction are critical.

The Story

The decision of the East Timorese to seek independence from Indonesia in August 1999 confronted the country with immense challenges. For almost three decades, East Timor had been administered by the Indonesian authorities through qualified Indonesian nationals; they could not be expected to carry on in an independent nation. Illiteracy rates were high among the Timorese, with the few who had been educated and possessed useful skills having mostly left for other countries. Added to this was the inherent difficulty of a multi-lingual society, where most young people of the Indonesian era speak Bahasa as a first language, while the older generation that would form the fledging government is comfortable with and has institutionalized Portuguese as the main working language.

The outbreak of violence that followed the independence referendum compounded these challenges with the burden of reconstructing what had been deliberately destroyed. More importantly, the Timorese needed to develop the determination and ability to live under and exercise the democratic process that they had voted for.

This is the context within which the UN Transitional Authority in East Timor has worked since 1999. Under the authority and in cooperation with the Timorese, some 3,000 UN volunteers from over 100 countries were recruited and deployed between 1999 and 2002 to work on projects in some 160 areas within the new government, particularly at the district level.

One important initiative involved the revival of fisheries. For generations, coastal communities had relied on fishing for their livelihoods. But at least 90 per cent of the East Timorese coastal fleet, fishing gear and onshore infrastructure was destroyed in 1999. While thousands of people, including fisher folk, fled the territory, those who stayed behind desperately needed to resume fishing activities, and in a sustainable way. A team of UN volunteers arrived to assist in setting up the Ministry of Agriculture and Fisheries; some were assigned to the Department of Fisheries and Marine Environment.

The volunteers started by focusing on maritime fishing, helping fishermen acquire nets and boat engines. They conducted workshops on boat building to draw other people into the sector, while ensuring the future repair or replacement of used vessels. By the end of 2001, local fishing reached 60 per cent of 1997 production. Inland hatcheries were also reconstructed in order to support freshwater fish production, and volunteers trained less-experienced East Timorese to raise more than 5,000 common carp fingerlings. They then approached rice farmers and, through field support and demonstration, encouraged them to optimize their use of land and water by breeding fish in rice fields. Across East Timor's 13 administrative districts, this fostered renewed confidence in the country's development potential. Simultaneously, at the department's central office, volunteers also trained a team of 18 fisheries officers, as a means to continuously support the initiative at the local, intermediate and national levels.

Much remains to be done. Technical staffing has touched barely 20 per cent of its level before independence. Yet the country's legal fishing grounds have now expanded considerably. The department's next task needs to be developing and implementing adequate legislation on fisheries and marine resources, with special attention to securing the interests of local communities while tapping the potential of industrial fisheries.

Another UNV project supported civic education. It began during the 1999 referendum when some 500 volunteers, together with teams of nationals, helped organize and supervise the electoral civic education and registration processes. The volunteers also trained and prepared the teams to lead the polling process. This initial investment paid off in subsequent electoral activities, when far fewer international volunteers were needed.

Civic education became all the more crucial after the outbreak of violence. In response, UNDP launched a programme to activate a two-way flow of information between the capital, Dili, and the districts and local communities. It also helped create space and opportunities for people's participation in governance and the wider development process. As part of this effort, volunteers were recruited to work with civil society organizations on developing plans for civic education; producing relevant materials, including those for mass information programmes; and organizing and coordinating financial grants. Throughout, they focused on raising local people's awareness and catalysing their commitment to human rights, democracy and citizenship.

The initiative relied on the strong links tying together civil society organizations in East Timor – mainly indigenous and international NGOs as well as the Catholic Church – and their daily contacts with the population. Particular emphasis was placed on developing the capacity of East Timorese local staff from various organizations to carry out civic education in the districts and sub-districts as part of their ongoing development activities. Fifteen people were fully trained on civic education, including substantive aspects and technical skills. Fifty organizations received grants and training as well. A network of civil society groups was subsequently established, along with resource centres in the three regions of the country. Today, the resource centres have become community-owned and managed, and operate as information focal points for interaction between the government and civil society.

Results and Critical Factors

- Both cases show how technical cooperation can support the development of capacities in post-crisis situations at the individual as well as institutional levels, through locally owned processes.

- In East Timor, the dynamic mobilization and support of civil society has stirred increased local engagement and a determination to foster democratic processes, both in developmental activities and governance. The local resource centres and the network of civil society organizations offer promising ground for increased ownership and sustainability.

- The profiles and approaches of the UN volunteers played a key role in these results; these are mid-career specialists from over 100 countries with 10-15 years of professional experience. They left their homes for a temporary – usually short-term – assignment in East Timor, coping with tough living conditions in rural areas. The volunteers' continued proximity with counterparts and local populations, their non-threatening interaction with them, and the confidence that resulted enabled them to energize local people's drive towards committed engagement in their own development process. Gradually, East Timorese took the lead.

- In any post-crisis situation, short-term results that can stimulate people's enthusiasm and commitment must mix with a longer term perspective reflected through appropriate mechanisms for sustainability and gradual scaling-up.

- It is necessary to involve the local population from the outset of increased autonomy. The human interaction approach of the volunteers is particularly appropriate towards this end.

Further information

United Nations Volunteers (UNV) Timor-Leste (www.unvolunteers.org/dynamic/cfapps/coun-tryprofiles/country.cfm?CountryID=TMP).

Tarik Jasarevic. 2002. "Reviving Fisheries in East Timor - Casting Nets for Development." In *UNV News,* 93 (www.unvolunteers.org/infobase/unv_news/2002/93/02_08_93TMP_fish.htm).

Government of East Timor (www.gov.east-timor.org/).

The authors gratefully acknowledge the contributions of William Adrianasolo, Douglas Campos, Josette Navarro and Kevin Gilroy, UNV.

↪ ECUADOR:
NATIONAL DIALOGUE RALLIES CONSENSUS ON SUSTAINABLE DEVELOPMENT

> ### In a Nutshell
>
> In Ecuador, under the aegis of the Dialogue 21 programme, information and communication tools have created room for a public discourse that has brought together social, political, governmental and economic forces around sustainable human development.
>
> Together, a spectrum of people have built consensus in a crisis situation, engendering trust and changing previously confrontational and suspicious mindsets. External agencies played a facilitating role, used flexible and adaptive aid instruments, built on the practices of local institutions, and inspired confidence among the different groups. The overall experience was so successful that it may offer a model for replication in other fragile states or post-crisis situations.

The Story

Dialogue 21 is an Ecuadorian national project that began in 1999. It encourages the use of information and communication for promoting sustainable development and initiating contact between the country's diverse (i.e. ethnic, racial, etc.) social actors. The project was designed to respond to Ecuador's climate of crisis, which is not only political, with four presidents in less than 18 months, but also economic and social. Different segments of Ecuadorian society have found themselves locked in a state of permanent confrontation.

The project works on three overlapping levels. The first develops capacity among local leaders through training and information awareness on matters relating to local sustainable development. Those with a high school education can study at the Universidad Politécnica Salesiana, where the curriculum includes learning about the theory of sustainable development in a local environment, project design, resource mobilization, communication for development and social participation techniques. Those without a formal education can take part in an informal education process called a "local dialoguers' network", which organizes training workshops, distributes monthly information bulletins and broadcasts a twice-monthly radio programme where students can join in.

At its second level, Dialogue 21 participates in the design, management and approval of public policies that will lead to legislation supporting local action. One significant result of this was the Law on Parochial Committees, which took effect in October 2000. Dialogue 21 helped prepare the regulations governing the committees and negotiate an annual budget.

The third and all-embracing level promotes a national culture of dialogue through television and radio. TV spots show social actors in different situations, such as the military or the Church, talking with ethnic leaders. Their message is clear: "Dialogue is possible, dialogue enriches whoever engages in it as long as it is based on respect for others." Radio spots are on specific sustainable development themes that are of interest to different provinces and localities. They are sent to community stations, and local personalities debate the subjects.

The synergy among all three levels of Dialogue 21 is of utmost importance. Training local leaders in sustainable development becomes significant to the extent that it is backed by national laws and a permanent culture of dialogue.

From its inception, Dialogue 21 has built systematically on the broader Capacity 21 methodology, used across Latin America and around the world to implement Agenda 21, the action agenda for sustainable development that emerged from the 1992 UN Conference on the Environment and Development. In developing Ecuador's local capacities for sustainable development, Capacity 21, as a neutral facilitator, has sparked confidence with its "horizontal style". It uses three principles of Agenda 21: participation, information and integration. Engaging in a flexible, agreed-upon planning process, it adapts to the context and specific needs of those participating, and applies the lessons learned about sustainable development gathered from other countries in the region.

Dialogue 21 has now developed its own methodology, called "Esquinas para el Dialogo" (dialogue corners). It is a common Ecuadorian cultural practice for people to congregate in the course of their daily activities – in the neighbourhood, the parish, street corners, local shops and markets. They gather, talk about themselves and whatever is happening, and, in general, trade gossip. The challenge for Dialogue 21 was to adopt this practice for exchanging information about sustainable development at local, provincial and national levels.

To date, 18 "Esquinas para el Dialogo" have taken place – 14 local, three regional and one national – with a total participation of 883 people. Thirty-two per cent were women, 12 per cent were members of indigenous communities, and 4 per cent were Afro-Ecuadorians. National training was given to 60 communities, and there is now a network of 44 leaders or local "dialoguers" in place.

The following have been identified as challenges for the future: to work on building individual, local, national and global links for sustainable development; to strengthen the connections between projects and processes in order to clarify Dialogue 21's role; to open lines of research on the relationship between self-esteem and the articulation of political opinions; and, as one of the best expressions of a strategy to develop local capacities, to work tirelessly on formal and informal education to train local leaders on sustainable development.

Results and Critical Factors

The progress that has been made towards generating consensus and commitment to the principles of sustainable development, and the ability of formerly suspicious groups to work together may be attributed to the following:

- Using dialogue as a strategic instrument for building consensus, engendering trust and changing previously confrontational mindsets among diverse groups to chart a course forward in a post-crisis situation

- Building on the experiences and practices of local institutions and processes, and adapting these to meet contemporary needs

- Engaging external agencies in a facilitating role, which inspires confidence among stakeholder groups

- Using flexible and adaptable aid instruments that ensured the programme could respond to changing circumstances and needs

- Working at different levels to mobilize and strengthen different capacities, and in so doing, building synergy between the skills development of individuals, a revamped policy framework, and new participatory processes for dialogue and exchange among state and non-state actors

Further information

Capacity 21. 2001. *From Projects to Processes. From Rio to Johannesburg: Latin American Experiences in Sustainable Development*. UNDP Regional Capacity 21 Coordination for Latin America. Mexico City.

————. n.d. *Communications: A Strategic Axis Towards Human Sustainable Development*. Capacity 21 Approaches to Sustainability Series (www.undp.org/capacity21).

Dialogue 21. 2001. *Work Report 2001*. Quito.

Reforming Technical Cooperation for Capacity Development. 2002. "Insights in 1000 Words" (http://capacity.undp.org/cases/insights/romero.htm).

The authors gratefully acknowledge the contributions of Jose Romero, Capacity 21 Latin America, UNDP.

➲ EGYPT:
A CONFIDENT COMMUNITY LEARNS TO MANAGE ITS ENVIRONMENT

In a Nutshell

A poor community in northern Egypt mobilized itself to improve waste water processing. The Geziret El Sheir project succeeded in establishing a regular and fully functional system for waste water collection and disposal. As confidence grew in its own ability to bring about change, the community embarked on improvements in other aspects of environmental management. All along, local authorities offered vital contributions not only to the project, but also in replicating and upstreaming the experience.

The Story

Geziret El Sheir, an island in the Nile that is part of El Qanater city in the governorate of Qalubia, has some 7,000 inhabitants living in six small settlements. They have electricity, potable water and household cesspits, but until recently, solid waste collection was inadequate, there was no proper waste water removal, and the cesspits often overflowed. Residents were supposed to take their garbage to public dumps, but they usually flung it in the street, along the Nile or into irrigation canals. Piles of garbage and pools of stagnant water were common.

To address these issues, a project was conceived based on local dialogue and community-based participatory planning. It drew upon the active contributions of women and worked closely with the administration of the Qalubia Governorate.

The initiative is one of many supported by UNDP's Local Initiative Facility for the Urban Environment (LIFE) programme and the German Technical Assistance Agency (GTZ), both of which encourage joint action between the local community and formal institutions, as well as the participation of marginalized groups such as women in needs assessments and planning.

The initiative began with the Community Development Association (CDA) conducting initial field research and then preparing a fact-finding questionnaire with help from LIFE/GTZ, which was administered to a sample of the population. Based on these findings, multi-stakeholder workshops were held to bring residents and other actors together, introduce the participatory planning approach, build consensus on priority needs and appropriate solutions, agree on a plan of action and foster women's participation. It was decided that 25 local volunteers – 15 of them women – would act as a link between residents and the CDA, which contributed more than $6,000 to the project. Using the ZOPP (*ziel orientere projekt planung*, or objectives-oriented project planning) methodology, workshop participants identified three priority problems ranked in descending order: cesspit overflow, lack of solid waste management and unemployment among youth.

In addition to improving the environment, the project had other, equally important social goals. These included stimulating long-term behavioural changes related to sanitation, and establishing sustainable dialogue between the community and the local authority, elected popular councils and the private sector.

Subsequently, a series of environmental awareness campaigns began urging positive attitudes towards environmental sanitation and disseminating best practices for hygienic procedures. LIFE/GTZ provided technical assistance to the CDA to prepare a management plan for waste water collection by truck, which required a database to design an efficient truck route, so houses in Geziret El Sheir were numbered for the first time. The local authority authorized the disposal of waste water in a drainage canal, and a plan was made to collect fees for regular cesspit emptying and cleaning. Paid to the CDA, the fees were decided by the community itself and were slightly higher than those that had been charged by the municipality. Residents were willing to pay because their participation in the decision-making process had given them a sense of ownership and a stake in the improvements that were taking place.

The launch of the system was celebrated in a ceremony attended by the Governor of Qalubia, members of the People's Assembly, some members of local popular councils and the CDA board, residents of the community, and representatives from other communities and NGOs who were keen to learn about the Geziret El Sheir experience.

It has since become clear that the role of local authorities was indispensable in the project's success. As partners in all its phases, they made available two workers in two shifts for the waste water collection system. They also provided technical training for the collection staff, maintenance services and equipment. And they paved half a kilometre of road to allow the truck easy access.

Once the problem of waste water collection was solved, other local initiatives began, including a solid waste management project that established a garbage collection system. But perhaps the greatest impact was the empowerment of young men and women through their work as community volunteers. They received training in how to conduct environmental awareness campaigns, disseminate a project concept, and act as a link between the CDA and the community. This training and their involvement in different project activities helped build their self-confidence and sense of empowerment. Two volunteers, one male and one female, have now become members of a Project Development Committee responsible for long-term project management after the LIFE/GTZ team has phased out. For young Egyptian women who have limited opportunities, this is a relatively acceptable and accessible way to exercise their authority and influence. At a second workshop at which 43 community representatives and local authority officials were present, women's participation was remarkable and very effective.

Results and Critical Factors

The Geziret El Sheir project created a cleaner living environment, while broadening the capacity of the community and inspiring self-confidence, including among women. Better organized community development associations and new partnerships with the local authorities have opened doors for creative initiatives and fuelled a willingness for further participation. Community volunteers, particularly youth and women, have gained the knowledge and skills to carry out environmental upgrading and citizen's awareness campaigns.

Factors that contributed to the success of the project include the following:

- The use of a systematic approach including appropriate technology, social mobilization, and community training to help small localities address big problems and benefit from a positive psychological impact

- The identification of problems clearly apparent in daily life, followed by considerable achievements, leading to bigger actions with fewer inputs and costs, and drawing upon the moral infrastructure, self-confidence and capacity

- The promotion of local dialogue as an effective means to organize communities for common action and for building effective partnerships

- The involvement of local authorities right from the beginning, which proved critical not only to the project but also in replicating and upstreaming the experience

- The employment of strategic "pre-actions" activities, such as area mapping, surveys, training of volunteers, etc., which contributed greatly to the success of the project and comprised a valuable social asset

Further information

Local Initiative Facility for the Urban Environment (LIFE). 2001. *External Evaluation of LIFE Global Programme.* Management Development and Governance Division. New York: UNDP.

Local Initiative Facility for the Urban Environment (LIFE) and German Technical Assistance (GTZ). 2001. *Geziret El Sheir: Joint Evaluation Report.*

German Ministry of Economic Cooperation (www.bmz.de).

United Nations Development Programme (UNDP). Forthcoming. *LIFE: A Decade of Lessons in Participatory Local Governance to Improve Living Conditions of the Poor.* New York: UNDP.

The authors gratefully acknowledge the contributions of Pratibha Mehta, UNDP/LIFE.

➲ EGYPT:
GOVERNORATE HUMAN DEVELOPMENT REPORTS PROVIDE
ANALYSIS AT THE COMMUNITY LEVEL

In a Nutshell

In 1993, Egypt became one of the first countries to produce a national human development report (NHDR). The process cultivated statistical capacities relating to human development indexes and other socioeconomic indicators; indeed, it was only after the 1996 NHDR that poverty terminology came into use. Today, the government's Five-Year Plan (2002-2006) incorporates analysis and planning from the human development standpoint. Human development indexes were disaggregated at the municipal level in 2002, and efforts are underway to prepare regional human development reports with disaggregation to the village level.

Clearly, the NHDR has become a major human development advocacy tool in Egypt, while facilitating capacity development with respect to poverty analysis and development planning.

The Story

Since its first NHDR in 1993, Egypt has produced a report almost every year, in collaboration with the Institute of National Planning (INP) and the local UNDP office. In the process, new statistical capabilities have flourished within the INP and its mother institution, the Ministry of Planning. NHDR contributions to capacity development for poverty analysis and development planning include the creation in 1996 of a methodology for calculating a national poverty line, and the production of the first reliable estimates of poverty in the country, disaggregated by region.

The reports have been adopted unofficially by the government and are being used in ILO and World Bank poverty-related analyses. They also provided the baseline information for the projections in Egypt's first MDG report, prepared by the UN Country Team in 2002. The NHDRs' calcuations of human development indexes at the regional or governorate level have been adopted by the Egyptian Social Fund for Development and other government local investment programmes, such as Shourok, as a method for earmarking resources.

By virtue of the visibility and quality of the reports, the then NHDR coordinator was appointed Minister of Planning in 2001. This has allowed him to continue the process of capacity development from within the government, where the concept and terminology of human development has become ever more apparent in processes, documents and events. The current Five-Year Plan, for instance, has incorporated human development analysis and planning, along with related targets and indicators. Through the parallel but coordinated work of the National

Council of Women and UNDP, gender sensitive budgeting has also appeared, while the progressive spread of human development concepts within the Ministry, and in the government more generally, opened the planning process to private-sector participation in 2002.

In recent years, the NHDR has become an even more influential document, retaining its quality without losing the autonomy and neutrality of its authors and content. In the 2003 report, following the disaggregation of human development indexes at the municipal level, a series of indicators was produced for each of 451 municipalities, and used by the UNDP office to devise an electronically search-able, map-centred geographic database.

The analysis of spatial development disparities has since prompted the Prime Minister to request that a programme be prepared, together with UNDP, for the dozens of municipalities that showed poor results. Because of its multidiscipli-nary nature and significant size, this initiative will promote coordination not only among UN agencies. It will also be one of the first actions envisaged in a National Poverty Reduction Action Plan that is being prepared by the Ministry of Planning with the support of the World Bank, UNDP and ILO.

The analytical and substantive capacities generated by the NHDRs have not remained confined to the INP or the Ministry of Planning. UNDP is now support-ing, with co-financing from the Danish government, the preparation of governorate reports, led by the Ministry of Local Development. The first seven reports appeared in 2003, with preparations for the remaining 20 underway. These have pushed HDI disaggregation to Egypt's 4,500 villages. Their detailed analysis will allow not only precision in tackling local development issues and pri-oritizing investments by type and size, but also the opportunity to sustain a process of local participatory development planning and monitoring, which has been a feature of report preparation. At the same time, awareness has grown swiftly among local authorities, who have started to adopt human development concepts, measurements and terminology.

Results and Critical Factors

The availability of pertinent data at the village, municipal and governorate levels has guided advocacy on human development across Egypt, allowing the targeting of pressing priorities. At the same time, capacity development for poverty analy-sis and development planning at the national level is now spreading to the sub-national arena. Besides contributing to Egypt's five-year planning process, the NHDR database makes socioeconomic information available for the first time through maps and a query system, providing a vital planning tool for government departments and donors. Factors that account for the success of the NHDRs include the following:

- From the outset, a national institution, INP, was charged with the responsibility for coordinating the preparation of the reports, with UNDP providing a critical support role.

- A strong commitment on the part of the director of INP ensured that HDR policy analysis was woven into national systems and procedures, which also strengthened individual and organizational capacities.

- Opportunities have been deliberately created to draw on in-country expertise that supports the development of the NHDRs, and to encourage the broad-based participation of different sectors of society in the formulation and review process, including in selecting the theme, conducting research and carrying out peer reviews.

Further information

Egypt Human Development Report 2003
(www.undp.org.eg/publications/ENHDR_2003/NHDR2003.htm).

Donors Assistance Group (DAG). 2001. Position paper on social development. Cairo.

UN Country Team. 2002. *Millennium Development Goals Report for Egypt*
(www.undp.org/mdg/egypt.pdf).

———. 2001. *Common Country Assessment* (www.undp.org.eg/rc/cca.pdf).

———. 2002. *United Nations Development Assistance Framework*
(www.undp.org.eg/programme/ccf.pdf).

Government of Egypt. 1997. *2017 Vision for Egypt*. Cairo.

The authors gratefully acknowledge the contributions of UNDP Egypt.

⮑ ESTONIA:
THE INNOVATIVE USE OF FOUNDATIONS TO IMPLEMENT NATIONAL POLICIES

In a Nutshell

Since 1996, Estonia has been using foundations as a legal and institutional mechanism to support national policies and programmes in areas as diverse as the environment, infrastructure development, facilitation of exports, entrepreneurship and foreign investment, educational reform, social integration, information technology, and preservation of art and culture.

While the jury is still out on the impact of foundations on national development, the case does offer food for thought, both in terms of the merits of providing targeted capacity development support to them, and, more importantly, in considering how they can strengthen a government and beneficiary groups.

The Story

In 1996, Estonia's Ministry of Culture and Education undertook a European Union funded programme for the reform of vocational education and training. The Union provided $4 million to work according to its system for decentralized implementation of programmes. This involved setting up an institution outside of the ministry. It was agreed to establish a mechanism that resembled a programme implementation unit, but ultimately was something more and different: a separate legal body.

The programme was able to do this through new legislation that regulated Estonia's non-governmental and non-profit sector. The Foundations Act, one of several laws regulating the non-profit sector, had come into force in 1996. It states that a foundation is a legal entity under private law. It has no members and administers assets to achieve the objectives specified in its articles of association. A foundation is not necessarily a mere endowment or a grant-bestowing institution, although the act allows it to serve these functions.

While the Foundations Act was not passed explicitly for the purpose of implementing national development programmes, foundations were soon adopted as a tool for funding and carrying out certain key state programmes, whether financed primarily from government funds, or, as was more likely, from a multitude of sources, including donors, the private sector and municipal governments. Foundations' legal and financial liability framework, the possibility of enhanced partnerships and stakeholder involvement, and the flexibility to determine foundation activities made them an increasingly popular choice.

From 1996 to 2002, about 500 foundations were registered, of which 74 were founded by the government or municipalities to implement development-related programmes. Of these, 30 have the government as a primary or only founder; 17

have the government as an indirect founder (i.e. through county governments, which are administratively beholden to the national level), and 27 have a municipality as a founder.

The membership of supervisory boards for development-related foundations is broad-based and ensures strong stakeholder participation and consensus. Typically, the boards include representatives of various government and sometimes municipal bodies, non-governmental organizations, the private sector, research institutes and universities, and beneficiaries. The right to membership brings with it legal and financial liabilities and responsibilities, which are shouldered by both the supervisory boards and the managing directors. Sectoral government ministers remain accountable to the Cabinet and the public for results.

The foundation approach is semi-governmental in nature. While legally the foundations are non-governmental bodies, the government by default has a more prominent role as either a primary founder or a co-funder in most cases. Depending on the particulars of a foundation's articles of association, a primary founder may possess certain entitlements that other partners do not have, such as the right to appoint members to the supervisory boards, even if boards have remained well harmonized and representative of stakeholders. Thus a balance can ultimately be achieved between alignment with national priorities and broad participation.

Results and Critical Factors

As an alternative model for national programme implementation, the Estonian experience could, with certain reservations, be considered positive. The approach has contributed greatly to national capacities and public administration in selected sectors: the Tiger Leap Foundation, for example, is sensitizing the Estonian education system on ICT, while the Integration Foundation addresses the social integration of ethnic minorities. Specific benefits have included:

- Close alignment with national priorities resulting from the relationship between the programme and the policy framework, and the fact that ultimate accountability rests with national authorities

- A government focus on policy and oversight as opposed to implementation, which has improved programme continuity and accommodated adjustments across changes in leadership

- Active stakeholder participation and broad consensus on policy and programme directions

- The pooling of resources and the ability to achieve cross-programme synergies in cases where a particular donor is unwilling or unable to take this approach

The use of foundations in Estonia is not without its challenges. The process of improving links between programmes and policies can slip into a heavy focus on outcome results, while the nature of cooperation between ministry, agency and foundation staff needs to be better delineated, especially where several sectors and/or beneficiary groups are involved. In spite of shared participation on supervisory boards, some perceptions exist that beneficiary influence should be enhanced and the government role reduced; otherwise, there is a risk that supervisory boards will cede to political whims. There is also a need to better integrate the financial management systems of foundations with those of national agencies. Concerns persist as well that there are too many foundations, raising fears of inefficiency and lack of coordination.

Further information

Jerzy Celichowski. 2001. *Estonian e-Democracy Report* (www.osi.hu/infoprogram/e-government%20in%20estonia%20proof%20read.htm).

The Foundations Act (www.legaltext.ee/text/en/X1014K3.htm).

The Integration Foundation (www.meis.ee).

Integration of Non-Estonians into Estonian Society: Setting the Course. UNDP integration-themed discussion paper (www.undp.ee/integrat/).

The Tiger Leap Foundation (www.tiigrihype.ee).

The authors gratefully acknowledge the contributions of Robert Juhkam, UNDP.

⮕ **ESTONIA:**
TIGER LEAP BRINGS THE BENEFITS OF ICT TO EVERYONE

In a Nutshell

The Estonian government has pursued a policy of integrating ICT into the everyday life of Estonians as well as using it to promote socioeconomic development and good governance. As a result, Estonia has achieved a high level of e-readiness over a short time, with one of the best rates of public access in Europe.

These achievements stem from partnerships developed between local and international stakeholders, the innovative use of foundations to provide a legal and institutional framework, and a strong national vision to harness the power of ICT for national development. In this context, donors have played a catalysing role, offering technical guidance and financial assistance to a locally driven process.

The Story

Estonia's connection to the wired world began with an initial focus on introducing ICT to the education sector through the now well-reputed "Tiger Leap" programme. Its success provided the impetus to extend integration to other sectors and walks of life.

Launched in 1996, Tiger Leap set out to develop IT infrastructure in schools, including Internet connections; help teachers acquire basic computer skills and learn to use ICT in subject teaching; support the updating of curricula and promote learning skills; and encourage the creation of Estonia-specific and Estonian language software. The programme eventually trained 10,900 out of the 17,000 teachers in Estonia; supplied 61 different educational software programmes to schools, including 39 in Estonian; and supported 172 development and training initiatives through project competitions.

At the beginning, the Tiger Leap Foundation was established to manage the programme, administering $13.5 million in resources from 1997 to 2002. Led by the Ministry of Education, its co-founders included ten private companies, an association of Estonian computer firms and 26 individuals.

In the wake of the success of the education project, the government invited UNDP to prepare a discussion paper on ICT as a socioeconomic catalyst, hoping to widen awareness and inspire public discussion that would ultimately result in policy development. For UNDP, this served as a timely upstream complement to an earlier and more downstream Internet project, which included setting up a public email server and the first four Internet access points in Estonia, three of which were in rural areas of Estonia's second largest island.

Five respected public figures from a variety of backgrounds prepared the discussion paper, entitled "The Estonian Tiger Leaps into the 21st Century". It recommended:

- Access for everyone, with Estonia aiming to become the first country where logging on to the Internet is a human right

- Creation of a total overall learning environment, with ICT skills as one cornerstone, so as to increase capacity and capabilities across the board

- Full virtualization of the public sector

The Tiger Leap Foundation thereafter initiated two ICT road shows in 1998 and 1999, known as the "Tiger Tours". In various towns and villages, huge tents were raised over 100 or so Internet-connected computers, with public access and hands-on training. Core funding was provided by the Estonian Union Bank; Microlink, a home start-up computer company that now spans the Estonia, Latvia and Lithuania markets and beyond; and the Estonian Telephone Company. Other sponsors included IT companies, several media firms, UNDP, the Soros Foundation and local governments.

All sides benefited. The bank netted new e-banking customers; Microlink probably sold more home computers; and the Estonian Telephone Company signed up people for Internet service packages. Rural and town residents crossed a knowledge gap. Gaining first-hand experience and new bits of information, they learned that everyday government, banking or self-education could be conducted via public access points.

Meanwhile, the government reaped rewards that continue to unfold. The sensitization of the wider population and imparting of skills helped create an audience eager to take advantage of the launch of the government's e-governance efforts. Examples include a direct democracy citizen portal; the e-Tax Board project, which provides a simple way to e-manage individual tax accounts and assists government receipt of taxes; steps taken towards offering Internet voting for the 2005 elections; and paperless government Cabinet sessions.

Countless other ICT projects and activities have sprung from the momentum and interest generated by the Tiger Leap programme. The ICT private sector has flourished, a college dedicated to IT has been founded, and a legal and regulatory framework now guides further development.

Results and Critical Factors

Estonia's relatively high level of e-readiness has emerged over a short time. Approximately 500 public access Internet points dot the country, with 36 per 100,000 persons. In 2002, some 40 percent of Estonians considered themselves Internet users, with a similar proportion conducting their daily banking via the Web. Through the e-governance initiative, the government has made itself more accessible, participatory and transparent. These developments in turn have made Estonia more competitive internationally, with its expertise attracting attention. Future challenges now include ensuring sustainability and maintaining momentum to garner additional benefits.

Estonia's achievements can be attributed to:

- Partnerships developed between local and international stakeholders; the part played by the government in proactively bringing different interest groups together; and the innovative use of foundations to manage the partnerships

- A strong national vision to harness the powers of ICT for national development, and a willingness among other local actors, including the private sector, to invest in the process

- The catalysing role of donors, who offered technical guidance and financial assistance at strategically important times

Further information

Jerzy Celichowski. 2001. *Estonian e-Democracy Report* (www.osi.hu/infoprogram/e-government%20in%20estonia%20proof%20read.htm).

ESIS Knowledge Base: Information Society Promotion Office (www.esis.ee/ist2000/esis/projects/tigertour.htm).

IT College (www.itcollege.ee/inenglish/index.php).

A. Meier. "Estonia On-Line" (www.time.com/time/europe/specials/eeurope/field/estonia.html).

A. Meier. "Estonia's Tiger Leap to Technology." In *UNDP Choices* (www.undp.org/dpa/choices/2000/june/p10-12.htm).

The Tiger Leap Foundation (www.tiigrihype.ee).

The authors gratefully acknowledge the contributions of Robert Juhkam, UNDP.

⮑ ETHIOPIA:
A PRSP ENCOUNTERS THE CONSTRAINTS AND PROMISES OF PARTICIPATION

In a Nutshell

The preparation of PRSPs offers interesting experiences in civic engagement in policy-making. While participatory policy formulation is highly desirable, its design has proven hard to fashion and continues to be dogged by flaws related to quality and depth, conditionality and ownership of the change process.

The preparation of Ethiopia's recent PRSP demonstrated all of these issues. While it built on lessons learned from earlier papers to attempt more genuine participation, large capacity gaps, government foot-dragging and donors' occasional undue influence all imposed constraints. Nevertheless, the paper has yielded a number of promising results. The government's leadership in moving from an interim to a full PRSP as well as the efforts of independent civil society think-tanks to capture the public mood and develop capacity for participation must count as highlights.

The Story

Nearly half of Ethiopia's population lives in poverty, and a chronic drought has persisted for many years, both factors that have countered reasonably robust economic performance. Against this backdrop, an interim PRSP (I-PRSP) paper was prepared in September 2000 outlining an agenda for policy reform and institutional change to reduce poverty. Observations and comments for improvements were provided by independent institutions of civil society, including the Christian Relief and Development Association (CRDA), Forum for Social Studies (FSS), the InterAfrica Group (IAG), the Ethiopian Economic Policy Research Institute (EEPRI) and the donor community.

The I-PRSP was subsequently presented for nationwide discussion in early 2002. Through regional and federal steering committees and consultative forums, government departments garnered an array of public perspectives. In particular, 6,000 people joined *woreda* (district council) consultations (in 117 out of 550 rural and urban *woredas*) to debate poverty. The participation of women was relatively high due to the efforts of the regional technical secretariat and sector bureaux.

Regional consultations followed among some 2,000 people. Parallel meetings with representatives from pastoral communities and discussions at the Ethio-Forum, organized by the Ethiopian Social Relief and Development Fund (ESRDF), provided vital inputs, while other civil society institutions organized their own independent forums. Eventually, a federal PRSP consultation brought together

450 persons representing different governmental and non-governmental stake-holders, following which the government officially released the full PRSP.

More than anything else, the PRSP exercise provided an opportunity for civil society to engage in the public policy process, making it more transparent. Public participation in the national conference revolved mainly around the nature of agenda and priority setting, as stakeholders attempted to persuade the government to include their concerns, and lobbied for allocations of sufficient resources within the PRSP framework. This helped make the PRSP more representative of the interests of a cross-section of society.

Another key feature was that organizations like IAG set about developing capacities for participation at the district and regional levels. This included train-ing of facilitators and rapporteurs, encouraging the media to raise public awareness of the PRSP, and working to sensitize parliamentarians. The FSS, an independent policy research institute, ran a programme of public debates and consultations involving government policy makers, civil society, representatives from the private sector, and the poor themselves for nearly two years. The key policy issues discussed were submitted in the form of the *Consolidated Report of FSS' Public Debates and Consultation* to aid the PRSP process. FSS also provided a forum for the poor to tell their own story to the public.

The final PRSP was quite an improvement over the I-PRSP. It incorporates the divergent views of many segments of civil society and the donor community. Offering a more thorough and comprehensive analysis of the poverty situation in the country along social and spatial dimensions, it probes incidence, depth and severity along gender, age, and rural and urban dimensions, based on reliable empirical data. Further, the policy recommendations and action plans have originated from rigorous assessments that include the suggestions forwarded by the different stakeholders

Ethiopia's PRSP subsequently inspired the preparation of a strategy paper for a Sustainable Development and Poverty Reduction Programme (SDPRP), in which the government has expressed its commitment to linking poverty with fast, broad-based, equitable and sustainable growth. The SDPRP identifies four core policies and strategies as building blocks for poverty reduction: industrialization led by agricultural development, judicial and civil service reform, decentralization, and empowerment and capacity building.

Some 12 bilateral agencies, as well as UNDP and the European Union, pledged $50,000 each towards the PRSP process between July 2001 and July 2002. The World Bank, IDA and the government of Japan provided $825,977, most of which was in the form of technical cooperation, while the African Development Bank offered $300,000. With these commitments, donors signalled their belief in the PRSP's potential to serve as a channel for more effective relationships among devel-opment partners in the country. They have now proposed a regular joint forum for monitoring and managing the paper, so that multi-stakeholder forums can be sustained.

It is anticipated that through a continuous and constructive engagement with the government of Ethiopia, the donor community will find it more appropriate to channel assistance through national processes, especially in the form of budget support.

Results and Critical Factors

PRSPs have been among the more debated innovations in the development discourse in recent times. Envisaged as instruments of consultative policy-making, they have had a mixed track record, from donor-dominated processes in Cambodia and Senegal to more genuinely participatory ones in Bolivia and Ethiopia. While the intent of the PRSP methodology is sound, criticism stems from the issue of "genuine" participation – in terms of coverage, time allowed for discussion, acceptance of divergent views and capacity gaps among the participants. Additionally, the "who leads" questions are central, as are the conditionalities. Ethiopia confronted these concerns, even as it clearly made progress. Some of the following issues were apparent:

- A strong coalition of civil society and the donor community helped formulate a broad-based PRSP. Despite their notable contributions, however, many civil society organizations had limited capacity to engage in rigorous socioeconomic research to the extent of influencing the economic policy-making process and outcomes.

- The government's commitment to a participatory policy process was the key to success. Initially, it did not embrace subjecting the I-PRSP to wider public discussion and consultation. However, this attitude was gradually but surely turned around.

- Civil society institutions that were involved in the consultations used innovative methods to influence the PRSP. The training of these organizations to participate was also a step forward.

- Best practices and experiences from other African countries helped improve participation. An examination of initiatives in East Africa yielded models for how to engage civil society. In particular, a round table discussion of the experiences of Kenya, Tanzania and Uganda imparted specific lessons on civil society organizations and PRSP design.

- A substantive outcome of the PRSP was the formulation of the SDPRP – a key policy document for Ethiopian society and the economy.

Further information

J. Abdel-Latif. 2003. Presentation at the International Symposium on Capacity Development and Aid Effectiveness, Manila (www.undp.org/capacity/symposium/documents/Civicet.ppt).

Abehe H. Gabreil. 2002. The PRSP Process in Africa (www.uneca.org/prsp/docs/ethiopia_prsp.htm).

C. Lopes. 2002 "Does the New Development Agenda Encapsulate Real Policy Dialogue?" Paper prepared for an EGDI publication. Stockholm.

"Poverty Reduction Strategies and PRSPs: Ethiopia." World Bank Poverty Net (http://poverty.worldbank.org/prsp/index.php?view=ctry&id=58).

The authors gratefully acknowledge the contributions of the InterAfrica Group, particularly of Jalal Abdel Latif and Abebe H Gabriel.

→ GUATEMALA:
COORDINATION AND FLEXIBILITY HELP CIVIL SOCIETY BROKER TRUST AFTER WAR

In a Nutshell

An experience in Guatemala bears lessons for engagement in post-conflict reconstruction. In this case, an assembly of civil society organizations played a key role in starting to rebuild a country devastated by civil war. They were assisted by donors, which devised a coordinated strategy, with one agency acting as facilitator. The careful construction of a process of dialogue, capacity mapping and eventually the commissioning of pilot development projects helped foster an atmosphere of trust that led to civic regeneration.

The Story

In 1996, Guatemala emerged from 36 years of unremitting civil war. As expected, the physical infrastructure was in ruins. But the years of fighting had also left a legacy of widespread mistrust, with psychological scars evident in every walk of life. Human development indicators had plummeted to levels that were among the worst in the world. There seemed little margin for hope, except for the fact that throughout the conflict, civil society organizations had kept the channels of dialogue and reconciliation open. This came at a price though, as many suffered human rights abuses.

When peace first gained a foothold, sincere recognition for civil society efforts followed with the establishment of a Civil Society Assembly, which both the government and the rebels recognized as an interim platform for negotiations and future planning, a middle ground in the hotly contested political space. A multitude of civil society organizations participated, including labour unions, women's organizations, indigenous people's groups and human rights advocates. Broad representation ensured that the Assembly considered diverse concerns, not merely those that the government or revolutionary commanders deemed important. In particular, marginalized communities, indigenous people and women's groups placed great trust in civil society organizations. So besides being a forum for negotiations, the Assembly quickly became a venue for rousing popular support for the peace accords and implementing essential rebuilding tasks.

While it was necessary to centrally involve civil society in development and national reconciliation, it was not at all clear at first how these organizations should or could be engaged in a coordinated fashion by the international community. The peace accord had mapped out an ambitious agenda for reconstruction, but in reality it hit many bumps. Principal among these was the completely withered capacity of the government and major institutions.

At this point, UNDP was asked to play the role of coordinating agency in the reconciliation and capacity development process, even though its own credibility first had to be re-established, because it was seen to have been pro-government during the war. Also, activities had to be carefully chosen so as to unite the full spectrum of civil society organizations.

A three-step process began, encompassing identification and mapping of civil society, assessment of capabilities and cooperation for action. The first stage involved preparing a directory of civil society organizations, which built confidence by teaching the community about itself. It also raised awareness among government agencies and donors about the huge variety of groups working on a vast number of issues.

The second stage assessed the capacities of these organizations, with mainly Guatemalan experts conducting wide-ranging research. They specifically looked at two categories of groups – those focusing on human rights and those representing the Mayan people. The assessments provided a fairly accurate map of civil society organizations, including their areas of operation and core capacities.

With an enhanced understanding of needs and priorities, UNDP helped mobilize funding for the third stage, seeking assistance from bilateral partners, including Norway, Sweden and the Netherlands, as well as from private foundations such as the MacArthur Foundation. Targeted capacity development interventions began – mainly aimed at building institutions and starting small with grants for pilots. This laboratory approach helped distil lessons for subsequent fast-track upscaling, as other donors soon gained confidence to engage with civil society groups. The reconstruction of Guatemala slowly but surely took its first few steps. Since then, the growth in civil society participation in a variety of arenas related to the peace accords, including demobilization, land issues and judicial reform, has been quite remarkable.

Results and Critical Factors

- This case underscores the importance of donor coordination in post-conflict societies with fragile institutional frameworks. Had each donor intervened with its own unique strategy and programming requirements, local capacities, in so far as these existed, would have been overwhelmed – leading to a donor- and development-industry-driven regime.

- A number of flexible aid instruments were applied – their essentially experimental nature allowed room for trial and error.

- The choice of civil society as the principal agent for building trust, and eventually for developing the capacity to deliver services, was a sound decision, given that this sector was the only one with credibility among the various parties to the conflict.

- The somewhat time-consuming participatory mapping exercise highlighted priority areas for engagement, identified potential implementation partners, and ensured that these partners (mostly civil society organizations) were representative of the full range array of stakeholders. Helping to develop civil society capacity in the priority areas made for smooth implementation and easy upscaling of pilot projects later on.

- UNDP played a pivotal role in anchoring the process in Guatemala, mediating between the factions, earning the faith of the various actors stepping forward as the conflict ended, and then helping to nurse smaller pilots until other donors were ready to work with civil society organizations. UNDP itself learned much about engagement with civil society – and more so under difficult circumstances.

Further information

A. Russell. 2000. "Reviving Civil Society in Guatemala: Learning from UNDP's Experience." In *Changing Policy and Practice from Below: Community Experiences in Poverty Reduction. An Examination of Nine Case-Studies.* Edited by Anirudh Krishna. New York: UNDP, Civil Society Team.

United Nations Development Programme (UNDP) Civil Society Division (www.undp.org/csopp/CSO/NewFiles/about.html).

The authors gratefully acknowledge the contributions of Andrew Russell, UNDP.

⮑ GUINEA BISSAU:
BUILDING A RESEARCH INSTITUTION IN AN INHOSPITABLE ENVIRONMENT

In a Nutshell

In Guinea Bissau, a group of motivated academics established a national research institute that became a model of sustainability. It introduced management arrangements that balanced fundamental research on the one hand, and consultancy and practical interventions on the other, with the latter funding much of the research. Contributions from external partners were systematically channelled to one-off operations such as training, infrastructure, equipment or time-bound events. Institutional priorities were considered above individual interests.

The institute became an anchor for professionals who wanted to further their academic knowledge and arrested brain drain. As well as a centre for debating crucial national issues, it ensured a place for democratic values, even amidst a difficult political transition.

The Story

Guinea Bissau's independence in the early 1970s was not accompanied by a proper transition for its public service. Its Portuguese rulers left it devoid of a civil service cadre, and the country came into its new status with a poor education system and only a handful of graduates from external universities. Despite this abysmal record, the former colony had a tradition of socio-historical research renowned in the West African subregion. This was due mostly to the dedicated and almost eccentric interest of a few Portuguese and Cape Verdian scholars organized around the Center for Studies of Portuguese Guinea, one of whom was none other than the eventual leader of the liberation struggle and the "father of Guinea Bissau and Cape Verde nationalities", Amilcar Cabral.

Motivated by this tradition and building on the sheer enthusiasm that bloomed with the establishment of a new country, a group of young academics, trained mostly in western universities, decided to create a new institution from scratch. The National Institute for Studies and Research (INEP in its Portuguese acronym) came into being one decade after independence, despite raised eyebrows about the feasibility of such a public enterprise in a country with so many competing priorities and poor capacity.

Impelled by a strong sense of ownership, this group wanted to be in charge of an alternative way of doing business. It was a time when external cooperation was huge and influential, and Guinea Bissau was benefiting from one of the largest per capita aid levels in Africa. The architecture of INEP was thus based on a set of ambitious principles: the greatest autonomy possible within the parameters of public service, collegial leadership, a strong mandate (for instance, to monopolize the ownership of governmental historical archives, set up a legal copyright registry and serve as the clearing house for expatriate research projects), and a new approach to civil service pay arrangements.

INEP soon put in place a mechanism that would allow its researchers to undertake well-defined, part-time consultancies, provided they fulfilled minimum research requirements. The consultancy remuneration would revert to the institute, which in turn would distribute it in the following portions: 40 per cent for the researcher(s), 20 per cent for remaining institute staff and 40 per cent for institutional development, which could include a library extension, buying a new photo lab or finalizing the microfilming of a particular archive. After just four years, INEP managed to cover 90 per cent of its recurrent expenditures from its own revenue, limiting the state subsidy to the base salary of its staff (which was very low) and the electricity bill. On the other hand, staff in all categories had an income ranging from three times the civil service pay to 25 times (in the case of the most entrepreneurial academics). Another important innovation was the authorization for civil servants to participate in INEP's consultancy or academic teams on a part-time basis. This often allowed higher ranking professionals to garner additional income, in a regulated and supportive framework.

The model and ethos of INEP rapidly attracted a lot of attention, both nationally and internationally. As a result, the institute was never short of partnerships, particularly with institutions that traditionally sponsor research in developing countries, such as the Canadian International Development Research Centre (IDRC), the Swedish Agency for Research Cooperation (SAREC, now integrated into Sida), and various Canadian and European NGOs. Their important contributions helped establish a modern library and training activities, and sponsored equipment (such as computers, cars, etc.) as well as seminars and events. Later, SAREC's funding was totally devoted to an ambitious publications drive.

In its life of nearly two decades, INEP has worked with all the major international organizations and bilateral agencies, including UNDP, UNICEF, UNESCO and the World Bank. The institute's focus has shifted over time from a socio-historic bias to a socioeconomic one. More recently, a strong emphasis on environmental issues resulted in a renewed partnership with the International Union for the Conservation of Nature (IUCN). INEP currently manages the only biosphere reserve in Gambia Bissau.

Today, the institute employs 60 staff, half of whom are professionals.

Results and Critical Factors
- INEP has been able to maintain a credible and sustainable research capacity by offering an alternative to the use of national talent by donor agencies. In so doing, it has also fostered an ethos that has swayed political

developments. It emerged as an institution that actors across the political spectrum wanted to preserve, because they had or could have access to it, but also because it became an important employment alternative for those with the qualifications to join it. This is attractive when important figures find themselves out of political appointments.

- During the civil war that erupted in Guinea Bissau in 1999, INEP was severely affected, with its installations ransacked, archives destroyed and a number of researchers fleeing the country. Despite this setback, INEP continued contributing in ways that will remain useful for a long time to come. It has already published hundreds of articles in its three journals. One of these, *Soronda,* is still active, covering the spectrum of issues related to development challenges in Guinea Bissau. The institute has issued more than 50 monographs on various subjects, ranging from environmental to anthropological to macroeconomic studies, and has been the initiator and leader of a host of participatory studies involving all key political players. Thanks to its track record, management systems, large library and overall image, INEP has also been asked to lead the establishment of Guinea Bissau's first university.

- INEP's innovation arrested potential brain drain. Even more importantly, in a continent where remuneration issues have been an intractable problem within the community of scholars and civil servants, the institute's revenue generation template provides an interesting departure meriting a closer study by policy makers across Africa.

Further information

C. Lopes, Carlos Cardoso and Peter Mendy. 1999. "Destruicao da memoria colectiva de um povo. " In *Lusotopies,* 6. Paris: Karthala.

National Institute for Studies and Research (INEP). *Soronda, Revista de Estudos Guineenses.* A journal published twice a year since 1985.

————. 1995. *Os primeiros dez anos. Monografia por ocasiao do 10. Aniversario.* Bissau: INEP

————. *Boletim de Informacao Socio-Economica.* A journal published since 1985 (25 numbers).

HONDURAS: DEMOCRACY TRUST BACKS NATIONAL CONSENSUS AMIDST VOLATILE POLITICS

In a Nutshell

The Democracy Trust was conceived as a policy advocacy tool to encourage commitment to the PRSP process among political parties. By ensuring that political parties publicly back policies of development and poverty eradication, the trust has granted the Honduran population a mechanism to hold elected officials to their obligations, and to demand their right to improved and sustainable services. As well, commitments to development thus become state policies and no longer belong solely to the government of the day.

Without capacity development, long-term strategies for poverty reduction are difficult to achieve. Thus, the Democracy Trust plays a crucial role in promoting the growth of social capital, expanding capabilities through the creation of formal and informal communications networks that exchange ideas as well as shared norms, goals and beliefs.

The Story

In 2000, after a broad-based "sounding out" of basic deficiencies within national development, government ministers, civil society representatives, ambassadors and development agency representatives identified the lack of political continuity in Honduras as a major stumbling block. It was severely threatening long-term commitments, particularly with respect to poverty reduction and achievement of the MDGs. The fact that these goals coincided with national agreements under the HIPC and PRSP initiatives provided an important opportunity for action.

Against this background, the Democracy Trust was conceived to build consensus on public policies. It was launched on 5 October 2000, with the President of the Republic signing the Democracy Trust Declaration, together with representatives of the UN system, embassies and international organizations. The Cardinal of Tegucigalpa was asked to preside over the trust's board, which now contains highly reputed civil society representatives, the Minister of Finance, and the Ambassadors of Argentina, France, Japan, Sweden, the United States and Venezuela. To date, 25 embassies and international organizations have committed themselves to participation, providing financial support for policy forums and civil society dialogue, think-tank activities, advocacy, and training of journalists on covering poverty-related themes.

The overall objectives of the Democracy Trust are to:

- Generate an open and de-politicized dialogue on issues pertaining to sustainable human development and poverty reduction, within an overarching process of democratic consolidation

- Identify policies and approaches aimed at transforming national policy and building social consensus

- Strengthen civil society's role in the follow-up and monitoring of the PRSP

- Involve the participation of all sectors of society: government, private enterprise, mass media, NGOs, political parties, academic and intellectual sectors, cooperatives and unions, religious organizations, ethnic groups and minorities

Since its inception, the Democracy Trust has achieved some notable results. It has opened an unprecedented public dialogue among political parties and leaders, as well as created space for national consensus building. An interactive methodology brings together different agents and social actors, with a view to assisting the government, civil society and the donor community in the design of policies, programmes and projects on sensitive areas of human development.

The trust encouraged social and political entities to prepare a 20-year vision for the country, with a view to generating farsighted policies instead of those that merely reflect the interests of the government in power. Consequently, leaders of political parties and civil society signed a series of longer term commitments and 16 other agreements on national transformation. The Democracy Trust is now working on facilitating compliance, follow-up and monitoring.

It is also leading a programme to facilitate the modernization of the five registered political parties in Honduras. Some initiatives include the redefinition and/or consolidation of political doctrines, the formulation of political programmes, and a greater incorporation of youth and women in politics. A training programme has begun for journalists, with a curriculum prepared in cooperation with Honduras' three leading universities. The course includes subjects such as the interpretation of the social and political context of the country; ethics and the process of generating news in strict adherence to the truth; and the responsibility of the media in providing the general population with constructive critical analysis of crucial problems.

Results and Critical Factors

The Democracy Trust has already proven itself to be an important tool for building social capital and consensus in the face of substantial change and the instability inherent in any developing country. In a short space of time, it has promoted dialogue and consensus on crucial issues for the advancement of democracy and poverty reduction; bolstered the capacities of civil society to prepare proposals on public policies; contributed to the strengthening and modernization of political parties; and developed the capacities of journalists for critical analysis on development and democracy. Factors that account for these accomplishments include:

- *Promotion of complementarity of efforts:* The trust has not sought to duplicate the concerted activities of existing institutions such as the

National Forum of Convergence, the Presidential Commission for Participation of Civil Society, and Interforos, among others. Instead, it has sought to generate a dialogue on development issues and democracy that will allow the creation of a social consensus oriented around constructing a country vision. This has minimized the risk of conflict flaring among organizations.

- *Incorporation of the five political parties and the various agencies of the international community:* Looking beyond just civil society, the trust extended a privileged space for the five political parties and the international cooperation agencies to plan initiatives, and to coordinate and receive information on the different social, political and economic processes that they observe in the country.

- *Pursuit of agreements and written pacts for the political parties and civil society:* The adoption of social agreements has been a step forward, along with a monitoring and tracking strategy.

- *The credibility and leadership of the trust's president:* Effective dialogue requires a great amount of integrity on the part of the entity organizing it. In the case of the Democracy Trust, the presidency was deliberately offered to one of the very few people in the country whose reputation is unharmed: the Cardinal of Tegucigalpa, who is also widely acknowledged as an extremely intelligent and articulate leader.

- *Facilitation and continued support:* UNDP has provided active support while maintaining adequate boundaries and autonomy. Its facilitation of the management of financial and technical resources, together with the strong social and political capabilities of the members of the trust, has resulted in a solid institution, reliable and capable within the public sphere of Honduras.

Further information

Foro de Fortalecimiento a la Democracia (FFD) (www.ffd.hn).

Foro de Fortalecimiento a la Democracia (FFD) and the Center of Documentation of Honduras (CEDOH). *The Electoral Process of 2001 and 2002. Monitoring from the Civil Society.* Tegucigalpa.

Foro de Fortalecimiento a la Democracia (FFD) and the National Forum of Convergence (FONAC). 2001. *Declaration of the Presidential Candidates on a Country Vision.* Tegucigalpa.

————. 2001. *National Agreements of Transformation for Human Development in the Twenty-First Century.* Tegucigalpa.

United Nations Development Programme (UNDP). 2000. *Honduras National Human Development Report.* Madrid: Mundi Prensa.

————. 2002. *Honduras National Human Development Report.* Madrid: Mundi Prensa.

The authors gratefully acknowledge the contributions of Gisella Camoriano and UNDP Honduras.

⊃ **INDIA:**
CITIZEN REPORT CARDS TO IMPROVE PUBLIC SERVICE
PERFORMANCE

In a Nutshell

Citizens grading government agencies for performance and publishing the results in the mass media: this is the essence of the report card methodology initiated by the Public Affairs Centre in Bangalore. The centre conducts client satisfaction surveys among lower income groups, assessing their approval of public service providers such as electricity and water supply departments. The findings are publicly shared as report cards, setting new standards of public accountability. A credible methodology of surveying, tabulation and quantitative analysis underpins the approach, and the report card experience has now been replicated worldwide.

The Story

In 1993, under the banner of the Public Affairs Centre, a small group of people in Bangalore who were concerned about the city's standards of public services initiated an exercise to collect feedback from users. Perceptions on quality, efficiency and adequacy were aggregated to create a report card that rated the performance of the city's major providers of telephone connections, water and electricity. The findings presented a quantitative measure of satisfaction and perceived levels of corruption, which, following coverage in the media, not only mobilized citizen and government support for reform, but also prompted the agencies themselves to respond positively to calls for improvement.

The exercise was repeated in 1999, and has been replicated in at least five other Indian cities, as well as in the state of Karnataka, where Bangalore is the capital. Subsequent rounds have taken a partnership approach, where findings are first shared with the agency in question and possible solutions explored before media campaigns begin. By systematically gathering and disseminating public feedback, the report cards have served as a surrogate for competition among monopolies – usually government owned – that previously lacked the incentive to respond to client needs. They have been a useful medium through which citizens can credibly and collectively inform agencies about their performance, and bring pressure for change.

Between 1994 and 1999, four of the eight agencies covered in the 1993 report card in Bangalore made attempts to respond to public dissatisfaction. The worst-rated agency – the Bangalore Development Authority – reviewed its internal systems for service delivery, introduced training for junior staff, and, along with the Bangalore

Municipal Corporation, began to host a joint forum of NGOs and public agencies to consult on solving high-priority problems such as waste management.

The Karnataka Electricity Board formalized periodic dialogues with resident associations to garner feedback. Two other agencies tried to strengthen their grievance redressal systems.

There have been lessons learned from the application of the report cards, and the Public Affairs Centre is engaged in refining the methodology to take these on board. One issue that came up was that the questions asked did not allow for flexible responses, especially when used in urban, low-income settlements. The focus on quantitative data did not permit qualitative responses, and queries tended to refer to men as the primary respondents. In lower income settlements, quite a few households are headed by women, who are generally available to answer questions. The centre is also working to eliminate subjectivity in ranking, especially between client groups of differing socioeconomic profiles.

Results and Critical Factors

- The report card approach is now used widely in the Bangalore public service sector. The initiative has led to the establishment of a *swabhimana,* or forum for citizen's voices, which civic bodies treat as a nonpartisan representative of citizens' groups and NGOs.

- Report cards have also been adapted for use by different agencies across the world, including the World Bank, UNDP and Transparency International. Report cards in Washington, D.C. and in major cities in the Philippines and Ukraine reflect the growing application of this approach in varied settings.

- The report cards have forced hitherto apathetic public agencies to listen and react to citizen concerns. While anecdotal evidence on the incompetence of public agencies has always existed, quantification of perceptions has brought with it a credible indicator that lays down the extent of (dis)satisfaction and allows interagency comparison, triggering internal reforms.

- In India, public awareness of the issues of quality service delivery and corruption has grown substantially, following heavy coverage of report findings in the mainstream media. In 1994, the country's premier daily, *The Times of India,* ran a weekly feature for two months focusing on one interesting finding at a time.

- Although report cards are a seemingly uncomplicated method of surveying citizen feedback, they require a competent intermediary that is technically versed in piloting and administering a poll.

- The process requires adequate financing, time and interest on the part of local residents, in addition to a conducive socio-political climate. These are all demanding requirements, and innovative ways will have to be sought if the exercise in developing countries is to be cost-effective and easily manageable.

Further information

N. Banerjee. 2002. "Public Expenditure Review: Citizens' Report Cards in India." In capacity.org, 15. ECDPM (www.capacity.org).

National Foundation for India (www.nfi.org.in.).

Public Affairs Centre, Bangalore (www.pacindia.org).

World Bank's participation site (www.worldbank.org/participation/accountpoor.html).

INDIA:
PUBLIC HEARINGS ARREST CORRUPTION IN RAJASTHAN

> ### In a Nutshell
>
> A small NGO, Mazdoor Kisan Shakti Sangathan (MKSS), led an initiative to challenge local government functionaries on disbursements of drought relief funds, and ended up carrying out one of the most energetic civil society campaigns in recent Indian history. It began with researchers sifting for information on projected disbursements as they appeared in government records. These were then corroborated by asking labourers and villagers how much they had actually received, or whether construction and other public works had actually taken place. The results were presented in public hearings, with government officials attending whenever possible so that organizers could ask them to return any missing funds.
>
> The initiative regularly confronted difficulties in acquiring access to government records, an experience that later led to the National Right to Information campaign, which now systematically advocates on different levels for making public disbursements transparent.

The Story

A civil servant quit her job in the Indian Administrative Service to form MKSS and start a campaign across a block (an administrative unit) in rural Rajasthan, India's westernmost state. The local population had been demanding to know the details of budget allocations on public works – how much was allocated, how much spent, on what projects, etc. – from the district administration. To support this initiative, the campaign devised a methodology: villagers, particularly those working as labourers, suppliers and contractors, would come together to compare two sets of data. The first would derive from MKSS' research at local government offices about amounts sanctioned and actually spent (including wages paid to labour). Labourers, contractors and suppliers would then be asked to verify if the money shown on paper had actually ended up with them, and whether construction took place as claimed. Additionally, MKSS would do some investigations on the ground. Discrepancies would be unveiled at a public hearing, and officials asked to return missing funds.

The playing out of this process, however, has been more intricate. Information on public works is hard to find, especially actual figures. Public officials – both elected functionaries and junior staff of the bureaucracy – are very reluctant to come to the hearings. At times, officials have tried to bring court stay orders against the divulging of public works information, although the courts have been quick to vacate these orders on being petitioned.

The law mandates that block-level data must be released within five days of a petition. But in one documented case, the actual information took a full year to arrive. In another, villagers had to organize a 40-day sit-in to get the figures they wanted – a long time for people barely scratching out a living on daily wages. The delays are largely due to the unwillingness of local officials to divulge information, as well as the poor quality of records in outlying government offices.

So far, the findings that have been gathered bolster the belief that corruption alone drains away a large portion of public expenditure. For example, between 1994 and 2000, of 98 projects done by the government in ten villages, evaluations could be done for only 31, due to incomplete records or late arrival of information. The outlay on these 31 projects amounted to rupees 65 lakhs (about $135,000). The villagers and the NGO discovered that officials and bureaucrats had siphoned off around rupees 45 lakhs (a little under $100,000)!

Since it began, the information initiative has become more institutionalized, with the community adopting a number of methods for public accountability. These include mounting posters demanding proper handling of funds and peoples' audits. While the functionaries directly in the line of fire have tried to stonewall at every step, a significant group of other actors, both in legislatures and the courts, has enthusiastically stood behind the project. It seems that while there will always be vested interests in the diversion of public funds, there is also always a counter force keen on good governance.

Results and Critical Factors

- The process started by MKSS has spread into broader public auditing within India, and is being watched with much interest elsewhere in development circles.

- A number of states in India have passed legislation, statutes and various administrative orders mandating disclosure of information on public works. The National Campaign for People's Right to Information (NCPRI) is calling for this to become a constitutional right.

- The scope of the right to information has broadened, and the spotlight now encompasses a wide range of development issues as well as human rights, judicial accountability, electoral processes, media ownership, nuclear and defence activities and even the functioning of NGOs themselves.

- MKSS has played a crucial role in sustaining the campaign for information and keeping people engaged. Even over time and interminable delays, it has kept the community focused on the mission. Most village hearings, for example, begin with a puppet show on corruption and development – this sparks initial interest, but more importantly explains development and corruption links in a simple manner easily grasped by the general populace.

Further information

Anne-Marie Goetz, and John Gaventa. 2001. "Bringing Citizen Voice and Client Focus into Service Delivery." Institute of Development Studies (IDS) Working Paper No. 128. Brighton: IDS (www.ids.ac.uk/ids/govern/citizenvoice/annexcs.html).

Bela Bhatia, and Jean Dreze. 1998. "Freedom of Information Is Key to Anti-Corruption Campaign in Rural India." A working paper presented in Berlin (www.transparency.org/working_papers/bhatia-dreze/bhatia-dreze.html).

Bunker Roy. 2000. "Villages as a Positive Force for Good Governance: The Right to Information and India's Struggle against Grass-Roots Corruption." In *UN Chronicle Online Edition,* 37. New York: United Nations (www.un.org/Pubs/chronicle/2000/issue1/0100p86.htm).

World Bank's participation site (www.worldbank.org/participation/accountpoor.html).

➲ INDONESIA:
DECENTRALIZATION STARTS WITH ASSESSING
CURRENT CAPACITIES

In a Nutshell

Indonesia is implementing a capacity development programme for local governments, with assistance from a group of external partners, as part of a wider decentralization effort. To help design an effective strategy, one that also promotes government-donor coordination, a capacity needs assessment tool was developed. It focused mainly on cross-sectoral issues and took stock at three levels. Field assessments, which brought together different local stakeholders, stimulated debate on key issues of local governance under decentralization.

Overall, the experience has helped forge better coordination among development partners. However, it was a complex process requiring significant financial and human resources. Crucially, its success depended on encouraging the involvement of senior government officials, which required articulating a shared understanding at the outset of the meaning of capacity development.

The Story

Between November 1999 and October 2000, GTZ and CLEAN Urban (a project funded by the United States Agency for International Development [USAID] that covers urban and financial management issues) conducted a study in Indonesia to assess the needs of local governments and legislatures for capacity-building support. It focused mainly on cross-sectoral issues, emphasizing links between them. Selected service sectors (urban, health and education) were also covered, since these represent the most important services delivered by local government to citizens.

The results of the study were expected to shape a framework for formulating capacity development programmes that would allow local governments, under Indonesia's current decentralization policy, to fully assume their new roles and functions. In addition, it was hoped that the experience would boost the capacity of central government agencies in charge of decentralization policy to undertake similar assessments without external assistance.

The study team used a conceptual approach that distinguished three levels of capacity: systems, entity and individual. The assessment was geared towards a qualitative analysis of major issues, perceptions and suggestions from a broad range of stakeholders, including senior officials from central government agencies, officials from local governments and provincial agencies, members of local parliaments, and representatives of local NGOs and community groups.

For each topic addressed, a normative framework provided the starting point. The frameworks were based on Indonesian policies and regulations as well as on international best practices. Consisting of generic principles of good local governance, they provided the basis for identifying the competencies required by both central and regional government organizations. They also acted as icebreakers in many meetings, allowing discussion leaders to present the approach, while respondents were able to relate to the principles.

The assessment process included three elements. First, talks took place with central government officials on the normative frameworks, as well as on their perception of local capacity-building needs. Second, field studies were conducted with five local governments. These included plenary sessions with local officials and parliamentarians, focus group discussions, site visits, individual meetings and interviews, and an analysis of local policy papers and regulations. At the end of each exercise, the study team presented its preliminary findings and recommendations to the different stakeholder groups consulted.

The third step was presenting the initial findings and recommendations to an inter-ministerial working group on capacity building. Meetings with officials from selected technical and sector agencies provided opportunities to delve into more details, in order to establish priorities. The findings were also provided to donors.

Several thematic and technical reports were produced, while the summary final report became a working document for a preliminary donor and consultative group meeting on decentralization. Tools and instruments for field assessments were documented and made available to other interested parties. The Web site for the project became a sought-after source of information for technical assistance officials, practitioners and advisors working in Indonesia on decentralization and local governance. A regular electronic report was also disseminated.

The study has since been used to discuss detailed capacity development programmes. For one local government, the field assessment has already yielded a new technical assistance project with GTZ. In other cases, findings have been integrated into technical assistance activities that are either currently ongoing or planned for the future. Because the studies often brought together different local stakeholders, they also opened space for debate on governance under decentralization, which in itself is a step towards capacity development.

As a follow-up, donor support was provided to an inter-ministerial working group on capacity development, established by presidential decree as one of the coordination teams for the implementation of the decentralization laws. What could not be achieved, however, was building capacity among central government agencies to undertake similar needs assessments along cross-sectoral or cross-agency lines. Persistent changes in the central government have resulted in the constant loss of counterparts and the need to routinely re-establish communication and working relationships with officials.

Results and Critical Factors

- Government ownership and the involvement of government officials in the conceptualization and management of the study was crucial to its success

- Exercises of this nature are complex and require adequate budgeting of time, financial resources and personnel. Access to qualified consultants combining country experience with the requisite technical expertise has been especially important.

- In view of the fact that government officials will often equate capacity development with training, a great deal of time and effort needed to be spent at the outset on developing a broader understanding of the concepts of capacity and capacity development.

- The normative frameworks provided an effective way to combine a relatively abstract approach with concrete institutional and individual implications that were easier to understand, especially for local government officials.

- An important aspect of the assessment was the consistent effort to make findings available to the public through the Internet and electronic media. While the international community was highly appreciative of this facility, such media are not yet sufficiently accessible to government officials in Indonesia, who are less used to them and often lack the requisite technical equipment.

- The fact that several technical assistance stakeholders conducted the study helped to forge better coordination among donors and donor-assisted projects in similar fields.

Further information

R. Rohdewohld. 2000. "Capacity-Building Needs Assessment for Local Governments in Indonesia." In capacity.org, 8. ECDPM (www.capacity.org/8/editorial1.html).

Support for Decentralisation Measures Programme (www.gtzsfdm.or.id).

UNDP. 1998. *Capacity Assessment and Development in a Systems and Strategic Management Context*. Technical Advisory Paper, 3 (http://magnet.undp.org/docs/cap/Main.htm).

The authors gratefully acknowledge the contributions of Rainer Rohdewohld, GTZ/CLEAN.

⮥ JORDAN:
DIVING CLUB EVOLVES INTO INFLUENTIAL ACTOR ON COASTAL MANAGEMENT

In a Nutshell

Through a gradual and organic process of capacity development, a Jordanian environmental NGO evolved from humble beginnings into an effective and respected institution with the capacity for research, advocacy, policy advice and community mobilization. The Jordanian Royal Ecological Diving Society (JREDS) has built partnerships with various public agencies, and with other NGOs and community organizations, both nationally and regionally. Starting as a beneficiary of the Global Environmental Facility's (GEF) Small Grants Programme, it has broadened its funding base to assure financial sustainability and independence. This has all been achieved despite little tradition of civic participation in Jordan, or of questioning state and commercial interests on safeguarding the natural environment.

The Story

Jordan is a comparatively small country facing many environmental and social development challenges. One of the most complex issues is the sustainable management of the fragile and over-exploited coastal area in Aqaba. This fragile ecosystem has unique features and is a centre of attraction for ecological divers. However, developments have engulfed the short beach in the last decades, with fierce competition between transport, tourism and industry sectors over occupying it. Only seven kilometres remain untouched, and environmental deterioration and pollution are major problems. In 2000, Aqaba was declared a "special economic zone", which threatened even greater environmental hazards. While the Aqaba Special Economic Zone Authority has devised environmental protection by-laws with stringent standards and regulations that are even more advanced than those provided under national law, success in sustainably managing a fragile ecosystem ultimately requires the integration of the efforts of various institutions and community groups.

The involvement of civil society started in 1995, with the establishment of JREDS. Evolving from a club for Jordanian ecological divers, it gained momentum as a full-fledged NGO. The project initiated a continuous coral reef monitoring programme together with the country's top marine ecology scientists, and supported an intensive public awareness campaign. Through its close cooperation with the Marine Science Station, a national scientific organization based in Aqaba, JREDS also built a comprehensive information database. It has played a role in subsequent awareness and capacity development efforts, as well as in conducting scientific research and advocating scientifically based views on economic development plans in Aqaba. This capacity readily attracted further support from donors, extended cooperation links with the Aqaba Special Economic Zone

Authority, and brought the local community into various activities. Throughout, staff took part in various training and capacity-building initiatives that enhanced considerably their skills in project management, public advocacy, and knowledge generation and distribution.

In 1998, JREDS organized a participatory multi-stakeholders' workshop to investigate new project ideas that are now technically and administratively coordinated by JREDS, while being implemented by grass-roots organizations. In 2002, the Small Grants Programme supported JREDS with a planning grant to crystallize its latest initiative, which aims to help boat operators in Aqaba upgrade their role in sustainable tourism. JREDS worked extensively with the operators' society in developing the proposal and concept.

Today, JREDS is an organization with some 250 members, 15 staff and eight ongoing projects. It has become the technical arm of the GEF Small Grants Programme in Aqaba, while managing to diversify its own donor base and to develop demand-driven projects covering various issues, including rehabilitation of water networks in poor urban areas. Three coral monitoring stations in the Gulf of Aqaba chart the well-being of the coral reef, and in terms of knowledge on the marine environment in Jordan, JREDS is now considered a one-stop shop.

In its brief history, JREDS has cooperated with almost all relevant stakeholders in Aqaba: the public sector, private concerns in industry and tourism, tourists, school children, fisher folk, local women and youth. It has also managed to work at regional levels, and was granted the responsibility of coordinating regional public awareness programmes in the Red Sea region in 2001. Through participation in regional networks, its activities now cover eight countries along the coastal ecosystem.

Reaching out to people as well as ecosystems, JREDS staff train community members and students at an education centre on how to use computers and the Internet to research information on the marine environment. In addition, the group has an active socioeconomic programme to improve the living standards of the less fortunate in Aqaba, especially fisher folk and people whose livelihoods depend on the sea, through income-generating projects and the production of environmentally sound local sea crafts.

Results and Critical Factors

JREDS has been the only NGO in Jordan to focus professionally on protecting marine ecosystems. It has shared its capacity with smaller NGOs working on other sustainable development projects, and proved to be vital in mobilizing human and technical resources for implementing projects and conducting advocacy campaigns.

- Capacity development at JREDS has involved a cumulative process rather than a pre-set product or outcome. Many stakeholders have contributed inputs.

- Projects have been constructed through a bottom-up approach. Multi-stake-holder meetings and planning grants have helped in focusing preparation, and ensuring a high level of civil society and local community participation.

- The capacity development process at JREDS has been institutionally and socially sustainable, with the knowledge gleaned readily available in databases and shared among the society's staff, as well as other stake-holders and interested sectors via the educational centre.

- Knowledge and experiences have been transferred to other NGOs by engaging in technical and administrative coordination of the Small Grants Programme projects in Aqaba. This does not impose JREDS' presence on smaller groups, but helps them to engage in their own capacity development cycles, while gaining self-confidence and a sense of ownership of projects.

- Although capacity development has not yet had a direct impact on policy in Aqaba, JREDS has been very active in filling the need for advocacy, human resource mobilization, public awareness campaigns and specific grass-roots initiatives.

- The GEF Small Grants Programme provided the needed financial and technical support for the nascent JREDS to mature. Carrying out the initial GEF-supported project was a learning process that facilitated and supported further capacity development initiatives.

- Capacity development has helped the group to broaden its funding base, ensuring the diversity and sustainability of its programmes. Staff have been well trained on attracting donor attention, and their professional track record has helped to impress various funders.

Further information

JREDS (www.jreds.org).

M. Adgham. 2002. *SGP Intervention in Aqaba, Jordan*. Amman: UNDP.

Small Grants Programme Jordan (www.gef-sgp.org.jo).

———. 2002a. *Lessons in Sustainable Development: Ten Years of Partnership between SGP and the Local Community in Jordan*. Amman: UNDP.

———. 2002b. *SGP Jordan Biennial Country Programme Review*. Amman: UNDP.

The authors gratefully acknowledge the contributions of Batir Wardam, Small Grants Programme Community Electronic Forum, Jordan.

➲ JORDAN:
A NON-THREATENING APPROACH TO INTERDISCIPLINARY COLLABORATION

In a Nutshell

In 2000, Jordan produced a National Agenda 21, as well as the country's first environmental impact assessment guidelines. It also became the first country in the Arab region to prepare a National Environmental Information Strategy and a National Awareness, Education and Communication Strategy, using the Agenda 21 methodology. Jordan harnessed the powers of ICT and used participatory planning techniques to mobilize local capacities, build new development concepts, and bring together groups that had never worked together to formulate bold national policies. External support facilitated innovative practices that strong national commitment and local policy "champions" carried forward.

The Story

Jordan's Capacity 21 programme produced its National Agenda 21 in 2000. It was launched under the patronage of Her Royal Highness Princess Basma Bint Talal, who is considered a key political figure in supporting development activities, and whose presence conferred priority and credibility. Subsequently, using the Agenda 21 methodology, Jordan passed its first environmental impact assessment guidelines, and the Arab region's first National Environmental Information Strategy and National Awareness, Education and Communication Strategy. To back implementation of the National Agenda 21, the Sustainable Development Networking Programme was set up, along with 28 information technology community centres and a community knowledge portal.

The process of preparing Jordan's National Agenda 21 was a learning experience for all concerned. Over two years, six task forces of technicians, decision makers, academics and representatives of local communities met regularly to share and debate ideas, and broker consensus on sustainable development priorities. Participants included staff members of the General Corporation for Environmental Protection – which has since been replaced by the Ministry for the Environment, based on the recommendations of Agenda 21 – and representatives of the Ministries of Agriculture, Water and Irrigation, Mineral Resources and Energy, as well as the Natural Resources Authority. Members of NGOs, including the Royal Scientific Society, Jordan Environment Society and Friends of the Environment, also took part, along with private consultants, engineers, and scholars from the University of Jordan and the Jordanian University of Science and Technology.

The degree of open exchange of information among such a wide range of experts from different disciplines had never been seen in Jordan before, providing an opportunity for collective thinking and facilitating genuine transparency in the ensuing formation of policy. While all the participants were experts in their respective fields, many were unfamiliar with the fundamental principles of sustainable development. A chemical engineer, for instance, who had no background in environmental issues, gained new ideas about the design of hazardous waste landfills, how other countries cope with waste management, and the role of environmental protection agencies. By the end, the participants had become conversant with the ideas and principles of Agenda 21 and other key international conventions – on subjects such as desertification, biological diversity and climate change – that followed the 1992 United Nations Conference on Environment and Development. In addition, each was required to contribute his or her specialized knowledge, so technicians learned from managers and policy makers and vice-versa.

The sharing of information soon generated some tangible results in important areas, such as solid waste management. Many people had not appreciated the importance of managing the collection, separation and disposal of municipal solid waste, and as a result, human and financial resources were being used inefficiently. To localize Agenda 21 concepts, a solid waste management programme began in Zarqa, Jordan's second largest city. Since then, Zarqa has become a model for action on this issue, and similar programmes are planned for other municipalities.

Since the National Agenda 21 debuted, the Sustainable Development Network Programme has carried it forward, continuing to provide a platform for development practitioners to exchange views and information electronically. Initially, ten institutions representing the public, private and non-governmental sectors were equipped with the necessary hardware and software. Subsequently, other institutions joined the programme, as well as local communities in remote areas through the information technology community centres and the community knowledge portal.

In 2002, the Ministry of Planning established a Sustainable Development Office to work on issues related to Agenda 21, particularly in mainstreaming them across economic, social and environmental programmes. A Liaison Office for Agenda 21 has been proposed for the newly established Ministry for the Environment to ensure proper follow-up and monitoring.

Results and Critical Factors
- Strong national commitment and the crucial role of national "champions" were key to progress.
- Capacity 21 offered the country a groundbreaking and non-threatening opportunity to test participatory approaches and partnership building among different stakeholder groups in policy-making and dialogue. The process was an inclusive learning experience.

- Access to information, facilitated by ICT, and opportunities created for multi-stakeholder dialogue were powerful tools in mobilizing local capacities, building ownership for new development concepts and bringing together groups that had never worked together.

- The interdisciplinary approach has now been used during consultations related to Jordan's signing of the Free Trade Agreement with the United States in 2000, the drafting of the new Environmental Protection Law in 2001, and the preparation of the national assessment for the 2002 World Summit on Sustainable Development.

Further information

Community Knowledge Center (www.ckc-undp.org.jo/).

Jordan Information Community Center (www.jitcc.gov.jo/).

Capacity 21 Evaluation Report 1993-2001 (www.undp.org/capacity21/docs/cap21GlobalEval2002.pdf).

Capacity 21 (www.undp.org/capacity21/).

Sustainable Development Network Programme (www.sdnp.jo/).

⮕ LAOS:
A TEAM APPROACH ALIGNED TO THE LOCAL
DECISION-MAKING STYLE

In a Nutshell

Project implementation often suffers from poor collaboration between the main actors – the recipient organization, project staff and the donor. A team-based approach to project management, where different stakeholders collectively share responsibility, may heighten the chance for success by creating a forum for ongoing capacity development, collective monitoring and a matching of expectations, in accordance with locally perceived priorities.

Such an approach was tried in Laos as part of the Governance and Public Administration Reform Programme. It proved particularly useful in governance-related projects, where technical skills, often provided by external consultants, need to be balanced with in-house knowledge of political sensitivities, as well as local styles of building consensus and making decisions. It fostered an environment where honest dialogue can flourish, based on the principle of mutual learning and respect.

The Story

Technical cooperation traditionally involves three players: the donor organization (bilateral, multilateral or trilateral), the recipient organization (usually but not necessarily a government agency) and sources of technical assistance (short-term or long-term, national or expatriate consultants, who may be individuals, consultancy firms or executing agencies). While technical cooperation calls all upon three to work together to achieve common objectives, real collaboration is the exception rather than the rule. In the classic case, one finds the donor on one side, the government or recipient stakeholder on the other side, and the project advisor(s) caught in between, trying to manage expectations.

By contrast, the Laotian authorities and UNDP have made serious progress in instilling project management with national ownership. Recipient organizations select short-term consultants and resident advisors from a list of proposed candidates, while national project directors have overall responsibility for managing financial resources, and are held accountable for results and disbursements. But not all donors follow this approach, and government staff often criticize the fact that they are not sufficiently involved in the decision-making. In general, the classic division between the government, project staff and the donor has so far been maintained in Laos. It became even more formalized when a donor coordination agency was established and became a de facto buffer between the donor and the government/project.

Yet the need to improve collaboration between the different parties has been clear, so the Prime Minister's Office decided to experiment with a more team-based approach for the Governance and Public Administration Reform Project, designed to assist ongoing reforms, with indirect support for reaching socioeconomic goals, transitioning to a market economy and achieving sustainable development. A small project management team was put together, composed of the national project director, his deputy and the national project manager; the resident project advisor for technical assistance; and the UNDP programme officer. Meetings took place once or twice a month, chaired by the national project director or, in his/her absence, the project manager. Minutes were made available to all interested parties, in order to increase transparency.

Project objectives and related outputs had been defined in a general way, leaving room for the team to adjust the pace of implementation to changing priorities and opportunities. The different participants collectively shared responsibility for decisions related to implementation. And rather than being an outsider responsible, on behalf of the donor, for controlling disbursements in line with approved work plans, the UNDP programme officer was considered a full member of the project management team.

All the parties involved welcomed this approach. In countries with a group-oriented management culture, such as Laos, a team is more in line with the local decision-making style. The project management group also created a forum for capacity development, where all parties learned from each other's experiences and skills, and provided a mechanism for ongoing and collective project monitoring by key partners. Having members work together on the basis of equality and mutual respect proved to be fundamental. Too often, projects falter not because they lack technical inputs, but because of too little cultural sensitivity and behavioural flexibility. There are numerous cases of highly qualified consultants, both from the North and the South, who fail because of attitude, despite their high level of competency.

Membership of a project management team can easily be extended to other stakeholders, such as co-funding donors, pilot groups, non-governmental organizations or even beneficiaries. However, the management team should remain small to allow for meaningful dialogue and efficient decision-making. To ensure national ownership, it is important that the majority of the team members are nationals.

Results and Critical Factors

- A team-based approach to project management is particularly useful in governance-related programmes, balancing technical skills often provided by external consultants with national knowledge of political sensitivities and the often complex processes of building consensus and making decisions.

- A team helps the project march to local time, rather than to externally defined timetables, which are not always in sync with realities on the ground.

- Such an approach also allows all parties involved to strike an appropriate balance between short-term success (imposed by the donors or by the political agenda of the host country) and long-term, sustainable results.

- Technical assistants can concentrate on substance rather than devoting a large portion of their time to shuttling between the donor and recipient.

- Donor agencies need to have adequate staff to participate proactively in project management teams and stay close to project implementation.

- On the recipient side, a successful team requires a culture of information sharing and a commitment to transparency in all aspects of project management.

Further information

United Nations Development Programme (UNDP). 2000. *Support to Governance and Public Administration Reform (1997-2000) Lao People's Democratic Republic.* Report of the final evaluation. UNDP.

Reforming Technical Cooperation for Capacity Development. 2002. "Insights in 1000 Words" (www.undp.org/capacity).

The authors gratefully acknowledge the contributions of Patrick Keuleers, UNDP Subregional Resource Facility, Bangkok, Thailand.

➲ **MALAWI:**
FACING CAPACITY EROSION IN THE PUBLIC SECTOR

In a Nutshell

HIV/AIDS imposes unique challenges for development. Among other things, the erosion of capacity through lives lost to the disease has been debilitating for the public services in countries like Malawi. Development agents are faced with multiple challenges in dealing with the depletion, including even assessing the value of this loss.

Towards this end, support was offered to the Malawi government to conduct an HIV/AIDS impact assessment study within the public service, covering four ministries and one department. Employees in these institutions account for over 70 per cent of civil servants. The study was among the first of its kind in Malawi, and has provided critical insights on how urgent action is needed to stop the whittling away of public sector capacity by HIV/AIDS.

The Story

The first case of HIV/AIDS in Malawi was diagnosed in 1985. Since then, the rates of infection have been on the rise. The 2001 Sentinel Surveillance Report puts prevalence among people aged 15-49 at 16 per cent. This being the most productive age group, there are serious implications for all sectors of the Malawi economy and public services.

Deaths of parents due to HIV/AIDS has orphaned over 300,000 children below the age of 15, and the number is likely to skyrocket in coming years. Opportunistic diseases are spreading, with the number of reported tuberculosis cases, estimated at 5,000 before the onset of HIV, now surpassing 23,000. Much of this increase is attributed to HIV.

With attrition growing in the public service, the government acknowledged the need to undertake an HIV/AIDS impact assessment to establish the exact trend of these deaths, knowledge that in turn would guide policies and interventions. To develop national research capacity, local consulting firms were invited to conduct the study. They reviewed existing documentation, interviewed stakeholders and collected primary data on the epidemic in four ministries and one department (the Ministry of Health and Population; the Ministry of Agriculture and Irrigation; the Ministry of Education, Science and Technology; the Ministry of Water Development and the Malawi Police). A steering committee comprising members from the Department of Human Resources Management and Development (DHRMD), the National AIDS Commission (NAC) and UNDP guided the consultants.

The study revealed that attrition in the public service had been soaring between 1990 and 2000, especially among technical cadres and frontline staff, whose work involves a lot of field travel. Total mortality rates rose from 3 per cent in 1990 to 16 per cent in 2000, an increase of more than 500 per cent. Women died at a much earlier age than men.

The resulting capacity erosion has curtailed service delivery, with productivity and performance faltering due to increased absenteeism, high numbers of vacancies and increased workloads for those in service. Increased stress, frustration, burnout and low staff morale are common. In particular, coverage and provision of services have suffered due to the loss of skilled workers such as agricultural research scientists, medical doctors and engineers.

There are also financial implications for HIV/AIDS-related mortality, morbidity and absenteeism in terms of training and recruitment costs, increased funeral expenses and the pay-out of death benefits. According to the study, the five organizations spent between $53.4 million and $78.1 million on HIV/AIDS-related costs during the period under review, while the government has been spending between $6.1 million and $8.9 million per annum for training and recruitment of a replacement workforce. Most of these financial expenditures were not in the budget.

As well, funeral attendance results in a two-day absence of at least 20 employees. From 1990 to 2000, a total of 8,105 deaths across the five organizations translated into a loss of 324,200 person days, or 14,736 months. Based on an average monthly salary of $2,790, total funeral attendance would have cost the five organizations $41.1 million, or just over $3.7 million per annum.

The study proposed three sets of recommendations. The first category covers the prevention and mitigation of HIV/AIDS in the workplace. For instance, proposals have been made to sensitize all staff members on HIV/AIDS; involve every person in HIV/AIDS prevention and mitigation activities; and provide anti-retroviral drugs (ARVs) to those who need them.

The second category of recommendations relates to improvements in the capacity of the public sector. To this effect, the study has suggested, *inter alia,* that DHRMD put in place a mechanism to facilitate the fast-tracking of recruitment into government; set up a comprehensive incentive package for skills that are difficult to replace; and use UN volunteers as a short-term replacement for critical capacities. In addition, it advised that the government increase the size of the Malawi Government Scholarship Fund to educate replacement workers.

The third category of recommendations seeks better management of information in the public sector. For instance, the government was asked to put in place systems for recording and monitoring morbidity, mortality and absenteeism. Each government institution should budget for and record funeral costs.

The development community can continue to play a vital role in helping arrest the erosion of public sector capacity in Malawi. It can seek full commitment at the highest level, especially from the Secretary to the President and the Cabinet, and advocate for adequate funds from the Treasury. The government has already announced an allocation of two per cent of each ministry or department's total budget for this effort.

Even beyond the budgetary shift, political commitment for change has been visible. The Vice President urged the Office of the President and the Cabinet to ensure that the recommendations from the study are implemented immediately, with the assistance of UNDP and a Public Sector HIV/AIDS Mainstreaming Committee comprising technical persons, principal secretaries and chief executives. A work plan to carry out the recommendations has been finalized. In order to speed capacity improvement, the government has embarked on a process of identifying vacancies that could be immediately filled by UN volunteers.

Results and Critical Factors

The Malawi study provides evidence of significant human resource capacity erosion in the country's public service between 1990 and 2000. At the same time, the government is spending enormous amounts of resources on both visible and invisible costs stemming from escalating levels of morbidity and mortality. Other issues include:

- While the human and social losses associated with HIV/AIDS are self-evident, the loss in capacity in areas like the public service are only now being understood due to studies like Malawi's.

- It is easy to comprehend the direct costs associated with an epidemic of this size, but the Malawi exercise also points to large invisible costs, such as employee absences for funeral attendance, the need for retraining, and the replacement of highly skilled employees such as doctors and agricultural scientists.

- Development partners will need to support a concerted strategy, while significant resources will be required for dealing with the complex challenges of mediating and arresting capacity erosion in Malawi.

Further information

Malawi Institute of Management and the United Nations Development Programme (UNDP). 2002. *The Impact of HIV/AIDS on the Human Resources in the Malawi Public Sector* (http://iiep.tomoye.com/ev.php?URL_ID=2214&URL_DO=DO_TOPIC&URL_SECTION=201&reload=1060977625).

E. Kadzamira, et al. 2001. *The Impact of HIV/AIDS on Primary and Secondary Schooling in Malawi: Developing a Comprehensive Strategic Response.*

B. K. Lodh. 1995. *The Demographic and Economic Impacts of HIV/AIDS in Malawi 1987-2022.*

United Nations Development Programme (UNDP). 2001. *HIV/AIDS: Implications for Poverty Reduction.* Background paper prepared for the UN General Assembly Special Session on HIV/AIDS. New York: UNDP.

United Nations Development Programme/Food and Agriculture Organization (UNDP/FAO). 2001. *The Impact of HIV/AIDS on Agricultural Extension Organization and Field Operations in Selected Countries of Sub-Saharan Africa, with Appropriate Institutional Response.* Geneva: UNDP/FAO.

The authors gratefully acknowledge the contributions of Fred Mwathengere, UNDP Malawi.

➲ MALAYSIA:
RAISING THE CAPACITY OF MARGINALIZED GROUPS TO FACILITATE CLASS MOBILITY

In a Nutshell

One of Malaysia's strengths is its ethnically diverse society, consisting of the majority Malays and indigenous groups (Bumiputera), as well as Chinese, Indians and others. Capacity development interventions have arisen from the need to advance Malaysia's standing as a new state, but also to address ethnic imbalances inherited from colonial rule.

Two priorities have been clear. The first involved increasing wealth among the Bumiputera so they could be entrepreneurs in their own right. The second sought to raise the number of Bumiputera in higher education so they could have a chance at class mobility. These initiatives have enabled hitherto marginalized ethnic groups to participate in mainstream development while contributing significantly to the transformation and relative peace and prosperity of their country.

The Story

Malaysia is today a middle-income country, and the world's 17th largest trading nation. Despite periodic economic downturns, it has achieved impressive growth, with poverty dropping from 49.3 per cent in 1970 (a figure that refers to peninsular Malaysia only) to 7.5 per cent in 1999. A multi-ethnic middle and business class has emerged, and while some tensions exist among Malaysia's different groups, as a society it upholds a culture of tolerance and accommodation.

Early on, during the period 1957-1969, capacity development in Malaysia was left mainly to individual and private initiative. As a result, equity ownership remained in the hands of foreigners and the Chinese, and income inequalities worsened despite economic growth. In higher education, Malays comprised less than a quarter of the students despite making up more than half the population. As tertiary education was considered a principal means for social mobility and entry into middle-class jobs, Malays could only occupy a small proportion of middle-class occupations.

Frustrations boiled over in the 1969 ethnic clashes in Kuala Lumpur. Consequently, capacity development for ethnic Malays became an urgent national priority, with the launch of the New Economic Policy (NEP) marking the beginning of active state intervention. The NEP had a two-pronged objective of eradicating poverty irrespective of ethnicity and restructuring society to level the economic playing field. It chose to focus on shifting wealth to the Bumiputera and increasing their numbers in higher education.

To address equity in terms of economic participation, the government established a number of state-owned enterprises, one of the most significant and successful being the National Equity Corporation. Placed under the jurisdiction of the Bumiputera Investment Foundation and chaired by the Prime Minister, it served as an investment house and fund manager for Bumiputera investors. The government provided it with large grants and interest-free loans. Within a few years, the corporation successfully took over a number of foreign-controlled conglomerates involved in sectors regarded as nationally strategic. It also acquired sizeable stakes in a number of public listed companies.

This acquisition of corporate wealth was transferred to Bumiputera individuals and institutions by means of a unit trust scheme, Amanah Saham Nasional (ASN), launched in 1981. By the end of 1982, ASN had attracted 1.1 million Bumiputera unit holders. By 1990, the number had increased to 2.44 million with investments in 60 companies listed on the Kuala Lumpur Stock Exchange. That year, ASN was replaced by Amanah Saham Bumiputera (ASB), which has been equally popular, attracting 4.7 million investors by December 1997. ASB's parent company has grown from a relatively small investment house in 1978 to become the largest and most successful unit trust fund manager in Malaysia today.

However, the NEP objective of 30 per cent Bumiputera ownership of corporate wealth has not been met, with the figure remaining at 19 per cent as of 1990. Increasing the number of units per investor so that participation becomes more equitable remains a major challenge.

The NEP's other focus, on education, was no less important. A fifth to a quarter of total public sector expenditure flows to education, with a large portion devoted to tertiary schooling. While before 1969, there was only one university, the University of Malaya, with Bumiputera comprising only a quarter of the student population, there are now 11 public universities and seven public university colleges, as well as eight private universities and almost 500 private colleges. To ensure a more equitable representation of students of various ethnic groups, the government has reserved 60 per cent of the seats in the public institutions for Bumiputera. At the same time, scholarships, bursaries and loans have been disbursed by the government to deserving students – particularly Bumiputera – to study in universities overseas.

In recent years the government has set up the National Higher Education Fund to further expand accessibility to higher education. This loan fund is available not only to students in public universities but also to those in private institutions. It has enabled more Bumiputera children to obtain a university education, which is swelling their ranks in professional and managerial positions.

Results and Critical Factors

Many governments have tried reservation and quota policies to create a level playing field among citizens of different races, ethnicity and creeds. The record of such actions has been mixed, which leads to the conclusion that selective reservations must be left to individual governments to decide. In Malaysia too, there is the recognition that the government needs to finely balance the accordance of equal opportunities to Bumiputera with the possibility of disaffection among other groups. Some key issues include:

- Active state intervention in the economy and society on behalf of the generally more disadvantaged Bumiputera – especially through capacity development initiatives targeting equity in economic participation and improved educational opportunities – has brought the Bumiputera into mainstream development and contributed significantly to the transformation and relative peace and prosperity of Malaysia.

- Although present day conventional free market wisdom favours shifting all economic activity to the domain of the private sector, state capitalism cannot entirely be discounted because it plays a role in the realm of political economy – which pure market forces are unable to factor in.

- That Malaysia has been able to maintain ethnic peace is indicative of the fact that its own leadership has struck the right balance and may need to uphold it until this kind of guidance becomes unnecessary.

Further information

Embong Abdul Rahman. 2002. *State-led Modernization and the New Middle Class in Malaysia.* Houndmills and New York: Palgrave.

E. T. Gomez and K. S. Jomo. 1997. *Malaysian Political Economy: Politics, Patronage and Profits.* Cambridge: Cambridge University Press.

Shari Ishak. 1995. "Industrialization and Poverty: The Malaysian Experience." In *Jurnal Antropologi dan Sosiologi* (Malaysia), 22: 11-29.

J. V. Jesudason. 1989. *Ethnicity and the Economy: The State, Chinese Business, and Multinationals in Malaysia.* Singapore: Oxford University Press.

Government of Malaysia. 2001. *Eighth Malaysia Plan 2001-2005.* Kuala Lumpur: Percetakan Nasional Malaysia Berhad.

The authors gratefully acknowledge the contributions of UNDP Malaysia.

➲ MONGOLIA AND MOROCCO:
MICROSTART BACKS BUSINESS PLANS OF LEADERS WITH VISION

In a Nutshell

Experiences from Mongolia and Morocco demonstrate the importance of backing breakthrough institutions in microfinance that can become industry leaders and engage in healthy competition in the market, while maintaining a focus on the overarching goal: reaching out to poor clients.

Past lessons indicate that while funders can invest and structure their assistance wisely, they do not create successful microfinance; managers with the vision to establish sustainable institutions do. Moreover, organizations with strong management are exactly the ones who are most likely to benefit from technical assistance – weaker institutions often cannot implement even the good ideas they receive.

The Story

By allowing poor people access to financial services, microfinance is an important tool to combat poverty. Comprehensive studies have demonstrated that it helps very poor households meet basic needs and protect against risks, while improving overall economic welfare and allowing the growth or stabilization of small enterprises. By supporting women's participation in particular, microfinance takes a step towards gender equality. In general, the magnitude of impact correlates to the length of time that clients have been in the programme.

Despite microfinance's track record, however, demand for these services remains largely unmet. Estimates of the number of potential clients globally range from 400-500 million households, of which only around 30 million could tap into microfinance in 2002. While there is an understanding among international agencies and governments that poor people want sustainable access to these services rather than time-bound projects or "experiments", only microfinance programmes achieving a high degree of sustainability have secured the funding they need to serve significant numbers of potential clients.

To pinpoint how some of these factors can translate into policies and programming, the Consultative Group to Assist the Poor, a donor consortium, has developed performance standards for microfinance. These are now widely accepted as industry norms, even as an increasing number of countries have made their policy and regulatory environments more conducive to supplying financial services for the poor. There is also a growing recognition among microfinance institutions that integration into the formal financial system is required to ensure continuity and expansion. Still, only around two per cent of an estimated 10,000 to 15,000 microfinance operations and institutions worldwide operate in a professional and fully sustainable manner. They serve more than 90 per cent of the active microfinance client base worldwide, however, and comprise professional financial institutions now independent of development aid and government subsidies.

In 1997, UNDP and the UN Capital Development Fund (UNCDF) launched the MicroStart programme in order to help build a new generation of microfinance institutions with solid institutional and financial performance. Individual country strategies have been influenced by the experience of mature markets such as those in Bangladesh and Bolivia, which underscored the importance of nurturing breakthrough microfinance institutions with the potential to become industry leaders and attract healthy competition to the market, while maintaining broad access. MicroStart programmes globally have confirmed this approach – the biggest advances have come from institutions with the vision, drive and capacity to rapidly upscale their operations. Often, 80 per cent of the results of these programmes come from 20 per cent of the institutions – the market leaders. Two examples illustrate this point.

In Mongolia, an experienced practitioner initially worked with two multi-purpose NGOs that wanted to pilot credit services. They soon realized that microfinance would consume all their internal management capacity. Preferring to continue their range of services, arrangements were made to set up a new institution dedicated to microfinance. The practitioner provided technical advice and served as a mentor to Xac, the name of the new organization, which achieved financial self-sufficiency within just 18 months following an initial, small investment of $1 million. In three years, Xac's share of the total loans issued by the financial sector in Mongolia reached 28.5 percent. Inspired by this success, a number of other financial institutions embarked on microloan lending, while Xac became the first microfinance institute ever to be licensed by the Bank of Mongolia. Six other financial companies were subsequently licensed. Competition is now spurring healthy development of the industry, improving corporate management and increasing the variety and quality of financial services.

Another success story can be found in Morocco, where MicroStart invested $1.5 million in seven microfinance institutions, while the Save the Children Federation provided technical advice and mentoring. In its first three years, the programme attracted 40,723 new clients, 86 per cent of whom came through a provider called Zakoura. It grew from 2,000 to 36,830 active clients while achieving financial self-sufficiency. Moreover, Zakoura increased the value of its outstanding loans from $300,000 to over $5,000,000 during the course of the programme, even though the monetary value of its assistance from MicroStart was only $215,000. The institution was able to finance this growth largely by borrowing from commercial sources that trusted its businesslike approach.

A mid-term evaluation found that evidence of the technical partner's influence abounds at Zakoura. The organization was far from a top performer at the beginning, and still has a long way to go. Yet it made productive use of the learning available through MicroStart. For donors and other investors, the key is to learn to distinguish between "small and promising" and "small and weak". In the space of a year, Zakoura was serving 80,000 active clients, with plans to continue doubling its clientele annually. A key factor driving this growth was stiff competition from Al-Almana, the other leading microfinance institution in Morocco, with roughly the same number of clients.

Results and Critical Factors

- Funders can support development of the microfinance sector by investing and structuring their assistance wisely. However, they do not create successful microfinance; managers with the vision to establish sustainable institutions do.

- The principal role of donors is to pick promising horses. For the most part, donors are bettors, not jockeys or trainers. The extent to which externally provided capacity development can help improve mediocre runners is often overstated.

- While weak organizations may need more assistance than strong ones, experience shows that organizations with skilful management are the ones more likely to put support to effective use. Poorly managed organizations often cannot implement even good ideas.

- Restricting investment to a particular geographic area will dramatically limit its impact and slow down the process of national coverage. It is better to start by identifying institutions that have the vision and capacity to grow to national coverage, and then back their business plans for expansion.

Further information

The Introduction of Micro-finance in Mongolia: XAC. 2001. Presentation by the former Deputy Governor, Central Bank of Mongolia, to the Global Meeting on Promising MFIs. New York, June.

Elisabeth Rhyne. 1998. "The Yin and Yang of Microfinance: Reaching the Poor and Sustainability." In *MicroBanking Bulletin.*

Elisabeth Rhyne and Jill Donahue. 1999. *MicroStart: Finding and Feeding Breakthroughs – Mid-Term Evaluation.* UNDP and UNCDF/Special Unit for Microfinance (www.uncdf.org/english/microfinance/ microstart/midterm/).

Richard Rosenberg. 1998. *Independent Review of UNCDF Micro-finance Activities.* Consultative Group to Assist the Poor (www.um.dk/danida/evalueringsrapporter/1999-5/a2.asp).

UN Capital Development Fund/Special Unit for Microfinance (UNCDF/SUM) (www.uncdf.org/sum).

United States Agency for International Development (USAID). 2002. *Clients in Context: The Impacts of Micro-finance in Three Countries. Assessing the Impact of Microenterprise Services (AIMS).* USAID (www.mip.org).

The authors gratefully acknowledge the contributions of John Tucker, UNCDF/Special Unit for Microfinance.

⮕ MOROCCO:
CLEAR DECISIONS ON TELECOMMUNICATIONS POWER ECONOMIC GROWTH

> ### In a Nutshell
>
> When the Moroccan government began deregulating its telecommunications industry, it first split post and telecommunications services and then set up a National Agency of Telecommunications Regulations. A cell phone license was issued that attracted international interest and earned the country $1.1 billion. The state-owned Maroc Telecom went private after extensive modernization, and phone access skyrocketed over a period of seven years, from 4.5 to 20 lines per 100 inhabitants.
>
> Morocco's successful transformation of its telecommunications industry can be attributed to strong national vision and leadership, sound regulations, total transparency and prudent use of international expertise to bolster local capacities.

The Story

Deregulation was first proposed in Morocco during a telecommunications workshop held in 1994. The subject stirred a vigorous debate – for Morocco, the choice was either to follow the international movement in this direction or remain on the fringe of competitiveness. Eventually, the former option held out, and in October 1996, the Moroccan Cabinet passed legislation to launch deregulation. It was guided by three principle objectives: splitting postal and telecommunications activities; separating regulatory functions and business activities; and establishing regulation, verification and arbitration bodies for the industry. An estimated $6-7 billion would be needed to reach a phone density of 15 lines per 100 inhabitants, a goal beyond the means of the state or the post and telecommunications authority. Capital from national and foreign partners was the only way to mobilize financing.

In 1997, post and telecommunications services were split through the creation of the Ittissalat Al Maghreb (IAM), a public limited company with the task of ensuring universal access. It was also mandated to set up one or more public telecommunications networks. A private company, Barid Al Maghreb (BAM), was designated for improving the postal services.

The separation of management and marketing duties, and the establishment of verification and arbitration mechanisms soon followed with the formation of the National Agency of Telecommunications Regulations (ANRT). This body, placed under the authority of the Prime Minister, and administered by a board and a management committee, is responsible for granting licenses, permits, agreements and registrations, and for ensuring appropriate oversight.

IAM then created its own trademark, Maroc Telecom, to provide cell phone services, while the ANRT launched an invitation to tender for a second cell phone license. The license was predicted to cost between $150-200 million, but 15 operators showed strong interest. Through competitive bidding, the professionalism of the ANRT, and the credibility and transparency that accompanied the entire process, the purchase price soared to $1.1 billion.

While during the first five years of cell phone operations there were only 120,000 subscribers, the sale of the second network accelerated development of the market in a way that even the most optimistic observers would not have forecast: from 600,000 at the start of the second license to 6 million in 2002. Two factors spurred this boom: first, the competition between the two operators and their very aggressive marketing strategies, and second, a prepaid card formula, which was very attractive and netted about 80 per cent of the subscriptions.

The privatization in December 2000 of Maroc Telecom – through the sale of 35 per cent of its assets, and the introduction of another segment on the local and international stock exchanges – was the largest such transfer to take place in Morocco. The preparation for privatization was accompanied by a thorough modernization. New value-added services were offered, including technological innovations such as short messaging service (SMS); the wireless application protocol (WAP), which allows Internet access; specialized connections, etc. The network is now 100 per cent digital and has more than 5,000 kilometres of fibre optic cables. For the first six months of 2000, a turnover of $500 million and a profit of $100 million were up 32 per cent and 48 per cent, respectively, compared with the same period the year before.

However, the privatization coincided with the world economic downturn. Since the spring of 2000, the value of industry stocks has crashed 40 per cent, reducing the financing capacity of buyers. Only Vivendi made an offer for Maroc Telecom, of $2.3 million, which was 15 per cent above the minimum price set by the state.

Throughout the deregulation process, ANRT leaders consistently stressed human resources capacity development. The European Union participated in creating the agency, contributing to its business plan and human resources training, with teamwork playing an important role. Once nominated, the ANRT director selected five university-educated people to take on different management positions. These were Moroccan nationals who did not have much experience initially. But they carefully studied the experiences of other countries, each one examining how a particular nation introduced the telecommunications industry to the free market. They also learned from highly qualified international advice on subjects such as markets, market strategy and preparation of specifications.

Results and Critical Factors

Liberalization resulted in the rapid development of a modern industry, with the number of phones soaring from 4.5 to 20 lines per 100 inhabitants between 1995 and 2002. Subscription prices, access and communication costs, and the waiting time to get a connection all dropped dramatically. Telecommunications has become one of the most important motors powering Morocco's economic development, pulling in $3.5 billion in foreign investments since 1999, or about two-thirds of the country's global foreign investments between 1998 and 2001. This achievement stems from a combination of critical factors:

- The government took a clear position on embracing deregulation, and implemented the necessary measures to facilitate a smooth transition, based on sound regulations and total transparency.

- Staunch political commitment combined with timely actions to split up the industry and establish the necessary regulatory mechanisms inspired confidence among international investors to take advantage of viable market opportunities.

- International expertise and experience were selectively used to enhance the work of local managers at the ANRT, and to strengthen the capacity and credibility of the organization.

Further information:

Département de la Poste et des Technologies de l'Information (www.septi.gov.ma).

S. Dutta, and M. Coury. *Global Information Technology Report 2002-2003*. Chapter 8, "ICT Challenges for the Arab World." World Economic Forum (www.developmentgateway.org/download/189102/Chapter_08_ICT_Challenges_for_the_Arab_World.pdf).

International Telecommunication Union. 2001. *Effective Regulation: A Case Study – Morocco* (www.itu.int/itudoc/itu-d/publicat/ma_ca_st.html).

————. 2002. *World Telecommunication Development Report: Reinventing Telecoms* (www.itu.int/ITU-D/ict/publications/wtdr_02/index.html).

Maroc Telecom (www.iam.net.ma)

Opérateur de la 2ème Licence GSM, Méditel (Médi Telecom) (www.meditel.ma).

Agence Nationale de Régulation des Télécommunications (www.anrt.net.ma).

World Bank. 1999. Introducing Telecommunications Competition through a Wireless License: Lessons from Morocco. (www.wds.worldbank.org/servlet/WDS_IBank_Servlet?pcont=details&eid=000094946_0 0022505304425).

————. 2000. *Morocco – Information Infrastructure Sector Development Loan Project (IIDSL)*. (www-wds.worldbank.org/servlet/WDS_IBank_Servlet?pcont=details&eid=000094946_00050205562567).

The authors gratefully acknowledge the contributions of Olivier Ranaivondrambola and UNDP Morocco.

⮕ **MOZAMBIQUE:**
BRINGING BACK JUSTICE, LAW AND ORDER TESTS LONG-TERM
COMMITMENT

In a Nutshell

UNDP technical cooperation in the area of public security and justice in Mozambique dates back to the mid-1990s, forming an integral part of a larger portfolio of support for post-crisis governance. The programme's primary objective is to ensure public safety and security by improving the quality of policing and the justice system.

The experience in Mozambique provides insights on capacity development in general, highlighting the importance of adopting a holistic approach and making operational linkages with other broad-based initiatives, such as public sector reform. Additional lessons include understanding the dynamics of change, building capacity on the basis of existing knowledge and systems, and being willing to commit to long-term engagement.

The Story

In December 1992, the Security Council approved the creation of the United Nations Operations in Mozambique (UNOMOZ), following the signing of the General Peace Agreement between the then President of Mozambique and the President of the Resistencia Nacional Mozambicana. The mandate of UNOMOZ covered four areas: political, military, electoral and humanitarian. Specifically, it called for the creation of new public security forces, and proposed steps to de-politicize and restructure the police force. The demobilization of some 71,000 combatants underscored the urgency of establishing an effective force to maintain order. Through Law 19/92, the Mozambique Republic Police (PRM) was set up as a paramilitary force composed of 20,000 ex-military personnel.

UNDP support to the PRM began after UNOMOZ left Mozambique in 1994. The scope and nature of assistance was based on a needs assessment undertaken by the Spanish Civil Guard, on behalf of UNDP and the government. The first project started in 1997, with bilateral assistance coordinated by UNDP and implemented by the Guard. It aimed to improve the capacity of the new police force for guaranteeing public safety, in strict observance of international norms of human rights and citizens' freedoms. Most of the support focused on functional and organizational re-engineering, rehabilitation of training facilities, curriculum development, training and reorientation of members of the police force. A second phase began in October 2001, emphasizing strategic planning and stronger management at the central command, the establishment of model policing units countrywide (including innovative facilities for assisting female victims), community policing, and continuing technical support to the police academy and training programme.

Assistance to the justice sector – encompassing the Ministry of Justice, the Supreme Court, the Attorney General's Office and the Administrative Court – followed in 1999, with the goal of modernizing the system and its institutions to become fair and timely. This complemented the work with the police force, as the administration of justice is inseparable from the maintenance of law and order. The first phase of the project included the establishment of the Legal and Judicial Training Centre for judges, prosecutors, court clerks and legal assistants, and modernization of the prison system. The current phase focuses on enhancing the individual skills of justice personnel, institutional development and decentralized administration of justice, with particular attention paid to cross-cutting issues that undermine capacity development in the sector, such as corruption.

Notwithstanding the relatively short period of intervention and the narrow objectives, the programme has made significant contributions. In human resources development, these have included the rehabilitation of police and legal training facilities; training needs assessments and subsequent development of new curricula; and individual training for about 5,000 police officers and 100 justice system officials. In terms of organizational development, achievements have encompassed a functional review of the police force and the justice sector; the development of policy and strategic plans – with inputs from civil society – for restructuring the police force; the creation of a new policy for the prison system and a framework for its implementation; a strengthened and more independent judiciary; and improved managerial and administrative capacity at the Ministry of Justice and the Attorney General's Office.

Results and Critical Factors

- Accomplishments related to social capacities have comprised modest improvement in the quality of the overall administration of justice, law and order; introduction of community policing and alternative local dispute resolution mechanisms; enhanced capacity for change within the police force as well as the justice sector; significant political support for capacity development at all levels related to public security and justice; stronger public dialogue on legal reform and the administration of justice, law and order; and enhanced participation of civil society on these issues through periodic surveys on the performance of the police and judiciary.

- It is arguable that not enough attention was paid to the peculiarities of the administration of justice, law and order in Mozambique during the programme's initial design. The model of the new police force is based on the Spanish Civil Guard, which is paramilitary in nature and clearly foreign. Its relevance over time and its sustainability in the Mozambican milieu is increasingly uncertain. Questions have been raised about its composition and suitability. The model in its current form is in fact not quite consistent with its desire to make justice, law and order widely accessible and people friendly.

- Capacity development cannot be undertaken in isolation from other transformational activities, including those immediately or seemingly outside the target institutions, such as the policy environment. In this case, the appalling remuneration and working conditions of the police, legal and justice personnel in Mozambique curtail capacity development, but can only be effectively addressed within the framework of larger public service reform.

- Capacity development requires a capacity for change, a capacity to manage change and a capacity to sustain change. These dimensions apply at all three levels – individual, institutional and societal – and cannot be taken for granted. They must be deliberately addressed in designing technical cooperation programmes that are holistic and based on a long-term horizon.

Further information

Amnesty International. 2002. *Policing to Protect Human Rights: A Survey of Police Practices in Countries of the Southern African Development Community, 1997-2002* (www.amnesty.org).

Richard Synge. 1997. *Mozambique: UN Peacekeeping in Action, 1992-94.* Washington, D.C.: United Nations Institute for Peace Press.

United Nations. 1996. *United Nations Operation in Mozambique.* New York: UN Department of Public Information.

United Nations Development Programme (UNDP). 2001. *UNDP and Security Sector Reform in Post-Conflict Situations.* New York: UNDP Evaluation Office.

United Nations Development Programme (UNDP) projects of the government of Mozambique. Project documents MOZ/95/015 and MOZ/00/007, Support to PRM, Phases I and II; MOZ/98/003, Support to Justice. Maputo: UNDP.

The authors gratefully acknowledge the contributions of Aeneus Chuma and UNDP Mozambique.

⮑ MOZAMBIQUE:
EFFECTIVE BUDGET SUPPORT FOR POST-FLOOD RECONSTRUCTION

In a Nutshell

Following the floods and cyclones of 2000 and 2001 in Mozambique, the government set in motion a post-flood reconstruction programme, quickly revealing its leadership as well as its ability to rally the international community and perform a number of functions efficiently and transparently. Strong government commitment to programme goals provided the incentive for donors to pledge significant resources and agree to work largely through the national system, including the government's budget. In turn, this helped strengthen accountability and transparency, while avoiding complex and multiple funding arrangements. Establishment of a parliamentary task force to oversee the programme further ensured that the government was not only held to account by its external partners but also by the country's legislators.

The Story

In 2000, media around the world reported on the massive devastation of floods and cyclones in Mozambique, mainly in the southern part of the country. Over a quarter of the population was affected in some way, while more than 700 people died. Many important connecting roads, bridges, power lines, schools, health centres, businesses and homes were completely destroyed. The next year, severe floods struck again, this time across more than double the area of the previous year. For a country classified as one of the poorest in the world, there was an urgent need to act quickly. To make an appeal for support, the government of Mozambique co-hosted a donors' conference with UNDP and the government of Italy in Rome. The conference document was wholly produced by Mozambique, and presented a clear and well-thought-out plan of action. Financial pledges of over $453 million soon came forth, 25 per cent more than the estimated cost of the proposal.

Upon returning from Rome, government officials signed new agreements with all donors that had pledged resources. This approach was innovative because pledges in international conferences and round tables have often been considered only somewhat binding. In this case, a legally binding contract was in place with a well-defined schedule of financial disbursements, matched by corresponding reconstruction activities and reporting procedures. Donors were encouraged to channel funds through the government budget and not through the establishment of a specific trust fund. While some wanted closer control over their contributions, funding through the treasury would give the government full responsibility for using the funds as well as for ensuring strict accountability and supervision. It also meant that the reconstruction programme would be fully integrated into the overall public sector financial management system. Fund management was consequently handled through existing administrative arrangements, with little additional capacity required. Assistance was disbursed rapidly, totalling over 90 per cent in late 2002. There have been remarkably few of the usual complaints about delays, unaccounted funds and opaque procedures.

As part of the efforts to ensure the programme's efficiency and adequate coverage, Mozambique's Parliament set up a task force to monitor the reconstruction activities. It had earlier created a committee to monitor the floods, and now called upon the Ministry of Finance and Planning to submit quarterly progress reports. The first of these appeared six months after the Rome conference and was widely circulated among donors. This kind of record of events as they unfolded may have played an important role in motivating quick dispersal of funds. UNDP continued to support the monitoring, keeping donors up to date with data provided by both the donors and the government.

The speed and magnitude of the international response to Mozambique's reconstruction needs marked donors' strong endorsement of the government's post-flood reconstruction programme. Many were bold enough to go well beyond a normal response, and commit themselves to something much bigger and more ambitious than would normally have been the case. During the Rome conference, a number noted that the scope of their assistance reflected their recognition of the prudent macroeconomic policies that Mozambique has pursued since 1995. As a result of these experiences, the government is now encouraging donors to consider new forms of support that harmonize their procedures around government systems and again channel funds through its budget.

Results and Critical Factors

The Mozambican experience with recovering from the floods brings out several practical lessons in capacity development, with the success of the reconstruction programme attributed to a handful of factors:

- Strong government ownership and commitment to the goals of the programme provided the incentive for donors to pledge significant resources and agree to work largely through the national system.

- Working through the budget was crucial in strengthening national accountability and transparency, while also avoiding complex and multiple funding arrangements.

- The binding commitments of donors to rapid disbursements ensured a reliable and consistent flow of resources, and locked donors and the government into a clearly spelled-out contractual relationship.

- Accountability to Parliament meant that the government was held to account for the use of public funds not only by its external partners, but also by the country's legislators.

- There was a willingness among donors to trust national systems, in terms of contributing funds through the national budget, simplifying and harmonizing reporting requirements, and relying upon UNDP as an intermediary.

Further information

Government of Mozambique. 2000. *Post-Emergency Reconstruction Programme.* International Reconstruction Conference. Rome, 3-4 May.

————. 2001. *Post Flood Reconstruction Programme for Central Mozambique.* Maputo.

United Nations Development Programme (UNDP). 2001. *Support to Mozambique's Reconstruction Programme.* Final report. Maputo: UNDP.

United Nations Development Programme (UNDP) and the Government of Mozambique. *2000 International Reconstruction Conference: Six Months Later.* Maputo.

The authors gratefully acknowledge the contributions of Alexander Aboagye and UNDP Mozambique.

⮑ THE PHILIPPINES:
ACCENTURE'S STRATEGY TO ATTRACT AND RETAIN LOCAL TALENT

In a Nutshell

Retention of local talent in developing countries is a challenge that requires an organization to understand the culture and motivations of individuals. For a private company, keeping local staff has definite business advantages, but there is also an associated societal responsibility in developing the nation's human resources. To hold on to local talent, public and private institutions must develop an integrated strategy encompassing skill-building, financial and cultural dimensions.

This is precisely what Accenture, a global management consulting firm, attempted in its operation in the Philippines. The firm set out to understand the perspectives and hopes of workers, with an operational strategy focused on providing fulfilling and challenging jobs, and an organizational culture designed to further connect staff members to their colleagues and community. The result was that any staff member considering migrating to work overseas would need to seriously weigh the opportunities (higher salary plus a potentially better lifestyle and future) against the challenges (cultural distance and displacement, and perhaps a less fulfilling job).

The Story

Management consulting is an industry that does not produce tangible products for wholesale or retail distribution, but provides advisory and project-based assistance to its clients. With this operating model, the substantive assets of a consulting firm are the knowledge and skills of its staff. Acquiring, developing and retaining valued personnel are fundamental functions, because attrition not only erodes institutional knowledge and morale, but carries a high financial replacement cost. A sound retention strategy is therefore vital for the success of the business.

For a global management consulting firm operating in developing countries, holding on to qualified local staff presents particular challenges, given the steady brain drain overseas. Aggressively marketed opportunities are pitched to skilled people, dangling high salaries for jobs in developed countries. Social and cultural issues, which include family financial pressures, revolve around the perception of a better lifestyle and future overseas, along with a desire in some cases to join family members there. Companies themselves need to balance the provision of effective career development in the hope of keeping staff with the associated risk of increasing opportunities for them to leave.

In the Philippines, Accenture developed an integrated retention strategy in response to these challenges, based on general corporate directives and covering four areas: the organization's model, career development, remuneration and cultural considerations. Regarding the first, the firm's typical approach to starting operations in a new country was to use skilled expatriate managers to run and develop the business, hire the best people possible from the local populace, and transfer managerial responsibilities to local staff as skills and experience evolved. This "develop local partners" model was premised on the understanding that local staff will always have a cultural and societal advantage in understanding, networking and selling to local businesses. It was driven by a long-term objective to build a sustainable local business. Other models prevalent in the industry include hiring expatriates to manage and run, or flying teams of expatriates in and out of the country on a project-by-project basis. However, these approaches are considered short term and not as effective in building a successful service business that draws on local staff and clients.

The retention strategy in the Philippines' married the "develop local partners" thrust with a strong emphasis on the second part of its strategy, structured career development as an effective way to reduce attrition. The firm recruited aggressively at the best universities in the Philippines, highlighting the advantages of skill-building and career development with a global multinational. The global "Win the War for Talent" campaign was localized to determine the best approaches to attracting top university graduates and experienced personnel.

In addition, Accenture offices in the Southeast Asia region annually recruited overseas to attract Asian students attending universities in Europe and the United States, akin to a reverse brain drain or returnee programme. Once any staff member came on board, the firm provided regular formal training, including annual sessions at a global training facility in the United States. In the Philippines, strategic assignment of individuals to projects elsewhere in the region helped enhance skills and experiences. Career development was also nurtured through a strong focus on knowledge sharing within Southeast Asia and a mentorship programme. The firm had no "glass ceiling" with respect to promoting local staff, and in general, the pace of promotion in consulting is rapid compared to the corporate world. Due to flat organizational structures, a "slot" does not need to open for an individual to move up. In the Philippines, it was clear to staff members that they had the opportunity to reach the top, as evidenced by a Filipino Managing Partner running the office, and the fact that 75 per cent of the partners based in Manila were Filipinos.

Remuneration was the third arm of the retention strategy. Accenture attracted recruits with initial salaries that were maintained in the top quartile of corporate businesses in the Philippines, and provided hiring bonuses for high-demand skills. In addition, annual salary increases were based on merit rather than linked to years of service, and outstanding performers could claim large salary increases. Nonetheless, this approach could not match the double, triple and beyond salary boosts a skilled consultant could obtain by migrating overseas.

The fourth component, cultural considerations, proved to be one of the strongest elements in aiding retention. The term "cultural" in this context includes organizational and team culture, as well as societal and family culture. To understand local sensibilities, Accenture provided incoming expatriates with training that covered general living challenges, alongside specific cultural, political, historical and business issues. This helped expatriates manage more effectively, make fewer cultural blunders, encounter fewer frustrations, and have a richer sense of understanding of the country and its people.

Accenture also fostered an organizational and team culture to develop skills and innovation. Staff felt a link to "the firm" through the global training centre, knowledge sharing, cross-national staffing of projects, and the pride of belonging to a large and successful multinational. To foster a team culture within the newly forming technology practice in the Philippines, both social and professional development activities took place. The group of staff shared experiences, project activities and personal aspirations, which further connected them to the local community and lessened the incentive to venture overseas.

Results and Critical Factors

Through the application of this strategy, the following retention results were achieved from 1995 through 1998 in the technology practice in the Philippines:

- Growth of the practice from eight to over 50 staff members.

- An average departure rate of 17 per cent (the industry average in the Philippines was between 25-30 per cent). The average departure rate of the highest rated staff was less than 10 per cent.

- Among staff who left, the great majority joined a Philippines-based organization or pursued further academic study, rather than migrating, therefore keeping their skills in the country.

- The management of the practice was successfully transferred to a Filipino colleague, who continues to succeed in building and growing it.

Accenture's four-pronged approach meant that staff weighed the potential benefits of working abroad against the large number of intangible benefits of remaining in their native country. Key factors for the success of this strategy included the organization's "develop local partners" model; career development based on knowledge sharing and without a "glass ceiling"; competitive remuneration based on merit; and, as one of the strongest elements, cultural considerations that covered team culture as well as societal and family cultures.

Further information

Accenture (www.accenture.com).

Charles Hampden-Turner, and Fons Trompenaars. 1997. *Riding the Waves of Culture: Understanding Diversity in Global Business.* New York: McGraw-Hill.

————. 2001. Building Cross-Culture Competence. New York: John Wiley & Sons (http://intermundo.net/print.pl?mid=4; ISBN: 0471495271).

The authors gratefully acknowledge the contributions of John Patterson, formerly with Accenture Philippines.

⟳ THE PHILIPPINES:
CIVIL SOCIETY PUTS A WATCH ON PUBLIC SPENDING

In a Nutshell

G-Watch, or Government Watch, is a civil society initiative in the Philippines for monitoring public sector expenditure. The group promotes transparency and citizen's participation in governance, helping to hold government departments accountable. Involving a wide variety of stakeholders, such as policy research institutes, academia and international agencies, the project has spotlighted a number of cases of government profligacy, non-existent projects and bad management. Working with young university graduates, who photograph and research public projects, G-Watch then compares these results to government facts and figures, and discusses discrepancies with officials in open forums.

The Story

Profligacy, poor management and corruption strangle public expenditure in developing countries. The Philippines is no exception. In 1998, for example, the Department of Education, Culture, and Sports claimed to have spent over $1.3 million under the Third Elementary Education Project to build two classrooms – about $670,000 each!

G-Watch was born to call public attention to these forms of waste. It was initiated by the Philippine Governance Forum, a collaborative project of the Ateneo School of Government, the Ateneo Centre for Social Policy and Public Affairs, and UNDP. Its fourfold objective is: to monitor selected government projects; to communicate the findings from these to the agencies concerned as well as to key stakeholders; to use the findings for dialogue and problem solving; and to develop monitoring skills and tools at the local level to facilitate stronger community vigilance.

The group conducted its first mission in 2000, covering three government departments on three of the main islands of the country: the Department of Education, Culture, and Sports; the Department of Health; and the Department of Public Works and Highways. Projects chosen for review were ones that were part of the agencies' principal mandates. G-Watch field researchers, fresh college graduates chosen to bring an "untrained eye" to the exercise, fanned out to agency offices to obtain and review documents, and go through budgets related to project allocations. From a list of these projects, the Philippine Governance Forum consulted with high officials to select the ones that they could best monitor, and that had either been finished or were nearing completion. After they picked the most appropriate cases, the researchers were dispatched to project sites. Armed with still cameras and documents, they undertook actual inspections and conducted interviews with key informants and local project managers to compare the information on paper with the results on the ground.

They discovered that in at least two cases, the Department of Education, Culture and Sports failed to achieve project outputs. Its Milk Feeding Programme, for example, was supposed to provide milk to 5,048 children in selected schools in one region from January to March 2000 – yet not a single drop was delivered. A school building, on record as newly constructed, turned out to have only two walls. With the Department of Public Works and Highways, the researchers discovered that the government had released $6.6 million in the 1999-2000 budget for a project that was already reported completed in September 1998, while six high-priority projects either overshot their original budgets, suffered delays, failed to meet standards in their original plan, had funds that were unaccounted for, or worse, were grossly overcompensated.

These findings were presented in a forum attended by government officials, Ateneo School of Government faculty and representatives of civil society groups. There were varied reactions, but no one seemed surprised by what was revealed. Some participants defended the anomalies that were uncovered, but none questioned their accuracy.

A second phase has since begun where G-Watch is collaborating with the Department of Budget Management and the World Bank to assess the Social Expenditure Management Programme, a social safety net plan that the government put in place in response to the Asian financial crisis. This second phase aims to make the monitoring process more systematic by examining the rationality of expenditures incurred, analysing agency processes, and computing opportunity costs of overruns and delays.

Results and Critical Factors

- G-Watch has demonstrated the constructive role that civil society can play in holding the government to account and in increasing the level of transparency in public expenditure tracking. Most evident is its ability to monitor agency performance and point out corruption.

- Initiatives such as G-Watch can usefully complement internal government and parliamentary monitoring mechanisms, as well as citizen watchdogs or user report card initiatives. It substantiates perceptions with on-the-ground information to clearly measure the quality and quantity of service delivery by public agencies.

- The methodology employed by G-Watch is fairly straightforward and does not involve any complex or theoretical tools. This makes it easy to use at the community level.

- G-Watch also provides a forum where different government agencies and civil society can interact to agree, refine and reflect on the findings of its investigations. The ultimate test is whether as a result of G-Watch enquiries, the Philippines' government takes action to address irregularities.

Further information
Philippine Governance Forum. Government Watch Programme
(www.pgf.org.ph/gwatch.html).

————. 2000. A forum newsletter, 1(1) (www.pgf.org.ph/forum/gwatchmonitor.html).

World Bank. *Filipino Report Card on Pro-Poor Services: Case Studies on Civic Engagement in Public Expenditure Management*
(www.worldbank.org/participation/web/webfiles/philipreport.htm).

The authors gratefully acknowledge the contributions of UNDP Philippines.

➲ THE PHILIPPINES:
THE LONG ROAD TO RELIABLE AGRICULTURAL STATISTICS

In a Nutshell

The Philippines' Bureau of Agricultural Statistics (BAS) was established in 1987 to provide reliable and timely agricultural statistics. It has since emerged as a vital contributor to improved agricultural policy-making, programming and project formulation, and enjoys a premier status as a producer and disseminator of high quality information. The BAS story is one of an institution receiving constant and incremental technical cooperation for capacity development, which was provided synergistically by a number of agencies over time, growing steadily in quality and sophistication.

The BAS today serves as the statistical arm of the Department of Agriculture. It is governed by the policies of the Philippine Statistical System and serves as an active partner in many inter-agency activities housed or initiated by the National Statistical Coordination Board. At the field level, it is a vital and credible source of data for the agriculture sector.

The Story

The BAS was created to serve as the official agency of the Philippines' government for the generation, compilation and release of statistics on agriculture, fisheries and related fields. To develop the whole range of capacities needed for such an organization to function efficiently and intervene in policy formulation, a series of technical cooperation inputs were acquired from the Asian Development Bank (ADB), FAO and USAID.

The bank's technical cooperation focused on statistical research with an emphasis on improving sampling frames, survey designs, and data collection and crop forecasting methods; setting up personnel training; and implementing a decentralized data-processing system.

Then came a more detailed, nine-year USAID technical cooperation package. This included training in agricultural statistics, technical report writing, computer operation and management of survey operations. There was a master's degree course in statistics for BAS personnel as well as some non-degree training courses. This investment helped BAS set up a strong base for planning and for implementing its various statistical programmes and activities. It also helped reorient existing BAS field offices from mere data collection sites to functional operation centres. Crop and livestock production surveys were redesigned and alternative mechanisms for estimating fruit and vegetable production were devised.

This paved the way for rationalizing BAS' marketing and price information system. The composition of market baskets, including procedures for price data collection, were subsequently modified to conform with observed marketing practices in the production and trading areas to suit the needs of data users. Data users and producers came together in a series of national, regional and provincial symposia and workshops that helped both parties understand different expectations and limitations. The workshops also established and strengthened links with agribusiness.

Beyond improvements in data collection, processing and analysis, the USAID project also helped the BAS develop its information dissemination capacity. A number of publications were produced: an agribusiness directory series, marketing bulletins, and situation and outlook reports. The project published comic magazines to teach farmers about important agricultural issues. AgStatView, a bulletin, presented analysis of information on basic agricultural variables in an easy-to-understand format. Early warning systems began, along with an electronic system of disseminating agricultural data called the Electronic Access to Statistical Information Board (EASIBoard). Finally, through the Local Area Production and Marketing Analysis Service (LAPAMAS), the BAS collaborated with farmers' cooperatives as well as with national offices and local government units to produce a localized version of the AgStatView. This was supplemented by comic book presentations of information on agricultural production and the market situation.

Some months after the launching of LAPAMAS, a related outreach service dealing with the cost of agricultural production was conceived. This entailed highly specialized technical assessments, but the agricultural survey system could not afford to do a regular cost of production survey. Following meetings with various stakeholders, a collaborative activity with cooperatives began. Interested members could participate in the "recording project", where they underwent orientation on the mechanics of farm recording using a structured recording form. However, the complexity of recording and data processing meant that there was a considerable time lag before farmers got to see the results. The high costs and the need for sophisticated skills made the project unviable. Yet given the benefits, farmers petitioned for its continuation.

At this point, the BAS turned to FAO for assistance, which led to the Philippine Project on Assistance in Processing, Analysis and Utilization of Farm Level Data.

This initiative procured and installed hardware and software for on-site process-ing of records. Initially, central office staff edited these, but eventually local staff took over this responsibility along with the cooperatives, with a data processing system installed on the latter's computers. The project invested in training and farm level consultations, with the services of local experts plus the advice and supervision of FAO officers. While initially the project was carried out according to the design introduced by the experts, BAS staff modified the system over time in accordance with user requirements, balanced by the available resources.

Besides these specialized inputs, FAO has also provided BAS with staff study visits to other Association of Southeast Asian Nations (ASEAN) countries. Through FAO-initi-ated regional forums such as the biennial Asia-Pacific Commission on Agricultural Statistics, expert meetings and seminars, BAS has the opportunity to inform FAO mem-ber countries of the results of its various capacity development initiatives.

Results and Critical Factors

The series of technical cooperation inputs that BAS received from the ADB, USAID and FAO significantly contributed to its efforts to be recognized as a dependable source of agricultural statistics, not only to support national agricultural policies, programmes and projects, but also in terms of wider sharing with the internation-al community. Despite limitations imposed by government budgetary constraints, BAS has managed to maintain the prestige it has carefully nurtured over the years.

- Capacity development projects at BAS have clearly improved the knowl-edge and skills of staff, thus increasing their confidence in linking up with different partners and collaborators for expanding the delivery of BAS products and services.

- The organization has acquired specialized skills and is able to carry out fairly sophisticated surveys and data processing that benefits the agri-cultural sector. While technical cooperation was used to import skills and equipment, BAS' personnel capacity was systematically and simultane-ously upgraded to the point where staff could modify various assessments and indicators to meet local needs.

- The dissemination of complex findings was done in easily comprehended formats such as comic books and radio broadcasts, a tactic that was especially important given that the primary clients for such information are farmers and farmers' cooperatives. The result was clear in the farm-ers' well-articulated demand for continuation of certain services.

- Donors and international agencies have demonstrated a willingness to stay engaged for the entire period that it takes to develop 360 degree capacities, and have continued to participate in the building of the BAS from time to time.

Further information

Bureau of Agricultural Statistics (BAS) (bas.gov.ph).

Association of Southeast Asian Nations (ASEAN) (www.aseansec.org).

Food and Agriculture Organization (FAO) (www.fao.org/).

The authors gratefully acknowledge the contributions of Romeo Recide, BAS, along with Hiek Som and Frederick Baker, FAO.

⮕ RWANDA:
UBUDEHE COLLECTIVE COMMUNITY ACTION HOLDS HOPE FOR REBUILDING A SHATTERED SOCIETY

In a Nutshell

Rwanda provides a promising example of working with rural communities on local development. During the national PRSP process, a pilot project turned to the traditional grass-roots practice of collaborative self-help, known as *ubudehe*, as a basis for planning and implementing development initiatives. The government and donors embraced the strategy, recognizing that communities were capable of defining their own problems, priorities and solutions, and should be backed by supportive policy actions and access to resources.

In the process, a major shift occurred through simplified procedures that made funds more accessible, and ensured that local ideas and commitment could be quickly translated into tangible results. Rwanda now intends to expand the pilot, strengthening community structures and capacities nationwide.

The Story

Prior to colonization, Rwanda had a highly organized traditional system of community development and self-reliance centred on collective action. It was known as *ubudehe*. During Rwanda's PRSP preparation, *ubudehe* was revived as a key strategy to address poverty and support decentralization, drawing on the understanding that the poor often best understand the problems they face and know their priorities, but do not have sufficient information or resources to design effective solutions.

A pilot initiative in the province of Butare involved direct funding of projects identified by communities, including livestock rearing, small animal husbandry and manure production, as well as simple infrastructure such as wells, public standpipes and market stalls. First a community would gather to pin down its most urgent problems, and then it would devise a cost strategy, keeping in mind the need to consider those among the poor who are most vulnerable.

In each instance, one poor family would be selected for consultation on its main concerns and proposals for a solution. Madame Mukagasana Liberata, for example, a 35-year-old widow in one village, had two sons and only one hen, placing her close to the bottom of the economic ladder. She concurred with the community that poor harvests due to infertile soil had become a pressing problem. But most rural people cannot afford to purchase fertilizers and receive limited extension services. So Madame Liberata's community, based on her input, decided to raise goats to provide manure for cultivation. They identified the activities required to carry out this project and calculated a time frame for each activity as well as a budget. With the facilitation of a community development worker, they devised team rules to guide their operations, including implementation and monitoring.

Even before the completion of the PRSP, community initiatives such as these became more meaningful when the government struck an arrangement with the European Union to offer on-site funding of up to $1,000 following a simple project process analysis. This was considered more directly effective than waiting for the consultation to finish and subjecting community initiatives to the bulky bureaucratic procedures of the government, NGOs and donors.

Working in this way has marked a departure from the heavy-handed, top-down style of the government and the largely prescriptive approach of many donors and NGOs in the past. Yet it has been successful: the government now intends to adopt the Butare pilot countrywide, which will help existing community structures and capacities to flourish. The risk, however, is in the way the system is tied to project grants; it may generate a culture of entitlements rather than genuine self-help.

Still, Rwanda is a nation with deep government commitment and a strong national belief in the importance of taking ownership of its own destiny. There has been political support from the highest levels for the PRSP process, which was launched by the President in 2000 in the National Assembly. This was a symbolic gesture of endorsement and a recognition of the need for partnership with all stakeholders. It also served to legitimize a country-driven process, giving it political momentum and the hope of sustainability. Without strong political backing, the PRSP and the community-based articulation of a local vision for development would not have been possible in a post-conflict country like Rwanda, where national unity, reconciliation and security concerns take precedence. Yet given Rwanda's history of uneven development and acute resource scarcity, a significant and rapid decline in poverty will be a key element in a stable future, one that involves rebuilding community cohesion along with overall national confidence and pride.

Results and Critical Factors
- Instead of introducing new practices and relying on outside expertise to promote local development, the Butare pilot integrated existing community strategies to address development challenges. This helped to empower local communities and ensured strongly anchored local ownership.

- The government's recognition of the need to encourage its people to take greater charge of their own destiny and its commitment to the PRSP process provided an incentive to donors to offer support through government channels, while giving communities the confidence to take the lead in their own development.

- By simplifying rules and procedures for accessing funds, and by allowing direct and rapid support for community projects even before the end of the PRSP preparations, mutual trust grew between local communities and external agents. The experience also expanded community capacities to communicate and negotiate the course of development from their own perspective.

- With assistance from the government and development partners where necessary, Rwanda now intends to adopt and replicate the community-based approach across the country. It will be used to develop a core training module, which will be integrated into the training component of the national decentralization programme. The Ministry of Local Government will also seek to institutionalize participatory planning and management through community development committees as one of the strategies for poverty reduction.

Further information

Samuel Wangwe. 2002. *The PRSP Process in Rwanda.*
Second Meeting of the African Learning Group on the Poverty Reduction Strategy Papers (PRSP-LG) (www.uneca.org/prsp/docs/rwanda_prsp.htm).

Government of Rwanda, National Poverty Reduction Programme and Ministry of Local Government and Social Affairs. 2001. *Ubudehe mu kurwanya ubukene (Ubudehe to Fight Poverty).* A paper presented by the Rwanda PRSP Team at the 2nd African Forum on Poverty Reduction Strategies (www.worldbank.org/wbi/attackingpoverty/activities/rwanda-nprp.pdf).

Government of Rwanda. 2002. *Local Governance for Poverty Reduction in Rwanda.* Paper presented at the 5th Africa Governance Forum. Maputo, 23-25 May.

Rwanda Poverty Reduction Strategy Paper (http://worldbank.org/poverty/strategies).

The authors gratefully acknowledge the contributions of Barbara Barungi, UNDP Subregional Resource Facility, Pretoria, South Africa.

⊃ SOLOMON ISLANDS:
CONNECTIVITY IS THE OPTION FOR REMOTE ISLANDERS

In a Nutshell

The People First Network, or PFnet, is an initiative providing email access through innovative, low-cost technology. Remote locations across the Solomon Islands connect to the Internet using a simple computer, short-wave radio and solar power. The network helps communities keep in touch, participate in governance, find educational opportunities and generate new sources of income.

This case illustrates how IT innovations can build on available local resources, making technology work for less privileged communities and bridging the digital divide.

The Story

The Solomon Islands consists of roughly 850 islands, mostly underdeveloped and flung out over several thousand square miles of the Pacific Ocean. The country has come through a period of ethnic unrest that left the economy near collapse and the nation in danger of further fragmentation.

Until recently, the only means of communication with the outside world for most remote islands were short-wave radios and satellite telephones. Short-waves often require hours of patient queuing and repeated connection attempts, at a cost that is still too high for rural people living in a no-cash, subsistence economy. Urgent messages are sent through word of mouth. Otherwise, with the postal system being very slow, the principal medium of communication has been letters carried by inter-island travellers. Satellite telephones, where available, are far beyond the reach of the local population, costing between $5 to $10 per minute, regardless of the location being called.

The Solomon Islands People First Network Initiative, an NGO, set out to address these problems with basic email services. It sought to improve connectivity while dramatically reducing the prices of communication, making it affordable for low-income users as well as sustainable over time.

PFnet has two components. One is the People First Internet Café in Honiara, which allows residents of the capital city to send emails or browse the Web. It also serves as a training facility for rural development stakeholders and the broader public. Opening in February 2001 with 12 workstations, it is already financially self-sufficient. A recent survey of customers revealed that most users are students and nearly 40 per cent are women.

The second part of PFnet is a network of email stations located on remote islands. The stations are usually hosted in provincial clinics, schools, or other accessible and secure public facilities, where operators assist customers in sending and receiving emails at a nominal cost. Each station is set up through consultation and an agreement with a village committee that drives the process, raises awareness and inspires a sense of ownership. Used to short-wave radio systems, residents feel comfortable with the technology and are able to do their own troubleshooting.

Typically, rural villagers use the stations to send text emails, which take about ten seconds to transmit. Routine sending of attachments is discouraged. Non-text files such as JPEG images can also be sent, although the user must compress them first. This facility has proven to be useful for NGOs working among rural communities: one group, for example, turns to PFnet to help rural crafts-people market their works with digital photographs, while another assists farmers on identifying pests through pictures.

Several times a day, each remote email station connects to the hub station in Honiara and transfers outgoing emails, which the hub then sends on to the Internet. At the base station, seven different modems operate simultaneously.

After the first remote station was opened in October 2001, seven more were set up by January 2003, and another two have received funds for deployment. With the system in place, it is very simple to add any number of stations on a modular basis; PFnet plans to deploy as many as 25 remote email centres across the nine provinces of the country. All of the selected locations target the most remote areas, where access and telephone service are not already available. The PFnet programme also includes training and capacity development to build the network and facilitate sharing between development stakeholders.

PFnet was set up with funding and technical support from the Solomon Islands Development Administration and Participatory Planning Programme (SIDAPP), a project of UNDP and the United Nations Office for Project Services (UNOPS). The diplomatic missions of China, Great Britain and Japan have also donated directly, while a number of other donors provided funding for the start-up and initial deployment, and continue to support the network's expansion on a station-by-station basis.

Currently, the partners of PFnet include the University of the South Pacific for distance learning trials at a rural community school; Kastom Garden Association (KGA), a community farmer's advice network; the Ministry of Commerce Online Business Information Service, which provides online business information to entrepreneurs and small to medium enterprises, especially in rural areas; and the Solomon Islands Institutional Strengthening of Lands Administration Project (SIISLAP), among others.

PFnet has won international recognition for its achievements: it was a finalist at the 2002 InfoDev/Worldbank/IICD ICT stories competition, and a finalist at the 2002 Stockholm Challenge in Sweden. It has also generated interest among other UNDP country offices in the Asia Pacific region for possible replication.

Results and Critical Factors

As an affordable telecommunications network, PFnet assists low-income groups in taking charge of their own development through improved information and knowledge. It gives rural people a voice in matters concerning their affairs and development, allowing direct contact with decision makers and the media. Other results include:

- In a country fragmented by ethnic strife, a fast and inexpensive communication system plays a role in peace-keeping by dispelling rumours and keeping the channels open between social groups.

- The network facilitates the exchange of information between NGOs, government offices, the media, businesses and other development stakeholders. PFnet is also helping people find new livelihoods, and improving agriculture and land administration.

- PFnet provides distance and vocational education, as well as training in basic information technology skills.

Some factors critical to the success of PFnet have been the adoption of appropriate technology, strong community involvement, the presence of a champion NGO and the demonstration of tangible benefits to the community. Designing the project so it generates its own revenue has been a major contributing factor towards sustainability and future growth.

Further information

ABC Radio Australia-Pacific Beat. n.d. "E-mail Expanding into Villages." A broadcast (http://abc.net.au/ra/pacbeat/stories/s778556.htm).

People First Network. Brochure (www.peoplefirst.net.sb/downloads/PFnet_Brochure.doc).

————. *Rural Community Email Networking in Solomon Islands* (www.peoplefirst.net.sb).

People First Network: The Solomon Islands' Rural E-mail Network for Peace and Development (www.undp.org.fj/PFnet.htm).

➲ SOUTH AFRICA:
POOR PEOPLE FIGHT FOR THEIR SPACE THROUGH
ORGANIZED FORA

In a Nutshell

Convened by the South African NGO Coalition (SANGOCO), the War on Poverty Forum collected numerous anti-poverty programmes around a common agenda: holding public hearings to solicit a wide range of perspectives from ordinary citizens on key policy issues such as health, the environment and housing. A large number of the responses called for redressing grievances, for which separate mechanisms were established. This voice mechanism proved capable of culling a rich and informative body of public opinion.

The Story

In 1997, amidst the frustration of seeing a host of agencies working on poverty eradication through a myriad of schemes, all of which added up to little impact, SANGOCO called together key actors to discuss ways to coordinate efforts. Besides SANGOCO, these included the South African Council of Churches, the Congress of South African Trade Unions and the Homeless Peoples' Federation. UNDP and the Department of Welfare were also represented. From this meeting, an idea was born: to launch a national War on Poverty Forum. The forum would allow ordinary citizens to express their views on critical development issues at public hearings called "speak outs".

As a starting point, SANGOCO commissioned seven thematic background papers on rural development and land matters, education, urban development and housing, welfare, economic development, environment and health. These provided participants at the hearings with quick summaries of policy issues related to each theme. Having reviewed the existing national policies, participants were better prepared to comment both on implementation failures and on policy reform.

A total of 35 day-long hearings were held in 29 locations across South Africa between 31 March and 19 June 1998. To maximize policy impact, important national organizations were assigned primary roles. Since the South African Human Rights Commission has the constitutional mandate to monitor the government's performance vis-à-vis the new Constitution, SANGOCO invited the commission to serve as co-host. Given that poverty and inequality have a strong gender dimension, the Commission on Gender Equality was asked to appoint its commissioners to the panels that ran the hearings. And because the church is committed to working with the poor, its leadership and congregations were called upon to actively participate. The Congress of Trade Unions also sent representatives, as did a number of other national umbrella organizations. An aggressive advertising campaign publicized the schedule of hearings, with radio messages employed as the principal medium, although other means, such as messages written on T-shirts, caps, mugs, etc., were also used.

Mechanisms were put in place for the benefit of those who did not have the time or the resources to attend a hearing. People were invited to make submissions by telephone via toll-free lines. Organizations and individuals could also record their submissions on tapes and forward these to a secretariat.

To expand public discussion even further, an essay writing and drawing competition took place in schools. Primary school children drew pictures depicting their personal experiences of poverty, and secondary school children wrote essays that dealt with various aspects of the issue. A private publishing house sponsored prizes for the best submissions. Photographs depicting poverty were collected and exhibited at hearing locations.

Large numbers of poor citizens came to each event, keen to participate and speak out. Volunteers stood at the door collecting statements, asking individuals whether they would like to make a formal submission, and then selecting those that appeared most useful for stimulating public discussion. Approximately ten per cent of those who gave statements then made presentations before the assembled gathering. Each speaker had ten minutes to talk, with 20 minutes for questions from the audience and the appointed commissioners.

To facilitate easy access, the hearings took place in community halls, churches and schools, mainly in rural areas. In each province, a local NGO was assigned responsibility for convening the hearing, but it was required to work with other organizations in order to publicize it and mobilize participants.

Between four and eight commissioners, selected from among participating organizations, officiated at the hearings. Each was conducted in at least three languages, and many were done in five. Cases were divided between those involving failures of implementation, and others for which wider changes, including policy reform, needed to be considered. For the former, submitters were referred to a local NGO, a government department, or some other organization that could assist.

A list of required interventions was prepared at the end of each day, with the commissioners taking charge of follow-up. Many problems were resolved locally. At a hearing held in Messina, for instance, a farmer was subpoenaed by the Human Rights Commissioners for ill-treating his farm workers. In other cases, information was compiled that improved service delivery by government line agencies. Referrals were made to legal experts on matters relating to miscarriages of justice, and school boards in many areas were requested to include basic legal rights within their curricula. After each hearing, the organizing team wrote to every submitter, providing them with a summary of the meeting report, and including a list of local and national organizations that could be helpful in providing assistance.

Results and Critical Factors

The War on Poverty Forum offers innovative elements both in terms of its outcome and process. These include:

- The creation of a voice mechanism for the poor to speak on policy issues is a large step in capacity development. It enhances a sense of ownership, and strengthens lines of accountability between the people and formal policy-making structures. It empowers people by allowing them to contribute to making meaningful policy.

- SANGOCO very skilfully managed a complex process. The case points to the importance of creating strategic partnerships between government and civil society organizations in order to combine different capacities and strengthen overall legitimacy.

- One key innovation was the careful separation of submissions related to grievance redress and those on substantive policy issues like school reform. This enabled the forum to be very effective for both constituencies. Participants were satisfied that volunteers listened to their grievances and raised these with appropriate authorities, while policy makers were privy to a unique "peoples' perspective" on issues affecting the poor.

Further information

V. Mthintso and Jacqui Boulle. 2000. *The War on Poverty Forum: The South African Experience with Poverty* (www.undp.org/csopp/CSO/NewFiles/toolboxcasesafrica.htm).

South African NGO Coalition (SANGOCO) and the United Nations Development Programme (UNDP) (www.undp.org.za/docs/pubs/povertyupdate.html).

Southern African Regional Poverty Network (sangoco.org.za/progs/fin_sust/natprogaction.htm).

The authors gratefully acknowledge the contributions of Vukani Mthintso and Jacqui Boulle.

➲ SOUTH AFRICA:
WOMEN ANALYSE THE BUDGET, AND PARLIAMENT HEEDS
THE GAPS

In a Nutshell

The South African Women's Budget Initiative analyses budgetary allocations across sectors of the South African economy and assesses whether these are adequate to meet specific policy commitments. A collaborative venture involving Parliament and civil society organizations, the initiative has a strong advocacy component, particularly around gender.

Besides demonstrating how this kind of partnership can increase accountability and transparency in public expenditure planning and monitoring, this case also shows how civil society expertise can complement a government's own capacities, in the process strengthening policy formulation overall.

The Story

The South African Women's Budget Initiative began in 1995 during the immediate aftermath of the apartheid regime. It was meant to provide quality analysis of the budget for use by both Parliament and civil society. Two independent think-tanks – the Institute for Democracy in South Africa (IDASA) and the Community Agency for Social Enquiry (CASE) – joined forces to set up the initiative with the National Parliamentary Committee for the Status and Quality of Life of Women.

Their premise from the start was that widespread poverty in South Africa is not always related to lack of spending: South Africa's development budget compares well with similar countries. Rather, it is the distribution of allocations between departments that is the problem. The budget initiative therefore began to examine budgets within specific departments and looked at how they may be re-allocated.

As is true in most developing countries, limitations on the availability of data mean that it is not possible to analyse each line item of every budget for its impact on women. Instead, Women's Budget Initiative experts prepare a series of policy briefs that touch on four themes: the gender issues facing the sector; how the state is involved in remedial measures; whether budget allocations meet policy commitments; and alternative measures to correct budgetary shortfalls.

Using these documents as a base, advocacy takes off through submissions to Parliamentary committees, national newspapers and the Internet. On the day the budget is actually announced, the initiative runs its own campaign on radio, especially community radio, which is heard widely by local interest groups. Additionally, analytical pieces are sent to the editorial and op-ed pages of newspapers. Throughout the year, researchers write articles on their findings, workshops are conducted, and technical assistance is provided to government departments and committees to help them understand the analysis and incorporate it in their operational plans. Crucial baseline research features regularly in Parliamentary submissions, and is used by many organizations working on sectoral policy.

Over the years, more and more organizations and individuals have coalesced around the initiative. Gradually, a loose coalition of sorts has formed that has considerable expertise on issues confronting women and related responses, along with a strong grounding in knowledge about budgetary affairs. Today, the Women's Budget Initiative produces in-depth research on about 30 government departments.

Results and Critical Factors

- It is not common to see a partnership of mutual gain between a Parliament and civil society. In this case, civil society has brought a level of research capacity that the Parliament itself lacks. And the legislature, in turn, provides a level of access to the upper echelons of government that civil society normally does not enjoy.

- Government involvement has meant that the initiative does not lack detailed data and information. Civil society participation ensures a healthy critique of gap areas and suggestions for remedial action.

- The initiative is grooming budget analysis experts; many of these "alumni" have gone on to initiate budget work within their own organizations and form a strong referral team for the original initiative.

- Due to the scope of advocacy, the government has, since 1997, committed itself to systematically monitoring women's quality of life, with the initiative working in this direction in close association with the Department of Finance and Central Statistical Services.

Further information

D. Cohen, R. de la Vega and G. Watson, eds. 2001. *Advocacy for Social Justice*. A publication of the Advocacy Institute and Oxfam. Bloomfield, Connecticut: Kumarian Press.

Institute of Development Studies, University of Sussex (www.ids.ac.uk/ids/govern/citizenvoice/annexcs.html).

World Bank Public Expenditure Review Group/Participation Group (www.worldbank.org/participation/tools&methods/casestudies).

➲ SUDAN:
FUTURE SEARCH TECHNIQUE CREATES A VISION FOR PEACE

In a Nutshell

Future search is a task-focused planning meeting used all over the world. Together, diverse groups of stakeholders explore their past, present and desired future, confirm common ground, and commit to joint action plans.

In Sudan, the United Nations Children's Fund (UNICEF) and Operation Lifeline Sudan (OLS) employed a future search to help imagine a vision of peace for the children in the south of the country, where war has raged for many years. UNICEF hoped this would help place consideration of the lives of children outside the context of political disagreements and inspire everyone to contribute to improving their future.

The Story

Southern Sudan is one of the world's poorest and most chronically underdeveloped areas. It has lost a generation of children to the turmoil engendered by a brutal civil war that has ravaged the region since independence from Britain in 1956. During the present phase, over a million people have died as a result of war and famine, while thousands more die from preventable diseases or grow up malnourished.

While the debate on Sudan's future has tended to focus on whether development should follow peace or vice-versa, the situation of children grows worse. Children can no longer wait for political leaders to declare peace. Against this background, and to mark the anniversary of the Convention on the Rights of the Child, a cross-section of southern Sudanese adults were invited to a conference to see whether they could put their differences aside and find common ground for the sake of the next generation.

The event was held in Nairobi in 1999. People came from many areas within southern Sudan, as well as from the Sudanese diaspora, and included health workers, NGO activists, elders, teachers, chiefs, women, administrators and academics. The result was a unique coming together of people who under normal circumstances would never meet. They were invited to leave their political perspectives at the door as they sat together and imagined new possibilities for their children.

An important part of the undertaking was to listen to children on their vision of the future. Some 40 children accompanied by their teachers came to Nairobi for their own conference, held just before the more general meeting. Aged 13-17, most had suffered displacement and separation from their families, and some had even fought in the war. For many, this was the first time they were able to meet people from different areas and tribes, in an atmosphere of calm and hope.

It became clear that all had suffered to a greater or lesser extent from the conflict. They were all poorly educated, yet they had something positive and unique to contribute. Working together, they analysed their past and present. The message they developed was clear: children want peace, they want access to health services, and above all, they want to go to school and learn.

The children approached their tasks with great maturity, humour and tolerance. This was displayed in the debate on which children should be selected to participate in the main conference. It centred on whether the ten children most capable of articulating a common vision should be chosen, or whether each region or ethnic group should be represented. The discussion was intense and lively, with the children finally deciding to select two representatives from each of five mixed groups so that each mixed group would be heard – even though this meant more boys than girls were selected and some regions were not included.

The inaugural ceremony for the main conference was an emotional occasion. Several participants were meeting for the first time in years. Many were overwhelmed when the children presented their painful experiences, bringing to life exactly how they had been affected by war and how much they yearned for peace in a way that stark statistics can never show.

The future search methodology was unknown to most people, and everyone had to take time to understand that the conference was not about presenting papers, analysing data and going over the same ground covered at umpteen earlier meetings. Once this was clear, participants threw themselves into the tasks with great will and enthusiasm. Given the deeply difficult past they all shared, which included bitter conflicts between some of the different ethnic groups in the room, the ease with which everyone focused was impressive.

Every participant had suffered trauma and loss as a result of the war. Personal tragedies – the deaths of children, parents or siblings; bombing of schools; fleeing in terror from attacks – were all recounted. The list of stories included the helplessness of parents unable to provide for their families during famine, as well as the inability to prevent widespread death or to provide adequate social services for children. However, when people discussed initiatives of which they were proud, it became apparent that they have tried, even under overwhelming circumstances, to improve their lives.

When the adults veered into politics, the children were there to bring attention back to what really mattered to them. The dream for the future of children created by the main conference was striking in its similarity to the dream of the children themselves. Peace and reconciliation came out very strongly, as did the pressing need for education and health services. The adult stakeholders also identified one other issue, which for them is key to securing a functioning society: good governance, with accountable structures that respect human rights.

Results and Critical Factors

The conference had a dramatic impact on the lives of some of the children. Sudanese living outside Sudan joined in a plan to develop curriculum material and deliver textbooks to villages. Another task force agreed to identify community members with existing teaching skills. A third group talked about training courses for agriculturists and farmers, while health care professionals collaborated to train health workers and assist local citizens in erecting buildings to be used as health centres. In the children's conference, regional action groups formed and discussed what they wanted to tell people back home about their experience in Nairobi, and the kinds of gatherings they could arrange.

Seven months later, 54 Sudanese NGO staff were trained in future search principles and methodology. Subsequently, UNICEF/OLS staff went to Southern Sudan and ran a future search on demobilizing child soldiers that included former child soldiers themselves, community representatives, and most significantly the local authorities and commanders from the Sudanese People's Liberation Army (SPLA). In February 2001, UNICEF announced that it had airlifted more than 2,500 child combatants out of conflict zones and into safe areas where a rehabilitation and family tracing process began.

In the first future search meeting in 1999, the children said that they desired peace in 2005 and peace through education. In 2002, a peace agreement was signed between the government of Sudan and the Sudanese People's Liberation Movement (SPLM). Over 50 schools have opened, including two boarding schools for girls, whose enrolment in these areas has tripled in one year.

The story of future search in Sudan offers three messages:

- First, the exercise helped children realize that their views count and they can make a difference. This was proven when their theme – peace through education – became a reality through the opening of new schools.

- Second, the future searches challenged the paradigm that development can happen only after peace is in place. In fact, as was shown here, development can lead to and prepare the ground for peace.

- Third, peace is not an event, it is a behaviour. Most conflicts start over disparities in resources, even when they may present themselves as ethnic or religious disputes. Education, therefore, can become the most important tool for peace. It provides an alternative to war.

Further information

Future Search. *Future Search and Its Realisation in Southern Sudan* (http://future-search.net/network/activities/special_features/sudan.cfm).

———. *Future Search to Demobilize Child Soldiers in South Sudan* (http://futuresearch.net/method/applications/world/africa/child_soldiers.cfm).

————. *Future Search Stories from Around the World* (http://futuresearch.net/method/applications/world.cfm).

————. *What is Future Search?* (http://futuresearch.net/method/whatis/index.cfm).

The authors gratefully acknowledge the contributions of Sandra Janoff, Future Search Network.

➲ **TANZANIA:**
FROM "TOP-UPS" TO SUSTAINABLE INCENTIVES FOR
CIVIL SERVANTS

In a Nutshell

The government and donors have come together in Tanzania to institutionalize a system of incentives within the public service. The Selective Accelerated Salary Enhancement scheme (SASE) offers a potentially sustainable solution to salary incentive problems within the wider context of pay reform, and is part of the overall government's Public Service Reform Programme (PSRP).

Aimed at addressing low motivation, uncompetitive salary structures and constraints on capacity development, SASE targets personnel with the greatest impact on service delivery. In providing an opportunity for donors to harmonize their practices around national systems, it also strives to reduce inducements that distort the local labour market.

The Story

In 1999, the government of Tanzania adopted a medium-term pay reform strategy as part of the PSRP. Recognizing the centrality of capacity development in improving public sector performance, the government considered enhancements in public service pay, especially in technical and professional grades, as a precondition for building and utilizing capabilities. While recognizing that more income in itself is not a sufficient condition for better performance, it reasoned that there was little likelihood of sustaining reforms without fair compensation for work and access to requisite skills.

Striving for a system perceived as fair, objective and transparent, the government came up with the SASE scheme. Qualification is selective, targeting personnel in positions having the greatest impact on service delivery and the wider reform efforts of government. Nominees sign performance agreements that serve as the basis for determining acceptable performance, and they have up-to-date job descriptions that specify outputs and time frames. Performance is appraised on an annual basis, using an objective assessment system.

SASE is being phased in starting with ministries, departments and agencies that have a leading role in change management and a potential impact on the socioeconomic well-being of the average Tanzanian. They must also be well advanced in formulating their strategic plans, and have been selected for inclusion in the performance improvement model that offers incentives to undertake institutional reforms.

From its inception, the plan for SASE implementation was as follows:

- The government would set a medium-term target pay structure covering the period 2000/01 through 2004/05, while donor budget support would, *inter alia,* supplement salaries of SASE-funded positions.

- All personnel of a particular grade and step/increment, whether a SASE scheme beneficiary or not, would be entitled to the same basic salary for a given fiscal year. The difference in compensation between SASE beneficiaries and non-beneficiaries would be the difference between the target salary and the basic salary for the given fiscal year.

- Donors would agree to phase out other supplementation arrangements. The SASE salary scales would serve as the benchmark for the payment of any salary supplements, as this would allow the government to internalize such supplementation as and when donor support was phased out.

- Each fiscal year, as the government would make salary adjustments, the gap between actual and target pay would be reduced, thus lowering donors' financial commitment as the government's ability to pay competitive compensation rose.

SASE was to start with 11 ministries, departments and agencies before being extended throughout the public service. However, a number of bottlenecks and constraints have meant that it has not been implemented as envisaged, and some of the anticipated benefits are now unlikely to accrue. Difficulties have arisen on both the donor and government sides. The latter has been unable to conduct performance reviews and adhere to the envisaged annual salary adjustments, which has reduced the willingness of donors to fund the scheme. Without the convergence of actual salary levels with the target salary levels, there is no clear time horizon for phasing out the salary supplement and no exit strategy for donor funding – which will up the costs of the initiative.

Implementation also started slowly, with the Civil Service Department being the only place to qualify for support in 2000/2001, although the Ministry of Health became eligible at the beginning of 2001/2002. By the second quarter of 2002, four additional institutional branches were able to join, with a major push on to get the remainder from the first phase to qualify by mid-2002/2003, nearly half way through the life of the plan.

The slow roll-out pace poses at least two problems. By the time that all the different ministries, departments and agencies are in a position to benefit from the scheme, its salary supplements are likely to be inadequate to induce any change in work behaviour. Gradual pay reform is likely to be the reality and traditional supplementary payments will persist. In this case, the shift of funds to the SASE scheme is unlikely to happen.

Results and Critical Factors

SASE has much going for it in seeking to provide a sustainable solution to the issue of salary incentives. In harmonizing the work of donors, it could curtail distortions in the local labour market. However, the case demonstrates the difficulties of implementing such a programme, and highlights some of the factors that can derail implementation.

- A complex system that ties the government and various donors to an agreed course of action only works when the partners are able and willing to combine their efforts. However, factors beyond the control of any stakeholder can result in the partners reneging on their commitments. This can in turn chip away at confidence in the system, and lead to a fall back on the practices the scheme intended to replace.

- Initiatives of this nature are time sensitive and technically complex, and any departure from the agreed schedule of implementation can undermine the whole roll out. Issues of the capacity to manage the system arise.

- It was originally envisaged that SASE would be funded through donors contributing to a common pool. As government sectors qualify, they may solicit sponsorship of their own SASE schemes directly from donors. Yet this type of financing arrangement runs the risk of "projectizing" whole ministries. Those viewed as unattractive would not receive support.

- A robust and transparent performance appraisal system is required to ensure that bogus applications for SASE entitlements are avoided, and that the system does not breed resentment. Either way, a scheme like SASE is likely to place extreme pressure on management to extend benefits even to those who do not necessarily merit them.

Further information

Government of Tanzania. 1999. *Public Service Reform Programme (PSRP)*. Dar es Salaam.

————. 2002. *Public Sector Reform Programme Quarterly Progress Report* (January-March 2002). Dar es Salaam.

Ted Valentine. 2001. *Revisiting and Revising Tanzania's Medium-Term Pay Reform Strategy.* Dar es Salaam: Crown Consultants International, DFID East Africa.

The authors gratefully acknowledge the contributions of Philip Courtnadge and UNDP Tanzania.

⤳ TANZANIA:
INDEPENDENT MONITORING HOLDS A GOVERNMENT AND ITS PARTNERS TO ACCOUNT

In a Nutshell
Relations between Tanzania and the donor community deteriorated during the early 1990s. A high-level group of experts, appointed to investigate the problems, proposed ways to put the relationship back on track. Seven years later, a radical change of rules has brought the two sides back together.

An independent monitoring mechanism now helps to hold the partners to account, recommending regular improvements based on impartial and transparent assessments. The group's findings are widely accepted and respected, providing a sound guide for the implementation of essential capacity development principles.

The Story
Tanzania remains heavily dependent on aid and is a priority country for many donor organizations. An effective partnership is critical both for development and the achievement of external cooperation objectives. In the late 1980s and early 1990s, however, donors expressed growing concern about poor administration, corruption, inadequacy of democratic processes and budget mismanagement. At the same time, the government viewed donors as inappropriately intrusive and demanding, and unable or unwilling to deliver on promises. A high-level independent working group composed of international and national experts was appointed to investigate what was going wrong. The results showed dissatisfaction on both sides and a high degree of mutual misunderstanding.

The group's report recommended that the government tighten and strengthen the operations of the Ministry of Finance; develop clear priorities for its investment and expenditure systems; and acquire and retain leadership in its own development efforts. As for the donors, substantial changes were needed in their operational culture, so as to reduce the gap between the rhetoric of "ownership" and the reality on the ground.

In January 1997, the government and donors met to draft a new way of doing business. The guiding principle was that Tanzania should take the lead, with a longer term vision for development, strengthened financial management and capacity development, open and honest dialogue, and independent stocktaking of progress towards agreed objectives.

In 1999, the same high-level working group conducted a more comprehensive assessment. This time, the report was mixed. It recognized a significant shift towards Tanzanian leadership, particularly in the sphere of macroeconomic management, and noted that donor attitudes and practices had changed noticeably, with more genuine dialogue taking place. Several donors were also contributing to "basket funds" in some sectors, the uses of which were determined under Tanzanian leadership. Budget and financial control systems were firmer, and corruption was being more aggressively addressed. However, reform of technical cooperation earned poor grades.

One significant recommendation was that the government and its external partners institute ongoing, independent monitoring of their relationship. As a step in this direction, the government, while developing its PRSP, also produced the "Tanzania Assistance Strategy." At the 2000 consultative group meeting, the government and donors reached a new agreement that in implementing the strategy, the performance of both sides should continue to be impartially evaluated. Doing so would help balance the aid relationship and lend real meaning to the aspirations for genuine partnership and open dialogue.

It was decided to appoint an independent monitoring group composed of three Tanzanians and three experienced non-governmental professionals from donor countries. The secretariat would be based in the Tanzanian Economic and Social Research Foundation.

There were elaborate discussions about the terms of reference of the group. With respect to donor performance, it was decided to focus on collective monitoring, rather than specific donor procedures as initially proposed. Under donor pressure, emphasis also shifted away from an earlier concern with ownership towards the concept of aid effectiveness. This was done to ensure the monitoring group looked at how aid contributed to PRSP outputs/outcomes rather than only at the transaction costs of delivering aid. Finally, local ownership now appears as only one of five explicitly mentioned ways of increasing aid effectiveness: the objective is to promote ownership, rather than to dub it the cornerstone of a development partnership.

The most recent report of the monitoring group in 2002, presented to the 2002 consultative group meeting, notes that by comparison with 1995, relations are much improved. On the Tanzanian side, progress can be attributed to the emergence of leadership with a demonstrated and sustained commitment to improvement and reform; increased openness, transparency and accountability; improvements in public expenditure management; and a demonstrated willingness to engage in dialogue.

For their part, donors now have greater trust in the government and have responded in various ways to improve their own policies and practices. Significant shifts include a willingness to be self-critical and accept independent assessment, as well as dissatisfaction with the past effectiveness of donor policies, such as the perceived limitations of a project-based approach and of tied technical cooperation. There is a new desire to adapt and respond flexibly to improvements on the government's side; to work with government systems and processes; to move away from reliance on conditionality towards a more coordinated and partnership-based approach; and to reduce government (and donor) transactions costs, for example, through better coordination arrangements.

However, the reports also observed that capacity and the use of technical assistance was an area where little progress had been made, with the topic considered highly complex and particularly sensitive.

Results and Critical Factors

The establishment of an independent mechanism to monitor the partnership between the donor community and a government is a considerable innovation, especially since it arose from a strained relationship. It has now become an established feature of the consultative group agenda, and merged with the Tanzania Assistance Strategy Action Plan. The seriousness with which the group's findings are treated bodes well for the future, and may prove helpful in tracking the implementation of capacity development principles. Crucially, this mechanism introduces accountability and transparency.

Factors that have helped ensure its success include the following:

- Despite the tensions that had emerged, there remained a deep-seated desire on both sides to see the relationship work more effectively.

- The appointment of trusted, respected and independent experts to review the situation was fundamental for ensuring that all sides were prepared to seriously consider their findings and work constructively towards a harmonized agenda under the government's leadership.

- The wider debate on aid effectiveness, ownership and capacity development taking place at the same time gave extra impetus, providing all parties with the incentive to find solutions and give practical meaning to a new aid paradigm.

- The arrival of fresh personnel on both sides of the relationship helped ensure that potentially defensive and reactive postures were replaced by a genuine desire for improvement.

Further information

Independent Monitoring Group (IMG). 2002. *Enhancing Aid Relationships in Tanzania: Report of the IMG.* Presented to the Tanzania Consultative Group. Dar es Salaam, December (www.tzdac.or.tz/IMG/IMG-main.html).

————. 2001. *Local Ownership and Donor Performance Monitoring: New Aid Relationships in Tanzania?* (www.sti.ch/pdfs/swap143.pdf).

Gerald K. Helleiner. 2000. "Towards Balance in Aid Relationships: Donor Performance Monitoring in Low-Income Developing Countries" In *Cooperation South,* 2, 21-35, published by UNDP.

Gerald K. Helleiner et al. 1995. *Report of the Group of Independent Advisers on Development Cooperation Issues Between Tanzania and Its Aid Donors.* Copenhagen: Royal Danish Ministry of Foreign Affairs.

S. Wangwe. 2002. *NEPAD at Country Level: Changing Aid Relationships in Tanzania.* Dar es Salaam: Mkukina Nyota Publishers.

The authors gratefully acknowledge the contributions of Philip Courtnadge and UNDP Tanzania.

➲ TANZANIA:
TWINNING INSTITUTIONS WITH TRUST AND EQUITY

In a Nutshell

In Tanzania, a twinning programme between a local research institute and a counterpart Norwegian group developed sustainable organizational capacities around the principle of equitable partnership. Following the Norwegian Agency for Development Cooperation's (NORAD) policy precept of "recipient responsibility", it was up to Tanzania's Institute for Development Management (IDM) to strike a suitable arrangement with Norway's Agder University College.

The foundations of a collaboration built on trust and common interest slowly grew as the two institutions got to know each other. Both learned from the other's advantages and disadvantages, and the notion of equity was given concrete expression by allowing the weaker partner, in terms of research competence, the stronger hand in control over resources.

The Story

IDM was established in 1972 to meet needs for skilled human resources in public administration, local government and rural development. It has, throughout its history, provided training of a practical rather than an academic nature, receiving considerable amounts of development assistance for investment in physical infrastructure as well as for consolidation and improvement of its training programmes.

Cooperation between IDM and Agder University College grew out of a long-standing relationship between IDM and NORAD, in which various approaches to institutional development have been pursued. These have included traditional technical assistance arrangements, on-the-job training, staff development programmes involving overseas training courses for IDM staff, and a twinning arrangement.

A major premise underlying these efforts has been that IDM's position as a training institution, and its sustainability under new conditions of market competition, can only be safeguarded through high academic quality. This requires not only top-level staff, but also a programme of management research to ensure that the training offered is relevant to Tanzanian realities.

The partnership with Agder University College has focused on research coop-eration, even though the college had neither a strong research programme of direct relevance to IDM, nor a well-established graduate programme. The college thus never viewed its relationship to IDM as one of mentor to fledgling. On the contrary, an equitable partnership emerged, in which the comparative strengths and weaknesses, advantages and disadvantages of the two institutions have com-plemented each other. Research and research training, in contrast to other possible fields of cooperation, involve quite specific activities and benchmarks for progress, and these have guided the collaboration.

The idea of partnership has been strongly supported by NORAD, the main for-eign donor supporting IDM. NORAD's policy precept of "recipient responsibility", which prompted IDM to define its own needs, and negotiate the scope and content of the arrangement with Agder University College, was a significant departure from IDM's first experience with a twinning arrangement in the 1980s. In that case, the Norwegian organization quickly became a consultant to NORAD rather than a genuine partner of the institute.

The relationship between IDM and Agder University College took several years to mature, during which it was based mainly on good personal relations (Agder University College staff members had been working at IDM) and growing mutual familiarity after several rounds of exchange visits. The first agreement signed was quite broad in terms of possible areas of cooperation and reflected a cautious approach. An elaborate management structure was adopted, involving yearly meetings between the leadership of the respective institutions, in addition to biannual consultations between project leaders. A rigid format for individual projects, governing time frames as well as expenses for both Norwegian and Tanzanian participants, was also introduced at an early stage.

In the interest of promoting the partnership, Agder University College agreed to an administrative model that did not cover all costs. This gave IDM full financial and administrative control, as well as a good deal in terms of price. The approach may not have been necessary in strictly operational terms, but it contributed significantly to establishing mutual familiarity and trust. Over time, a system evolved that now encom-passes joint target and priority setting, as well as the definition of common interests.

On this basis, the second phase of cooperation has concentrated on a smaller number of projects that are judged to be more directly relevant to IDM's mission, while allowing Agder University College to focus its academic resources more nar-rowly. The expected pay-offs for Tanzania are improved academic quality, increased relevance of research to national circumstances, and an enhanced com-petitive advantage in the market for training and consultancy services.

Results and Critical Factors

- Since IDM controls all funds and Agder University College has no independent access to NORAD, the partnership has been an equitable one, with IDM free to manage the agreement on its own professional terms. The practical problems encountered (e.g. cumbersome banking services) have been solved.

- Both institutions have gained. IDM staff have improved their skills with respect to designing and executing research projects, through training courses in research methodology and arrangements for supervision. Agder University College has benefited in terms of international exposure and actual research experience in a developing country.

- Partnerships must be built on the self-interest of partners. It takes a long time to instil confidence, and the cautious approach adopted in this case was essential in establishing a foundation of trust and common interest.

- Equity must be given concrete expression, such as the balance here between research capacity and control over resources. Partners need not, however, provide the same inputs or expect to receive the same outputs.

- Research cooperation, if properly carried out, provides a suitable platform for genuine partnership, since it involves well-defined activities and widely accepted benchmarks for progress. Not all fields of activity may benefit so clearly.

Further information

Stein Kristiansen. n.d. *North-South Academic Institutional Collaboration: The Case of Mzumbe University, Tanzania, and Agder University College, Norway.* School of Management, Agder University College (www2.ncsu.edu/ncsu/aern/steinkp.html).

Estomih J. Nkya. *Local Government Research Programme: Public-Private Sector Partnership and Institutional Framework at Local Level. The Case of Solid Waste Management in the City of Dar es Salaam, Tanzania.* Research report no. 17. Agder University College, Institute of Development Management Collaboration (www.tzonline.org/pdf/researchreport171.pdf).

Research Capacity Building Through Partnership: The Tanzanian-Norwegian Case. 2000. In capacity.org, July (www.capacity.org).

More on the cooperation between the Institute of Development Management (IDM) and Agder University College (www.cmi.no/public/1999/awp99-04.htm).

The authors gratefully acknowledge the contributions of Johan Helland, Chr. Michelsen Institute.

➲ **TURKEY:**
CITY DWELLERS TRANSFORM MUNICIPAL GOVERNANCE

In a Nutshell

Turkey has developed an innovative way for fostering interaction and dialogue among community members and municipal authorities in local decision-making. Across a number of cities, through a combination of locally driven initiatives and national level support, consultative mechanisms have sprung up to engage an array of local actors.

In many cases, this has changed the landscape of municipal governance. And while securing the approval of the central government has been crucial, the wider Local Agenda 21 initiative, as well as international events such as the 1996 Habitat II conference, boosted the confidence of local actors enough so they were willing to try a new approach.

The Story

The seeds of participation at the municipal level were sown in Turkey in 1996, during the United Nations Second International Conference on Human Settlements (Habitat II), held in Istanbul. It marked the first major international event where civil society organizations claimed equal participation in local decision-making. Inspired by this message, a number of Turkish NGOs started organizations at the neighbourhood level, only to see them languish from lack of structure and focus. Capacity 21's Local Agenda 21 programme stepped in to provide guidance as well as technical and financial support.

Today, 50 Turkish municipalities have active Local Agenda 21 initiatives, with city councils that usually meet quarterly and are drawn from a wide spectrum of local partners. They include ex-officio members such as the governor, mayor and parliamentarians of the province, as well as representatives of foundations, professional associations, private sector organizations, trade unions, academic institutions and neighbourhood groups.

In more than half the participating cities, the majority of the members of the councils and Local Agenda 21 secretariats are women. Under them, working groups prepare city action plans to address local problems, ranging from solid waste management and the environmental protection of a mountain or river basin, to education and child care. More and more municipal authorities are including the recommendations of the working groups on the municipal agenda, and even formally adopting them.

In Ankara, for example, the City Council persuaded the municipal government to clean up two polluted lakes, while in Izmit, the council and the municipality are collaborating on an action plan entitled "Rehabilitation-Reconstruction After the (1999)

Earthquake". In Antalya, the council established a permanent residence for street children, refurbished and operated entirely through donations from local stakeholders.

A distinct advantage of the system is that it is not associated with any political party. This makes people more willing to provide ideas and work towards consensus. In the past, participatory platforms often failed because they were associated with one party, and adherents of other groups withdrew. Now, most people can find a place for themselves.

Traditionally, governance in Turkish cities has rested securely in the hands of mayors who had little connection with the local population. But with today's multi-party democracy, mayors can be elected with only 25 per cent of the vote. This means that even those who are sceptical about participation recognize that it can strengthen their base of support. In some cities, Local Agenda 21 activities created such high expectations that when change did not come quickly, the mayor was voted out of office.

All of this activity, however, would not have been possible without the approval of the central government. Initially, it was difficult to establish participatory mechanisms because the governorates – who are provincial authorities representing central ministries, with jurisdiction over the municipalities – challenged them. After a series of appeals, the Ministry of Interior issued the 1998 Local Agenda 21 Law, urging all of Turkey's governorates to become partners in Local Agenda 21. Not only was the problem of the "legality" of participatory platforms overcome, but the active involvement of public agencies in the Local Agenda 21 process was secured.

Results and Critical Factors

- Through a combination of locally driven initiatives and external ideas, municipal governance has opened to the participation of local stakeholders, who work in partnership with authorities. By mobilizing the capabilities of the general population, municipalities increase their own capacities.

- Securing central government approval bolstered ownership, while the Local Agenda 21 Law ensured the engagement of public agencies. Technical know-how, financial resources and lessons learned from the wider Local Agenda 21 programme, and international events such as Habitat II, played a catalytic role role in supporting local actors as they tried out a new approach.

- Participation has spread across the country, as those who were initially less convinced have seen what can be achieved through joint decision-making and local partnership. Once the political pay-off of participatory approaches is recognized, local politicians tend to be quick to champion the process – at the same time, a key to success is ensuring that local City Councils remain non-partisan.

Further information

Capacity 21 Country Study: Approaches to Sustainability. Local Agenda 21 in Turkey: Moving from Local to National. 2000 (www.undp.org/capacity21/docs/ats/ats-turkey-en.pdf).

Capacity 21 Evaluation Report 1993-2001. 2002 (www.undp.org/capacity21/docs/cap21GlobalEval2002.pdf).

Turkey's Local Agenda 21 (http://yerelgundem21.org).

Capacity 21 (www.undp.org/capacity21/).

The authors gratefully acknowledge the contributions of Sadun Emrealp, International Union of Local Authorities, and Esra Sarioglu, UNDP Turkey.

➲ UGANDA:
DEVELOPING THE CAPACITY FOR DECENTRALIZATION AND LOCAL GOVERNANCE

In a Nutshell

Support to decentralized governance in Uganda began in 1995 with the District Development Project (DDP), which explored ways to empower local governments and communities to identify, deliver and sustain locally determined investment priorities. It also offered practical lessons that could feed into the development of national policy and procedures. The pilot defined, tested and applied participatory planning, allocation and investment management procedures, and developed a system of incentives and sanctions for local governments linking capacity development with improved performance, increased transparency and better service delivery.

The Ugandan government has since declared the DDP a success, considering it an important and sustainable vehicle for implementing the 1997 Local Government Act and Local Government Financial and Accounting Regulations. The recently approved Fiscal Decentralization Strategy has moreover endorsed a system of development grant transfers that is explicitly modelled on the DDP experience.

The Story

The DDP debuted in 1995, supported by UNCDF. The government of Uganda then turned to the DPP to develop a pilot system for implementing and "testing" the recently passed Local Government Act, and to assess operations that would fall under the government's financial and accounting regulations.

Following institutional analyses, research and consultations with stakeholders at all levels, the pilot was approved in 1997. The consultations reviewed existing practices, local knowledge, and alternative methods and systems for implemention, while their participatory nature spread understanding and ownership of the project objectives among local governments and communities. Meanwhile, discussions took place between the government, UNCDF and the World Bank, with the last expressing interest in the initiative, but wanting to review the pilot before committing support.

Consistent with the provisions of the Ugandan Constitution (1995) and the Local Government Act, the DDP embarked on ways to devolve development planning and budgeting in seven districts by focusing on participatory planning, allocation and management of development resources for service delivery and infrastructure. Four key elements set the project apart from similar initiatives:

- A system linking participatory planning and budgeting
- A stable discretionary development fund for local governments to use in planning processes, based on an agreed allocation formula
- Minimum conditions and performance measures to trigger the disbursement of funds, with penalties for falling short of the requirements and rewards for meeting and/or exceeding them
- A capacity-building fund to support learning related to decentralized local governance

The DDP tested how each of these elements contributed most effectively to decentralized planning and financial management. Annual internal reviews brought together central and local governments, politicians and community leaders. They took stock of experiences and bottlenecks; assessed the design and relevance of the projects in relation to government rules, regulations and procedures; and adjusted the programme accordingly.

Evaluations of the DDP pilot have been generally positive, and UNCDF has worked on other initiatives, including some supported by the World Bank and DFID, to replicate the model for an additional 51 local governments, including those in urban areas.

The second phase, launched in 2002, is now building on the first portion by piloting activities to harmonize the different participatory planning and budgeting methodologies that continue to be used at the district level; identifying ways to enhance local revenue generation without penalizing the poor; exploring gender budgeting to assess the impact of public expenditures on women and men; and building the capacity of local council courts to administer justice in areas of key concern to women and marginalized groups.

The process has evolved from a technically assisted pilot, to a programme management unit, to a government initiative with its own coordination unit and on-demand technical assistance. The next step will be comprehensive government management with technical support as needed.

The DDP has achieved several significant capacity development results, starting with its formulation of systems for decentralized planning and finance that have helped empower communities to take greater control over the allocation of development funds. It has also demonstrated ways to promote transparency and accountability, while fostering more open dialogue between local governments and communities.

In terms of policy impact, the DDP has provided a model for development grant transfers to local governments, which forms the basis of the recently approved Fiscal Decentralization Strategy. It has also devised systems and procedures that have been adopted by the government as policy, leading to the amendment of legislation and the regulatory framework.

Concerning donor replication, the World Bank's Local Government Development Programme (phases I and II) absorbed all the main features of the DDP approach, including allocation strategies, planning, investment methodologies and the capacity-building fund. The second phase will further extend local revenue enhancement throughout the country, learning lessons from part two of the DDP. As well, the DDP methodology for assessing local government performance has been taken up by the central government as the approach to be followed in districts supported by other donors.

Overall, the DDP has contributed to orienting central government around its new role vis-à-vis local government, and has generated political support and commitment to decentralization.

Results and Critical Factors

The positive impact the DDP has had on Uganda's decentralization stems from the following factors:

- The government's clear vision for devolving power and commitment to implementing the decentralization policy

- The government's willingness to draw on the expertise of international organizations in order to test different approaches as a basis for national systems

- A project design process that involved extensive consultations with different stakeholders, which built support for the proposed objectives, followed by a process-consulting approach that increased a sense of responsibility and moved decision-making into the mainstream of the government decentralization process

- Continuous dialogue and cooperation among funding agencies, which led to the replication of the DDP experience throughout the country

- The introduction of a system linking capacity development support to performance, which provided a mechanism for poorly performing local governments to improve their operations and record of service delivery

Further information

D. Porter and M. Onyach-Olaa. 1999. "Inclusive Planning and Allocation for Rural Services." *In Development in Practice,* 9(1-2): 56-67 (www.uncdf.org/local_governance/reports/risks/background/03.html).

L. Kullenberg and D. Porter. 1998. *Accountability in Decentralized Planning and Financing for Rural Services in Uganda.* Entwicklung und Ländlicher Raum (www.uncdf.org/english/about_uncdf/corporate_policy_papers/taking_risks/background_papers/03.html).

UN Capital Development Fund (UNCDF). 1998. *Taking Risks.* New York: UNCDF (www.gm-unccd.org/FIELD/Multi/UNCDF/UNCDFtaking.pdf).

————. *2001a. Mid-term Evaluation of DDP* (www.uncdf.org/english/consultants/impact/uga_eval.pdf).

————. 2001b. *Project Concept Paper DDP 2.*

————. 2002. *Project Document: DDP 2.*

UN Capital Development Fund (UNCDF) and the Government of Uganda. 1998 and 1999. *Internal Reviews of DDP.*

UN Capital Development Fund (UNCDF) Uganda (www.uncdf.org/english/countries/uganda/index.html).

The authors gratefully acknowledge the contributions of Joyce Stanley and Hitomi Komatsu, UNCDF.

➲ UKRAINE:
LEADERSHIP TRANSFORMS AWARENESS AND ROLES IN THE
FIGHT AGAINST HIV/AIDS

In a Nutshell

Ukraine faces one of the world's fastest growing HIV/AIDS epidemics. Glimpsing the potential enormity of the impact on present and future generations, it has turned to UNDP's Leadership for Results Programme, used around the world to shift perspectives and develop the capacity to take action.

The strategy is simple yet effective: bring together key change agents and influential community members; offer them the opportunity to respond to the epidemic in a deeper and more systematic way; invest in developing their ability to be compelling and innovative leaders; and expand their capacity to coordinate and manage large-scale, multi-sectoral HIV/AIDS programmes.

The Story

On the threshold of a nationwide HIV/AIDS epidemic, with one per cent of its adult population living with the virus, modern Ukraine may be facing its greatest challenge. Given the experiences of other countries, where HIV/AIDS prevalence exploded from this critical flashpoint, and with Eastern Europe as a region now the site of the world's most rapidly escalating epidemic, the future could be one of devastating economic, demographic and social impacts.

Ukraine has therefore resolved to embark on a strong national response, turning to the international community to complement local efforts. UNDP's Leadership for Results Programme, a large scale, multi-dimensional, strategic approach that draws together an array of actors and sectors, is one initiative providing valuable support to Ukraine's efforts to staunch the epidemic.

The programme works at country and regional levels to strengthen capacities for effective leadership, strategic planning, large-scale programme management and coalition building, promoting the collaboration of leaders at all levels and institutions across all sectors. It also enhances understanding among key stakeholders of the fundamental causes that fuel the HIV/AIDS pandemic, and enlarges the capacity of community leaders (particularly from civil society groups, private-sector concerns, networks of people living with HIV/AIDS, the media, the arts and religious institutions) to maximize impact. A focus on "commitment in action" is woven into Leadership for Result's capacity development approach.

In Ukraine, programme activities in 2002 included about 200 participants from civil society, national and sub-national governments, the National AIDS Commission, UNDP and the UN Country Team. A programme team contacted the National Association of Ukrainian Pharmacies, for example, because pharmacies are located in every city and are frequented most often by a primary target audience of the campaign: women aged 20-40. The association was invited to become a partner, distributing information on HIV to women clients of this age group. It readily agreed, passing out at no cost an even greater volume of leaflets than originally envisioned.

Media initiatives have enjoyed particular success. Journalists were invited to participate in a two-day meeting to examine the role of mass media in stopping HIV/AIDS. Sessions explored how media can cover HIV/AIDS issues in an informed and sensitive manner; examined how it projects or mirrors societal values, symbols and norms that can help or hinder responses to the epidemic; and investigated a new paradigm of leadership in Ukraine.

With programme support, a series of radio call-in programmes on HIV/AIDS aired on local FM stations. As well, one participant initiated weekly call-in programmes financed entirely by local sponsors. As the broadcasts took off, hosts reported a significant change in their attitudes and those of the callers. Whereas in the beginning, callers were few and the tone often negative, their number gradually increased and they became more tolerant and supportive of people living with HIV/AIDS. The topics evolved as well. Early questions largely concerned modes of transmission, while later queries revolved around the rights of people living with HIV/AIDS. More calls came from people personally affected by HIV/AIDS who felt able to share their experiences. As a result of the programmes' popularity, local stations have committed to continuing them.

Results and Critical Factors
The year-long Leadership for Results Programme has unleashed a process that is shifting points of view and fuelling constructive actions. Specifically, the programme has elevated commitment, highlighted individual responsibility, nurtured leaders, encouraged tolerance, and fostered confidence and capacity. Individuals, institutions and communities have found ways to explore strengths and weaknesses, individual and societal motivations, and plans and commitments. As a result, a number of breakthrough initiatives have been achieved:

- A group of participants from one of the worst affected regions in Ukraine created a club for people living with HIV/AIDS, where people meet and feel comfortable communicating freely. It is the first of its kind in Ukraine.

- NGO participants from the region with the highest prevalence of AIDS cases partnered with government representatives to design an initiative to provide care and support for people in the final stages of AIDS.

- The Association of Gays, Lesbians and Bisexuals set up the first-ever voluntary testing campaign by and for men who have sex with men.

- A team of government employees conducted workshops on leadership for the heads of various working groups to invigorate their HIV/AIDS prevention work. In addition, using their own resources, they published 2,000 booklets aimed at teenagers, parents and teachers.

- Government employees, using local budgetary funds, designed a campaign called "Sensible Choice, Sensible Person", with computer games, cartoons and a Web site for young people. They organized three trainings for medical workers and 40 lectures at educational establishments, reaching 2,000 young people.

- A team of participants from a border region with non-Ukrainian speaking minorities worked with the communities to craft and disseminate booklets on prevention in Hungarian, Polish and Romanian. Participants in another border region set up a service that reaches out to young people seeking work abroad, offering them HIV/AIDS information and counselling.

Further information

United Nations Development Programme (UNDP) on HIV/AIDS (www.undp.org/hiv/docs/results.pdf).

United Nations Development Programme (UNDP) Ukraine (www.un.kiev.ua/en/undp/).

"Ukraine Breaks Down Barriers and Builds Leadership against HIV/AIDS." 2002. *In UNDP Newsfront*, 15 May (www.undp.org/dpa/frontpagearchive/2002/may/15may02/).

The authors gratefully acknowledge the contributions of Serra Reid, UNDP.

➲ VENEZUELA:
THE OIL INDUSTRY FLOURISHES, ALONG WITH NATIONAL CAPACITIES TO SERVE IT

In a Nutshell

Over the last two decades, Venezuela has developed its fledgling oil sector, at first heavily dependent on foreign expertise, into a major global energy player with progressively higher levels of indigenization. This took place through a combination of prudent policy-making and effective corporate management strategies.

Capacity development has been most spectacular in the sub-sector of oil-related engineering and construction, which has involved joint ventures and development of technological capabilities. The result is an internationally competitive engineering and construction sector in Venezuela, with a share of the total contracting hours in the engineering services of the state-owned oil company that has risen from ten per cent at the beginning of the 1980s to 90 per cent today.

The Story

Venezuela is a significant player in the global energy market. It possesses 77.8 billion barrels of oil reserves and 148.3 trillion cubic feet of gas reserves; has the capacity per day to produce 4 million barrels, refine 3.3 million barrels and export 2.8 million barrels; and can produce 8 million tons of petrochemicals per year. By 2001, annual capital expenditure in the oil sector was around $8 billion.

Petroleos de Venezuela, S.A. (PDVSA), the state-owned oil company, was created in 1976, after the oil industry was nationalized. It is now an important global energy corporation, with business in oil, gas and coal, as well as in chemicals and petrochemicals. Appropriate policies and sound corporate management strategies have been crucial to this success, while significant and relatively constant levels of both public and private investment have yielded strong and competitive private companies across the energy sector.

Currently, the strategy of PDVSA is not only the development of competitive suppliers but also the consolidation of an efficient energy cluster, where operators, contractors and suppliers, institutions, universities, technology centres and government bodies interact and contribute to sustainable economic growth. All related initiatives are being integrated into the Domestic Capital Development Programme.

A good illustration of how this corporate policy bears fruit can be found in the development of the oil-related engineering and construction sectors. Before PDVSA intervened, oil industry operators largely used imported goods and services. Existing engineering companies were small and mainly involved in civil works such as construction of buildings, roads and bridges. Consultancies concentrated around areas like soil engineering, structural analysis and basic geology. Experience in project management was minimal.

The Engineering, Consulting and Project Management Development Programme was consequently set up to develop Venezuelan expertise in these areas. PDVSA's plan, across all levels of operations, was to promote partnerships and joint ventures by implementing a "performance requirement" in the contracting process. It was very straightforward. Foreign companies were encouraged to partner with existing Venezuelan companies, and in the process, technology transfer and personnel training took place, especially in key areas such as design and project control systems; complex project management; integrated engineering, procurement and construction projects; and specialized technology management.

PDVSA also established complementary contracting practices that enabled capacity development. Some of these involved the segregation of projects according to the scale and capabilities of contractors, and the implementation of reimbursable cost and cost-plus schemes, which were designed to overcome the limitations of local companies in the areas of financial resources, capability and scale.

By working closely with foreign firms, Venezuelan companies were able to incorporate better engineering standards and practices; carry out the training of key personnel; implement appropriate design and project control systems; and establish a shared management decision system. For foreign companies, this approach fit well with the strategic business model of overcoming access barriers in emerging markets. Partnering with a local company helped lower natural obstacles of language and culture, and eased negotiation of the terrain of national laws and regulations.

In a few years, local firms attained significant levels of participation in the total number of engineering hours contracted by PDVSA. Since 1986, the levels of participation have always been above 70 per cent. In years when very complex refining projects were undertaken, although the relative participation of local firms fell, their capacities were almost completely absorbed. Currently, partnering and joint ventures remain a common practice in contracting procedures at PDVSA.

Results and Critical Factors

Venezuela successfully built indigenous capacity in the oil sector by focussing on the key sub-sectors of engineering and construction. This pumped up overall efficiency, while capacity advances meant that companies could become more than just suppliers and contractors, going on to develop new business opportunities as operators and/or investors in partnership with PDVSA. In turn, the growth of the oil industry has yielded benefits for the economy through employment and income generation in the area of non-traditional exports.

- Several decisions, made within a comprehensive and coherent policy framework, underpin Venezuela's success, including the performance requirements for foreign firms. Both industrial and commercial policies addressed important issues, such as the need for supporting technology and innovation, the development of a network of small and medium enterprises, staggered contracting practices, and the preservation of the space for active policies in trade negotiations.

- At the corporate level, there was a high degree of commitment from the top of PDVSA. The project management approach accorded equal importance to analysis, design, implementation, monitoring and evaluation.

- PDVSA's role in the area of corporate social responsibility and sustainable development has been stellar: in 25 years of existence, its efforts have covered initiatives such as quality assurance and supplier development programmes, joint ventures and export promotion in core and non-core energy-related activities, and the promotion of foreign direct investment in areas of downstream industrialization.

Further information

Petroleos de Venezuela, S.A. (PDVSA) (www.pdvsa.com.ve; www.pdvsa.com).

Romulo Betancourt. 1979. *Venezuela: Oil and Politics*. Boston: Houghton Mifflin Company.

Jan Black and Martin Needler. *The Latin American Oil Exporters and the US*. Chapter 3.

William H. Gray. 1982. *Venezuela, Uncle Sam, and OPEC*. Smithtown, New York: Exposition Press.

Historia del Petróleo en Venezuela (www.matersalvatoris.org/petroleo/temas/historia/).

Evolución Histórica de la Economía Petrolera Venezolana (www.geocities.com/unilatinasiglo21/Principal/union_pensamiento/articulos_pensamiento/historia-petr.html).

Alexander's Gas and Oil Connections. News and Trends: Latin America, 6(12) (www.gasandoil.com/goc/news/ntl12749.htm).

Bibliography of Venezuelan oil history
(www.la.utexas.edu/chenry/mena/bibs/oil/1996/0070.html).

The authors gratefully acknowledge the contributions of Cesar Hernandez and Dr. Werner Corrales, Domestic Capital Development Group, PDVSA.

⮑ YEMEN:
PRSP PREPARATION PAVES THE WAY FOR INCLUSIVE
POLICY-MAKING

In a Nutshell

The process of preparing PRSPs has served as an opportunity for enhancing participation and civic engagement in national policy-making processes in many countries. In some cases, they have helped develop other capacities just by dint of their rigour and requirements. The PRSP for the Republic of Yemen is a case in point; preparation called for the government to upgrade its capabilities in a number of areas. In the process, it seeded a new, more inclusive culture of policy-making, and helped donors to fine-tune their coordination, monitoring and reporting.

The Story

The 2002 *Human Development Report* ranked the Republic of Yemen 144 among 173 countries in terms of the human development index. The Yemeni government is, however, pursuing a number of strategies to accelerate economic growth and progress in human development, and recently prepared a PRSP.

Anchored in the Ministry of Planning and Development, it builds on a host of national planning and strategic exercises launched in earlier years, including the National Action Programme for Poverty Eradication, which aimed at improving policy formulation. Its output was later used in the preparation of Yemen's National Strategic Vision (2025) and Second Five-Year Development Plan (2001-05). Gradually, the agencies responsible for formulating these various frameworks – notably the Ministry of Planning and Development, the Ministry of Finance, the Central Bank of Yemen and the Central Statistical Office – have acquired the necessary capacities for policy analysis and review.

At the start of the PRSP, additional capacity needs were identified in relation to the collection and analysis of baseline information on poverty and human development. Another element that required attention was consensus building around the PRSP formulation process, which would require consultation with stakeholders in prioritizing, implementing and monitoring poverty reduction targets.

As well, Yemen's policy of decentralization provides both a challenge and an opportunity in terms of a mechanism for rolling out the PRSP at sub-national levels. Both central and local government systems continue to require support to coordinate poverty reduction efforts. At both levels, stronger data collection, analysis and dissemination would go a long way towards instilling a culture of evidence-based decision-making. Some of the particular gaps are in the areas of generating reliable databases; monitoring implementation of poverty reduction;

and conducting better analysis and dissemination of data in order to reach planning, capacity development and governance goals.

With a view to addressing these weaknesses, the government in 2002 established a mechanism for carrying the PRSP forward. It comprised three organs: a ministerial committee for overseeing the execution of the paper; a technical team for monitoring; and a technical unit called the PRS Follow-up and Monitoring Unit, supported by UNDP, the World Bank and Oxfam. The three groups were asked to coordinate government ministries, departments and agencies as well as local authorities, civil society organizations, donors and the private sector. Donor support has been forthcoming in several other areas as well, including for information technology in the Ministry of Planning and Development as well for training of governorates' (a unit of local government) personnel, both supported by GTZ. With assistance from UNDP and the World Bank, the technical unit will eventually operate a Web-based socioeconomic database linked to other sectoral databases.

These activities, as well as those involved in preparing both the Second Five-Year Development Plan and especially the PRSP, have initiated a new way of working on development planning in Yemen. Previously, national exercises involved a small cadre of government functionaries supplemented by national and international consultants, with Parliament exercising some review over the final product. However, during the PRSP preparation, ten workshops were carried out in different areas of the country to explain the purpose and proposed content of the paper and seek feedback. Participants came from a broad cross segment of Yemeni society, and at some events the international community was also invited to participate. A "Voice of the Poor Study" was conducted among men and women and integrated into the PRSP, while a newly approved programme, Assistance to the Government of Yemen to Coordinate and Monitor Implementation of the PRS Initiative, will introduce gender budgeting through a partnership with Oxfam.

Advocacy relating to the PRSP (and the National Action Programme for Poverty Eradication preceding it) and participation have taken place among targeted groups, including civil society organizations, while the second *National Human Development Report* (2001/02) had the theme of civil society participation. A number of TV and radio programmes were conducted and cluster meetings held even in remote areas. A shorter version of the PRSP has also been produced in order to improve pro-poor planning and monitoring. Consequently, there is far greater awareness in and outside government of the importance of focusing development efforts on poverty reduction, and venturing beyond economic growth to embrace key governance and human rights issues.

Prior to the preparation of the Second Five-Year Development Plan and the PRSP, it was difficult for the government to lead aid coordination. In addition to capacity limitations, priorities were unclear, both for the government and the international community. Nonetheless, at the sectoral and thematic levels there have now been some good examples of government-led coordination, albeit with significant support from a lead donor. These include on the issues of poverty monitoring and reporting; support to the electoral process; development and conservation; HIV/AIDS and reproductive health; and basic education.

Results and Critical Factors

The PRSP ushered in a new "work culture" within the Yemeni official machinery – one that went beyond civil servants and consultants to a mode of wide-ranging consultation. This has given rise to new perspectives among the country's policy makers, who have begun to look at development as more than economic growth indicators.

- The first achievement was in the area of developing capacity for policy formulation, which required generating, processing, analysing and applying quality data. The results were visible in the Second Five-Year Development Plan and Vision 2025 documents. Enhanced participation in policy formulation was another key outcome.

- The government's capacity for effective aid management through donor coordination was on view for the first time in response to the challenges posed by the PRSP, which required the government to clearly spell out its strategies, focus and priorities.

- One specific area where government capacity was challenged to rise above the status quo was in monitoring and reporting systems – which the government had to upgrade in order to report on its progress on its poverty reduction strategy as well as on the MDGs.

Further information

World Bank Poverty Reduction Strategy and Poverty Reduction Strategy Papers (PRSPs) (http://poverty.worldbank.org/prsp/country/187/).

International Monetary Fund (IMF). 2002. Republic of Yemen Poverty Reduction Strategy Paper 2003-2005 (www.imf.org/External/NP/prsp/2002/yem/01/).

United Nations Development Programme (UNDP) Yemen. 2003. "The PRSP in Yemen." In the *UNDP Poverty Reduction Practice Newsletter,* March (www.undp.org/newsletters/povertymar03.htm).

Yemen Poverty Reduction Strategy Paper (PRSP) (www.mpd-yemen.org/english/PRSP203_2005_2.pdf).

The authors gratefully acknowledge the contributions of James W. Rawley and Moin Karim, UNDP Yemen.

⮑ AFRICA:
AFRIQUE EN CRÉATION SUPPORTS CULTURAL EXPRESSION AND EXCHANGE

In a Nutshell

Sustain and nurture creativity, promote artists, encourage new talents and innovative aesthetics, strengthen and network cultural organizations: these are the watchwords of the Afrique en Création programme, launched by the French Ministry for Foreign Affairs through the French Association for Artistic Action (AFAA). The programme supports the professional training of Africa's artistic talents in the stage and visual arts, and in so doing helps build upon the continent's rich cultures.

By contributing to a better knowledge of African creativity, paving the way for artistic exchanges within Africa and with northern countries, and bringing together civil initiatives, Afrique en Création underscores the contributions of Africa to worldwide cultural exchange. Moreover, it recognizes culture as an important means of communication between peoples that supports to the wider development process, with the potential for playing a role in improving education and reducing poverty.

The Story

Cultural and artistic activity has blossomed in Africa and is now spreading to the world stage through the growing presence of African artists at international events. While remaining rooted in their cultural heritage, these artists are avidly exploring new avenues of creativity and setting their sights firmly on a global audience.

The Afrique en Création initiative has fostered this evolution by helping to develop a vision and an agenda to promote contemporary arts and culture, especially nationally and regionally. An international forum held in 1990 brought together several hundred artists and cultural representatives to chart the future of African cultural development, and to define the role that cultural cooperation could play.

Over the subsequent decade, artists redefined their position in modern African society, as they progressively broke their dependence on the state and political circles. Young emerging artists began to see themselves as "entrepreneurs" offering a new form of societal expression and playing a more direct role in advancing development.

The initiative aims to professionalize the arts by supporting creativity and the development of cultural expression, offering opportunities to African artists to participate in major international events, and providing exposure to new techniques and production methods. The programme has focused on creating a network of African cultural organizations; professionalizing African artistic companies; sponsoring artistic events in Africa; and improving the know-how of artists and cultural entrepreneurs

But in achieving their autonomy and freedom of expression, artists have lost many traditional forms of support. Today, they need to devise innovative ways to sustain themselves, even in the midst of harsh economic realities and a lack of encouraging policy and legal frameworks. Financial and technical assistance therefore continues to be critical in furthering their development. In 2001, an updated and reformulated Afrique en Création programme, implemented on behalf of the French Ministry of Foreign Affairs by AFAA, was launched with this need in mind. A principal source of funding has been the French government's Priority Fund for Solidarity (FSP), totalling some $2 million.

Results and Critical Factors

According to a recent evaluation, Afrique en Création is helping to raise the status of cultural and artistic cooperation projects. The promotion of artistic productions, the artists themselves and cultural organizations has increased noticeably.

A total of 184 activities have occurred in at least 25 countries, while many artists and cultural entrepreneurs have presented their works across the continent as well as in Europe, especially in France. Key achievements include the organization of events in Bamako and Antananarivo, the international recognition of the creative dynamism of African visual arts, and the formation of the informal network of cultural organizations, which has complemented the direct support provided to many cultural agencies and artists. The programme has also given visibility, credibility and opportunities to many hitherto unknown cultural organizations.

Factors that have contributed to the success of Afrique en Création include:

- Continuous and close dialogue between the project team and African partners has helped ensure the relevance of assistance. While providing technical and financial support, the programme has emphasized the importance of building existing capacities, networks and information sources. It has mobilized local expertise to provide training and support, as well as to assist with major events. This has ensured that support remains rooted in local experience and adapted to local realities.

- Diverse intervention strategies have been employed to stimulate the sector, ranging from small-scale financial support for individual artists and companies to the organization of international events. Assistance of this nature must be viewed as a long-term process requiring multi-year and flexible funding arrangements.

- Stimulation of complementary support took place: for every 1 Euro spent from the FSP funding, an additional 1.36 was raised. Moreover, local partners have been encouraged to diversify their financial partnerships with other northern organizations. More effort is needed to build synergy among northern funders in order to rationalize and optimize available sources of assistance.

- More could be done as well to involve formal institutions at the country and regional level that can influence the long-term development and sustainability of the arts in terms of access to funding, as well as the promotion of wider public interest and support.

Further information

Afrique en Création (www.afaa.asso.fr/site_aec/index.php).

Various articles relating to Afrique en Création contained in the AFAA magazine, *Rezo International*, 8, and other issues (www.afaa.asso.fr/site/part_3_ress/pdf_rezo/rezo-no-8.pdf).

The authors gratefully acknowledge the contributions of Valérie Thfoin, Association française d'action artistique (AFAA), and the Department of Cultural Cooperation and Evaluation, French Ministry for Foreign Affairs.

➲ AFRICA:
PRIVATE SECTOR GROWTH BEGINS WITH BETTER MANAGERS

In a Nutshell

In 1989, the Africa Training and Management Services Project was established to build management capacity in Africa's private sector. A relatively complicated architecture was put together, resulting in a limited liability company to implement the project, and a foundation to mobilize and dispense funds. With support from multilateral development institutions, bilateral donors and the private sector, the initiative has now seconded experienced managers and set up management development and training programmes for over 255 companies in 25 African countries.

At first, the project encountered difficulties in convincing would-be clients of the merits of its largely commercially provided services. Yet recent evaluations suggest that clients are satisfied, with many saying that they have been able to improve their management and operating practices.

The Story

Sub-Saharan Africa remains one of the world's most challenging frontiers for economic development and poverty reduction. In recent decades, research studies as well as regional and international conferences have consistently identified poor management capacity as a critical challenge. Experts argue that without adequate capabilities, improved economic performance cannot be achieved.

Responding to this challenge, UNDP, along with other multilateral agencies and development finance institutions, initiated the Africa Training and Management Services Project. Its main objective is to build management capacity in order to improve private sector performance.

The project's relatively complex architecture put together UNDP and its resident missions, host governments, the development finance institutions and multinational companies. A public-private partnership was born with a dual purpose: to operate as a commercial entity and to be an instrument for private sector development.

On an invitation from the Dutch government, the African Management Services Company (AMSCO) was formed in 1989 as a limited liability company to implement the project, under the execution of the International Finance Corporation (IFC). The IFC, African Development Bank and the development finance institutions from seven donor countries all became shareholders, along with 53 international private companies.

In parallel, the foundation Stichting ATMS was established under Dutch law to hold donors' funds and to make grants to client companies, enabling them to cover part of the cost of AMSCO's commercial services. UNDP, the World Bank

Group, the African Development Bank and 11 donor countries now support the foundation, which, like AMSCO, has its own board.

Currently, donor assistance constitutes between 15-20 per cent of AMSCO's earnings; clients contribute the rest. The Netherlands and the African countries in which AMSCO operates provide tax exemption to company personnel, including AMSCO managers seconded to client firms. Although Amsterdam remains the corporate headquarters, operations are being gradually transferred to Africa, with regional offices in Abidjan, Accra, Harare and Nairobi. There is a country office in Lagos and an Africa head office will open in Johannesburg.

Filling the management gap in Africa requires both immediate hands-on involvement as well as training and development. To intervene in private and state-owned companies, and to encourage them to train and develop their staff, there must be an adequate commercial incentive. Initially, it was difficult for AMSCO, without any track record, to prove to African companies that they should be interested.

It took some trials and errors and millions of dollars in donor funding to meet the costs of experienced managers and the various training and development activities. The project had to ensure that the risks and liabilities of its supporters remained limited, and early on learned to assess the prospects of clients and negotiate to offer them appropriate support. It had to promise and deliver better performance, quality enhancement and improved governance, with the aim of increasing the viability of client companies and making them more internationally competitive.

To this end, AMSCO began engaging experienced managers and other experts for periods of two, three and sometimes five years. Clients pay the bulk of the associated costs. Those unable to meet the full amount – particularly the small and medium enterprises that make up 70 percent of the portfolio – can turn to donor assistance.

While the experts serve as chief executives and are in overall charge of their respective companies' operations, many step into functional positions as technical and operations managers, chief financial officers, quality control experts, etc. Their loyalties are to the client companies, but AMSCO monitors their performance against the business or operation plans approved by each firm.

AMSCO managers also participate in and implement the client company's staff development and training programme, including a needs assessment, the preparation and implementation of a plan, and evaluation of activities. Over time, it has been possible to expand client-specific training to benefit other companies with similar needs.

AMSCO has also experimented with business development models. One of them is *temps partage,* the secondment of a manager to more than one company, where his or her time is shared along with the costs. Managers also participate in improving corporate governance and the performances of boards of directors, with the ability to easily serve as a non-executive director of a third or fourth company.

Regular regional and subregional events for managers and client company executives take place to facilitate business communication, networking and the swapping of ideas. Several firms have benefited simply from learning what has been tried elsewhere in Africa.

Results and Critical Factors

- In spite of a sluggish start-up and substantial initial losses, AMSCO's activities and market outreach have expanded since the mid-1990s, exceeding targets set by sponsors. It has operated in 25 African countries, serving some 255 clients and training close to 4,000 people.

- Independent evaluators have found that the rationale for AMSCO remains valid: Africa still needs experienced, qualified and trained managers. A majority of AMSCO's clients are satisfied with its services, which have been found to be relevant to the development needs of over half the clients.

- The project has allowed many companies to improve their management and operating practices due to higher motivation, newly acquired skills and changes in governance. Sales and profitability have increased, surpassing the costs to clients and subsidies from donors. As competitors witness this improved performance, they too contact AMSCO for management support.

- Despite these achievements, AMSCO's sustainability is not assured. Its commercial activities are still not adequately priced because many clients and would-be clients are unable or unwilling to pay the full costs. Many still consider AMSCO a donor agency that comes with grants and subsidies. But this reliance cannot continue indefinitely.

- Retaining the public-private partnership remains a critical factor. Good corporate governance practices are also essential if all stakeholders' interests and rights are to be protected. The volume of African voices driving the project forward needs to increase, and more efforts should be made to involve more African private sector participation and adapt the concept to the African context or encourage indigenous business development support.

Further information

DFC Ltd. 2003. *Evaluation of the African Management Services Company.* London: DFC Ltd (www.ifc.org/oeg/publications/Studies/AMSCO_Evaluation_Report.03.01.15.Rev.pdf).

Normal International. 1998. *AMSCO Impact Study.*

PLS Consult. 1999. *AMSCO Review Report.* For the Danish Agency for Development Assistance (DANIDA).

African Management Services Company (AMSCO) (www.amsco.org).

The authors gratefully acknowledge the contributions of Charles A. Minor, AMSCO.

➲ EASTERN EUROPE:
IPF INITIATIVE FACILITATES RESEARCH AND CURBS BRAIN DRAIN

In a Nutshell

Inadequate capacities for policy analysis in transition countries continue to hinder progress. The innovative International Policy Fellowships (IPF) initiative provides policy leaders with the chance to work with mentors on policy projects while remaining in their home countries.

Since 1998, more than 150 fellows and alumni have turned to the programme to investigate alternative ways of ushering in much needed reforms. Many have gone on to influence specific policies, promote participatory policymaking, or establish regional or local institutes.

The Story

International scholarship and fellowship programmes for researchers and activists from transition countries have often been associated with brain drain, as highly trained human resources move elsewhere. In Central and Eastern Europe and the former Soviet Union, the IPF programme of the Open Society Institute provides leaders from all sectors with a year of opportunities to work with mentors on policy projects, while remaining in their home countries. As a result, fellows not only conduct original field research to benefit their communities, but also establish and maintain ties with local policy-making organizations.

There are enormous challenges and opportunities for innovative and independent researchers in transition countries, where gaping holes persist in local social science field research and policy analysis. Launched in late 1998 in affiliation with the Centre for Policy Studies of the Central European University in Budapest, IPF has a budget of approximately $1 million for 50 to 55 fellows per year. Its mission is to identify the next generation of leaders in Central and Eastern Europe, the former Soviet Union, and other regions of interest to the Soros Foundation's network, and support their policy research. The programme also aims to improve the quality of independent analysis and help prevent "brain drain" by ensuring leaders can conduct research in their home countries while maintaining mobility and intellectual freedom. It seeks to develop the capacity of participants to write professional policy documents and advocate policies, basic skills that frequently need to be sharpened. In turn, the Soros Foundation can employ participants' ideas and policy papers for the development of programme strategies for itself and other organizations.

The fellowship programme's success draws from a number of elements. To start, a competition to select participants is publicized through extensive advertising campaigns via the Internet, newspapers, offices of the Soros Foundation, local institutions and recruiting events. The competition itself, which is transparent and multi-tiered, includes application screening by programme staff, evaluations by experts and colleagues to ensure that research objectives correspond to donor programme objectives, and conference call interviews of all finalists.

Once the grants are allocated, funds are disbursed in two instalments that cover monthly stipends, research expenses, required laptop computers and other technical equipment, local language as well as English publication expenses, and travel and training costs. Additional funding is available for last-minute conference participation and necessary budget amendments. Participants sign contracts that state clear project goals and their audience.

Over the course of the year, fellows participate in three to four professional policy trainings, while social activities set the stage for future collaboration and exchange among alumni. Following comprehensive Web site development training, participants post project reports on individual home-pages. At least two expert mentors are appointed by specialists or fellows themselves to oversee projects and complete interim and final mentor critique forms. The mentors are leading policy makers and experts in the fellow's particular field of study, and often work with influential international organizations, governments or universities. While providing participants with supervision and feedback, they also benefit by obtaining first-hand knowledge of research projects that often challenge mainstream concepts and assumptions about social issues and public policy.

Results and Critical Factors

- In countries with a history of authoritarian regimes, highly educated and competent researchers interested in doing policy analysis often lack the necessary resources, such as well-researched data, and skills, such as the ability to assess relevant factors and options in a non-ideological way, and clearly present feasible recommendations for action. Appropriate policy training, networking and research opportunities can open possibilities for the development of new resources and skills, taking the researchers far beyond their local bureaucratic setting. Seed funding for these kinds of initiatives often yields far greater returns in the development of sustainable policy-making capacity than project funding for policy experts working outside the local context.

- The more than 150 IPF fellows and alumni to date have explored issues of reform in countries in transition and sparked public discussion on problems that previously were inadequately addressed. A majority has gone beyond the stated contract goals to impact specific policies and promote participatory policy-making.

- Other IPF alumni have established regional or local policy-making institutes with local and other sources of funds. Recently, they have joined forces to set up the Institute for Public Policy Analysis in Georgia, the

Centre for Public Policy Strategies in Lithuania, the Poznan University Centre for Public Policy in Poland, the European Policy Forum in the Czech Republic and the Press Freedom Centre in Hungary.

- Fellows have published hundreds of articles and papers, both locally and overseas. They have organized press conferences and written books compiling original field research for leading Western publishers. Based in part on the IPF model, several Soros Foundation country offices and other organizations have established their own national policy fellowship programmes.

Further information

International Policy Fellowships (www.osi.hu/ipf).

Centre for Policy Studies (www.ceu.hu/cps/oth/oth_welcome.htm).

Open Society Institute Budapest (www.osi.hu/).

The Soros Foundation (www.osi.hu/).

The authors gratefully acknowledge the contributions of Pamela Kilpadi, Open Society Institute.

➲ SOUTH-EAST EUROPE:
A VIRTUAL MEETING PLACE FOR EDUCATION REFORMERS

In a Nutshell

The South-East Europe Education Cooperation Network (SEE-ECN) is a broad-based, low-cost regional project. It supports the exchange of information, ideas, and know-how for the reform and improvement of education in 11 countries.

The network began with a sense of urgency over the need to enhance education standards, and took off through strategic kick-starting from external finance. As a virtual meeting place, it has brought people together and mobilized capacities across the region, stimulating a kind of East-East cooperation, while providing a framework for donor support.

The Story

SEE-ECN emerged with the end of the Kosovo conflict in 1999, which brought fresh opportunities and interest in cooperation among ex-Yugoslav republics. The Stability Pact political framework, brokered that year, highlighted the region and the commitments of donor countries to assist post-conflict reconstruction, development and integration of the region within Europe and globally.

During the late 1990s, cross-border and regional cooperation in education in the Balkans was driven largely by donor-led initiatives, experts and agendas. Otherwise, contact between countries was fragmented and in some cases frosty, with almost no formal relation among some neighbouring states and entities – for example, between Albania and Serbia, or Kosovo and Bosnia-Herzegovina. The quality of education varied widely from place to place.

In the post-conflict period, ministries of education, schools and universities shared the challenge of having to respond quickly and flexibly to profound democratic, economic and social transition. Many countries grappled with deteriorating infrastructure and low teacher salaries, rural-urban migration, refugee return or non-return and brain drain, political instability, and weak and outmoded institutions. Citizens everywhere held high expectations for "European standards" in education. These common issues and needs over a relatively small geographic region, with shared languages across some borders, provided the impetus for greater cooperation among policy makers and the donors seeking to support them.

In 2000, the Open Society Institute and the network of Soros foundations teamed up with the leading education reformers in Slovenia to conceive an indigenous network for education cooperation that would increase the regional information flow about education, incorporate local languages, engage education experts across borders, and provide a focal point for dialogue and capacity development on education reform. Slovenia was well positioned to lead the formation of the network, with its steady experience of restructuring education and relative political stability since gaining independence in 1991. The Center for Education Policy Studies at the university in Slovenia's capital, Ljubljana, became the network's base.

The Open Society Institute and the government of Austria provided seed funding of approximately $200,000. A virtual governing board was formed to oversee the network and decide priorities. Over the next year, the SEE-ECN identified a local coordinating organization for each country or entity in the region, thus extending the network through Albania, Bosnia-Herzegovina, Bulgaria, Croatia, Kosovo, Macedonia, Moldova, Montenegro, Romania and Serbia. Local coordination was set up in existing organizations – mostly local education institutes, think-tanks, and non-governmental organizations. The start-up funds financed a staff coordinator in Ljubljana and reimbursed local coordinators for direct costs.

As a first priority, the network collected and translated education policy documents from and about the region. Jointly over the first year, they built a virtual library, which now houses more than 1,500 items and is already accessed by around 10,000 users monthly. An online expert database supports the exchange of specialists across the region. The network has worked with the OECD in preparing and making available reviews of each national education system; this work was linked to the efforts of the Stability Pact to raise education as a priority and attract donor assistance.

In 2001, the SEE-ECN, with the Open Society Institute, sponsored its first regional event for capacity development, on drafting education legislation. A vast e-library of education laws from within and beyond the region was collected, and country teams of ministry officials, parliamentarians, lawyers, and policy analysts came together to exchange experience and practical know-how. Six months later, the UNESCO International Bureau of Education partnered with the SEE-ECN on a similar process to increase capacity for managing large-scale curriculum reform.

In the past, international agencies had mostly invited local stakeholders to seminars they thought were needed, but with the new network, it became possible to turn the process around, with local stakeholders setting the agenda.

An e-survey conducted in 2002 has helped assess the value of the network to users. Around 200 institutional and 100 individual members are registered in it; all ministries of education have been enthusiastic. Major donors, agencies and researchers active in South-East Europe routinely consult it and seek referrals, while the number of sponsoring donors and partners has tripled since the start-up.

Results and Critical Factors

- A common interest and a sense of urgency to enhance education standards motivated participants to work together across borders.
- External finance played a strategic role in kick-starting the SEE-ECN initiative, but did so by responding to rather than leading the agenda.

- The network has since provided a framework within which donors can more easily identify needs and engage with local partners.

- Using ICT to mobilize expertise and create a virtual meeting place for the exchange of ideas has significantly increased access to information resources at a comparatively small cost, and works on a demand-driven basis.

- Physical hubs located in different institutions in participating countries have reinforced the virtual network, ensuring that activities and initiatives can be followed up.

Further information

The South-East Europe Education Cooperation Network (www.see-educoop.net).

Open Society Education Programmes: South-East Europe (www.osepsee.net/1.htm).

United Nations Educational, Scientific and Cultural Organization (UNESCO) International Bureau of Education (www.ibe.unesco.org/).

The authors gratefully acknowledge the contributions of Terrice Bassler, Open Society Education Programs, South-East Europe.

⮕ WEST AFRICA:
ACTION RESEARCH TEACHES PROBLEM SOLVING ON THE JOB

In a Nutshell
The daily reality of overwhelmed health and social services in many developing countries confronts staff in these fields with seemingly insoluble problems. While many contribute considerable knowledge and skills, they often lack the encouragement to act self-reliantly and effectively to address the issues that arise. Action research offers a way out of this dilemma, because it elicits existing knowledge and then devises appropriate responses to challenges, in tandem with all concerned.

Since 1991, the Centre International de Formation en Recherche Action (CIFRA) in Burkina Faso has conducted action research training courses for health and social workers across West Africa. Participants are better able to analyse routine problems and resolve them with few resources. Many have acknowledged the effectiveness of this approach.

The Story
To strengthen the capacities of district health systems, donors often finance short-term courses to sharpen the skills of workers in first-line health services and support structures. Such training has become a kind of reward system and can be effective. Nevertheless, a gap often remains between its content and the realities on the ground: health teams must deal with problems that are often specific to the setting they are in, and little research is available on how to resolve them.

Often these problems seem overwhelming, causing even dedicated health workers to give up. In other cases, despite well-developed skills and considerable knowledge about the people they care for, staff struggle to use their understanding proactively. There is little emphasis on problem-solving techniques, or encouragement to improve care and working conditions.

This is where action research comes in, because it is about investigating one's own work environment, and then developing and implementing appropriate solutions for the problems identified. It teaches skills that can be applied across a host of different situations and can help bring about continuous system development. It focuses on teams of professionals rather than individuals; addresses the capacity needs of these teams in their environment; and helps actors, such as health professionals, to solve problems together with the people concerned, such as their clients.

CIFRA has promoted action research in Burkina Faso as part of a supra-regional project. Since 1991, it has conducted training courses to provide health and social workers – managerial staff, doctors, advisors, nurses and midwives – with skills to systematically analyse and resolve problems encountered in the workplace. Each year an international training is held in Burkina Faso, involving a basic course, a practical study segment and an evaluation seminar:

- *The basic course* introduces the action research methodology. It teaches situation and problem analysis techniques, with participants delving into solutions appropriate to their working environment. Methods of action research such as interviews, observation and focus group discussions are learned in theory, then tested and put into practice in case studies.

- During the subsequent *practical study segment*, participants conduct an action research study independently in their workplace, dealing with a concrete problem they face on a daily basis. Together with colleagues, clients and decision makers, they analyse the case, devise solutions, and identify and take appropriate actions.

- Finally, in an *evaluation seminar,* participants present the results of their study. Together, they review their practical experiences and prepare themselves to implement their conclusions.

Since the start of action research training at CIFRA, numerous participants have graduated – such as an array of staff from Togo's rural and urban health services as well as from NGOs. When GTZ assisted health project managers to explore the broader impact of this training, they found that former trainees in Togo had become very effective in their workplaces. A configuration was worked out with CIFRA that included the training of trainers during the international courses and follow-up regional courses in the country. Two senior staff members of the regional health management teams in Sokode (Central Region) and Lome (the capital city) participated in the 1999 and 2000 international courses.

Their practical study segments were carried out with members of the regional health management teams and narrowed in on the problems these teams had identified in their annual action plans. The results were then discussed during a follow-up planning exercise and presented to the research unit of the medical faculty of the University of Lome. The trainers also organized a course for 30 participants: two members of each of the district health teams (four in Central Region and five in Lome), the two regional health teams and some members of NGOs that were collaborating with these groups.

Results and Critical Factors

- So far, 11 supra-regional courses with over 450 participants have been organized in Burkina Faso, with participants from 14 countries in West and Central Africa, the Maghreb and Europe. Several regional courses have taken place in Burkina Faso, as well as in Benin, Chad, Guinea, Mali and Togo for over 250 participants. Since the middle of 2001, courses have also been offered in anglophone countries.

- According to the instructors, participation in the courses is above average. Students are highly motivated because the course offers them real opportunities to influence their work. The action researchers are proud of the awards the 1997, 1998, 2000 and 2001 studies received at the Journées Scientifiques du Houet (Bobo Dioulasso, Burkina Faso).

- A 1997 project progress review found that, after training, participants are more likely to conduct an objective analysis of problems and resolve them, often with few resources. Many are more motivated, develop their own initiatives and can perform their management functions even under difficult circumstances.

- An impact evaluation in 2001 found that three out of four participants from Burkina Faso and Togo managed to implement at least one of the actions identified during their training. Approximately half of all actions were effective. Two out of ten participants integrated the action research model into their daily work and had already used it at least a second time for problem solving.

- A critical element of the Togo experience was the lack of the transmission of acquired knowledge to other district health team members. This was counterbalanced by the fact that a critical mass of two members (out of five or six) of the district and regional health management teams were trained. As a result, the new knowledge was used in preparing the national health development plan. This took place in a bottom-up manner through the district and regional health development plans, with the trained team members performing well due to their enhanced decision-making capacity.

- All participants acknowledged that the course had influenced their way of dealing with their daily workload and problems. This was especially evident in Togo, where success factors seem to include the long-term stability of the staff as well as their high professional and ethical standards.

Further information

German Technical Assistance (GTZ). *Action Research – A Robust Hands-On Approach* (www.gtz.de/action-research/english/intro/intro.html).

List of projects carried out in the context of the Centre International de Formation en Recherche Action (CIFRA) International Course on Action Research in Health (www2.fhs.usyd.edu.au/arow//cifra/projects1.htm).

Overview of the Centre International de Formation en Recherche Action (CIFRA) International Course on Action Research (www2.fhs.usyd.edu.au/arow//cifra/french/french.htm).

Project summary: Centre International de Formation en Recherche Action (CIFRA) – Action Research Training Course (www.shared-global.org/projectsummary.asp?Kennummer=4689).

The authors gratefully acknowledge the contributions of the staff of the GTZ supra-regional sector project Promotion of Reproductive Health of Difficult to Reach Population Groups.

⮑ WEST AFRICA:
HARVESTING A NEW RICE THROUGH SOUTH-SOUTH COOPERATION

In a Nutshell

Capacity development involving South-to-South transfer of technology, resources and personnel is not a new concept. But it is increasingly talked about as an alternative to conventional technical cooperation models, where the resource imbalance between the North and South is further accentuated by the asymmetry of modern scientific knowledge. The following case illustrates how capacity development took place through transfers and cooperation between Asian and African countries, with donors playing a facilitating rather than supervisory role.

The experience involved the cross-breeding of African and Asian rice to produce a high-yield, high-protein variety that grows well in difficult ecosystems in Africa. An umbrella organization of 17 African countries played a critical role, overseeing the technical, social and commercial aspects and managing the transnational collaboration. Donors, research institutes, private foundations and universities worked together to ensure that the rice variety was widely adopted.

The Story

Poor farmers in West Africa missed the Green Revolution, which changed the lives of their counterparts in Asia. High-yield varieties of rice, the staple of Asia's leap towards food security, required external inputs like fertilizers, which were not readily available in West Africa. There the challenge was to boost agricultural productivity without a major increase in external inputs; conserve and even improve the environment; benefit poor farmers; and most importantly, incorporate indigenous knowledge systems while encouraging farmers to participate in and take ownership of the changes. Essentially, West Africa needed to develop technologies adapted to the Sub-Saharan environment, rather than modifying the environment to fit the technologies.

The African indigenous rice strain, while resistant to local diseases and suited to the fragile upland ecosystems of the region, did not produce the high-yield crops of the Asian strains. However, demand for rice in West Africa was far outstripping production. A response was urgently needed.

It came in the form of the West African Rice Development Association (WARDA), a regional institution born of technical cooperation support from donors. Comprised of 17 West and Central African member states, its mission is to contribute to food security and poverty eradication, particularly in West and Central Africa, through research, partnerships, capacity strengthening and policy support related to rice.

In considering the introduction of new strains of rice, WARDA played a convening role, bringing all the actors together and marshalling appropriate resources. The first challenge was to develop a variety that combined the resilience of the African strain with the productivity of the Asian version. WARDA achieved this by turning to resident researchers from FAO, the Japanese International Cooperation Agency (JICA), and UN volunteers from Myanmar and the Philippines.

Once the strain was developed, the challenge was to put it through trials and then distribute it widely. Field pilots were conducted under the aegis of a Japan/US collaborative programme with additional technical cooperation from Japan, the UNDP Technical Cooperation for Developing Countries (TCDC) programme and the Rockefeller Foundation. Specialist inputs poured in from Cornell University, the French Institut de recherche pour le développement (IRD, a research institute), the International Rice Research Institute Philippines, the Colombian Rice Research Institute, the universities of Tokyo and Kyoto, the Japan International Research Centre for Agricultural Services, and Chinese research agencies. Through these efforts, the generic strain New Rice for Africa (NERICA) was born. Today, it has 3,000 lines.

Over the long term, the stability and resistance of NERICA is expected to reduce the risk associated with rain-fed rice cropping and increase productivity. This will give farmers incentives to use more inputs, intensify land use and gradually abandon the practice of shifting cultivation, thereby improving the sustainability of cropping in Africa's fragile uplands.

All along, the idea has been not to replace local varieties, but rather to promote the integration of NERICA into existing farms, with complementary technologies, sound natural resource management, and improved rice marketing and distribution systems. With the new strain, an innovative field trial and assimilation process, called the Participatory Varietal System, has been designed to enable "mix-and-match" options for farmers as they assess optimal outputs. This ensures that they do not forfeit traditional rice varieties completely.

Another issue relates to seed production and distribution, notorious bottle-necks in the dissemination of new crop varieties, as national seed systems are too often under-resourced and therefore unable to meet production needs. Since the rapid adoption of NERICA has fomented a demand for efficient seed multiplication, an alternative supply mechanism for small-holder farmers has been introduced. It involves certification only of the foundation seed, rather than waiting for mass quantities to be produced. This reduces the time required for seeds to reach farmers, and depends on farmers' practices and indigenous knowledge for mass production.

While NERICA has been an essentially endogenous process, an ever-growing number of donors have poured funds into some aspect of its development and spread. The World Bank and the African Development Bank are the latest to join a now long list. Yet farmers have also embraced the new varieties. In Guinea, for example, 116 farmers planted NERICA varieties in 1997. In 1998-99, the number jumped to 1,000, and by the end of 2000, 20,000 farmers were planting the seed. The expected output of 15,000 tons was valued at $2.5 million.

Results and Critical Factors

- The NERICA experiment demonstrates how Southern countries can devise their own solutions. There was quick cognizance of the problem, the creation of an efficient and collaborative institution, and cross-national buy-in.

- Beyond highlighting how a series of highly supportive donors can do exactly enough without being overbearing, the case demonstrates that a good idea can attract the best resources from across the world, irrespective of Northern or Southern affiliations. A plethora of research institutes, government departments, NGOs and universities came together, ranging from nationalities as diverse as Colombia and Japan, and including organizations like Cornell University and DFID.

- The NERICA experiment turned the most significant critique of the Green Revolution on its head, proving that new, high-yield crop strains need not be based on intensive use of water and fertilizer, nor do they need to be become a blanket replacement of indigenous crop strains.

- NERICA goes to the heart of the food security issue in West and Central Africa. It is therefore an intensely political issue – with happy outcomes. The social dividend is that because the variety eliminates weeds, it directly benefits women and children – who do most of the weeding in fields. The environmental dividend is that a low-input rice crop eases the impact on fragile upland ecosystems, with inter-cropping with legumes a further stabilizing factor.

- The seed distribution strategy developed for NERICA represents effective strategic planning for downstream activities – an area of weak capacity in many Southern countries.

- Finally, the NERICA experience encapsulates the positive benefits of listening to farmers and those on the ground in defining both the policy problems as well as the operational solutions.

Further information

Ministry of Foreign Affairs in Japan. n.d. *Japan's Food and Agricultural Cooperation in Africa: NERICA* (www.mofa.go.jp/region/africa/nerica.pdf).

Kenayo Nwanze, et al. 2001. "Rice in West Africa: South-South Cooperation on Food Security." In *Cooperation South*, 2 (http://165.65.20.17/tcdcweb/coopsouth/2001_2/114-131.pdf).

United Nations Development Programme (UNDP) Japan. 2002. News, events and press releases: NERICA and the Tokyo International Conference for African Development (TICAD) side events at the World Summit on Sustainable Development, Johannesburg (www.undp.or.jp/news/WSSDsideevents31Aug.htm).

West African Rice Development Association (WARDA). 2001. *NERICA – Rice for Life.* WARDA-Consultative Group on International Agricultural Research (www.warda.cgiar.org/publications/NERICA8.pdf).

The authors gratefully acknowledge the contributions of the TCDC unit at UNDP.

⮑ GLOBAL:
CORPORATE SOCIAL RESPONSIBILITY AT THE BODY SHOP

In a Nutshell

Businesses globally have come under close scrutiny for their degree of social and environmental responsibility, an examination that pushes them beyond their conventional obligations to shareholders. Not many have managed the job of returning healthy bottom lines while paying the higher costs that come with fair wages and environmentally sustainable production policies. The few that have continue to face questions about the veracity of their claims.

The Body Shop typifies such a case. Its community trade programmes support sustainable development by sourcing ingredients and accessories from disadvantaged communities around the world, while adhering to fair-trade principles like decent wages and good working conditions. The company also runs a number of community-oriented projects, from Nicaragua to Somalia. However, some critics contest the claims that it makes about its products.

The Story

Multinational corporations are among the most controversial organizations in modern times. An oft-repeated critique claims they exploit disadvantaged people and developing countries. But the Body Shop has deliberately chosen a different approach, becoming an internationally lauded proponent of the view that corporations can and should make helpful contributions to the developing world.

The Body Shop was created in 1976, when founder Anita Roddick started producing soaps and lotions using herbal ingredients. Today, a chain of 1,200 shops does business in more than 45 countries, and the company is widely known as a pioneer for its staunch commitment to social and environmental concerns. In 1994, it formalized its conviction by modifying its mission statement to "help achieve positive social and environmental change by informing, inspiring, involving and empowering employees, customers and the community".

The Body Shop produces biodegradable products, promotes recycling and requires each of its stores to get involved in community projects. The company has recently joined forces with Greenpeace and the Intermediate Technology Development Group, for example, to lobby the government of the United Kingdom through the Choose Positive Energy campaign, which supports clean, sustainable, renewable energy. At the 2002 World Summit on Sustainable Development, campaign members presented a petition with over 1.6 million signatures, calling on governments to get serious about climate change and to set a timetable as well as targets for renewable energy use.

As part of the Body Shop's Trade Not Aid Project, a number of micro-enterprise initiatives were launched, illustrating the potential of fair trading practices. The project establishes direct trading links with producer communities in developing countries so that they can sustainably finance their own social and economic development. It also strives to protect a community's traditional way of life as well as the environment. For example, workers are given free lunch and health care along with their families at a factory producing wooden and cotton products in Tirumangalam, in southern India. Every time a product is bought from this factory, a 20 percent premium is added to the price. This extra revenue funds the local primary school, day care centre, and a clinic that offers family planning and HIV/AIDS awareness education.

The aim of another Body Shop programme – on community trade – is to support sustainable development by sourcing ingredients and accessories from disadvantaged communities around the world. One such example is henna, used in the new range of hair colour products that debuted in 2000. The henna is gathered by nomadic people in Somalia and supplied by Asli Mills, the trading arm of Candlelight for Health and Education, an NGO. Candlelight's initiative has given some 70 nomadic people an additional income as well as access to education and health programmes, from which they would not normally benefit. Henna leaves are collected from trees that grow wild in mountainous regions, and Candlelight/Asli Mills monitors the harvest to ensure that the trees and local environment are not damaged.

The Body Shop's corporate purchasing policy includes an environmental checklist that employees consult for these kinds of issues when buying new supplies. It looks at ecological life-cycle assessments that take into account the waste impacts of raw material sourcing on biodiversity, human and animal rights, and endangered species. The company has also been a lead innovator in corporate auditing, which assesses a firm's environmental and social impacts in order to improve its practices. In a survey published in December 2001 by the *Financial Times*, media and non-governmental organizations ranked the Body Shop second among the world's best companies for managing environmental resources. In 1990, Roddick's support of sustainable development was recognized with the United Nations' "Global 500" environmental award.

Despite all of these highly public activities, however, London Greenpeace has called into question a number of the Body Shop's claims, including its promise to use only natural ingredients and make products that have not been tested on animals. The group contends that many products actually contain chemical ingredients and some include ingredients that have been tested on animals by other companies. And not all the Body Shop's projects have gone according to plan. In Brazil, the firm buys Brazil nut oil for use in hair conditioners from the Kayapo Indians, an Amazon tribe. The nuts were already cultivated by the Kayapo, but at $8 a kilo were not providing enough revenue. The company gave the Indians machines that would turn them into oil, which sells for $38 a kilo. Yet some critics point out that only some Indians have benefited, causing strife within the community. Others have called into question the ethical issues involved in using the Indians for media campaigns without remuneration.

Genuine progress towards sustainable development requires a willingness on the part of businesses to be held accountable for economic, ecological and social performance, and to respond to the concerns of shareholders. The Body Shop's maverick approaches were not in the mainstream when it started selling environmentally friendly beauty products in 1976. Even beyond some of the criticism that has flowed in its direction, the company has done much to demonstrate how a corporation can be both responsible and profitable. Today, progressive business practices have begun to permeate day-to-day operations in many firms, and leading MBA programmes have incorporated social impact management into their curricula.

Results and Critical Factors

- In 1999, the Body Shop brand was voted the second most trusted brand in the United Kingdom by the Consumers' Association. The 1997 Interbrand survey criteria named the company the 28th top brand in the world, second in the retail sector. In a 1998 report, a survey of international chief executives in The *Financial Times* ranked The Body Shop the 27th most respected company in the world.

- The Body Shop illustrates that fair-trade practices are compatible with building a globally competitive company. The issue of fair prices and wages for grass-roots producer groups is a particularly important principle given that there is currently so much debate in the world on the pros and cons of globalization.

- Similarly, the Body Shop demonstrates that a multinational corporation need not necessarily be antagonistic to the environment or develop its products through controversial means like testing on animals.

- The controversy sometimes surrounding the Body Shop affirms that companies that claim to be practitioners of ethical business walk a very fine line in the court of public credibility. They need to make extra efforts to ensure that the claims they make check out factually, and that they keep a close watch over the fallout and implications of their business practices for producer communities, the environment and so on.

Further information

The Body Shop Community Trade programme (www.thebodyshop.com/web/tbsgl/values_sct.jsp).

The Body Shop link with a cooperative in Nicaragua (www.ndtc.org/bmzp/proposal1.html).

Sample critique on the Body Shop (www.mcspotlight.org/beyond/companies/bs_ref.html).

The Body Shop (www.thebodyshop.com).

⮑ GLOBAL:
TRAINING MOVES IN NEW DIRECTIONS THANKS TO ICT

In a Nutshell

This case highlights ways in which ICT and distance learning can support capacity development. Drawing on the experience of the Global Development Learning Network (GDLN), it demonstrates how new technologies have created opportunities for transforming the sharing and use of knowledge. Training in particular has benefited immensely from the information revolution, which has yielded cost-effective opportunities for linking training providers and their students, and significantly increased the relevance and impact of training for adults.

The Story

The GDLN harnesses ICT to support capacity building in developing countries. Based on the World Bank's own global communications infrastructure, the three-year-old network connects development providers with their counterparts in governments, NGOs, civil society and businesses. Some 50 distance learning centres have affiliated themselves to the GDLN, creating a unique partnership of government agencies, universities, training institutes and multilateral organizations that share a mission to develop capacity among government officials as well as other agents of change.

Beginning with a straightforward conversion of traditional training courses into the distance-learning format, whereby training costs could be reduced through savings in travel and by reaching more participants, the creators of the GDLN soon realized that much more could be done in terms of development impact. By eliminating the need for travel, training did not have to be delivered in a concentrated period of time. This would allow participants to read more background material; prepare real, rather than simulated assignments related to their actual work; and learn with their colleagues as a team. Direct links to participants' daily work meant courses could connect into government reform programmes or the development initiatives of partners such as donors or NGOs. Objectives could be written in the form of outcomes within the life cycle of a project.

GDLN consequently designed a learning methodology based on the development needs of client countries and the learning styles of target audiences, and with the objective of attaining tangible outcomes. In general, the approach can be summarized as being oriented around learners and action; viewing participants as part of a team, rather than as individuals; and enabling teams to develop comprehensive action plans by building skills related to design, development and implementation. The learning activities are planned as a blended combination of weekly, highly interactive videoconference sessions with international experts; local discussion sessions before or after the videoconferences; readings of some print materials; group assignments between sessions that apply learning to programme implementation; Internet resources accessed at the learner's pace and discretion; and email communication between experts and participants.

GDLN's Controlling Corruption course is a particular example of how distance learning can transform traditional course delivery with a more comprehensive, action-oriented, participatory approach. Previous attempts to address this issue focused on regulation, with strict attention to accountability and transparency. But these did not address fundamental causes and effects, or look at exactly how to build an accountable, transparent and self-regulating infrastructure to stem corruption. The emphasis turned to training, capacity building and technical assistance for high-level ministry officials brought to World Bank headquarters for a ten-day programme. The course was built around a daily nine hours of lectures and discussion covering topics related to the consequences of corruption. But the exercise did not achieve its expected results.

Finally, an approach was tested that blended learning methodologies and technologies. After protracted discussions with distance-learning and adult-learning specialists, experts on the subject agreed on a new curriculum involving the GDLN. It was more learner centred and action oriented, with course designers asked to think not in terms of the information that needed to be transmitted in order to understand corruption, but rather, what individuals working in government needed to know in order to actually control corruption. Instead of a global focus, it was decided to select a few countries – initially, seven in Sub-Saharan Africa. Invitations were sent to key ministerial personnel, who were invited to attend and participate as a team.

The goal was to enable each country team to develop a comprehensive action plan to control corruption, so the programme focused on the skills required to design, develop and implement a strategy. The curriculum included a combination of traditional, face-to-face workshops, followed by a regular series of seminars convened via videoconferencing technology. Print materials and email communications supported the strategy preparation. The result: each of the seven countries produced a government plan, which was presented at a conference in Durban.

Results and Critical Factors

In the three years that have elapsed since the GDLN initiative was launched, several lessons have been learned about its potential for development applications.

- Distance learning delivery systems are not only effective but highly competitive and efficient when compared with traditional ways of learning.

- GDLN is not just a training tool. Not only is the delivery of courses by distance learning more cost effective than by traditional methods, but the use of the technology itself, in conjunction with adult learning principles, can provide additional benefits in terms of learning gains. These start with allowing participants to learn by doing over time.

- Objectives set for the training can reach beyond learning and aim at practical outcomes. Through peer-to-peer communication, a community of practice can coalesce and last well beyond the course.

- New applications can be developed that would not be called training per se, but which can have a significant impact on capacity building. An example is a GDLN product line called Development Dialogues. Typically, these are short, two-hour videoconferences between two or more countries that can be designed around a policy topic and include international expertise, very often on a South-South basis. Used as an integral part of planning and implementing development projects, this brings "just-in-time" expertise to policy makers who would not have the time or the inclination to participate in regular training courses.

Further information

Global Development Learning Network (GDLN) (www.gdln.org).

International Centre for Distance Learning (http://icdl.open.ac.uk/).

An online list of journals and newsletters related to distance education (http://cctc.commnet.edu/HP/pages/darling/journals.htm).

World Bank (http://web.worldbank.org/WBSITE/EXTERNAL/WBI/0,,pagePK:208996~theSitePK:213799,00.html).

The authors gratefully acknowledge the contributions of Monika Weber-Fahr and Michael Foley, World Bank Institute/GDLN.

Authors biography

Carlos Lopes has a masters in development economics from the University of Geneva and a Ph.D. in history from the University of Paris1-Panthéon-Sorbonne. After serving in the civil service of his native Guinea Bissau, he taught or conducted research in several universities, including in Lisbon, São Paulo, Mexico, Uppsala and Zurich, before joining the United Nations Development Programme in 1988 as a development economist. He is currently Resident Coordinator/Resident Representative in Brazil. Mr. Lopes was previously the Acting Director of UNDP's Bureau for Development Policy. He has authored or edited 20 books on subjects related to development.

Thomas Theisohn is policy advisor with UNDP's Capacity Development Group. He has coordinated the "Reforming Technical Cooperation for Capacity Development" research initiative since 2001. The research findings have been published in several books. In 1997, Mr. Theisohn joined the Bureau for Development Policy in New York. Previously, he held UNDP posts in Angola and Ethiopia, and undertook missions to numerous African countries. His experience includes crisis and post-crisis reconstruction, environmental management, operational policy, programming, aid management, capacity development, outreach and training, with an educational background in theology, political science and environmental science.

Index

Page references in *italics* refer to figures, tables and boxes. Those followed by 'n' refer to notes.